COUNTDOWN
TO ZERO DAY

COUNTDOWN TO ZERO DAY

STUXNET AND THE LAUNCH OF THE WORLD'S
FIRST DIGITAL WEAPON

KIM ZETTER

Crown Publishers
New York

Copyright © 2014 by Kim Zetter

Published in the United States by Crown Publishers, an imprint of the Crown Publishing
Group, a division of Random House LLC, a Penguin Random House Company, New York.
www.crownpublishing.com

CROWN and the Crown colophon are registered trademarks of Random House LLC.

Portions of this work were originally published in different form in "How Digital
Detectives Deciphered Stuxnet, the Most Menacing Malware in History" copyright
© Wired.com. Used with permission. First published July 2011.

Cataloging-in-Publication data is on file with the Library of Congress.

ISBN 978-0-7704-3617-9
eBook ISBN 978-0-7704-3618-6

PRINTED IN THE UNITED STATES OF AMERICA

Book design by Anna Thompson
Jacket design by Oliver Munday
Jacket photograph: DigitalGlobe/Getty Images

10 9 8 7 6 5 4 3 2 1

First Edition

For SC and for my parents—with love and great gratitude, though gratitude is insufficient for all that you've done.

CONTENTS

Prologue: The Case of the Centrifuges   1

1.   **Early Warning**   5

2.   **500 Kilobytes of Mystery**   19

3.   **Natanz**   33

4.   **Stuxnet Deconstructed**   52

5.   **Springtime for Ahmadinejad**   69

6.   **Digging for Zero Days**   88

7.   **Zero-Day Paydays**   99

8.   **The Payload**   116

9.   **Industrial Controls Out of Control**   129

10.   **Precision Weapon**   166

11.   **A Digital Plot Is Hatched**   190

12.   **A New Fighting Domain**   205

13.   **Digital Warheads**   227

14.   **Son of Stuxnet**   249

15.   **Flame**   276

16.   **Olympic Games**   308

17.   **The Mystery of the Centrifuges**   336

18.   **Qualified Success**   359

19.   **Digital Pandora**   371

Acknowledgments   407

Index   413

COUNTDOWN TO ZERO DAY

THE CASE OF THE CENTRIFUGES

It was January 2010 when officials with the International Atomic Energy Agency (IAEA), the United Nations body charged with monitoring Iran's nuclear program, first began to notice something unusual happening at the uranium enrichment plant outside Natanz in central Iran.

Inside the facility's large centrifuge hall, buried like a bunker more than fifty feet beneath the desert surface, thousands of gleaming aluminum centrifuges were spinning at supersonic speed, enriching uranium hexafluoride gas as they had been for nearly two years. But over the last weeks, workers at the plant had been removing batches of centrifuges and replacing them with new ones. And they were doing so at a startling rate.

At Natanz each centrifuge, known as an IR-1, has a life expectancy of about ten years. But the devices are fragile and prone to break easily. Even under normal conditions, Iran has to replace up to 10 percent of the centrifuges each year due to material defects, maintenance issues, and worker accidents.

In November 2009, Iran had about 8,700 centrifuges installed at Natanz, so it would have been perfectly normal to see technicians decommission about 800 of them over the course of the year as the devices failed for one reason or another. But as IAEA officials added up the centrifuges removed over several weeks in December 2009 and early January, they realized that Iran was plowing through them at an unusual rate.

Inspectors with the IAEA's Department of Safeguards visited Natanz an average of twice a month—sometimes by appointment, sometimes unannounced—to track Iran's enrichment activity and progress.[1] Anytime workers at the plant decommissioned damaged or otherwise unusable centrifuges, they were required to line them up in a control area just inside the door of the centrifuge rooms until IAEA inspectors arrived at their next visit to examine them. The inspectors would run a handheld gamma spectrometer around each centrifuge to ensure that no nuclear material was being smuggled out in them, then approve the centrifuges for removal, making note in reports sent back to IAEA headquarters in Vienna of the number that were decommissioned each time.

IAEA digital surveillance cameras, installed outside the door of each centrifuge room to monitor Iran's enrichment activity, captured the technicians scurrying about in their white lab coats, blue plastic booties on their feet, as they trotted out the shiny cylinders one by one, each about six feet long and about half a foot in diameter. The workers, by agreement with the IAEA, had to cradle the delicate devices in their arms, wrapped in plastic sleeves or in open boxes, so the cameras could register each item as it was removed from the room.

The surveillance cameras, which weren't allowed inside the centrifuge rooms, stored the images for later perusal. Each time inspectors visited Natanz, they examined the recorded images to ensure that Iran hadn't removed additional centrifuges or done anything else prohibited during their absence.[2] But as weeks passed and the inspectors sent their reports

---

1 The number of inspection visits to Natanz has increased since this period. Beginning in 2010, inspections increased to once a week, and after a new agreement with Iran in late 2013, inspectors are now on-site at Natanz every day.

2 IAEA inspectors are not allowed to remove the recorded images from Natanz and can only view them on-site, where they are stored.

back to Vienna, officials there realized that the number of centrifuges being removed far exceeded what was normal.[3]

Officially, the IAEA won't say how many centrifuges Iran replaced during this period. But news reports quoting European "diplomats" put the number at 900 to 1,000. A former top IAEA official, however, thinks the actual number was much higher. "My educated guess is that 2,000 were damaged," says Olli Heinonen, who was deputy director of the Safeguards Division until he resigned in October 2010.

Whatever the number, it was clear that something was wrong with the devices. Unfortunately, Iran wasn't required to tell inspectors why they had replaced them, and, officially, the IAEA inspectors had no right to ask. The agency's mandate was to monitor what happened to uranium at the enrichment plant, not keep track of failed equipment.

What the inspectors didn't know was that the answer to their question was right beneath their noses, buried in the bits and memory of the computers in Natanz's industrial control room. Months earlier, in June 2009, someone had quietly unleashed a destructive digital warhead on computers in Iran, where it had silently slithered its way into critical systems at Natanz, all with a single goal in mind—to sabotage Iran's uranium enrichment program and prevent President Mahmoud Ahmadinejad from building a nuclear bomb.

The answer was there at Natanz, but it would be nearly a year before the inspectors would obtain it, and even then it would come only after more than a dozen computer security experts around the world spent months deconstructing what would ultimately become known as one of the most sophisticated viruses ever discovered—a piece of software so unique it would make history as the world's first digital weapon and the first shot across the bow announcing the age of digital warfare.

---

3 Inspectors visiting Natanz and other nuclear facilities around the world rotate on a regular basis, so the same IAEA inspectors don't visit every time. This is why the large number of decommissioned centrifuges didn't get noticed until after several reports of changing numbers arrived in Vienna and got viewed in the aggregate by analysts and officials there.

CHAPTER 1

EARLY WARNING

Sergey Ulasen is not the sort of person you'd expect to find at the center of an international incident. The thirty-one-year-old Belarusian has close-cropped blond hair, a lean boyish frame, and the open face and affable demeanor of someone who goes through life attracting few enemies and even fewer controversies. One of his favorite pastimes is spending the weekend at his grandmother's country house outside Minsk, where he decompresses from weekday stresses, far from the reach of cell phones and the internet. But in June 2010, Ulasen encountered something unusual that soon propelled him into the international spotlight and into a world of new stress.[1]

It was a warm Thursday afternoon, and Ulasen, who headed the antivirus division of a small computer security firm in Belarus called Virus-BlokAda, was seated with his colleague Oleg Kupreev in their lab in downtown Minsk inside a drab, Soviet-era building about a block from the Svisloch River. They were sifting methodically through suspicious computer files they had recently found on a machine in Iran when something striking leapt out at Kupreev. He sat back in his chair and called Ulasen over

---

1 Ulasen and his team encountered the malware the week of June 24, 2010.

to take a look. Ulasen scrolled through the code once, then again, to make sure he was seeing what he thought he saw. A tiny gasp escaped his throat. The code they had been inspecting the past few days, something they had until now considered a mildly interesting but nonetheless run-of-the-mill virus, had just revealed itself to be a work of quiet and diabolical genius.

Not only was it using a skillful rootkit to cloak itself and make it invisible to antivirus engines, it was using a shrewd zero-day exploit to propagate from machine to machine—an exploit that attacked a function so fundamental to the Windows operating system, it put millions of computers at risk of infection.

Exploits are attack code that hackers use to install viruses and other malicious tools onto machines. They take advantage of security vulnerabilities in browser software like Internet Explorer or applications like Adobe PDF Reader to slip a virus or Trojan horse onto a system, like a burglar using a crowbar to pry open a window and break into a house. If a victim visits a malicious website where the exploit lurks or clicks on a malicious e-mail attachment containing an exploit, the exploit uses the security hole in the software to drop a malicious file onto their system. When software makers learn about such holes in their products, they generally produce "patches" to close them up and seal the intruders out, while antivirus firms like Ulasen's add signatures to their scanners to detect any exploits that try to attack the vulnerabilities.

Zero-day exploits, however, aren't ordinary exploits but are the hacking world's most prized possession because they attack holes that are still unknown to the software maker and to the antivirus vendors—which means there are no antivirus signatures yet to detect the exploits and no patches available to fix the holes they attack.

But zero-day exploits are rarely found in the wild. It takes time and skill for hackers to discover new holes and write workable exploits to attack them, so the vast majority of hackers simply rely on old vulnerabilities and exploits to spread their malware, counting on the fact that most computer users don't often patch their machines or have up-to-date antivirus software installed, and that it can take vendors weeks or months to produce a patch for a known hole. Although more than 12 million viruses and other malicious files are captured each year, only about a dozen or so zero-days are found among them. Yet here the attackers were using an extremely valuable zero-day exploit, and a skillful rootkit, for a virus that, as far as Ulasen and Kupreev could tell, had been found only on machines in Iran so far. Something didn't add up.

THE MYSTERY FILES had come to their attention a week earlier when a reseller of VirusBlokAda's security software in Iran reported a persistent problem with a customer's machine in that country. The computer was caught in a reboot loop, crashing and rebooting repeatedly while defying the efforts of technicians to control it.[2] VirusBlokAda's tech-support team had scanned the system remotely from Minsk to look for any malware their antivirus software might have missed, but came up with nothing. That's when they called in Ulasen.

Ulasen had been hired by the antivirus firm while still in college. He was hired to be a programmer, but the staff at VirusBlokAda was so small, and Ulasen's skills so keen, that within three years, at the age of twenty-six, he found himself leading the team that developed and maintained its antivirus engine. He also occasionally worked with the research team that deconstructed malicious threats. This was his favorite part of the job, though it was something he rarely got to do. So when the tech-support team asked him to weigh in on their mystery from Iran, he was happy to help.[3]

Ulasen assumed the problem must be a misconfiguration of software or an incompatibility between an application installed on the machine

---

2 Ulasen has never disclosed the name of the reseller, but a link on VirusBlokAda's website for its distributor in Iran points to vba32-ir.com, a site owned by the Deep Golden Recovery Corporation, a data-recovery firm in Iran.

3 Information about VirusBlokAda's encounter with the malware comes from interviews with Sergey Ulasen and Oleg Kupreev, as well as from an account published by Kaspersky Lab in 2011, after the Russian antivirus firm hired Ulasen away from VirusBlokAda. That interview, "The Man Who Found Stuxnet—Sergey Ulasen in the Spotlight," was published November 2, 2011, at eugene.kaspersky.com/2011/11/02/the-man-who-found-stuxnet-sergey-ulasen-in-the-spotlight.

and the operating system. But then he learned it wasn't just one machine in Iran that was crashing but multiple machines, including ones that administrators had wiped clean and rebuilt with a fresh installation of the operating system. So he suspected the culprit might be a worm lurking on the victim's network, reinfecting scrubbed machines each time they were cleaned. He also suspected a rootkit was hiding the intruder from their antivirus engine. Ulasen had written anti-rootkit tools for his company in the past, so he was confident he'd be able to hunt this one down if it was there.

After getting permission to connect to one of the machines in Iran and remotely examine it, Ulasen and Kupreev zeroed in on six suspicious files—two modules and four other files—they thought were the source of the problem.[4] Then with help from several colleagues in their lab, they spent the next several days picking at the files in fits and starts, hurling curses at times as they struggled to decipher what turned out to be surprisingly sophisticated code. As employees of a small firm that mostly developed antivirus products for government customers, they weren't accustomed to taking on such complex challenges: they spent most of their days providing routine tech support to customers, not analyzing malicious threats. But they pressed forward nonetheless and eventually determined that one of the modules, a driver, was actually a "kernel-level" rootkit, as Ulasen had suspected.[5]

Rootkits come in several varieties, but the most difficult to detect are kernel-level rootkits, which burrow deep into the core of a machine to set up shop at the same privileged level where antivirus scanners work. If you think of a computer's structure like the concentric circles of an archer's target, the kernel is the bull's eye, the part of the operating system

---

4 A module is a stand-alone component. It is often interchangeable and can be used with various programs.

5 Drivers are software programs that are used as interfaces between a device and a computer to make the device work with the machine. For example, a driver is required to allow a computer to communicate with a printer or digital camera that is connected to it—different drivers are available for different operating systems so that the same device will work with any computer. In this case the drivers were actually rootkits designed to install and conceal malicious files on the machine.

that makes everything work. Most hackers write rootkits that operate at a machine's outer layers—the user level, where applications run—because this is easier to do. But virus scanners can detect these—so a truly skilled hacker places his rootkit at the kernel level of the machine, where it can subvert the scanner. There, it serves as a kind of wingman for malicious files, running interference against scanners so the malware can do its dirty work unhindered and undetected. Kernel-level rootkits aren't uncommon, but it takes sophisticated knowledge and a deft touch to build one that works well. And this one worked very well.[6]

Kupreev determined that the rootkit was designed to hide four malicious .LNK files—the four other suspicious files they'd found on the system in Iran. The malware appeared to be using an exploit composed of these malicious files to spread itself via infected USB flash drives, and the rootkit prevented the .LNK files from being seen on the flash drive. That's when Kupreev called Ulasen over to have a look.

Exploits that spread malware via USB flash drives aren't as common as those that spread them over the internet through websites and e-mail attachments, but they aren't unheard of, either. All of the USB exploits the two researchers had seen before, however, used the Autorun feature of the Windows operating system, which allowed malicious programs on a USB flash drive to execute as soon as the drive was inserted in a machine. But this exploit was more clever.[7]

---

6 The reboot problem didn't occur on other machines later found to be infected by the malware. So some researchers suspect the problem may have been an incompatibility between one of the malware's drivers and VirusBlokAda's antivirus software. The malware used the driver to install itself, and researchers at Kaspersky Lab in Russia suspected that when the driver injected the malware's main file into the memory of the machines in Iran, this caused some machines to crash. Researchers at Kaspersky Lab later tried to reproduce the problem but got inconsistent results— sometimes a machine crashed, sometimes it didn't. The irony is that the attackers had put a lot of effort into testing their malware against antivirus scanners from Kaspersky, Symantec, McAfee, and others, precisely to make sure their code wouldn't be detected by the scanners or crash machines. But they apparently hadn't tested it against VirusBlokAda's scanning software. So if VBA's scanner *was* the problem, it meant this tiny Belarusian firm had been their undoing in more ways than one.

7 Autorun is a convenience feature in Windows that allows programs on a USB flash drive, CD-ROM, or DVD, to automatically launch when the devices are inserted into a computer. It's a known security risk, however, because any malicious program on the device will automatically launch as well.

Windows .LNK files are responsible for rendering the icons for the contents of a USB flash drive or other portable media device when it's plugged into a PC. Insert a USB flash drive into a PC, and Windows Explorer or a similar tool automatically scans it for .LNK files to display the icon for a music file, Word document, or program stored on the flash drive.[8] But in this case, the attackers embedded an exploit in a specially crafted .LNK file so that as soon as Windows Explorer scanned the file, it triggered the exploit to spring into action to surreptitiously deposit the USB's malicious cargo onto the machine, like a military transport plane dropping camouflaged paratroopers onto enemy territory.

The .LNK exploit attacked such a fundamental feature of the Windows system that Ulasen wondered why no one had thought of it before. It was much worse than Autorun exploits, because those could be easily thwarted by disabling the Autorun feature on machines—a step many network administrators take as a matter of course because of Autorun's known security risk. But there is no way to easily disable the .LNK function without causing other problems for users.

Ulasen searched a registry of exploits for any others that had used .LNK files in the past, but came up with nothing. That was when he suspected he was looking at a zero-day.

He took a USB flash drive infected with the malicious files and plugged it into a test machine running Windows 7, the newest version of the Microsoft operating system. The machine was fully patched with all the latest security updates. If the .LNK exploit was already known to Microsoft, patches on the system would prevent it from dropping the malicious files onto the machine. But if the .LNK exploit was a zero-day, nothing would stop it. He waited a few minutes to examine the computer and, sure enough, the malicious files were there.

He couldn't believe it. VirusBlokAda, a tiny security firm that few in the world had ever heard of, had just discovered that rarest of trophies for

---

8 If Autorun is disabled for security reasons, then the malicious code on the flash drive that exploits this feature will not be able to launch automatically but will launch only if users specifically click on the file to open it.

a virus hunter. But this wasn't just any zero-day exploit; it was one that worked against every version of the Windows operating system released since Windows 2000: the attackers had bundled four versions of their exploit together—in four different .LNK files—to make sure their attack worked against every version of Windows it was likely to encounter.[9]

Ulasen tried to wrap his head around the number of machines that were at risk of infection from this. But then something equally troubling struck him. The malicious driver module, and another driver module that got dropped onto targeted machines as part of the malicious cargo, had installed themselves seamlessly on their test machine, without any warning notice popping up on-screen to indicate they were doing so. Windows 7 had a security feature that was supposed to tell users if an unsigned driver, or one signed with an untrusted certificate, was trying to install itself on their machine. But these two drivers had loaded with no problem. That was because, Ulasen realized with alarm, they were signed with what appeared to be a legitimate digital certificate from a company called RealTek Semiconductor.[10]

Digital certificates are trusted security documents, like digital passports, that software makers use to sign their programs to authenticate them as legitimate products of their company. Microsoft digitally signs its programs and software updates, as do antivirus firms. Computers assume that a file signed with a legitimate digital certificate is trustworthy. But if attackers steal a Microsoft certificate and the private cryptographic "key" that Microsoft uses with the certificate to sign its files, they can fool a computer into thinking their malicious code is Microsoft code.

Attackers had used digital certificates to sign malicious files before.

---

9 The exploit worked against seven versions of Windows: Windows 2000, WinXP, Windows 2003, Vista, Windows Server 2008, Windows 7, and Windows Server 2008 R2.

10 With Windows Vista and Windows 7, a driver that isn't signed with a trusted digital certificate that Microsoft recognizes will have trouble installing on the machine. On 32-bit Windows machines that have Vista or Windows 7 installed, a warning will display, telling the user the file is not signed or is not signed with a trusted certificate, forcing the user to make a decision about whether to let it install. On 64-bit Windows machines using either operating system, a file not signed with a trusted certificate simply won't install at all. The malware VirusBlokAda found only worked on 32-bit Windows machines.

But they had used fake, self-signed certificates masquerading as legitimate ones, or had obtained real certificates through fraudulent means, such as creating a shell company to trick a certificate authority into issuing them a certificate under the shell company's name.[11] In both scenarios, attackers ran the risk that machines would view their certificate as suspicious and reject their file. In this case, the attackers had used a valid certificate from RealTek—a trusted hardware maker in Taiwan—to fool computers into thinking the drivers were legitimate RealTek drivers.

It was a tactic Ulasen had never seen before and it raised a lot of questions about how the attackers had pulled it off. One possibility was that they had hijacked the computer of a RealTek software developer and used his machine and credentials to get their code secretly signed.[12]

But it was also possible the attackers had simply stolen the signing key and certificate, or cert. For security reasons, smart companies store their certs and keys on offline servers or in hardware security modules that offered extra protection. But not everyone did this, and there were possible clues to suggest that RealTek's cert had indeed been nabbed. A timestamp on the certificates showed that both of the drivers had been signed on January 25, 2010. Although one of the drivers had been compiled a year earlier on January 1, 2009, the other one was compiled just six minutes before it was signed. The rapid signing suggested the attackers might have had the RealTek key and cert in their possession.

---

11 Certificate authorities dole out the signing certificates that companies use to sign their code and websites. The CAs are supposed to verify that an entity requesting a certificate has the authority to do so—to prevent someone other than Microsoft from obtaining a code-signing certificate in Microsoft's name, for example—and to ensure that if someone applies for a signing certificate for a company they claim is theirs, it's a real company producing real code. Some certificate authorities don't do due diligence, however, and certificates are sometimes issued to malicious actors. There are also companies that, for a fee, will use their key and certificate to sign code for others. Hackers have used these companies in the past to sign their malware.

12 In September 2012, this is exactly what happened to Adobe. The software giant, which distributes the popular Adobe Reader and Flash Player programs, announced that attackers had breached its code-signing server to sign two malicious files with an Adobe certificate. Adobe stored its private signing keys in a device called a hardware security module, which should have prevented the attackers from accessing the keys to sign their malicious files. But they compromised a build server—a server used for developing software—which had the ability to interact with the code-signing system and get it to sign their files.

The implications were disturbing. The use of a legitimate digital certificate to authenticate malicious files undermined the trustworthiness of the computer world's signing architecture and called into question the legitimacy of any file signed with digital certificates thereafter. It was only a matter of time before other attackers copied the tactic and began stealing certificates as well.[13] Ulasen needed to get the word out.

Responsible disclosure dictated that researchers who find vulnerabilities in software notify the relevant vendors before going public with the news to give the vendors time to patch the holes, so Ulasen dashed off e-mails to both RealTek and Microsoft, notifying them of what his team had found.

But after two weeks passed with no response from either company, Ulasen and Kupreev decided they couldn't keep quiet.[14] The rest of the security community needed to know about the .LNK exploit. They had already added signatures to VirusBlokAda's antivirus engine to detect the malicious files and were seeing infections pop up on machines all over the Middle East and beyond. The worm/virus was on the run and spreading quickly. They had to go public with the news.[15]

So on July 12, Ulasen posted a brief announcement about the zero-day to his company's website and to an online English-language security

---

13 Ironically, on July 12, 2010, the day Ulasen went public with news about the malware, a researcher with the Finnish security firm F-Secure published a conference presentation about digital certificates, stating that, as of then, malware using stolen certificates had yet to be discovered. He noted, however, that this would inevitably happen now that new versions of Windows treated unsigned drivers with suspicion, pushing hackers to steal legitimate certificates to sign their malware. (See Jarno Niemela, "It's Signed, Therefore It's Clean, Right?" presented at the CARO conference in Helsinki, Finland; available at f-secure.com/weblog/archives/Jarno_Niemela_its_signed.pdf.) Indeed, not long after VirusBlokAda's discovery of the RealTek certificate, other hackers were already attempting to use the same tactic. In September 2010, antivirus firms discovered Infostealer.Nimkey, a Trojan horse specifically designed to steal private key certificates from computers. This was followed over the next two years by a number of malicious programs signed with certificates apparently stolen from various trusted companies.

14 Ulasen contacted Microsoft through a general e-mail address used for its security team. But Microsoft's security response team receives more than 100,000 e-mails a year, so it was understandable that an e-mail sent to its general mailbox from an obscure antivirus firm in Belarus got lost in the queue.

15 The malware, researchers would later discover, was a combination of a worm and virus. The worm portion allowed it to spread autonomously without user action, but once it was on a system, other components infected files, like a virus would, and required user action to spread.

forum, warning that an epidemic of infections was about to break out.[16] He divulged few details about the hole it was attacking, to avoid giving copycat hackers information that would help them exploit it. But members of the forum grasped the implications quickly, noting that it had the potential to be "deadly to many."

Three days later, tech journalist Brian Krebs picked up the announcement and wrote a blog post about it, summarizing what little was known about the vulnerability and exploit at the time.[17] The news raced through the security community, causing everyone to brace for a wave of assaults expected to come from the worm and copycat attacks using the same exploit.[18] In the meantime, the head of an institute in Germany that researched and tested antivirus products brokered an introduction between Ulasen and his contacts at Microsoft, prompting the software company to begin work on a patch.[19] But with news of the vulnerability already leaked, Microsoft decided to release an immediate advisory about the critical flaw to customers, along with a few tips advising them how to mitigate their risk of infection in the meantime. In the absence of a patch, however, which wouldn't be released for another two weeks, it was far from a cure.[20]

The computer security industry also rumbled into action to address the worm that now had a name—"Stuxnet," an alias Microsoft conjured from letters in the name of one of the driver files (mrxnet.sys) and another part of the code. As security companies added signatures to their engines to detect the worm and its exploit, thousands of malicious files started showing up on the machines of infected customers.[21]

---

16 Ulasen published his note on his company's site at anti-virus.by/en/tempo/shtml and at the Wilders Security forum at wilderssecurity.com/showthread.php?p=1712146.

17 Krebs, a former *Washington Post* reporter, runs the KrebsonSecurity.com blog, which focuses on computer security and cybercrime. He published his post July 15, 2010, at krebsonsecurity .com/2010/07/experts-warn-of-new-windows-shortcut-flaw.

18 Lenny Zeltser, "Preempting a Major Issue Due to the .LNK Vulnerability—Raising Infocon to Yellow," published July 19, 2010, at isc.sans.edu/diary.html?storyid=9190.

19 Andreas Marx, head of AV-TEST.org in Germany, brokered the introduction with his direct contacts at Microsoft.

20 Microsoft's advisory appears at technet.microsoft.com/en-us/security/advisory/2286198.

21 Most antivirus companies have automated reporting systems that will notify them when a malicious file is detected on a customer's machine if the customer has opted for this feature. In most

Almost immediately, another surprise emerged. On July 17, an antivirus firm in Slovakia named ESET spotted another malicious driver that appeared to be related to Stuxnet. This one was also signed with a digital certificate from a company in Taiwan, though not from RealTek. Instead, it came from a company called JMicron Technology, a maker of circuits.

The driver was discovered on a computer by itself, without any of Stuxnet's other files, but everyone assumed it must be related to Stuxnet since it shared similarities with the other drivers that VirusBlokAda had found.[22] There was something notable about the compilation date of this driver, however. When hackers ran their source code through a compiler to translate it into the binary code that a machine could read, the compiler often placed a timestamp in the binary file. Though attackers could manipulate the timestamp to throw researchers off, this one appeared to be legitimate. It indicated that the driver had been compiled on July 14, two days *after* VirusBlokAda had gone public with news of Stuxnet. Had the Stuxnet hackers unleashed the driver in a new attack, completely oblivious to the fact that an obscure antivirus firm in Belarus had just blown their cover? Or had they known their stealth mission was about to be exposed and were racing to get Stuxnet onto more machines before it would be blocked? There were clues that the attackers had missed a few steps while signing the driver with the JMicron cert, which suggested they may indeed have been in a hurry to get their attack code out the door and onto machines.[23] One thing was clear, though: the attackers had needed this new

---

cases all that gets sent to the company is a "hash" of the file—a cryptographic representation of the contents of the file composed of a string of letters and numbers produced by running the file through an algorithm—with no indication of who the victim is, other than the sender's IP address. But in other cases companies can obtain the entire malicious file itself if the victim decides to send it or the antivirus firm determines through the IP address who the victim is and requests a copy of the file.
22 Researchers speculated that the driver might have been used with a new version of Stuxnet the attackers unleashed after tweaking the code to prevent antivirus signatures from detecting it. No later version of Stuxnet has ever been discovered, but see page 357, footnote 41, for further discussion about a later version of Stuxnet.
23 See Costin G. Raiu and Alex Gostev, "A Tale of Stolen Certificates," published in *SecureView*, 2nd Quarter 2011, a quarterly newsletter from Kaspersky Lab. The mistakes appear in the digital signature block on the certificate, where a company provides information about itself. In this case, the attackers mistyped the URL for JMicron so that it returned a "server not found" error if someone tried to visit the website. They also failed to fill in several fields for the company's name,

certificate to sign their driver because the RealTek certificate had expired a month earlier, on June 12. Digital certificates have a limited life-span, and once RealTek's expired, the attackers could no longer use it to sign new files. The certificate was also revoked by certificate authorities once Stuxnet was exposed, which meant that Windows machines would now reject or flag any files that had already been signed with it.[24]

The discovery of the second certificate led to more speculation about how the hackers had obtained these security documents. RealTek and JMicron were both headquartered just two blocks away from each other in the Hsinchu Science and Industrial Park in Hsinchu City, Taiwan. Given their geographic proximity, some speculated that the attackers may have physically broken into the two offices to steal the digital signing keys and certs. Others speculated that the People's Republic of China was behind the Stuxnet attack and had hacked the two Taiwanese companies to get their digital signing keys and certificates.

Whatever the scenario, it meant the attackers likely had other stolen digital certificates in their arsenal. And if they had gone to this much trouble to make sure their attack would work, it likely meant they had a serious goal and considerable means at their disposal. Many in the security community were left feeling very uneasy and perplexed. "We rarely see such professional operations," ESET researcher Pierre-Marc Bureau remarked online.[25]

As antivirus firms examined the Stuxnet files pouring in from customers, they got another surprise. Based on dates in some of the files, it appeared that Stuxnet had been launched in the wild as early as June 2009, which meant it had been lurking on machines for at least a year before VirusBlokAda discovered it. It also appeared that the attackers had un-

---

copyright ownership, and other data. In eight of the fields, the words "change me" appeared instead of information.
24 The RealTek certificate was valid from March 15, 2007, to June 12, 2010. The JMicron certificate was valid until July 26, 2012, but once it was revoked by certificate authorities, the attackers couldn't use it anymore.
25 Pierre-Marc Bureau, "Win32/Stuxnet Signed Binaries," published August 9, 2010, at blog.eset .com/2010/07/19/win32stuxnet-signed-binaries.

leashed their attack in three different waves—in June 2009, and in March and April 2010—changing the code slightly in each of these waves.

One thing that was still a mystery, though, was Stuxnet's intention. Researchers could find no sign in any of the files that Stuxnet was stealing bank account passwords or other credentials the way so much other malware was designed to do. Neither could they find signs of any other obvious motive in the code. That is, until a researcher in Germany found one possible clue suggesting Stuxnet's aim.

"Hi guys," Frank Boldewin wrote to the online forum where Ulasen had first published his notice about Stuxnet, "has anyone . . . taken a deeper look at the malware?" Boldewin had unwrapped the first layer of covering on one of Stuxnet's files and found unusual references inside to software made by the German firm Siemens. The attackers appeared to be searching for computers that had one of two Siemens proprietary software programs installed—either Siemens SIMATIC Step 7 software or its SIMATIC WinCC program. Both programs are part of an industrial control system (ICS) designed to work with Siemens programmable logic controllers (PLCs)—small computers, generally the size of a toaster, that are used in factories around the world to control things like the robot arms and conveyor belts on assembly lines.

Boldewin had never seen malware targeting an industrial control system before. There was no obvious financial gain to be made from hacking factory equipment like PLCs, at least not the kind of quick cash that could be made from hacking bank accounts and credit card systems. It could mean only one thing to him. "Looks like this malware was made for espionage," he wrote.[26] The attackers must have been looking to steal a competitor's factory design or their product blueprints.

It was an assessment that many in the tech community were all too happy to embrace. Stuxnet appeared to be targeting only systems with the Siemens software installed, which meant that any computer not using the Siemens programs was presumably safe, and their owners could

---

26 Boldewin published his note at wilderssecurity.com/showthread.php?p=1712146.

relax. The systems in Iran that were caught in the reboot loop didn't have the Siemens software installed, Ulasen discovered, and aside from the system crashes they experienced, it appeared that Stuxnet had caused them no lingering harm.

So within a week or so after the mysterious worm's brief brush with fame, it appeared that Stuxnet was on its way out the door to lasting obscurity. Microsoft was still working on a patch to fix the security hole the .LNK exploit breached, but as far as most security companies were concerned, once they added signatures to their scanners to detect the worm's malicious files, Stuxnet held no further interest.

The story of the world's first digital weapon might well have ended here, except that a few security researchers weren't quite ready to let it go.

CHAPTER 2

500 KILOBYTES OF MYSTERY

In the six years Liam O'Murchu had been analyzing viruses and worms, he'd never seen anything like the code he was looking at now. It was using techniques that went way beyond anything he'd ever seen other malware do. This wasn't at all what he'd expected when he sat down at his computer in Symantec's Southern California office and pulled up the Stuxnet files that had arrived overnight from his colleagues in Europe.

It was Friday, July 16, the day after the news of Stuxnet had broken in the tech community, and O'Murchu was in the midst of what he thought would be a routine and perfunctory review of the code. The thirty-three-year-old Irishman was manager of operations for the Security Response team in Symantec's Culver City office, and it was his job to review new malware that came in to determine if it merited closer scrutiny.

Analysts in the company's office in Dublin, Ireland, had got hold of the Stuxnet files late in their afternoon but only had a couple of hours with the code before it was time to hand it off to O'Murchu's team in California, who were just waking up. Symantec's threat-analysis team is spread across multiple continents so that anytime an important threat pops up, someone somewhere is awake to jump on it. Then as the sun sets on one office and rises on another, workers in one time zone hand off their notes, like tag-team wrestlers, to those in the next zone.

Not all malware gets this follow-the-sun coverage. Of the more than 1 million malicious files Symantec and other security firms find each month, most are copycats of known tools that hackers simply tweak to alter their fingerprints and try to outrun antivirus scanners. These standard threats get piped through algorithms that tear through the code looking for signatures or behavior that matches known malware. Code gets kicked out of the queue for researchers to examine manually only if the algorithms find something they can't reconcile. Malware containing, or suspected of containing, a zero-day exploit always gets examined by hand, which is the only reason Stuxnet landed on O'Murchu's desk.

O'Murchu is an avid snowboarder with a lyrical accent and closely cropped brown hair sculpted vertically in front like the lip of a small half-pipe. A fairly recent transplant to the United States from Dublin, he'd only been in Symantec's California office about two years before Stuxnet struck, but he'd worked for the company since 2004. He led a team of highly skilled malware analysts and reverse engineers who were engaged in a constant battle against an onslaught of digital threats, each one often more advanced than the last. None of them, however, prepared him for what he found in Stuxnet.

O'Murchu expected their examination of the code would be merely routine, just to confirm the presence of the zero-day exploit that Ulasen and Kupreev had already found. So he passed the code off to a junior engineer, thinking it would be a good opportunity to train him on zero days, and only examined the code himself to backstop his colleague and make sure he didn't miss anything. But as soon as he opened the files, it was immediately clear there was something strange going on with the code.

The main Stuxnet file was incredibly large—500 kilobytes, as opposed to the 10 to 15 KB they usually saw. Even Conficker, the monster worm that infected more than 6 million machines the previous two years, was only 35 kilobytes in size. Any malware larger than this usually just contained a space-hogging image file that accounted for its bloat—such as a fake online banking page that popped up in the browser of infected machines to trick victims into relinquishing their banking credentials. But there was no image file in Stuxnet, and no extraneous fat, either. And, as O'Murchu began to take the files apart, he realized the code was also much more complex than he or anyone else had previously believed.

When you've seen as much malware as O'Murchu has, you can glance at a virus or Trojan horse and know immediately what it does—this one is a keystroke logger that records everything a victim types; that one is a banking Trojan that steals login credentials to online banking accounts. It's also easy to see whether a piece of code was slapped together sloppily or crafted skillfully with care. Stuxnet was obviously the latter. It appeared to be a dense and well-orchestrated collection of data and commands that contained an enormous amount of functionality. What those functions were was still a mystery, but O'Murchu's interest was immediately piqued.

O'MURCHU'S FIRST ENCOUNTER with malware occurred in 1996 when he was studying computer science at University College Dublin and a fellow student unleashed a homemade virus that infected all the machines in the school's computer labs. On the Ides of March, the virus seized control of the terminals and locked everyone out. Users could only log in after answering a series of ten questions that flashed on the screens. Most were annoyed by the interruption, but O'Murchu just wanted to get his hands on a copy of the virus to take it apart. It was part of his DNA to deconstruct things. Growing up in the country outside the small town of Athy in County Kildare, he was the kind of kid who was less interested in playing with toy cars than in tearing them apart to see how they worked.

O'Murchu didn't set out to become a virus wrangler. He began his college career dutifully taking physics and chemistry classes for the science degree he planned to pursue, but then enrolled in a computer science course and became obsessed. He quickly abandoned the chemist's lab for the computer lab. Hacking was a growing problem at the university, but O'Murchu never considered computer security a possible career path until intruders began breaking into servers belonging to the school's computer club, and a team of students was tasked with patching the servers to kick them out. O'Murchu was fascinated by the cat-and-mouse game that ensued, as he watched the intruders repeatedly outmaneuver the defenders to get back in.

That lesson in breaking digital barriers came in handy when he and a group of friends traveled to the United States after college and briefly got jobs testing internet kiosks for a San Diego start-up. They were hired to see if they could bypass the kiosk's paywall in order to steal internet access. But instead of getting the normal computer users the company thought it was getting, it had inadvertently hired a team of skilled hackers. After half a dozen kiosks were set up in the warehouse where the systems were being assembled, O'Murchu and his friends were told to go at them. They were only supposed to test the system for two weeks before the company planned to ship the kiosks out to customers, but O'Murchu and his friends kept finding new ways to break the paywall. After two months passed and they were still finding holes, the company canceled the testing and just shipped the kiosks out.

O'Murchu spent the next couple of years traveling the world and snowboarding with a vague desire to get into security but without any plan for doing it. Then in 2002, he got a job with the anti-spam company Brightmail in Dublin. He only took it to earn money to support his traveling, but when Symantec bought the firm in 2004, he saw it as a chance to leap into security. During a tour of Symantec's Dublin office given to the Brightmail employees, O'Murchu could barely contain his impatience at being shown around the various departments. All he wanted to see was the virus research team that he hoped to join. But when he finally met Eric Chien, the American who managed the team, his dream of being hired was dashed. O'Murchu thought Symantec had hundreds of analysts stationed around the world and that it would therefore be easy to get a job. But Chien told him only half a dozen people worked on the team, and all of them had been on the job for years. "Nobody really leaves," Chien said. "Everyone loves their work."

otprint. Once unpacked and decompressed, the main module expanded
1.18 megabytes in size.

With the packer now removed, O'Murchu was able to easily spot
he Siemens strings Frank Boldewin had seen. But more important, he
lso spotted an encrypted block of code that turned out to be Stuxnet's
mother lode—a large .DLL file (dynamic link library) that contained
about three dozen other .DLLs and components inside, all wrapped together in layers of encryption like Russian nesting dolls. He also found a
massive configuration file containing a menu of more than four hundred
settings the attackers could tweak to change everything from the URL
for the command-and-control servers Stuxnet contacted to the number
of machines Stuxnet would infect via a USB flash drive before the USB
exploit would shut down.[1] Curiously, O'Murchu also found an infection
stop date in the file—June 24, 2012. Every time Stuxnet encountered a
new machine, it checked the computer's calendar to see if the June date
had passed. If it had, Stuxnet would halt and not infect it. Any payload
already installed on other machines would continue to work, but Stuxnet
wouldn't infect any new machines. The stop date had been set for three
years after Stuxnet infected its first machines in Iran and was presumably
the date by which the attackers expected to achieve their goal.[2]

What most stood out to O'Murchu, however, was the complex way
that Stuxnet concealed its files on infected machines and hijacked normal
functions to perform its nefarious deeds. It took O'Murchu nearly a day to
work out the details, and when he finally did, he was astounded.

Normally, the code for performing common tasks on a Windows machine, such as opening and reading a file or saving its contents to disk,
is stored in .DLLs in the operating system. When the operating system
or another application needs to perform one of these tasks, they call up
the relevant code from the .DLL—like a library patron checking out a

---

1 The .LNK exploit on USB flash drives was configured to spread Stuxnet to only three new
machines before it would shut down and delete the files from the USB flash drive.
2 Forensic evidence found inside the versions of Stuxnet Symantec examined indicated that the first
infection in Iran occurred June 23, 2009.

O'Murchu was undeterred. He taught himself the tools
used to decipher malicious code and write signatures, and v
plosion of spyware and adware burst onto the scene several m
he was ready when Symantec needed to expand its team. He v
next four years in Symantec's Dublin office—where the con
maintains its largest research group—before transferring to C
in 2008.

Over the years, O'Murchu and the Symantec team had wor
number of high-profile and complex threats. But none was as fas
or as challenging as Stuxnet would turn out to be.

WHEN O'MURCHU EXAMINED Stuxnet's main file, he imme
came up against several layers of encryption masking its many par
inner core. Luckily the first layer was a simple "packer" that was
cracked.

Packers are digital tools that compress and mangle code to ma
slightly harder for antivirus engines to spot the signatures inside and
forensic examiners to quickly determine what a code is doing. Malw
run through a packer morphs a little differently on its surface each time
packed, so the same code run through a packer a thousand times will cr
ate a thousand different versions of the code, though beneath the packe
layer they will all be the same at their core. Antivirus engines can tel
when a malicious file has been run through a known packer and can then
unpack it on the fly to hunt for the signatures beneath. To thwart this,
smart attackers design custom packers that aren't easily recognized or removed. But Stuxnet's creators hadn't bothered to do this. Instead they
used an off-the-shelf packer called UPX—short for "Ultimate Packer
for eXecutables"—that was easily identified and eliminated. Given the
sophisticated nature of the rest of the threat—the zero-day exploit and
the stolen digital certificates—it seemed an odd choice for Stuxnet's creators to make. So O'Murchu assumed their primary reason for using the
packer must have been to simply compress the files and reduce Stuxnet's

book—and run it in the machine's memory. Conventional hackers would try to store code for their malicious activities in the Windows .DLLs too, but antivirus scanners can spot code in a library that shouldn't be there, so Stuxnet placed its malicious code in the machine's memory instead, where antivirus programs were less likely to detect it. That alone wasn't remarkable, since a lot of smart hackers stored their malicious code in memory. But the *way* Stuxnet got its code to run was.

Usually, malicious code that lurks in memory will still need to ask the system to load additional code from files that it stores on the computer's disk. But antivirus engines will spot this behavior as well, so Stuxnet did it one better. Stuxnet kept all of the code it needed to operate inside itself, stored as virtual files with specially crafted names. Ordinarily this wouldn't work because when Stuxnet tried to call up this code, the operating system wouldn't recognize the names or would look for the oddly named files on disk and not be able to find them. But Stuxnet "hooked" or reprogrammed part of the Windows API—the interface between the operating system and the programs that run on top of it—so that anytime it called on these oddly named files, the operating system would simply go to Stuxnet, sitting in memory, to obtain the code instead. If an antivirus engine grew suspicious of the files in memory and tried to examine them, Stuxnet was prepared for this as well. Because it controlled parts of the Windows API responsible for displaying the attributes of files, it simply tricked the scanner into thinking the files were empty, essentially telling it, "Nothing to see here, move along."[3]

But this wasn't the end of it. Normal malware executes its code in a straightforward manner by simply calling up the code and launching it. But this was too easy for Stuxnet. Instead, Stuxnet was built like a Rube Goldberg machine so that rather than calling and executing its code directly, it planted the code inside another block of code that was already

---

3 Nicolas Falliere, Liam O'Murchu, and Eric Chien, "W32.Stuxnet Dossier" (report, February 2011), 13–15, available at symantec.com/content/en/us/enterprise/media/security_response/ whitepapers/w32_stuxnet_dossier.pdf. Symantec's extensive dossier describes in detail Stuxnet's technical specs and what each function in the code is designed to do.

running in a process on the machine, then took the code that was running in that process and slipped it inside a block of code running in *another* process to further obscure it.

O'Murchu was astounded by the amount of work the attackers had invested in their heist. Even the most complex threats he'd seen in recent years didn't go to such lengths. The average malware writer did just the minimum of what he needed to do to make his attack work and avoid detection; there was little to be gained from investing a lot of time in code that was just meant to do a quick smash-and-grab of passwords or other data. Even the advanced espionage tools that appeared to come from China didn't bother with the kinds of tricks he was seeing in Stuxnet. Red flags were popping up all over the code, and O'Murchu had only examined the first 5 KB of the 1 MB threat.

It was clear this wasn't a standard attack, and needed to be examined more closely. But the size and complexity of the code meant it was going to take a team of people to reverse-engineer and decipher it. So the question running through O'Murchu's mind was should they even bother doing it? No one would blame Symantec if the researchers dropped the code and moved on to other things. After all, the primary task of any antivirus firm was to halt infections before they began or to rid infected systems of malware that was already on them. What malicious code did to computers once it was on them was secondary.

But even though their primary work stopped at the point of detection, any customer infected with Stuxnet would still want to know what the malware had done to their system, even if Symantec had already detected and deleted its malicious files. Had it pilfered credentials or important documents? Altered or deleted crucial data? O'Murchu felt it was their duty to find out.

But this wasn't the only reason he wanted to continue digging through the code. The truth was, Stuxnet appealed to him because it was a huge adrenaline rush of a puzzle—a virus far too complex to be merely a tool for espionage, and far too sophisticated to be the work of mere cybercriminals. He just had to figure it out.

———

AS THE END of that first day drew near, O'Murchu typed up his notes describing what he had uncovered so far and sent them off to Symantec's team in Tokyo, regretting that he didn't have more time to spend with the code.

The Tokyo team worked part of that weekend, mapping Stuxnet's components and doing a high-level analysis of the code so that everyone could get a handle on what they were dealing with. Back in California, where O'Murchu lived with his British girlfriend near the beach in Marina del Rey, he tried to push the code out of his mind, but couldn't. Memories of the complex way it hijacked a system invaded his mind until he started to question whether he was right about what he had seen. To silence his doubts, he returned to the office to look at the code again until he was satisfied that he was correct.

By the time Monday morning arrived, he was impatient to get to the office to meet with his colleague Eric Chien and report what he had found. Like O'Murchu, Chien had transferred from Symantec's Dublin office to Culver City and was now technical director of the company's Security Response team. Chien decided they should call Nicolas Falliere, a young senior software engineer and analyst in Symantec's Paris office who was a whiz at deconstructing difficult code. The three of them worked out a plan for tackling the project.

Stuxnet was so large, with so many different parts, but the obvious place to start was the command-and-control servers. So while Falliere familiarized himself with the parts of Stuxnet that O'Murchu had already seen, Chien and O'Murchu focused on the servers.

Each time Stuxnet infected a system, it "phoned home" to one of two internet domains masquerading as soccer fan sites—mypremierfutbol.com and todaysfutbol.com. The domain names, registered by someone who used fake names and fraudulent credit cards, pointed to servers in Denmark and Malaysia that served as command-and-control stations for the attack. Each time Stuxnet infected a machine, it contacted the servers to announce its conquest and communicate intelligence about the latest victim. The communication was encrypted to prevent anyone from casually reading it, but the encryption the attackers had used was surprisingly weak and easily cracked. Once Chien and O'Murchu unlocked it, they were able to see that Stuxnet was reporting the machine's computer and domain names to the attackers, as well as the internal IP address, the version of Windows it was running, and whether or not it had the targeted Siemens software installed on it.[4]

Each piece of data presumably helped the attackers determine if Stuxnet was closing in on its target. This was important because they were essentially flying blind in their attack. Once unleashed, a self-propagating worm like Stuxnet has a life of its own, and the attackers would have had no real control over where their malicious code traveled. The data coming back to the servers would have helped them track its path to some degree as it crawled through networks in search of its quarry.

But of all the information Stuxnet reported to its masters, the Siemens data was the most important because, as the researchers would soon learn, if Stuxnet found itself on a system that *didn't* have the Siemens software installed, it simply shut itself down. It still sought other machines to infect, but it wouldn't launch its payload on any machine that didn't have

---

4 A machine's domain name and external IP address—the outer-facing address of machines connected to the internet—can reveal the name of the organization or company that owns the infected machine, based on who owns the block of IP addresses in which the machine's address falls. This could help the attackers determine how fast and far Stuxnet spread. This information would also have told the attackers when Stuxnet traveled way off track as it began to show up in geographical regions far from its target. Internal IP addresses, on the other hand, are addresses that companies assign internally to machines to map them and route traffic between them. These IP addresses can be useful if the attackers possessed a map of the infected company or organization's internal network, perhaps stolen from a system administrator's computer, which indicated the internal IP address assigned to each machine on the network. If this was the case, the attackers could have tracked Stuxnet's path as it slithered inside a network infecting machine after machine, reporting back to the command-and-control servers each time it infected one that was connected to the internet. As for the computer name, it could have helped the attackers identify which employee or work group inside an organization owned the machines that were infected. One machine, for example, was named GORJI-259E4B69A, another was PEYMAN-PC. But many of the infected systems shared the same generic name: "ADMIN-PC," "USER-PC," or "home laptop," making it difficult to distinguish between them.

the Siemens software installed. Any system without the software was just a means to Stuxnet's end.[5]

O'Murchu contacted the DNS (domain name system) service providers for the two command-and-control domains and asked them to stop the traffic going to the attackers and divert it to a sinkhole—a computer dedicated to receiving hostile traffic—that Symantec controlled instead. DNS providers are the traffic cops of the internet, who make sure that e-mail and browsers reach their destinations, so that anytime someone types "nytimes.com" into their browser or clicks on a link for a website, they will arrive at the proper IP address.[6] By diverting the traffic to their sinkhole, the researchers could now collect the real-time data that Stuxnet, like a good soldier, was supposed to be reporting to the attackers. By Tuesday morning, July 20, a flood of traffic was coming to their sinkhole.

As each infected machine called in, O'Murchu and Chien mapped the domains and countries from which they reported and examined the data that Stuxnet sent in, looking for common characteristics—including the number of victims carrying the Siemens software. By the end of the week, more than 38,000 infected machines from dozens of countries had contacted the sinkhole, and at a rate of 9,000 new infections a day, the number was swiftly growing. They would eventually track more than 100,000 infections in more than 100 countries.[7] Stuxnet was still spreading, despite

---

5 Alex Gostev, chief malware expert at Kaspersky Lab in Russia, found that Stuxnet sent to the command servers a file—named Oem6c.pnf—that identified not only which Siemens program was installed on the computer (the Siemens Step 7 programming software or the WinCC program, which operators use to monitor conditions on their PLCs) but also included a list of any Step 7 project files on the machine and the path string that showed where on the computer the files were located. The Step 7 project files contain the programming commands for PLCs. Gostev suspects that anytime the attackers found project files on a machine, they may have sent a separate tool to the computer to steal the files and examine them for configuration data to determine if Stuxnet had found the systems it was seeking.

6 The DNS providers had already dead-lettered the traffic to the two domains so that it was going nowhere when Symantec approached them. They had pointed the traffic to the IP address 127.0.01, which is commonly used to return traffic to the sender's machine.

7 The 100,000 figure is the number that Symantec tracked during the first six months after Stuxnet was discovered. But the total number of infections, based on figures that other antivirus companies compiled as they added detection to their tools, eventually climbed to more than 300,000, according to Kaspersky Lab.

signatures distributed by antivirus firms to stop it, indicating that many victims didn't have the latest antivirus software installed. Among the infected machines calling in to their sinkhole was an occasional hit from an antivirus firm—a sign that researchers at some competing firms were still running Stuxnet on their test-beds.

As O'Murchu and Chien mapped the geographical location of each infection, an unusual pattern began to emerge. Out of the initial 38,000 machines they tracked, more than 22,000 were based in Iran. Indonesia was a distant second, with about 6,700 machines, followed by India with 3,700 infections. The United States had fewer than 400 infections, and the numbers in other countries dropped steeply from there. Only a small number of all of the infected machines had the Siemens software installed, and the majority of those were in Iran as well—217, as opposed to a mere 16 machines in the United States.[8]

The infection numbers were way out of sync with previous patterns of worldwide outbreaks, in which Iran never placed high, if at all, in the infection stats. Even in outbreaks that began in the Middle East or Central Asia, Iran never tracked high on the charts. It seemed clear that they were looking at a targeted attack focused on the Islamic Republic. But if the attackers were primarily interested in Siemens machines installed in Iran, then Stuxnet had spread far beyond its target. And why was it spreading farther in India and Indonesia than in the United States and Europe? What did the three nations have in common that made the infections concentrate there? Given the time and money that had obviously gone into producing the code, they knew they weren't looking at someone who was out to steal pharmaceutical recipes or the production secrets of an automobile plant, as Boldewin had speculated. The attackers had to be aiming to steal intelligence about critical systems, perhaps with strategic political importance to the region. The Siemens software that Stuxnet sought wasn't

---

8 At a US Senate hearing in November 2010, Dean Turner, director of Symantec's global intelligence network, testified that the number of unique infections in the United States had by then reached 1,600. Of these, 50 machines had the Siemens WinCC software installed on them.

just used in industrial plants, it was also used in critical infrastructure systems. Chien did a quick Google search on Iran and India to see what the two countries had in common and found recent stories about a natural gas pipeline that was being built to connect the two nations. The so-called Peace Pipeline involved a 1,700-mile pipeline running from Iran's South Pars gas field in the south of the country through Pakistan and into India, a plan the United States strongly opposed. The project had gone through a number of ups and downs over the years due to shifting geopolitical winds and funding issues, with India pulling out of it in 2009 under pressure from the United States. But in May 2010, just two months before Stuxnet was discovered, India had rejoined the project. Also that month, Iran was set to begin design and construction on the final portion of the pipeline to be built inside its borders.

But there was also something else dominating headlines about Iran— its rapidly expanding nuclear program. Iran was about to open a nuclear reactor at Bushehr, in the south of the country, which had been a source of great tension with Israel and the West for a number of years. But even more controversial than the reactor was a uranium enrichment plant in a place called Natanz that had been built to supply the reactor with nuclear fuel. The UN had voted for sanctions against Iran over the plant, and there was also talk about a possible air strike against the plant.

A disturbing geopolitical picture was beginning to emerge. The so- phisticated nature of the malicious code, plus the stolen certificates and Iran's place at the center of the outbreak made it appear that Stuxnet might be the product of a covert government spy mission—albeit one that had clearly run amok. Given that something in Iran appeared to be the target, the list of likely suspects was small—Israel, China, Russia, or the United States.

Chien paused to consider the implications. If Stuxnet *was* the product of a government spy mission, specifically a US spy mission, it made their sinkhole pretty audacious. By intercepting data the attackers were expect- ing to receive from infected machines in Iran, they had possibly landed themselves smack in the middle of an international incident and also may have helped sabotage a classified operation. The potential ramifications were daunting.

But Chien couldn't dwell upon this right now. Symantec's job wasn't to help protect covert government operations, no matter which country might be behind them. Their job was to protect the machines of customers. It didn't matter who launched the code or what it was targeting; as long as it was affecting Symantec customers, the malicious code had to be stopped.

Although machines in Iran, where Symantec didn't have customers, appeared to be the malware's primary target, Stuxnet had infected thousands of computers in other countries as well and was still on the loose, continuing to spread. And the researchers still didn't know what its malicious payload was designed to do or if it contained any bugs that might affect nontargeted machines.

They also couldn't rule out the possibility that Iran was actually the source of the attack instead of its target. Perhaps Iranian engineers had been writing Stuxnet to target machines in the United States and had lost control of it in a lab, which would have helped explain all of the infections in Iran. If it now spread to critical systems in the United States—an electric plant or the control system for a dam or railroad—what would happen then?

Chien and O'Murchu decided they had to press on.

Whatever the political implications of their decision might be, these would have to wait for consideration another day.

CHAPTER 3

NATANZ

While Chien and O'Murchu contemplated their new role in international politics, thousands of miles away in Iran, technicians at Natanz were still struggling over problems with their centrifuges. Though about 1,000 of the devices had been replaced months earlier, the cascades were only operating at 45 to 66 percent capacity, being fed much less uranium gas than they were capable of enriching. It was unclear to IAEA inspectors whether the problems were due to the natural growing pains that come with raising a new plant to maturity—Natanz began enriching uranium in 2007, but technicians were still installing new cascades and working out the kinks—or if something sinister was at play. The latter wouldn't have been a surprise. Natanz was the focus of intense international scrutiny, and it was no secret that there were many who would do anything to shut it down. In fact, they'd been trying to do so for nearly a decade.

THE ANCIENT TOWN of Natanz is located about two hundred miles south of Tehran and is home to the shrine of the thirteenth-century Sufi sheik Abd Al-Samad Esfahani, a model of early Persian architecture with elegant terracotta bricks and intricately patterned cobalt tiles. Although it sits on the edge of the Dasht-e Kavir Desert in the shadow of the Karkas Mountains, the elevated garden town has an invigorating mountain climate and is filled with natural springs. It has long been known for its fertile orchards in general, and its succulent pears in particular. But on August 14, 2002, it became known for something else. That's the day the National Council of Resistance of Iran (NCRI), a coalition of Iranian opposition groups in exile, convened a press conference at the Willard InterContinental Hotel in Washington, DC, two blocks from the White House, to announce that Iran was building an illicit nuclear facility near Natanz.

About two dozen reporters and representatives from NGOs, think tanks, and Iran watch groups filed into the Taft Room on the hotel's second floor to hear what the group had to say. Among them was a twenty-nine-year-old blond woman named Corey Hinderstein who worked for the Institute for Science and International Security (ISIS), a nonprofit nuclear nonproliferation group that tracked nuclear activities in Iran and elsewhere.

As guests sat down and a cameraman for C-SPAN took up position in the back of the room, Alireza Jafarzadeh, spokesman for the group, wasted no time getting to his point. "Although on the surface, [Iran's] main nuclear activity revolves around [the] Bushehr nuclear plant . . ." he said into the bank of microphones, "in reality, many secret nuclear programs are at work without any knowledge of [the] International Atomic Energy Agency. . . . Today, I am going to reveal to you two top-secret sites of the Iranian regime that they have succeeded to keep secret until today."[1]

Hinderstein and others shifted to attention.

Iran's nuclear power reactor at Bushehr, an ancient coastal city overlooking the Persian Gulf, had been under construction on and off for thirty years. It was one of three sites that Iran had identified as nuclear facilities

---

1 Alireza Jafarzadeh's speech is available in C-SPAN's library at: c-spanvideo.org/program/172005-1. A nonofficial transcript of his comments is also available at: iranwatch.org/privateviews/NCRI/perspex-ncri-topsecretprojects-081402.htm.

under its safeguards agreement with the IAEA, the UN agency that tracks nuclear activities around the world to make sure that countries like Iran don't use civilian nuclear facilities for covert nuclear weapons production.

For years Iran had insisted that its program at Bushehr, which was expected to be operational in 2005, was entirely peaceful in nature.[2] But there had long been rumors of secret nuclear facilities in Iran, including a covert uranium enrichment plant that might be used to create material for nuclear weapons. In 2001, US and foreign government sources had told Hinderstein's colleagues at ISIS that secret nuclear sites did exist in Iran, but provided no details that would help them investigate. Now it seemed that Jafarzadeh's ragtag group of dissidents might finally offer the proof that ISIS, and others, had been seeking.

Jafarzadeh, a thick dark mustache covering his upper lip, revealed the names of the two nuclear facilities, both of which were far north of Bushehr. One was a heavy-water production plant being built on the banks of the Qara-Chai River near Arak. "Anybody who has any kind of nuclear plans for nuclear weapons, they would definitely want to have heavy-water projects," he said.[3]

The other was a nuclear fuel manufacturing plant being built near an old highway that linked the town of Natanz to the town of Kashan. It was a joint operation of Iran's Atomic Energy Organization (AEOI) and its Supreme National Security Council. To hide the plant's true purpose, however, front companies had been established to secretly procure materials and technology for it. One of these was a company called Kala Electric

---

2 Although nuclear nonproliferation specialists weren't too concerned about plutonium from the light-water reactor at Bushehr being used to create nuclear weapons, because the material wasn't ideal for that purpose, there were other concerns related to the reactor. Deputy Assistant Secretary of Defense Marshall Billingslea told the Senate on July 29, 2002, that there were concerns that Bushehr was "a pretext for the creation of an infrastructure designed to help Tehran acquire atomic weapons"—meaning that materials acquired for Bushehr might be used for secret nuclear activites instead.
3 Heavy water is water with a high amount of the hydrogen isotope deuterium. Heavy water has nonweapons applications as a coolant and moderator in power plants and in research reactors for the production of medical isotopes. But spent fuel from such plants contains plutonium and other materials that, when reprocessed, can be used for nuclear weapons. Heavy-water reactors are a better source of plutonium than light-water reactors like Bushehr.

(also known as Kalaye Electric Company), which would later factor into Stuxnet as one of the companies believed to have been infected by the digital weapon.[4]

Construction on the Natanz complex, which Jafarzadeh said covered 100,000 square meters of land and had cost $300 million already, began in 2000 and was expected to be completed in three months, at which point workers would begin to install equipment. The cover story for the plant was that it was a desert-eradication project. But if this was true, then it was an extremely important desert-eradication project, because a former prime minister of Iran had toured the site earlier that month as a representative of the Supreme National Security Council, and the head of the AEOI made monthly visits to nearby Kashan just to keep tabs on the project. Workers at the plant also were not allowed to discuss the project with local officials. A major argument had in fact recently broken out between the AEOI and the Kashan Governor's Office because the AEOI would not discuss information about the site with the office, Jafarzadeh said. And when the deputy governor general of the province tried to visit the construction site at Natanz, he was turned away.

As Jafarzadeh rattled off details about the site and pointed to poster boards at the front of the room showing the network of front companies and individuals who were running the project, Hinderstein scribbled away in her notebook. With the general location of facilities cited, as well as the names and addresses of front companies revealed, it was the first solid evidence ISIS had received about Iran's illicit nuclear program that might be independently verified.

The timing of the revelations wasn't lost on Hinderstein. Iran was a signatory to the Treaty on the Nonproliferation of Nuclear Weapons, and under its safeguards agreement with the IAEA it was obligated to disclose the existence of any new nuclear facility 180 days before introducing nuclear material to the site so that inspectors could begin monitoring it. If the Natanz plant was indeed ninety days away from completion, then

---

4 For more information, see page 97.

Jafarzadeh's group had exposed it just in time for IAEA inspectors to demand access to it before it opened.

All of this raised obvious questions about how the NCRI got their hands on top-secret intelligence that had seemingly eluded the world's top spy agencies for years. Jafarzadeh insisted that his group obtained the information from people inside Iran who were directly associated with the program, as well as through extensive research and investigation by his group. But more likely it had come from US or Israeli intelligence agencies.[5] Israel had a history of leaking intelligence by proxy in order to sway public opinion without tainting the intelligence with its own political agenda. Israel was naturally the country with the most to fear from a nuclear-armed Iran, but it had obvious integrity issues when it came to calling out the nuclear activities of other nations, since it had long maintained its own covert nuclear weapons program, which it has never publicly acknowledged.[6] For this and other reasons, it conducted its political machinations behind the scenes by feeding intelligence to Western governments, the IAEA, and groups like Jafarzadeh's.

If the information did come from the United States or Israel, Jafarzadeh's group was an odd choice to leak it. The NCRI was the political arm of the Mujahedin-e Khalq, or MEK, an Iranian opposition group once known for its anti-Israel and anti-US stance. It was accused of killing six Americans in Iran in the 1970s as well as setting off bombs in Iran in 1981 that killed more than 70 people, including the Iranian president and prime

5 Jafarzadeh said the NCRI received the intelligence just days before the press conference and that it came from members of the resistance inside Iran. "These are people who were directly associated or involved with this, [and] had access to information directly about these kinds of activities," he told reporters in the room. "Certainly, these are people who have access to this information within the regime." Asked if his group had shared the intelligence with US authorities, Jafarzadeh parsed his words carefully. The data "have been prov . . . ," he started to say, "have been available to the proper authorities in this country. I'm not aware of their reaction yet." Two years later, CIA Director George Tenet said about these and other revelations from the NCRI, "I want to assure you that recent Iranian admissions about their nuclear programs validate our intelligence assessments. It is flat wrong to say that we were 'surprised' by reports from the Iranian opposition last year." He was speaking at Georgetown University on February 5, 2004. A transcript of his talk is available at: https://www.cia.gov/news-information/speeches-testimony/2004/tenet_georgetownspeech_02052004.html.

6 Israel secretly joined the ranks of nuclear powers in 1967.

minister. The group had been on the US State Department's list of terrorist organizations since 1997 but had been trying to rehabilitate its image to get off the list ever since. Helping to expose secret nuclear facilities in Iran would no doubt earn it support in Congress to achieve that aim.[7]

The NCRI had made provocative claims about Iran's nuclear program in the past, but some of them had proved to be false. There were questions about the accuracy of this new information as well. Jafarzadeh had identified the Natanz facility as a fuel-manufacturing plant, but this didn't make sense to Hinderstein and her colleagues at ISIS. Iran was already planning to build a fuel-manufacturing plant not far from Natanz, so it didn't seem logical to build a second one so close. Nonetheless, they were willing for now to accept the revelations as true. To help verify them, however, Hinderstein decided to seek out satellite images to see if she could spot evidence of construction that matched Jafarzadeh's description.

Hinderstein had been with ISIS for six years—she'd come to the job straight out of college—and over time had become its resident expert on satellite imagery, an emerging tool that only recently had become available to groups like hers. For decades, satellite imagery, particularly high-resolution images, had been the sole domain of governments and intelligence agencies. The only time anyone else could see pictures from space was if a government agency or research institute decided to release them, which rarely occurred. Images only became available for the public to buy in the mid-1990s, but these weren't very sharp. It wasn't until several years later that images at 1.6-meter resolution—the resolution at which you could actually see details clearly—became available.

ISIS was one of the first nongovernmental organizations to invest in the expensive software needed to analyze the images, recognizing early on the important role they could play in nonproliferation work. Hinderstein's first experience analyzing satellite images came in 1998, after Pakistan con-

---

7 The NCRI's lobbying campaign worked. With the aid and support of a number of US lawmakers, as well as former leaders of the FBI and CIA, the group got its name removed from the terrorist list in 2012. Supporters called the group a loyal ally of the United States and cited its role in helping expose Iran's covert nuclear program as one of the reasons to remove it from the list.

ducted six underground nuclear tests in response to underground atomic detonations made by India. Working with a satellite imagery expert, she learned how to identify pixelated objects in the images and interpret shadows and gradations in order to decipher depth in the two-dimensional pictures.

About two months after the press conference, armed with the details from Jafarzadeh and extensive additional research, Hinderstein logged into their account at Digital Globe, one of two commercial providers of satellite images in the United States, to scour the archive for available images.[8] Today, satellites have imaged nearly every part of the Earth, with most pictures available to anyone via Google Earth. But in 2002, the only way to find images in Digital Globe's archive was if someone had already commissioned the company to photograph a site, or if Digital Globe had taken images of a location on its own initiative, such as Niagara Falls or the Grand Canyon—images the company knew would sell well. To commission an image that wasn't in the archive cost about $10,000, but once an image existed, it became available for others to purchase at one-third the price.

The Digital Globe interface that Hinderstein used looked like Google Maps, with small gray boxes that popped up on-screen wherever satellite images were available. But clicking on a gray box produced only a browsing image—a rough image of 16-meter resolution, which meant that every pixel showed 16 meters of ground. To see more detail, you had to buy the 1.6-meter version.

Hinderstein couldn't believe her luck when she found images for both Arak and Natanz available in the archive. Jafarzadeh hadn't provided exact coordinates for either of the two sites, so Hinderstein had to first locate Arak on the Digital Globe map, then move slowly outward from the town, searching in concentric circles until a gray box popped up. When she clicked on the image, it was clear this was a heavy-water production

---

8 The other company was GeoEye.

plant as Jafarzadeh described. ISIS had identified such a plant in Pakistan a couple of years earlier, and the site near Arak looked very similar.

When she searched the region of Natanz, however, she found two possible locations in the middle of the desert where images were available. At each of the sites, three gray boxes stacked on top of each other popped up, indicating multiple images were available for both sites. It was as if someone had left a giant arrow directing her to them. The dates on the images indicated they had all been snapped September 16 and 26—weeks after Jafarzadeh's press conference. It was clear that someone else had been seeking the same information that she was seeking. Hinderstein suspected it was the IAEA. The IAEA had established a satellite imagery analysis lab of its own the previous year, and it would have made sense for the agency to commission images after Jafarzadeh's revelations.[9]

Hinderstein clicked on the gray boxes at one of the sites and quickly eliminated it as the nuclear facility. It was nowhere near the 100,000 square meters Jafarzadeh described and looked more like a water-purification or sewage plant than anything to do with nuclear fuel. The other site, however, was more suspect. It was much larger than the first and showed obvious signs of massive, ongoing excavation. Despite the blurry 16-meter image, Hinderstein could make out what looked to be a collection of buildings and large mounds of churned earth inside two layers of security fences. She also noted a single road leading out to the site, suggesting the area had restricted access.

After she purchased and loaded the 1.6-meter image into their viewing tool, she could see numerous pipes laid out on the ground as well as large piles of gravel for mixing concrete. There was also a traffic roundabout that had already been partially paved. But as she studied the image more closely, she noticed something odd. Jafarzadeh had said the site was a fuel-manufacturing plant, but fuel-manufacturing was a very industrial process and tended to involve aboveground facilities with large smokestacks. There were no smokestacks at the Natanz site, however, and what's more,

---

9 An IAEA source confirmed to me that the agency did commission the images.

there were three large buildings that were being built deep underground, with a tunnel connecting them. The buildings were in the final stage of construction. She could also make out what appeared to be a series of circles around the perimeter of the site, suggesting the future location of anti-aircraft guns.

The images had been captured at just the right time to catch Iranian workers still in the process of covering the rooftops of the underground buildings with several alternating layers of earth and cement. A few weeks later and they would have been completely obscured from above, yielding no obvious sign of their existence. Someone had carefully planned the outing of Natanz at just the right moment to capture the evidence.

Two of the underground buildings were each about the size of half a dozen football fields and were heavily reinforced with concrete walls about six to eight feet thick. The Iranians were obviously fortifying them against a possible air strike. The tunnel leading down to the buildings was also built in the shape of a U instead of a straight line—a common tactic to prevent missiles sent into the mouth of a tunnel from having direct aim at a target on the other end.

Hinderstein showed the images to her boss, David Albright, a physicist and former weapons inspector in Iraq who founded ISIS. The two were certain now that this wasn't a fuel-manufacturing plant. Iran would have no reason to build such a plant underground, since there would be little interest in bombing it. The only logical conclusion, they reasoned— one that would explain the underground construction and the evidential plans for antiaircraft guns—was that this was the elusive uranium enrichment plant they had been seeking.

IT WAS A quiet day in Vienna when news from Jafarzadeh's press conference filtered back to Olli Heinonen in the IAEA's headquarters overlooking the Danube River. During August, most of Europe was on holiday, and Vienna was no exception. Heinonen's boss, Dr. Mohamed ElBaradei, the IAEA's director general, was on vacation in Egypt, and much of the organization's other staff members were out of town as well. So Heinonen, a Finn in his early fifties with wire-framed glasses and a boyish mop of reddish-brown hair, was alone in his office when he read the news. Heinonen was head of Division B of the IAEA's Safeguards Department and had only three months before he was taken on the IAEA's Iran portfolio after having been the agency's chief inspector of North Korea and other parts of Asia for several years. It was a return to familiar territory for him, since he'd managed the IAEA's Iran portfolio before from 1992 to 1995. A Persian rug marking the period still decorated the floor of his office.

A veteran nuclear inspector, Heinonen had come to the IAEA in 1983 from a nuclear research center in Finland. With a PhD in radiochemistry from the University of Helsinki, he had a higher level of subject expertise than early generations of IAEA inspectors, who tended to have little scientific training. He also had a reputation for quiet confidence and steadfast determination that made it clear to the nations he inspected that he had little patience for duplicity.

As he took in the news from Jafarzadeh, he was struck by the level of detail it revealed. Heinonen had been waiting for information like this for a while. Like his counterparts at ISIS, he immediately suspected the Natanz facility wasn't a fuel-manufacturing plant at all but a uranium enrichment plant. Two years earlier, government sources had told the IAEA that Iran tried to secretly purchase parts from Europe in the 1980s to manufacture centrifuges for uranium enrichment.[10] Based on this, Heinonen had suspected that Iran had an illicit centrifuge plant hidden somewhere within its borders, but he never knew its location, and the IAEA couldn't confront the Iranians without exposing the source of the intelligence. The IAEA had also been wary of acting on information received from government sources, ever since an intelligence agency had told the IAEA in 1992 that Iran was secretly procuring prohibited nuclear equipment but hadn't provided any details. When the IAEA confronted Iran about the claims,

---

10 David Albright, *Peddling Peril: How the Secret Nuclear Trade Arms America's Enemies* (New York: Free Press, 2010), 187.

officials denied the accusations and invited inspectors to visit their nuclear sites to see for themselves. But the inspectors found nothing to support the claims and ended up leaving Iran embarrassed.[11]

The revelations this time, however, were different. They had been publicly disclosed, so Heinonen didn't have to hide the source of the information, and they included precise and specific details, naming actual facilities and locations. This meant the IAEA could independently verify their existence and demand that Iran open them to inspection.[12]

Heinonen picked up the phone and called his boss in Egypt, who agreed that he should send a letter immediately to Ali Akhbar Salehi, the Iranian ambassador to the IAEA, demanding an explanation about what Iran was doing at Natanz. Salehi was outraged by the letter's accusatory tone, saying the IAEA had no business questioning Iran about unverified claims, especially ones that came from a known terrorist group. Gholam Reza Aghazadeh, Iran's vice president and head of its Atomic Energy Organization, told the IAEA that Iran had not been hiding Natanz, but had simply planned to disclose its existence to the IAEA at a later date.[13] If the IAEA was patient, all would soon be revealed, he said. For now he would only say that Iran planned to build several nuclear power plants over the next twenty years and needed nuclear fuel to operate them. He didn't say if Natanz was a uranium enrichment plant being built to help produce such fuel, but this appeared to be the implication.

The IAEA pressed Iran to open Natanz immediately to its inspectors, and after a bit of back and forth Iranian officials reluctantly agreed to a

---

11 Author interview with Heinonen in June 2011.
12 There are differing reports about what the IAEA knew when. According to Mark Hibbs, a former leading journalist on nuclear issues who is now a policy analyst, about two months before the NCRI's press conference, the United States gave the IAEA coordinates for the suspect sites in Iran, which the United States had been tracking since at least the beginning of 2002 (Hibbs, "US Briefed Suppliers Group in October on Suspected Iranian Enrichment Plant," *NuclearFuel*, December 23, 2001). David Albright of ISIS says, however, that although US sources gave the IAEA coordinates for sites, they didn't say that the Natanz site was a uranium enrichment plant. Mohamed ElBaradei, in his book *The Age of Deception*, acknowledges that in mid-2002 the IAEA received information about the Natanz facility, but doesn't say if the IAEA knew it was a uranium enrichment plant.
13 Iranian officials would later say that the only reason they had concealed their activities at Natanz was because the West had tried to thwart their efforts to build a civilian nuclear program.

date in October. But just as the IAEA was preparing for the trip, Iran canceled the visit, saying the date would not work. A second visit was scheduled for December, but that too got canceled. Heinonen suspected Iran was trying to buy time to move incriminating evidence out of Natanz.

When ISIS founder David Albright learned that Iran was stalling, he decided to take the satellite images to the media to pressure Iran into opening Natanz to inspectors. It was one thing for Iran to rebuff claims made by an opposition group with a political agenda. It was another to respond to stark images of secret sites broadcast worldwide on CNN. So on December 12, CNN ran a story, along with the satellite images provided by ISIS, saying that Iran was believed to be building a secret enrichment plant at Natanz that might be used to produce fissile material for nuclear weapons. Iran's ambassador to the United Nations denied that Iran had a nuclear weapons program and told CNN that "any satellite photographs of any facility that you may have" were for a peaceful nuclear energy program, not a weapons program.[14]

The images had the desired effect, however: after the CNN story ran, Iranian officials committed to an inspection date in February.

ALTHOUGH THE NATANZ facility was new, Iran's nuclear activities actually went back more than forty years. They had their roots in the regime of the former shah, Mohammad Reza Pahlavi, during a time when the United States and other Western nations fully supported Iran's nuclear aspirations.

Iran launched its public and approved nuclear program in 1957, more than a decade after the United States detonated the first atomic bombs over Japan. It was during a time when other nations were clamoring to join the exclusive nuclear club the United States had founded. In an effort to redirect the nuclear ambitions of these nations, the Eisenhower admin-

---

14 A transcript of the CNN piece is available at http://transcripts.cnn.com/
TRANSCRIPTS/0212/13/lol.07.html.

istration promoted what it called the Atoms for Peace program, whereby countries would receive help to develop nuclear technology as long as they used it for peaceful purposes only. As part of the program, Iran signed an agreement with the United States to receive help to build a light-water nuclear research reactor at Tehran University. The United States also agreed to supply enriched uranium to fuel it.[15]

But despite US efforts to limit the development of nuclear weapons, four other nations pushed their way into the elite nuclear club after the war—the Soviet Union, Great Britain, France, and China. To curb the proliferation madness, the Treaty on the Nonproliferation of Nuclear Weapons was developed in the 1960s to prevent more countries from following suit and to work on reducing the weapons that nuclear-armed nations already possessed.[16]

Under the treaty, which divided the world into nuclear haves and have-nots, the nonweapons nations would be given aid to develop civilian nuclear programs as long as they agreed to foreswear building nuclear weapons and similarly agreed to regular inspections by the IAEA to ensure that materials and equipment intended for the civilian programs were not diverted for nuclear weapons development. The problem with this arrangement, however, was that many of the components and facilities for civilian nuclear programs were dual-use and could also be used for a nuclear weapons program, making it difficult to police a country's operations. As Hannes Alfvén, a Swedish Nobel laureate in physics once said, "Atoms for peace and atoms for war are Siamese twins."

Iran was one of the first countries to sign the treaty in 1968, and by 1974 it had established its own Atomic Energy Organization and developed a grand scheme to build twenty nuclear reactors with support from

15 Digital National Security Archive, "US Supplied Nuclear Material to Iran," January 29, 1980, available at nsarchive.chadwyck.com (registration required). See also Dieter Bednarz and Erich Follath, "The Threat Next Door: A Visit to Ahmadinejad's Nuclear Laboratory," *Spiegel Online*, June 24, 2011, available at spiegel.de/international/world/the-threat-next-door-a-visit-to-ahmadinejad-s-nuclear-laboratory-a-770272.html.

16 Anne Hessing Cahn, "Determinants of the Nuclear Option: The Case of Iran," in *Nuclear Proliferation in the Near-Nuclear Countries*, eds. Onkar Marway and Ann Shulz (Cambridge: Ballinger Publishing Co., 1975), 186.

Germany, the United States, and France, who all stood to gain from the sale of equipment to the shah's regime. The first two reactors were to be built at Bushehr. In 1975, German engineers with the Siemens subsidiary Kraftwerk Union broke ground on the $4.3 billion construction project, which was slated to be completed in 1981.[17]

There were concerns at the time that Iran's endgame might be nuclear weapons. The shah himself hinted at one point that his nuclear aims weren't solely peaceful in nature, asserting in an interview that Iran would get nuclear weapons "without a doubt . . . sooner than one would think" if conditions in the Middle East made it necessary.[18] But US leaders weren't worried, because they considered the shah a friend and couldn't seem to fathom a day when he or his regime wouldn't be in power.[19]

That day came pretty quickly, however, when the Islamic Revolution erupted in 1979 just as one of the reactor buildings at Bushehr was nearing completion. The revolutionaries who ousted the shah and seized power with the Ayatollah Ruhollah Khomeini took a narrow view of the behemoth reactors being erected at Bushehr, considering them a symbol of the shah's alliance with the West. The United States, alarmed by the unstable political situation, withdrew support for the project, and the German government eventually forced Kraftwerk Union to pull out of its contract for Bushehr.[20]

The subsequent Iran–Iraq war wasn't kind to the abandoned reactors. Throughout the eight-year war, which ran from 1980 to 1988, Iraq bombed the two towers more than half a dozen times, leaving them in

---

17 Ali Vaez, "Waiting for Bushehr," *Foreign Policy*, September 11, 2011.
18 John K. Cooley, "More Fingers on Nuclear Trigger?" *Christian Science Monitor*, June 25, 1974. Iranian officials later denied that he made the statement.
19 In fact, Iran discussed plans with Israel to adapt surface-to-surface missiles to fit them with nuclear warheads. See Paul Michaud, "Iran Opted for N-bomb Under Shah: Ex-Official," *Dawn*, September 23, 2003. Also, according to Akbar Etemad, head of Iran's Atomic Energy Organization under the shah, he had been tasked with creating a special team to track the latest nuclear research so that Iran would be ready to build a bomb if and when it was necessary. He disclosed the information during an interview with *Le Figaro* in 2003, according to Elaine Sciolino, "The World's Nuclear Ambitions Aren't New for Iran," *New York Times*, June 22, 2003.
20 John Geddes, "German Concern Ends a Contract," *New York Times*, August 3, 1979. See also Judith Perera, "Nuclear Plants Take Root in the Desert," *New Scientist*, August 23, 1979.

ruins.[21] During the war, the commander of Iran's Revolutionary Guard urged the Ayatollah Khomeini to launch a nuclear weapons program to fend off Iraq and its Western allies. But Khomeini refused, believing that nuclear weapons were anathema to Islam and a violation of its basic moral principles. He apparently changed his mind, however, after Saddam Hussein unleashed chemical weapons on Iranian troops and civilians, killing about 25,000 and injuring more than 100,000 others. Incensed by the UN's passive reaction, and alarmed at rumors that Iraq was seeking to build nuclear weapons of its own, Khomeini decided to revive Iran's nuclear program. This included developing a uranium enrichment program.[22]

To launch the program, Iran turned to a Pakistani metallurgist named Abdul Qadeer Khan for help. Khan had been instrumental in helping Pakistan build its nuclear weapons program in the mid-1970s, using centrifuge technology he had stolen from Europe. Khan had worked for a Dutch company that conducted centrifuge research and development for Urenco, a consortium formed by Germany, Great Britain, and the Netherlands to develop centrifuges for nuclear power plants in Europe. As part of his job, Khan had access to sensitive centrifuge designs that he copied and took back to Pakistan. He also absconded with lists of suppliers, many of whom were willing to secretly sell Pakistan parts and materials to make the centrifuges for its program.

Centrifuges are metal cylinders with rotors inside that can spin at speeds in excess of 100,000 revolutions per minute to enrich uranium hexafluoride gas, produced from uranium ore found in earth and seawater. The hexafluoride gas is piped into "cascades" of centrifuges—groups of centrifuges connected by pipes and valves. And as the rotors inside them spin, the centrifugal force separates the slightly lighter U-235 isotopes in

---

21 Vaez, "Waiting for Bushehr."
22 Institute for Science and International Security, "Excerpts from Internal IAEA Document on Alleged Iranian Nuclear Weaponization," October 2, 2009. The ISIS report is based on an IAEA internal document titled "Possible Military Dimensions of Iran's Nuclear Program," available at isisnucleariran.org/assets/pdf/IAEA_info_3October2009.pdf.

the gas—the fissile isotopes needed for atomic energy—from the heavier U-238 isotopes, in a process likened to panning for gold.[23] Gas containing the heavier isotopes gets pushed to the outer wall, while gas containing lighter isotopes gathers closer to the center. Coils wrapped around the outside of the centrifuge that are filled with heated water create a varying temperature that sets the gas in vertical motion, in an oval pattern along the wall of the centrifuge, to further separate the isotopes. Scoops divert the gas containing the concentration of lighter isotopes into other centrifuges at a "higher" stage in the cascade, where further separation occurs, while the heavier gas, the depleted uranium, is diverted into a second set of centrifuges in a lower stage of the cascade for further separation. When additional U-235 isotopes are separated from this gas, it gets fed back into the higher stages to be recombined with the other U-235 isotopes while the depleted gas is sent to "waste"—that is, the tail end of the cascade, where it gets discarded. This process gets repeated until gas containing the desired concentration of U-235 isotopes is achieved.[24]

In 1987, after Iran revived its nuclear program, officials there contacted a German engineer-turned-black-marketeer, who was a key supplier of equipment for Pakistan's illicit nuclear program. He helped arrange a secret meeting in Dubai between Iranian officials and other members of the Khan supply network. In exchange for $10 million, the Iranians walked away with two large suitcases and two briefcases filled with everything they needed to kick-start a uranium enrichment program—technical designs for making centrifuges, a couple of disassembled centrifuge prototypes, and a drawing for the layout of a small centrifuge plant containing six cascades.[25] Apparently as a bonus, the marketeers threw in a fifteen-page document describing how to turn enriched uranium into uranium metal

---

23 The U-235 isotope has three fewer neutrons than the U-238, which makes it lighter.
24 Charles D. Ferguson, *Nuclear Energy: What Everyone Needs to Know* (New York: Oxford University Press, 2011).
25 Dennis Frantz and Catherine Collins, *The Nuclear Jihadist: The True Story of the Man Who Sold the World's Most Dangerous Secrets* (New York: Free Press, 2007), 156. The items were listed on a handwritten document the IAEA obtained that was described in IAEA Board of Governors, "Director General, Implementation of the NPT Safeguards Agreement in the Islamic Republic of Iran, GOV/2005/67" (report, September 2, 2005), 5.

and cast it into "hemispheres," the core component of nuclear bombs.[26] Khan later told Pakistani television that he helped Iran develop its nuclear program because he thought if both Pakistan and Iran became nuclear powers, they would "neutralize Israel's power" in the region.[27]

The disassembled centrifuges the Iranians received were based on one of the designs Khan stole from Urenco. In Pakistan the centrifuge was known as a P-1, but in Iran it became known as the IR-1. Initially, Iran lacked money to do much of anything with the designs, but in 1988, after the Iran–Iraq war ended and its resources were freed up, the country began pouring money into an enrichment program, buying high-strength aluminum and other materials to build its own centrifuges, and secretly importing nearly two tons of natural uranium—including uranium hexa-fluoride gas—from China.[28]

Khan later secretly gave Iran components for five hundred P-1 centri-fuges, as well as instructions for setting up a quality-assurance program for making and testing the centrifuges. The latter was badly needed because Iran was having trouble with the centrifuges it had created from Pakistan's prototypes. Sometimes they spun out of control and crashed; other times they didn't work at all.[29] By 1994, Iran had succeeded in operating only one centrifuge successfully at "nearly full speed."[30]

As a result, the Iranians accused Khan of selling them a bill of goods. So in 1996, he handed over drawings for Pakistan's P-2 centrifuge, a more

26 In November 2007, according to the IAEA Board of Governors, Iran gave the IAEA a copy of the fifteen-page document, "Implementation of the NPT Safeguards Agreement and relevant provisions of Security Council resolutions 1737 (2006) and 1747 (2007) in the Islamic Republic of Iran" (report, February 22, 2008), 4. Iran claimed it had not requested the document but received it unsolicited from the black marketeers.
27 Erich Follath and Holger Stark, "The Birth of a Bomb: A History of Iran's Nuclear Ambitions," *Der Spiegel*, June 17, 2010.
28 IAEA Board of Governors, "Implementation of the NPT Safeguards Agreement in the Islamic Republic of Iran" (report, November 10, 2003), 5.
29 In 1992, the former head of Iran's Atomic Energy Organization, Masud Naraghi, left Iran and provided the CIA with some information about Iran's program. Naraghi had helped negotiate the deal in 1987 between Iran and A. Q. Khan to obtain the first centrifuges for Iran's enrichment program. He told the CIA, for example, that Iranian researchers were having trouble with the IR-1 centrifuges that they were trying to build from Khan's design. See Frantz and Collins, *Nuclear Jihadist*, 202. See also Albright, *Peddling Peril*, 76–81.
30 *Nuclear Jihadist*, 213.

advanced centrifuge based on another design stolen from Urenco.[31] The P-2 was much more efficient than the IR-1 and could enrich about two and a half times the amount of uranium in the same amount of time. It also used a rotor made from maraging steel—a more resilient material than the breakage-prone aluminum rotors in the IR-1.

While Iran was busy developing its secret uranium enrichment program, its public nuclear program continued in parallel. In 1995, the country signed an $800 million contract with Russia to resume construction of a reactor at Bushehr. The two countries also discussed building a uranium enrichment plant to produce fuel for the reactor, but the Clinton administration intervened and convinced Russia to drop it. So Iran simply built a secret enrichment plant on its own.[32]

Around this time, Europe began tightening export controls on dual-use equipment and components. The controls didn't deter Iran, however; they just forced its covert program further underground. To protect research and production facilities from being discovered, officials began spreading the work out among various sites around the country, some of them on protected military grounds, others hidden in plain sight in unassuming offices and warehouses. As part of this effort, it moved its centrifuge-manufacturing operations out of the Tehran Nuclear Research Center, where it had been launched, and into factories that once belonged to the Kalaye Electric Company, a former watch factory in an industrial part of Tehran that the Atomic Energy Organization had purchased as a front operation. It was the same company that Jafarzadeh would later mention at his press conference in 2002.

Sometime around 1999, Iran conducted its first successful enrichment tests at the Kalaye factory using small cascades of centrifuges and some

---

31 IAEA Board of Governors, "Director General, Implementation of the NPT Safeguards Agreement" (report September 2, 2005), 5.

32 It's believed that designs for a separate uranium conversion plant at Esfahan—for converting milled uranium ore into gas—may have come from China. In 1997, the Clinton administration announced that it had halted a deal that China had made to sell Iran a conversion facility, but Iran still obtained blueprints for the plant from the Chinese. See John Pomfret, "U.S. May Certify China on Curbing Nuclear Exports," *Washington Post*, September 18, 1997.

of the uranium hexafluoride gas purchased from China.[33] It was a major breakthrough, proving once and for all the viability of a program that had taken a decade to develop. Officials with Iran's Atomic Energy Organization went full tilt at this point, ordering workers to begin large-scale production of 10,000 centrifuges for a sprawling enrichment plant they planned to build at Natanz. At the same time, they began ramping up procurement efforts to obtain parts and materials in Europe and elsewhere.[34] Sometime in 2000, workers broke ground on the complex at Natanz, and Iran was on its way to becoming a nuclear nation.

---

33 Iran released the details of its nuclear history piecemeal over a number of years, and they were relayed in IAEA reports as the agency received them, beginning in 2004. The details from Iran, however, did not always jibe with information the IAEA and reporters received from other sources.
34 Albright, *Peddling Peril*, 185.

CHAPTER 4

STUXNET DECONSTRUCTED

In the first days after the news of Stuxnet broke, nearly a dozen Symantec researchers on three continents were involved in the company's initial analysis of the code. But very quickly that dropped down to just three—Chien, O'Murchu, and Falliere—as other analysts fell away to focus on new threats that were coming in. Now, nearly a week after Stuxnet had been exposed, the three analysts were still picking apart the "missile" portion of the attack and hadn't even begun to examine the payload yet.

Like conventional weapons, most digital weapons have two parts—the missile, or delivery system, responsible for spreading the malicious payload and installing it onto machines, and the payload itself, which performs the actual attack, such as stealing data or doing other things to infected machines. In this case, the payload was the malicious code that targeted the Siemens software and PLCs.

With so much work on Stuxnet still to be done, Chien had the task of convincing his managers that he and his team should continue digging through the code, even though it was already becoming yesterday's news. Every Wednesday, he had a video conference call with the company's threat managers around the world to review all of the major infections they were investigating at the time and to talk about strategy. The first Wednesday after Stuxnet was exposed, the puzzling attack was at the top of their agenda.

Symantec's offices in Culver City occupy a large and airy building on a nine-acre business campus dotted with palm trees and desert shrubs. The modern, five-story structure is a stark contrast to VirusBlokAda's cramped Communist-era office, with a spacious, high-ceilinged atrium and large cement-tile floors that clink like hollow glass when visitors walk on them, due to tunnels beneath that house the building's power and ventilation systems. The Symantec office complex is LEED–gold certified for its environment-friendly architecture, with solar-reflecting roof to ward off the relentless Southern California sun and a glass façade designed to give every occupant a view, or at least what passes for one in this uninspired neighborhood of shopping malls and freeways near the Los Angeles airport.

The videoconference room was a small, windowless space tucked into a forgotten neighborhood of the building's third floor that was reached via a circuitous route from the malware lab. Inside the room, three large video screens, mounted at eye level on a wall in front of a row of tables, made it appear as if the virtual visitors were seated directly across from Chien.

Chien laid out a summary of O'Murchu's early findings for his managers—the code's abnormally large size, its sophisticated method for loading and hiding its files, and the mysterious payload that seemed to target only Siemens PLCs. He also revealed the bizarre geographic pattern of the infection data pouring into their sinkhole. The possible political implications of the attack, however, remained unspoken.

"We want to put Nico on this full-time," Chien then told his managers, referring to Falliere in France. "And I think Liam and I should continue working on it as well." There was one catch, however. He had no idea how long it would take them to finish analyzing the code.

Typically, the company's research teams analyzed about twenty malicious files a day, so devoting three top analysts to a single threat indefinitely didn't make any business sense. They'd done this only once before, with the Conficker worm in 2008. But Conficker was a shape-shifting worm that infected millions of machines around the world and left a lot of still-unanswered questions in its wake, including why the worm had been created in the first place.[1] Stuxnet, by contrast, infected only a fraction of Conficker's numbers and had a targeted focus on an even smaller subset— the Siemens PLCs. Yet something about the mysterious code cried out for further investigation, and Chien's managers agreed they shouldn't drop it just yet. "But keep us posted on what you find," they said, with little idea that their weekly meetings would be dominated by talk of Stuxnet for months to come.

Chien and his colleagues seized the opportunity to dive into the code, taking it on as a personal obsession. But no sooner had they begun the operation than they realized they were headed into uncharted territory with little help to guide them.

SYMANTEC IS A large, international corporation, but Chien and O'Murchu worked out of a small satellite office, going at it primarily alone with little input. They worked in Symantec's Threat Intelligence Lab in Culver City, the cyber equivalent of a biodefense lab, where researchers

---

1 Despite the fact that Conficker spread so rapidly and so successfully, it never really did anything to most of the machines it infected, leaving an enduring mystery about the motives for creating and unleashing it. Some thought the attackers were trying to create a giant botnet of infected machines to distribute spam or conduct denial-of-service (DoS) attacks against websites—a later variant of Conficker was used to scare some users into downloading a rogue antivirus program. Others feared it might install a "logic bomb" on infected systems that would cause data to self-destruct at a future date. But when none of these scenarios materialized, some thought Conficker might have been unleashed as a test to see how governments and the security industry would respond. The attack code morphed over time and used sophisticated methods to remain several steps ahead of researchers to prevent them from stamping out the worm altogether, leading some to believe the attackers were testing defenses. After Stuxnet was discovered, John Bumgarner, chief technology officer for U.S. Cyber Consequences Unit, a consulting firm with primarily government clients, claimed Conficker and Stuxnet were created by the same attackers, and that Conficker was used as a "smokescreen" and a "door kicker" to get Stuxnet onto machines in Iran. As proof, he cited the timing of the two attacks and the fact that Stuxnet used one of the same vulnerabilities Conficker had used to spread. But Symantec and other researchers who examined Stuxnet and Conficker say they found nothing to support Bumgarner's claim. What's more, the first version of Conficker avoided infecting any machines in Ukraine, suggesting this may have been its country of origin.

could unleash malevolent code on a "red" network—a sandboxed system air-gapped from Symantec's business network—to observe its hostile behavior in a controlled environment. To reach the ground-floor lab, workers passed through several sets of security doors, each with progressively more restrictive rules. The final gateway kept all but a handful of workers out and physically isolated the red network from computers connected to the outside internet. Portable media were prohibited here—no DVDs, CD-ROMs, or USB flash drives were allowed—to prevent workers from mindlessly slipping one into an infested machine and inadvertently carrying it out of the lab with a malicious specimen stowed away on it.

The term "threat intelligence lab" conjures a sterile workshop with scientists in white coats bent over microscopes and Petri dishes. But Symantec's lab was just a nondescript office space filled with mostly empty cubicles and a handful of workers who stared intently at their monitors all day, mostly in silence, doing methodical and seemingly tedious work. There were no pictures on the walls; no Nerf guns or other goofy office games that workers sometimes play to blow off steam; no plants, fake or otherwise, to give the space a homey feel. The only greenery came courtesy of a wall of windows overlooking a grassy, tree-covered hill—the kind that business parks manufactured to simulate nature for shut-in workers.

O'Murchu's cubicle was barren of any personal touch, aside from a lone panoramic shot of the Grand Canyon, bathed in pink and mauve sunset hues, that commemorated a road trip he took with his father the previous year. He had two research computers on his desk that were attached to the red network and a third, for reading e-mail and surfing the web, that consisted of just peripherals—a keyboard, monitor, and mouse—connected via snaking cables to a hard drive secreted outside the lab in a server closet, safely quarantined from the hostile network.

Chien's cubicle, which shared a wall with O'Murchu's, was only slightly more personal, with an odd assortment of art postcards and pirate flags next to an enamel-coated door sign that read CHIEN LUNATIQUE—a pun on his name. Translated loosely from the French it meant "Beware of Dog," but Chien preferred the more literal translation, "Mad Dog."

Chien was thirty-nine years old but looked a decade younger. Tall, with a lanky frame and wire-rimmed glasses, he had a wide, engaging grin with cavernous dimples that sank deep into his cheeks whenever he laughed, and he talked in rapid-fire bursts whenever he got excited about a topic he was discussing. Chien had enjoyed a long and successful career in security, but in a highly competitive field where professionals often hyped their skills and experience to stand out among competitors, he was the opposite, modest and understated, preferring to focus on the forensics instead of the flash.

Of the three of them, he had worked at Symantec the longest. It was his first job out of college, but he fell into it completely by chance. In the early '90s at UCLA, he studied a mix of genetics, molecular biology, and electrical engineering, and like O'Murchu was well on his way to a career in science. But after graduating in 1996, he followed a few friends to Symantec, intending to stay just a couple of years to earn money for grad school. But he never left.

Cybersecurity was still a nascent field and it was easy to get a job without training or experience. Chien knew nothing about viruses at the time, but had taught himself x86 assembly, the programming language most malware is written in, and that was enough. The best analysts weren't trained computer engineers anyway. Engineers built things, but virus wranglers tore them apart. Even with computer security an established profession built on training courses and certifications, Chien favored job candidates who had no experience but had an unquenchable curiosity and a nagging need to solve puzzles and tear things apart. It was easy to teach someone how to code virus signatures, but you couldn't teach curiosity or instill in someone a passion for knowing how things worked. The best researchers had an obsessive streak that made them dog a piece of code until it relinquished its secrets.

When Chien joined Symantec, antivirus researchers were like the Maytag repairman in those iconic ads—they had a lot of downtime. Viruses were still rare and tended to spread slowly via floppy disks and the "sneaker net"—carried from one computer to another by hand. Customers who thought they were infected with a virus would mail the suspicious file on a floppy disk to Symantec, where it might sit in a desk tray for a week or more before Chien or one of his colleagues wandered by and picked it up. Most of the time, the files turned out to be benign. But occasionally, they found a malicious specimen. When that occurred, they dashed off some signatures to detect it, then threw them onto another floppy disk and mailed it back to the customer along with instructions for updating their virus scanner.

It wasn't long, though, before malware evolved and the landscape changed. The introduction of Microsoft Windows 98 and Office, along with the expanding internet and proliferation of e-mail, spawned rapid-spreading viruses and network worms that propagated to millions of machines in a matter of minutes. The Melissa virus in 1999 was one of the most notorious.[2] Launched by a thirty-one-year-old New Jersey programmer named David Smith, it came embedded in a Word document that Smith posted to the alt.sex.usenet newsgroup. Smith knew his target audience well—he enticed them to open the file by claiming it contained usernames and passwords to access porn sites. Once opened, Melissa exploited a vulnerability in the macro function of Microsoft Word and e-mailed itself to the first fifty contacts in the victim's Outlook address book. Within

---

2 Melissa wasn't the first prolific attack, however. That honor is reserved for the Morris worm, a self-propagating program created by a twenty-three-year-old computer science graduate student named Robert Morris Jr., who was the son of an NSA computer security specialist. Although many of Stuxnet's methods were entirely modern and unique, it owes its roots to the Morris worm and shares some characteristics with it. Morris unleashed his worm in 1988 on the ARPAnet, a communications network built by the Defense Department's Advanced Research Projects Agency in the late 1960s, which was the precursor to the internet. Like Stuxnet, the worm did a number of things to hide itself, such as placing its files in memory and deleting parts of itself once they were no longer needed to reduce its footprint on a machine. But also like Stuxnet, the Morris worm had a few flaws that caused it to spread uncontrollably to 60,000 machines and be discovered. Whenever the worm encountered a machine that was already infected, it was supposed to halt the infection and move on. But because Morris was concerned that administrators would kill his worm by programming machines to tell it they were infected when they weren't, he had the worm infect every seventh machine it encountered anyway. He forgot to take into account the interconnectedness of the ARPAnet, however, and the worm made repeated rounds to the same machines, reinfecting some of them hundreds of times until they collapsed under the weight of multiple versions of the worm running on them at once. Machines at the University of Pennsylvania, for example, were attacked 210 times in twelve hours. Shutting down or rebooting a computer killed the worm, but only temporarily. As long as a machine was connected to the network, it got reinfected by other machines.

three days the world's first mass-mailing virus had spread to more than 100,000 machines, a spectacular record at the time, but quaint by today's standards. In addition to spreading via Outlook, it slipped a nerdy Scrabble reference into documents on infected machines: "twenty-two, plus triple-word-score, plus fifty points for using all my letters. Game's over. I'm outta here." Melissa was relatively benign, but it opened the way to other fast-moving viruses and worms that would dominate headlines for years.[3]

As the threat landscape expanded, Symantec realized it needed to halt infections faster, before they began to spread. When the company first entered the antivirus business, it was considered a good response time to turn a threat around—from discovery to delivery of signatures—within a week. But Symantec aimed to reduce this to less than a day. To accomplish this, the company needed analysts in multiple time zones to spot viruses in the wild when they first appeared and get signatures out to US customers before they woke up and began clicking on malicious e-mail attachments.

Chien had already surpassed his two-year plan with Symantec by then. He'd saved enough money for grad school and planned to move to Colorado to snowboard and cycle before applying to science programs. But Symantec dangled an enticing offer—a post in the Netherlands instead. The company had a tech support and sales office outside Amsterdam but wanted a team of malware analysts too. Chien couldn't say no. He landed in the Netherlands days before the Love Letter worm crippled the internet in May 2000. The worm began as a college student's mischievous class project in the Philippines but then spread rapidly to millions of machines worldwide. It was the perfect test for Symantec's new European rapid-response team, even if that team consisted of just one. Within a record twenty minutes Chien had analyzed the code and crafted signatures to detect it. (Sadly, the achievement was all for naught, since Love Letter sucked up so much internet bandwidth that customers couldn't reach Symantec's servers to download the signatures.) As soon as the crisis passed,

---

3 Self-replicating worms—Conficker and Stuxnet being the exception—are far rarer than they once were, having largely given way to phishing attacks, where malware is delivered via e-mail attachments or through links to malicious websites embedded in e-mail.

Chien hired four more researchers to complete his Amsterdam team, and they were all in place when the next big threat—the Code Red worm—hit the following year.

He moved to Tokyo for a brief period to open another research office. Then, in 2004, Symantec moved its European headquarters from Amsterdam to Dublin, and Chien went with it. Shortly after, he bulked up the research team with more than a dozen new hires, including O'Murchu. In 2008 he returned to the United States, along with his new wife, a Frenchwoman who had worked in Symantec's Netherlands office. He was later joined in California by O'Murchu.

Now in Culver City, the two of them and Falliere faced a daunting task in deconstructing Stuxnet.

THE FIRST OBSTACLE the researchers encountered occurred when they tried to decrypt all of Stuxnet's code. As O'Murchu had already discovered, the core of Stuxnet was a large .DLL file that got deposited onto machines. This came packaged with dozens of smaller .DLLs and components inside of it, all wrapped together in layers of encryption that had to be cracked and removed before they could decipher the code. Luckily, the keys for unlocking them were in the code itself; every time Stuxnet landed on a Windows machine, it used the keys to decrypt and extract each .DLL and component as needed, depending on the conditions it found on the machine. At least this was how it was supposed to work. Some of the keys weren't getting activated on their test machine—the final ones needed to unlock the payload.

O'Murchu dug through the code, trying to find the reason, and that's when he discovered references to specific brands of Siemens PLCs. Stuxnet wasn't *just* hunting for systems with Siemens Step 7 or WinCC software installed; they also had to be using a specific line of Siemens PLCs—the company's S7-315 and S7-417 programmable logic controllers. Only this combination of software and hardware triggered Stuxnet's keys to unlock and release the payload.

The only problem was, Chien and O'Murchu had neither—the Siemens software nor the PLCs. Without them, they had to use a debugger to poke and prod the code to find the keys and manually unlock the payload.

The debugging program, a mainstay for reverse engineers, let them walk through the code step-by-step—like a stop-motion camera—to isolate each function and document its activity. Using this, they singled out each section of code that contained commands for decrypting the malware and followed the commands to find the keys. But locating the keys was only half the trick. Once they had all the keys, they had to find the encryption algorithm that each key unlocked. It took several days of digging, but when they had all the parts unlocked, they could finally see every step that Stuxnet took during its initial stages of infection.[4]

One of the first things Stuxnet did was determine if the computer was a 32-bit or 64-bit Windows machine; Stuxnet only worked with 32-bit Windows machines. It also determined if the machine was already infected with Stuxnet. If it was, Stuxnet made sure the resident malware was up to date and simply swapped out any old files for the latest ones. But if Stuxnet found itself on a new machine, it began an elaborate infection dance, racing rapidly through a succession of steps to scope out the landscape of the machine and determine the best way to proceed.

During this process, one of its rootkits quickly took up position on the machine to blind the system to Stuxnet's files on the USB flash drive. It did this by hooking the system so the file names couldn't be seen by virus scanners—the equivalent of hiding them in a scanner's shadow. If the scanner tried to read the contents of the flash drive, the rootkit intercepted the commands and served back a modified list that didn't include Stuxnet's files. But some scanners couldn't be bypassed in this way. Stuxnet knew which scanners were trouble and modified its methods accordingly

---

4 Once virus wranglers extract the keys and match them to the algorithms, they also write a decryptor program so they can quickly decrypt other blocks of code that use the same algorithm. For example, when they receive new versions of Stuxnet or even other pieces of malware that might be written by the same authors and use the same algorithms, they don't have to repeat this tedious process of debugging all of the code to find the keys; they can simply run their decryptor on it.

if it found one of these on a machine. If Stuxnet determined it couldn't bypass a scanner at all, it halted the infection and shut itself down.

But if Stuxnet decided to proceed, the second driver then got activated. This one had two tasks—the first was to infect any USB flash drive that got inserted into the machine, which it would do for only twenty-one days after Stuxnet infected the machine.[5] The second, and most important, task was to decrypt and load the large .DLL, and its various components, into the machine's memory using the novel techniques O'Murchu had documented. First it unwrapped and decompressed the .DLL to release the smaller .DLLs inside, then it loaded them into memory. Because the files were running in memory, any time the machine rebooted, the files got wiped away, so the driver also had to reload them in memory after each reboot.

Once the large .DLL and its contents were all unpacked and loaded into memory, Stuxnet searched for new machines to infect and called home to the command-and-control servers to report its new conquest— but unless it found the Siemens Step 7 or WinCC software installed on the machine, Stuxnet would go dormant on the machine once these steps were done.

So now the Symantec researchers knew how Stuxnet propagated and loaded its files, but they still didn't know why it was created or what it was designed to do. The answers to these questions were still buried within its payload.

As O'Murchu reflected on what they had uncovered so far in the missile portion of the code, he couldn't help but admire the artful handiwork the attackers had put into their attack—the clever ways they solved problems they expected to encounter, and the numerous scenarios they had to test before releasing their code. Not all of Stuxnet's features were impressive on their own, but as a whole the attack posed a formidable threat.

Aside from the complex ways Stuxnet loaded its files and bypassed security software, it used an extensive checklist to ensure all conditions were

---

5 In some versions of Stuxnet the attackers had increased the time period to ninety days.

ideal on a machine before unleashing its payload. It also carefully tracked all of the resources it used on a machine and made sure to free up each as soon as it was no longer needed to reduce the amount of processing power Stuxnet consumed on the machine—if Stuxnet used too much power, it ran the risk of slowing the machine down and being discovered. It also overwrote many of the temporary files it created on a machine once they were no longer needed. All software programs create temporary files, but most don't bother to delete them, since they'd just be overwritten by the temporary files other applications create. The attackers didn't want Stuxnet's files lingering on a system for long, however, because it raised the risk that they'd be seen.

But despite all the extra effort the attackers put into their code, there were several parts that seemed oddly underdesigned. O'Murchu wasn't the only one who thought so. As the Symantec researchers published their findings about Stuxnet over several weeks, members of the security community began grumbling online about the code's many failings, insisting that its authors weren't nearly the elite cadre of hackers original reports made them out to be. Their technical prowess was inconsistent, some said, and they made a number of mistakes that allowed investigators to see more easily what they were trying to do.

Stuxnet, for example, would have been much more difficult to decipher had the attackers used better obfuscation to thwart the researchers' forensic tools—such as more sophisticated encryption techniques that would prevent anyone except the target machines from unlocking the payload or even identifying that Stuxnet was targeting Siemens Step 7 software and PLCs. Stuxnet also used weak encryption and a standard protocol to communicate with its command-and-control servers instead of custom-written ones that would have made it more difficult for researchers to establish their sinkhole and read the malware's traffic.

Cryptographer Nate Lawson's comments dripped with disdain when he wrote in a blog post that Stuxnet's authors "should be embarrassed at their amateur approach to hiding the payload" and their use of outmoded methods that criminal hackers had long since surpassed. "I really hope it wasn't written by the USA," he wrote, "because I'd like to think our elite cyberweapon developers at least know what Bulgarian teenagers did back in the early 90s."[6] The mix of state-of-the-art tactics and Hacker 101 techniques made Stuxnet seem like a "Frankenstein patchwork" of well-worn methods, others said, rather than the radical skunkworks project of an elite intelligence agency.[7]

But O'Murchu had a different take on Stuxnet's inconsistencies. He believed the attackers deliberately used weak encryption and a standard protocol to communicate with the servers because they wanted the data traveling between infected machines and the servers to resemble normal communication without attracting unusual attention. And since communication with the servers was minimal—the malware transmitted only limited information about each infected machine—the attackers didn't need more advanced encryption to hide it. As for securing the payload better, there may have been limitations that prevented them from using more sophisticated techniques, such as encrypting it with a key derived from extensive and precise configuration data on the targeted machines so that only those machines could unlock it.[8] The targeted machines, for example, may not have had the same exact configuration, making it difficult

---

6 Nate Lawson, "Stuxnet Is Embarrassing, Not Amazing," January 17, 2011, available at rdist.root .org/2011/01/17/stuxnet-is-embarrassing-not-amazing/#comment-6451.
7 James P. Farwell and Rafal Rohozinski, "Stuxnet and the Future of Cyber War," *Survival* 53, no. 1 (2011): 25.
8 One method for doing this, as Nate Lawson points out in his blog post, is to take detailed configuration data on the targeted machine and use it to derive a cryptographic hash for a key that unlocks the payload. The key is useless unless the malware encounters a machine with the exact configuration or someone is able to brute-force the key by reproducing all known combinations of configuration data until it achieves the correct one. But the latter can be thwarted by deriving the hash from an extensive selection of configuration data that makes this unfeasible. Stuxnet did a low-rent version of the technique Lawson describes. It used basic configuration data about the hardware it was seeking to trigger a key to unlock its payload, but the key itself wasn't derived from the configuration data and was independent of it. So once the researchers located the key, they could simply unlock the payload with the key without needing to know the actual configuration. Researchers at Kaspersky Lab did, however, later encounter a piece of malware that used the more sophisticated technique to lock its payload. That payload has never been deciphered as a result. See pages 296–97.

to use a single payload encryption key, or there may have been concerns that the configuration on the machines could change, rendering such a key useless and preventing the payload from triggering.

Stuxnet's failings may also have been the consequence of time constraints—perhaps something caused the attackers to launch their code in a rush, resulting in last-minute work that seemed sloppy or amateurish to critics.

But there was another possible explanation for the patchwork of techniques used in the threat—Stuxnet was likely created by different teams of coders with different skills and talents. The malware's modular nature meant development could have been done by different teams who worked on various parts simultaneously or at different times. O'Murchu estimated it took at least three teams to code all of Stuxnet—an elite, highly skilled tiger team that worked on the payload that targeted the Siemens software and PLCs; a second-tier team responsible for the spreading and installation mechanisms that also unlocked the payload; and a third team, the least skilled of the bunch, that set up the command-and-control servers and handled the encryption and protocol for Stuxnet's communication. It was possible the division of responsibilities was so well defined and the teams so compartmentalized that they never interacted.

But although each of the teams had varying levels of skill and experience, they were all at least uniform in one thing—none of them had left any clues behind in the code that could be easily used to track them. Or so it seemed.

ATTRIBUTION IS AN enduring problem when it comes to forensic investigations of hack attacks. Computer attacks can be launched from anywhere in the world and routed through multiple hijacked machines or proxy servers to hide evidence of their source. Unless a hacker is sloppy about hiding his tracks, it's often not possible to unmask the perpetrator through digital evidence alone.

But sometimes malware writers drop little clues in their code, intentional or not, that can tell a story about who they are and where they come from, if not identify them outright. Quirky anomalies or footprints left behind in seemingly unrelated viruses or Trojan horses often help forensic investigators tie families of malware together and even trace them to a common author, the way a serial killer's modus operandi links him to a string of crimes.

Stuxnet's code was more sterile than the malware Chien and O'Murchu usually saw. But two things about it did stand out.

Chien was sifting through the notes they had taken on Stuxnet's initial infection dance one day, when something interesting caught his eye—an infection marker that prevented Stuxnet from installing itself on particular machines. Each time Stuxnet encountered a potential new victim, before it began the process of decrypting and unpacking its files, it checked the Windows registry on the machine for a "magic string" composed of a letter and numbers—0x19790509. If it found the string, Stuxnet withdrew from the machine and wouldn't infect it.

Chien had seen "inoculation values" like this before. Hackers would place them in the registry key of their own computers so that after unleashing attack code in a test environment or in the wild, it wouldn't come back to bite them by infecting their own machine or any other computers they wanted to protect. Inoculation values could be anything a hacker chose. Generally, they were just random strings of numbers. But this one appeared to be a date—May 9, 1979—with the year listed first, followed by the month and day, a common Unix programming format for dates. Other number strings that appeared in Stuxnet, and that the researchers knew for certain were dates, were written in the same format.

Chien did a quick Google search for the day in question and was only half surprised when one of the results revealed a connection between Israel and Iran. The 1979 date was the day a prominent Iranian Jewish businessman named Habib Elghanian was executed by firing squad in Tehran shortly after the new government had seized power following the Islamic Revolution. Elghanian was a wealthy philanthropist and respected leader of the Iranian Jewish community until he was accused of spying for

Israel and killed. His death marked a turning point in relations between the Jewish community and the Iranian state. For nearly forty years, while Mohammad Reza Shah Pahlavi had been in power, Iranian Jews had enjoyed a fairly amicable relationship with their Muslim neighbors, as did the Islamic nation with the state of Israel. But Elghanian's execution, just three months after the revolution ousted the shah, was a "Kristallnacht" moment for many Persian Jews, making it clear that life under the new regime would be very different. The event sparked a mass exodus of Jews out of Iran and into Israel and helped fuel hostility between the two nations that persists today.

Was the May date in Stuxnet a "Remember the Alamo" message to Iran from Israel—something like the missives US soldiers sometimes scribbled onto bombs dropped on enemy territory? Or was it an effort by non-Israeli actors to implicate the Jewish state in the attack in order to throw investigators off their trail? Or was it simply a case of Chien having an active imagination and seeing symbols where none existed? All Chien could do was guess.

But then the Symantec team found another tidbit that also had a possible link to Israel, though it required more acrobatic leaps to make the connection. This one involved the words "myrtus" and "guava" that appeared in a file path the attackers left behind in one of the driver files. File paths show the folder and subfolders where a file or document is stored on a computer. The file path for a document called "my résumé" stored in a computer's Documents folder on the C: drive would look like this—c:\documents\myresume.doc. Sometimes when programmers run source code through a compiler—a tool that translates human-readable programming language into machine-readable binary code—the file path indicating where the programmer had stored the code on his computer gets placed in the compiled binary file. Most malware writers configure their compilers to eliminate the file path, but Stuxnet's attackers didn't do this, either by accident or not. The path showed up as b:\myrtus\src\objfre_w2k_x86\i386\guava.pdb in the driver file, indicating that the driver was part of a project the programmer had called "guava," which was stored on his computer in a directory named "myrtus." Myrtus is the genus of a family of plants that includes several species of guava. Was the programmer a botany nut, Chien wondered? Or did it mean something else?

Chien searched further for information about myrtus and found a tangential connection to another prominent event in Jewish history, when Queen Esther helped save the Jews of ancient Persia from massacre in the fourth century BCE. According to the story, Esther was a Jewish woman who was married to the Persian king Ahasherus, though the king did not know she was Jewish. When she learned of a plot being hatched by the king's prime minister, Haman, to kill all the Jews in the Persian Empire with the king's approval, she went to the king and exposed her identity, begging the king to save her and her people. The king then had Haman executed instead and allowed the Jews in his empire to battle all the enemies that Haman had amassed for their slaughter, resulting in a victory for the Jews and 75,000 of their enemies dead. The Purim holiday, celebrated annually by Jewish communities around the world, commemorates this deliverance of Persian Jews from certain death.

On its face, the story appeared to have no relevance to Stuxnet at all. Except that Chien found a possible connection in Esther's Hebrew name. Before changing her name and becoming the queen of Persia, Esther had been known by the name Hadassah. Hadassah in Hebrew means myrtle, or myrtus.

The parallels between ancient and modern Persia were not hard to draw, in light of current events. In 2005, news reports claimed that Iranian president Mahmoud Ahmadinejad had called for Israel to be wiped off the face of the map. Though subsequent reports determined that his words had been mistranslated, it was no secret that Ahmadinejad wished the modern Jewish state to disappear, just as Haman had wanted his Jewish contemporaries to disappear centuries before.[9] And on February 13, 2010, around the same time that Stuxnet's creators were preparing a new version

---

9 University of Michigan Professor Juan Cole and others pointed out that the Persian language has no such idiom as "wipe off the map," and that what Ahmadinejad actually said was that he hoped the Jewish/Zionist occupying forces of Jerusalem would collapse and be erased from the pages of history.

of their attack to launch against machines in Iran, Rav Ovadia Yosef, an influential former chief rabbi of Israel and a political powerhouse, drew a direct line between ancient Persia and modern Iran in a sermon he gave before Purim. Ahmadinejad, he said, was the "Haman of our generation."

"Today we have a new Haman in Persia, who is threatening us with his nuclear weapons," Yosef said. But like Haman and his henchmen before, he said, Ahmadinejad and his supporters would find their bows destroyed and their swords turned against them to "strike their own hearts."[10]

None of this, however, was evidence that the "myrtus" in Stuxnet's driver was a reference to the Book of Esther. Especially when read another way, as some later suggested, myrtus could easily have been interpreted as "my RTUs"—or "my remote terminal units." RTUs, like PLCs, are industrial control components used to operate and monitor equipment and processes. Given that Stuxnet was targeting Siemens PLCs, it seemed just as possible that this was its real meaning.[11] But who could say for sure?

The Symantec researchers were careful not to draw any conclusions from the data. Instead, in a blog post written by Chien and a colleague, they said simply, "Let the speculation begin."[12]

---

10 "Rabbi Yosef: Ahmadinejad a New Haman," Israel National News, February 14, 2010, available at israelnationalnews.com/News/Flash.aspx/180521#.UONaAhimWCU.

11 John Bumgarner, chief technology officer for US Cyber Consequences Unit, supports this interpretation and also says that "guava" in the driver's file path likely refers to a flow cytometer made by a California firm called Guava Technologies. Flow cytometers are devices used to count and examine microscopic particles and are used, among other things, to measure uranium isotopes. Bumgarner believes they may have been used at Natanz to help scientists gauge the enrichment levels of uranium hexafluoride gas as the U-238 isotopes are separated from the U-235 isotopes that are needed for nuclear reactors and bombs. Guava Technologies makes a flow cytometer called Guava EasyCyte Plus that can be integrated with PLCs to provide operators with real-time data about the level of isotopes in uranium. Flow cytometers are a controlled product and would have to be registered under the Trade Sanctions Reform and Export Enhancement Act of 2000 before being sold to Iran. See John Bumgarner, "A Virus of Biblical Distortions," December 6, 2013, available at darkreading.com/attacks-breaches/a-virus-of-biblical-distortions/d/d-id/1141007?.

12 Patrick Fitzgerald and Eric Chien, "The Hackers Behind Stuxnet," Symantec, July 21, 2010, available at symantec.com/connect/blogs/hackers-behind-stuxnet.

CHAPTER 5

SPRINGTIME FOR AHMADINEJAD

A caravan of black, armor-plated Mercedes sedans sped out of Tehran, heading south toward Natanz at ninety miles an hour. Seated separately in three of the cars were Olli Heinonen; his boss, IAEA director Mohamed ElBaradei; and a third colleague from the agency. It was a crisp winter morning in late February 2003, six months after Alireza Jafarzadeh's group blew the lid off the covert plant at Natanz, and the inspectors were finally getting their first look at the site. Riding with ElBaradei was an elegant professorial man with white hair and a closely trimmed salt-and-pepper beard: Gholam Reza Aghazadeh, who was vice president of Iran and president of its Atomic Energy Organization.

Two weeks earlier, Iranian president Sayyid Mohammad Khatami had finally acknowledged that Iran was building a uranium enrichment plant at Natanz, confirming what ISIS and others had suspected all along about the facility. Iran was in fact developing a number of facilities for every stage of the fuel-production cycle, the president said in a speech, and Natanz was just one of them. But he insisted that Iran's nuclear aspirations were purely peaceful.[1] If you had faith, logic, and all the advantages that a

---

1 Khatami was speaking in Tehran on February 9, 2003, during a meeting between the Ministry of Science, Research and Technology and university chancellors. Parts of his speech were reported at: iranwatch.org/library/government/iran/iran-irna-khatami-right-all-nations-nuclear-energy-2-9-03.

great nation like Iran possessed, you didn't need weapons of mass destruction, he said. What he didn't say, however, was why, if Iran had nothing to hide, it was burying the Natanz plant deep underground. If nothing illicit was going on, why fortress it beneath layers of cement and dirt? And why enrich uranium at all if fuel for Iran's nuclear reactors could be purchased from other countries, as most nations with nuclear reactors have done and as Iran had already done in a contract with Russia? These and other questions were lingering in the minds of the IAEA officials as they drove out to Natanz.

The IAEA had come a long way since its inauguration in 1957, when it was created to promote the peaceful development of nuclear technology. Its other role as nuclear watchdog—to ensure that countries didn't secretly apply that technology to weapons development—was supposed to be secondary. But in the five decades since the agency's inception, the latter task had gradually become its most critical, as one nuclear crisis arose after another. Unfortunately, the agency's ability to fulfill this role was often thwarted by its limited authority to investigate or punish countries that violated their safeguards agreements.

Because the agency had no intelligence arm to investigate suspicious activity on its own, it had to rely on intelligence from the thirty-five member states on its board, like the United States—which made it susceptible to manipulation by these countries—or on whatever information inspectors could glean from their visits to nuclear facilities. But since inspectors only, for the most part, visited sites that were on a country's declared list of nuclear facilities, this left rogue states free to conduct illicit activity at undeclared ones. Even when armed with evidence that a nation was violating its safeguards agreement, the IAEA could do little to enforce compliance. All it could do was refer the offending nation to the UN Security Council, which could then vote on whether to levy sanctions.[2]

These weaknesses became glaringly apparent in 1991 after the end of

2 The thirty-five member countries on the IAEA's Board of Governors can vote to open an inquiry or refer a country to the UN Security Council for sanctions.

the first Gulf War, when inspectors entered postwar Iraq to sort through the rubble and discovered that Saddam Hussein had built an advanced nuclear weapons program under their noses. Prior to the war, the IAEA had certified that Hussein's cooperation with the agency was "exemplary."[3] So inspectors were shocked to discover after the war that they had been completely duped. By some estimates, Iraq had been just a year away from having enough fissile material to produce a nuclear bomb and two to three years away from having a full-scale nuclear arsenal.[4] Even more shocking was the realization that the illicit activity had been conducted in rooms and buildings next door to declared facilities the inspectors examined, but under the rules could not inspect spontaneously.[5]

Infuriated by Iraq's duplicity, the IAEA developed a so-called Additional Protocol to augment the safeguards agreement that countries signed. This increased the kinds of activities they had to report to the IAEA and also granted the agency leeway to ask more probing questions, request access to purchasing records for equipment and materials, and more easily inspect sites where illicit activity was suspected to have occurred. There was just one catch. The Protocol applied only to countries that ratified it, and in 2003 when the inspectors visited Natanz, Iran wasn't one of them. As a result, the inspectors were limited in the kinds of demands they could place on Iran.[6]

THE THREE-HOUR DRIVE from Tehran to Natanz dropped the inspectors at their destination midmorning on that February day. Along the

---

3 Prior to the war, the IAEA's deputy director in charge of compliance told Leonard Weiss, staff director of the Senate Committee on Governmental Affairs, that not only was Iraq's cooperation with the IAEA exemplary but that the IAEA had no hint from anyone that Iraq was doing anything untoward. See Leonard Weiss, "Tighten Up on Nuclear Cheaters," *Bulletin of Atomic Scientists* 47 (May 1991): 11.

4 David Albright and Mark Hibbs, "Iraq's Nuclear Hide and Seek," *Bulletin of Atomic Scientists* 47 (September 1991): 27.

5 Douglas Frantz and Catherine Collins, *The Nuclear Jihadist: The True Story of the Man Who Sold the World's Most Dangerous Secrets* (New York: Free Press, 2007), 188.

6 In 2004, Iran agreed to sign the Additional Protocol but didn't ratify it. Later, in 2006, after the IAEA referred Iran to the UN Security Council for noncompliance with its safeguards agreement,

way, they passed the Hoz-e-Soltan Lake on their left, a salt lake that evaporated in the summer and was knee-deep with brackish water in the winter, and the city of Qom on their right, a center of Shi'a learning and one of the holiest cities of Islam.

Once they passed Qom, an endless vista of sand and highway greeted them for 60 miles until they reached the town of Kashan. Another twelve miles after that, in a wilderness composed of varying shades of brown and beige, a collection of buildings emerged on the horizon, as if sprung from the desert floor.

When they reached Natanz, Heinonen was startled to see that construction at the sprawling complex was much further along than he'd expected. In addition to the underground halls, a maze of buildings aboveground was already erected, including a cluster of five prefabricated structures with aluminum siding that fanned out from one another like the beams of a disjointed cross. A large electric substation had also been erected to power the buildings and the centrifuges. One of the five buildings turned out to be a pilot fuel-enrichment plant, a research facility where technicians could test new centrifuge models and cascades before installing them in the underground production halls. Once installed in the halls, the centrifuges would be expected to spin for years on end, so the pilot plant was crucial for verifying beforehand that the technology and enrichment process worked.

Although the underground halls were still a long way from being operational, technicians already had about 160 centrifuges spinning in the pilot plant, and components for hundreds of other centrifuges were waiting to be assembled there.[7] The pilot plant was slated to begin operation in June, still four months away, but Iran expected to have 1,000 centrifuges installed in it by the end of the year, with the first batch of low-enriched uranium produced within six months after that.

As Aghazadeh led them around the plant, he took pains to insist that

---

Iran retaliated by announcing it would no longer adhere to the Protocol.

7 David Albright, *Peddling Peril: How the Secret Nuclear Trade Arms America's Enemies* (New York: Free Press, 2010), 192.

no uranium hexafluoride had been introduced to Natanz yet, and no enrichment tests had been conducted using gas, either. Testing, he said, had only been done using computer simulations. It was an important distinction to make, since enriching uranium without notifying the IAEA would have violated Iran's safeguards agreement. But Heinonen wasn't buying the story. The idea that Iran had spent $300 million to construct a uranium enrichment plant without first testing cascades with actual gas to make sure the enrichment process worked stretched the boundaries of belief.

From the pilot plant, the inspectors were next taken to a showroom where the Iranians had carefully laid out, like a high-end science project, all of the individual components of an IR-1 centrifuge, as well as a pair of fully assembled ones. Aghazadeh told the inspectors that Iran had produced the IR-1s from a design of its own making. But when Heinonen moved in for a closer look, he noticed that they resembled an early-generation Urenco design that the consortium had made in Europe years earlier. He didn't know yet that Iran had actually purchased the stolen design from A. Q. Khan, but he was already suspicious of the tales Aghazadeh was spinning.

After they finished examining the showroom, the inspectors were driven down the U-shaped tunnel that Corey Hinderstein had spotted on satellite images, to view the two cavernous halls buried seventy-five feet beneath the ground. Iran didn't plan to begin filling the halls with centrifuges until 2005, but at 32,000 square meters each, they were expected to hold about 47,000 centrifuges when filled.[8] For the time being, however, they were empty shells.

Throughout the visit, interactions between the inspectors and Iranian officials had been cordial. But things grew tense when the caravan returned to Tehran in the afternoon and Heinonen asked his hosts to show

8 David Albright and Corey Hinderstein, "The Iranian Gas Centrifuge Uranium Enrichment Plant at Natanz: Drawing from Commercial Satellite Images," ISIS, March 14, 2003, available at isis-online.org/publications/iran/natanz03_02.html. See also IAEA Board of Governors, "Implementation of the NPT Safeguards Agreement in the Islamic Republic of Iran" (report, June 6, 2003), 6.

him their secret cache of uranium. Aghazadeh was taken aback by the question and pleaded ignorance. Heinonen had come armed, however, with intelligence from Western government sources that in 1991 Iran had secretly imported uranium from China, including uranium hexafluoride.[9] He brandished a letter from Chinese officials confirming the transaction. When the Iranians later produced the uranium, saying they had forgotten they had it, Heinonen and his colleagues noticed that the containers were lighter than expected and that some of the uranium hexafluoride gas seemed to be missing. The Iranians said it must have evaporated through leaks in the containers, but Heinonen suspected it had been used for secretly testing centrifuges.

That's when Heinonen insisted on seeing the Kalaye Electric watch factory as well. At its press conference in August, the NCRI had identified Kala Electric, a slightly different spelling, as one of the front companies Iran had been using for its secret nuclear program. The NCRI hadn't said what role the company played in the program, but shortly before the IAEA inspectors arrived in Iran to visit Natanz, the NCRI conveniently announced that the Kalaye facilities were used for researching and developing centrifuges. This, plus the undisclosed uranium, gave Heinonen the ammunition he needed to insist on a last-minute visit to the factory.

The Iranians reluctantly showed them the Kalaye office building, a mostly empty structure, but insisted they couldn't find the keys to open the factory itself. The inspectors were scheduled to leave Iran the next day, so they extracted a promise to see the factory on their next visit. Unfortunately, by the time they returned to Iran more than a month later, the Iranians had had plenty of time to do spring-cleaning. The inspectors noticed obvious signs of freshly painted walls in one of the factory buildings, as well as doors that had been replaced and floor tiles that had been newly grouted. Suspicious that the Iranians were covering something up, the in-

---

9 The uranium in question included uranium hexafluoride, uranium tetrafluoride, and uranium oxide.

spectors asked to collect environmental samples from the building to test for traces of enriched uranium.[10] Environmental sampling was something the IAEA had added to its repertoire after its failure to detect Iraq's illicit nuclear program. Inspectors used special cotton squares and swabs to collect dust from walls and surfaces that could be tested to detect uranium particles as small as a picogram, determine the type of uranium that was present, and even gauge whether it had been enriched and to what level.[11] But the Iranians refused to let them collect any samples.

Months later, when they were allowed to collect samples at the factory, as well as from the pilot enrichment plant at Natanz, they found low- and highly enriched uranium particles that were not on Iran's list of declared materials.[12] Confronted with evidence of this deception, officials finally admitted that they had enriched uranium gas at Kalaye, a violation of Iran's safeguards agreement with the IAEA. But they said the gas was enriched only to test the centrifuges and was enriched only to 1.2 percent. This didn't jibe with the particles the IAEA had collected, however, which ranged from 36 percent to 70 percent enriched.[13]

Uranium in its natural state contains less than 1 percent of U-235, the isotope needed for reactors and bombs. Most nuclear reactors need uranium enriched to just 3 to 5 percent. Highly enriched uranium is enriched to 20 percent or more. Although 20 percent enrichment can be used for crude nuclear devices, in addition to some types of nuclear reactors, weapons-grade uranium is enriched to 90 percent or above.

Iranian officials insisted the highly enriched particles must have come from residue left inside used centrifuges that Iran had purchased—an

---

10 US satellite imagery had captured images of trucks visiting the site, suggesting that Iran had hauled away evidence before the inspectors arrived. See Frantz and Collins, *Nuclear Jihadist*, 293.

11 IAEA, "Tools for Nuclear Inspection," a two-page pamphlet published by the agency's Division of Public Information, which describes the environmental sampling process. Available at iaea.org/Publications/Factsheets/English/inspectors.pdf.

12 IAEA Board of Governors, "Implementation of the NPT Safeguards Agreement in the Islamic Republic of Iran" (report, November 10, 2003), 6–7.

13 Sharon Squassoni, "Iran's Nuclear Program: Recent Developments" (CRS Report for Congress, November 23, 2005), 3.

admission that the centrifuge design wasn't Iran's own, as they had pre-viously stated, and that some other nation was helping Iran build its pro-gram. Suddenly, concern over the nuclear program ratcheted up.

The environmental samples weren't proof that Iran was working on a covert nuclear weapons program, but they were indications that inspec-tors had a lot of work ahead of them to try to uncover the scope of Iran's nuclear program. They were also indications that nothing Iranian officials said could be trusted. It was the start of a long and exhausting dance that would occupy the IAEA the rest of the decade as inspectors tried to piece together the history of Iran's nuclear ambitions and gauge its nuclear weapons capability.

Just as the IAEA was beginning this dance, the NCRI announced in May 2003 that it had evidence of additional secret nuclear sites in Iran, including one at a village called Lashkar Ab'ad. Iran admitted it had a pilot plant there for conducting laser enrichment experiments—another method for enriching uranium.[14] And a couple of months later, the NCRI announced the existence of two more nuclear sites, including one in a warehouse district outside Tehran that was surrounded by auto junkyards to disguise it. The NCRI said it was a secret pilot enrichment plant that Iran had set up after the IAEA's February visit to Natanz so that techni-cians could conduct enrichment experiments in secret, away from the pry-ing eyes of inspectors.[15]

With so many public revelations in rapid succession, it was clear that someone was trying to keep the fire beneath Iranian officials stoked. But the revelations kept IAEA inspectors busy as well, since they now had to add more facilities to their list of sites to monitor. In addition to Bushehr and two reactor facilities already on the list, the IAEA added the pilot and

---

14 The Institute for Science and International Security maintains a comprehensive page that details Iran's laser enrichment activity. It's available at isisnucleariran.org/sites/by-type/category/laser-enrichment.

15 The information comes from a transcript of an announcement made by NCRI spokesman Alireza Jafarzadeh. "Iran-Nuclear: Iranian Regime's New Nuclear Sites," available at ncr-iran.org/en/news/nuclear/568-iran-nuclear-iranian-regimes-new-nuclear-sites.

commercial enrichment plants at Natanz, the reactor being planned for Arak, and a uranium conversion plant at Esfahan, about a hundred miles southwest of Natanz, where Iran planned to convert uranium into gas to be enriched at Natanz.

WHILE QUESTIONS ABOUT its nuclear program were being raised, Iran defiantly pressed forward with its uranium enrichment plans. In June, workers at Natanz began feeding the first batch of uranium hexafluoride gas into ten centrifuges at the pilot plant, setting off more alarms. Foreign ministers from the EU3—France, Germany, and the UK—urged Iran to suspend its enrichment activities until the IAEA could learn more about its nuclear program. A round of negotiations ensued and Iran agreed in October to suspend its enrichment activities temporarily. It also agreed to produce a detailed history of its nuclear program to remove "any ambiguities and doubts about the exclusively peaceful character" of it.[16] Iran stuck to the latter agreement to a degree, but when officials delivered their detailed history to the IAEA, acknowledging that the centrifuge program had been in development on and off for eighteen years, they left a number of important details out.[17] The IAEA only knew this because while the agency had been trying to extract information from Iranian officials, it had also begun learning more about the secret nuclear program from the CIA.

A few years earlier, the CIA had infiltrated the nuclear supply network of A. Q. Khan by securing the allegiances of a few of his key European suppliers and turning them into moles. From them, the CIA learned that Khan had sold the designs for Pakistan's P-1 centrifuge—the design stolen from Urenco—to Iran and had also sold prototypes for its more advanced

16 Reza Aghazadeh, vice president of Iran, in a letter to the IAEA on October 21, 2003, as quoted in IAEA Board of Governors, "Implementation of the NPT Safeguards Agreement in the Islamic Republic of Iran" (report, November 10, 2003), 4.
17 Ibid., 8.

P-2 centrifuge to Libya. If Khan sold the P-2 design to Libya, Heinonen reasoned, he must have given it to Iran as well. Iran hadn't mentioned the advanced centrifuge in its detailed history, but if it did possess the centrifuges, then it was possible that Iran's uranium enrichment program was much further along than Heinonen suspected. The IAEA pressed Iran to come clean about whether it was producing P-2 centrifuges, and officials admitted that they had indeed received a design for the P-2 centrifuge in 1996. Workers had tried to develop centrifuges from the design around 2002, officials said, but had abandoned the project shortly thereafter, after encountering problems making the centrifuge rotors. Iranian officials insisted to the IAEA that they hadn't been trying to hide their work on the P-2s, but had simply planned to disclose it later.

Things grew worse over the next few months after questions arose about yet another secret facility in Iran, this one a building at the Physics Research Center in Tehran.[18] By the time inspectors got access to the site to examine it, however, the building had been razed and the topsoil trucked away, thwarting efforts to collect environmental samples for testing.[19] That April, Iran announced plans to begin conducting tests at Esfahan to convert milled uranium ore, or yellowcake, into uranium hexafluoride gas. The EU3 considered this a violation of Iran's temporary suspension agreement, since converting ore to gas was a precursor to enriching the uranium, but decided not to press the issue, fearing that Iran would cancel the already delicate suspension agreement altogether.

Then that May, the IAEA was suddenly gifted with a large cache of documents, of mysterious provenance, that further intensified concerns about Iran's nuclear program.

It began when Heinonen got a call from a woman with an American

---

18 The NCRI had exposed the site in 2003, but said at the time that it was being used for a biological weapons program. Information obtained by IAEA, ISIS, and others in 2004, however, suggested it was being used for nuclear activity, which led the IAEA to request an inspection.
19 Iran claimed the site had been razed beginning in December 2003 due to a land dispute between the Ministry of Defense and the city of Tehran. The site was razed in order to return the land to the city. See ISIS, "The Physics Research Center and Iran's Parallel Military Nuclear Program," February 23, 2012, available at isis-online.org/uploads/isis-reports/documents/PHRC_report_23February2012.pdf.

accent who said her name was Jackie. He suspected she was from the CIA but didn't ask. She knew details about his investigation into Iran's nuclear program and said that she had information that would be of interest to him. Heinonen was wary of being manipulated by the CIA, but agreed to meet her at a Starbucks.[20]

When he arrived at the coffeehouse, a young Asian woman was waiting to speak with him. She told him she would arrange a meeting for him with two of the CIA's moles who had been inside the Khan nuclear supply network and who could brief him about Khan's dealings with Iran. She also said she had a stash of documents about Iran's nuclear program that she wanted to show him. The documents came from a businessman in Tehran who had worked for the government in the steel and concrete industries—activity that took him to Natanz and Esfahan and put him in touch with the people behind Iran's nuclear program. Somehow he had gained access to a large cache of highly sensitive documents about the nuclear program and had been passing them along to Germany's intelligence agency, the BND. "Dolphin," as the BND dubbed him, had planned to use the documents as a ticket to asylum in the West for him and his family. But before he could execute his plan, Iranian intelligence agents arrested him. His wife and children managed to flee across the border to Turkey, however, taking the documents with them.

When Heinonen read the documents, he couldn't believe his eyes. Dolphin's cache laid out in a very concise manner a series of projects that purportedly composed Iran's secret nuclear weapons program. They included the country's ambitious plans to make its own nuclear fuel by mining uranium ore from a mine in southern Iran, then processing it to produce uranium concentrate (or "yellowcake"), and finally converting the yellowcake into uranium tetrafluoride and uranium hexafluoride gas.

---

20 Information about the meeting and the documents comes from an author interview with Heinonen, December 2011. See also Catherine Collins and Douglas Frantz, *Fallout: The True Story of the CIA's Secret War on Nuclear Trafficking* (New York: Free Press, 2011), 112; and Erich Follath and Holger Stark, "The Birth of a Bomb: A History of Iran's Nuclear Ambitions," *Der Spiegel*, June 17, 2010.

Uranium tetrafluoride can be used to make uranium metal, which can be used for nonweapons applications but also for bombs.[21]

None of this alone was evidence of a nuclear weapons program. But the most alarming documents in the Dolphin stash were ones that described precision tests for detonating highly explosive materials. There were also sketches and instructions for building a reentry vehicle for Iran's fleet of Shahab-3 missiles that would contain a heavy round object—suspiciously similar to a nuclear warhead—as well as a three-minute video showing a simulated explosion of a warhead at 1,970 feet, played to the cheesy Vangelis soundtrack from *Chariots of Fire*.[22] A detonation at such a high altitude made no sense for releasing a chemical or biological weapon, Heinonen reasoned, so the warhead being designed must be intended for a nuclear weapon.[23]

Were the documents authentic? Heinonen couldn't be sure, but they corroborated other information the IAEA had been receiving from member states about Iran's activities. If he was correct in his interpretation of the documents, then they were the most damning evidence yet that Iran was indeed working on a nuclear weapons program.

The IAEA later confronted Iranian officials about the documents and demanded an explanation, but officials said the documents describing the explosives tests were just as applicable to conventional warheads as to nuclear ones and denied that the tetrafluoride project existed at all. They accused the IAEA of fabricating the documents to get sanctions passed against Iran and to build a case for justifying a US and Israel air strike against Natanz.[24]

---

21 Nuclear weapons are created by shaping uranium metal into two hemispheres and embedding them in an explosives device outfitted with detonators. The detonators are rigged to explode uniformly and simultaneously in order to send the two spheres smashing violently into each other and produce a chain reaction.

22 Iran developed the missile, which had a 900-mile range, in 1998 and conducted successful tests in May 2002. Iran was also developing a missile with a 1,200-mile range.

23 Follath and Stark, "The Birth of a Bomb."

24 ElBaradei opposed releasing the documents publicly since the IAEA was unable to verify their authenticity, and memories of the United States' use of discredited documents to support the invasion of Iraq were still fresh in his mind. The IAEA, however, pressed Iran repeatedly over subsequent years to provide information about the programs described in the documents, but no

Just when it seemed that tension over its nuclear program couldn't get any worse, Iran agreed again in late 2004 to suspend its uranium conversion plans at Esfahan as well as all of its other enrichment activities and to commit to formal talks about its nuclear program. The suspension agreement didn't last very long, however. In June 2005, Mahmoud Ahmadinejad, the mayor of Tehran, was elected president of Iran, and government support for the suspension and talks began to erode. Iran's nuclear program was becoming an issue of national pride, and hardliners in the government were beginning to view the suspension and talks as weak capitulation to the West. No matter what they did to appease the West it would never be enough, they said, because the real goal of Israel and the United States was to topple the Iranian regime.

As the war in Iraq dragged on and the United States lost the upper hand there, Iranian leaders became bolder in their defiance. In August 2005, just two months after Ahmadinejad's election, international talks over the program reached an impasse, and Iran announced it was revoking the suspension agreement.[25] Iran wasted no time removing seals that the IAEA had placed on equipment at the Esfahan plant during the suspension, and proceeded with its plans to convert uranium oxide into uranium hexafluoride gas. Conditions went from bad to worse in December, when Ahmadinejad ignited a firestorm by declaring in a public speech that the Holocaust was a myth.[26]

Things were spiraling out of control. Iran's neighbors in the Middle East were so spooked by the growing tension between Iran and Israel that Kuwait's Ministry of Health decided to install fifteen radiation-detection

---

answers were forthcoming in some cases or incomplete information was provided in others. Some of the information in the documents later found its way to ISIS. See David Albright, Jacqueline Shire, and Paul Brannan, "May 26, 2008 IAEA Safeguards Report on Iran: Centrifuge Operation Improving and Cooperation Lacking on Weaponization Issues," May 29, 2008, available at isis-online.org/uploads/isis-reports/documents/ISIS_Iran_IAEA_Report_29May2008.pdf.
25 Mohamed ElBaradei provides a good behind-the-scenes description of the negotiations in his memoir and explains why Iran felt cheated by them and justified in rejecting them. *The Age of Deception: Nuclear Diplomacy in Treacherous Times* (New York: Metropolitan Books, 2011), 141–47.
26 Karl Vick, "Iran's President Calls Holocaust 'Myth' in Latest Assault on Jews," *Washington Post*, Foreign Service, December 15, 2005.

systems throughout the country and at border sites to provide early warning of any nuclear activity in the region.[27] Efforts to gauge how close Iran was to being able to build a bomb, however, were scattershot. No one had a clear view of its covert program. But Iran didn't actually have to build a nuclear weapon to be a threat. All it had to do was master the enrichment process and produce enough low-enriched uranium to make a bomb should it choose to. Once it reached this breakout point, Iran could perch on that threshold indefinitely—all the while maintaining truthfully that it possessed no nuclear weapons—until the day it decided to convert the enriched uranium into weapons-grade material and build a bomb. Estimates about how long it would take Iran to reach the breakout point varied. The US National Intelligence Estimate of 2005 concluded that Iran was six to ten years from having enough material to produce a bomb. But Israel was less optimistic. Officials there estimated it was closer to five years.[28]

Enriching uranium is one of the most difficult processes to master in making nuclear weapons. It is a delicate undertaking in the best of circumstances, fraught with trial and error, and Iran had little experience doing it. Add to this the difficulties involved in manufacturing workable centrifuges, and it was easy to see why Iran's program had taken so long to reach the point that it had. Indeed, it appeared that technicians at Natanz were still having problems with their centrifuges, as Ariel Levite, deputy director general of the Israel Atomic Energy Commission, told the United States in early 2006. It would later be revealed that some of the problems were due to sabotage of components that Iran had obtained from Turkey.[29]

Regardless of the obstacles, in early 2006, Iran resumed enrichment at the pilot plant at Natanz. The move prompted Israeli officials to revise

---

27 "06Kuwait71, Kuwait's Country Wide Radiation Monitoring System," US State Department cable from the US embassy in Kuwait to the State Department in Washington, DC, January 2006. Published by WikiLeaks at wikileaks.org/cable/2006/01/06KUWAIT71.html.

28 The assessment comes from Ariel (Eli) Levite, deputy director general of the Israel Atomic Energy Commission, in a September 2005 US State Department cable from the Tel Aviv embassy, published by WikiLeaks at wikileaks.org/cable/2005/09/05TELAVIV5705.html.

29 "06TelAviv293, Iran: Congressman Ackerman's January 5 Meeting at," US State Department cable from the US embassy in Tel Aviv, January 2006. Published by WikiLeaks at wikileaks.org/cable/2006/01/06TELAVIV293.html. See page 200 in this book for an explanation of the problems.

their previous estimate, saying now that Iran was just two to four years from nuclear weapons capability.[30] They warned the United States that Iran must not be allowed to master its enrichment process or it would be "the beginning of the end." Once that occurred, Iran would be able to enrich uranium in secret facilities anywhere in the country.[31] Centrifuge plants, unlike other parts of the fuel cycle, didn't require special facilities to operate. So once technicians worked out all of the kinks with the process, they could hide cascades of centrifuges anywhere they wanted—even in converted office buildings. "We know Iran is moving elements of its program right now," Gideon Frank, director general of the Israel Atomic Energy Commission, warned US officials in early 2006.[32] Factories able to produce parts for centrifuges were already "all over the place," he said, and other parts of the nuclear program were being housed inside heavily fortified military facilities, where IAEA inspectors would not be able to examine them, and being sequestered underground where air strikes likely would not be effective.

Then in May, Iranian officials announced that technicians at the pilot enrichment plant at Natanz had succeeded in enriching their first batch of uranium to 3.5 percent, using a full cascade of 164 centrifuges. This was followed by another announcement that technicians would finally begin installing the first of 3,000 centrifuges in one of the large underground halls. It appeared that Iran had finally overcome its difficulties, and that nothing, short of an air strike, could stop it now.

Concerned that its ability to monitor Iran's nuclear program was rapidly declining, the IAEA declared Iran in noncompliance with its safeguards agreement after years of being urged to do so by the United States. The UN Security Council adopted a resolution in July 2006, demanding

---

30 Privately, Israel and Russia both told the United States they believed Iran could actually master its enrichment difficulties within six months. See "06Cairo601, Iran; Centrifuge Briefing to Egyptian MFA," US State Department cable, February 2006, published by WikiLeaks at wikileaks. org/cable/2006/02/06CAIRO601.html.
31 "06TelAviv688, Iran-IAEA: Israeli Atomic Energy Commission," US State Department cable, February 2006, published by WikiLeaks at wikileaks.org/cable/2006/02/06TELAVIV688.html.
32 Ibid.

that Iran suspend its enrichment by the end of August or face sanctions. Ahmadinejad refused. "Those who think they can use the language of threats and force against Iran are mistaken," he said. "If they don't realize that now, one day they will learn it the hard way."[33]

Western intelligence agencies suddenly noticed an uptick in Iranian efforts to secretly procure centrifuge components in Europe and elsewhere using a network of foreign and domestic front companies.[34] They were "trying to buy like mad," recalls David Albright of ISIS. They were seeking valves, pipes, and vacuum equipment, as well as components that could be used for missile development.[35]

Rumors began swirling about plans for an air strike, but privately, Secretary of State Condoleezza Rice told the IAEA's ElBaradei that she didn't think it would come to this. Iran, she said, would surely "buckle." But Iran wasn't buckling.

At the end of 2006, with no choice than to follow through on its threat, the UN Security Council adopted a resolution applying sanctions against Iran, banning the supply of materials and technology that could be used for nuclear development. Months later it voted on more sanctions to freeze the assets of individuals and organizations believed to be involved in the nuclear program.[36] Still, Iran remained undeterred.

In February 2007, Iranian officials announced to the IAEA that technicians at Natanz had already begun to install the first centrifuges in one of the underground halls. It had taken more than a decade for Iran to reach this point, but it had at last overcome all the obstacles—technological and manmade—that had been in its way. With nothing left to stop them,

---

33 "Iran Defiant on Nuclear Deadline," BBC News, August 1, 2006, available at news.bbc.co.uk/2/hi/5236010.stm.
34 "07Berlin1450, Treasury Under Secretary Levey Discusses Next," US State Department cable from the embassy in Berlin, July 2007, published by WikiLeaks at wikileaks.org/cable/2007/07/07BERLIN1450.html. The cable mentions that at least thirty Iranian front companies had been established for procurement. Also per author interview with David Albright in January 2012.
35 Albright, *Peddling Peril*, 200–1.
36 The UN Security Council applied economic sanctions against Iran in December 2006, and in March 2007 it voted unanimously to freeze the financial assets of twenty-eight Iranians linked to its nuclear and military programs.

technicians had two cascades installed in one of the underground halls by the end of the month, and another two were in the final stages of installation. They had also transferred nine tons of uranium hexafluoride gas into the hall to begin enrichment.[37]

By June 2007, 1,400 centrifuges were installed at Natanz and enriching uranium. All of the centrifuges were IR-1s, but technicians had also begun producing IR-2 centrifuges, the more advanced centrifuge based on Pakistan's P-2 design. Iran had revived production of the IR-2s after its initial failure to produce rotors for the centrifuges.[38] Iran was also developing even more advanced IR-4 centrifuges.[39]

Tension between the United States and Israel flared. Israel accused the United States of dragging its feet with regard to Iran's program and placing too much trust in sanctions and diplomatic efforts. Israeli prime minister Ehud Olmert warned in a public address that if Iran's program wasn't halted, Israel would act on its own. "Anyone who threatens us, who threatens our existence, must know that we have the determination and capability of defending ourselves," he said. "We have the right to full freedom of action to act in defense of our vital interests. We will not hesitate to use it."[40]

But something happened in December 2007 to throw a wrench not only in US diplomatic efforts but in Israel's attack plans as well. The US National Intelligence Estimate (NIE) came out that month with a startling conclusion about Iran's nuclear program. It stated with "high confidence" that Iran did have a nuclear weapons program at one time but had halted the program back in the fall of 2003, following the US-led invasion

37 Just when matters with Iran were at their most tense, North Korea tested a nuclear device. The deteriorating nuclear situation on multiple fronts prompted the *Bulletin of Atomic Scientists* on January 17, 2007, to move the minute hand of its famous Doomsday Clock two minutes closer to midnight. Instead of seven minutes to Doomsday, it was now set to five.

38 Due to export controls and other difficulties producing the rotors from maraging steel, as the centrifuge design required, Iran had abandoned production of the IR-2s in 2002. But Iranian scientists modified the design to substitute a carbon fiber rotor instead and sometime after 2004 resumed production.

39 Collins and Frantz, *Fallout*, 259.

40 "Prime Minister Ehud Olmert's Address at the 2007 Herzliya Conference," January 24, 2007. A translation is available at pmo.gov.il/English/MediaCenter/Speeches/Pages/speechher240107.aspx.

of Iraq. This suggested that Iran was "less determined to develop nuclear weapons" than previously believed. NIEs, coordinated by the Office of the Director of National Intelligence, are based on information gleaned from US and foreign intelligence. But this one seemed to contradict what Adm. Michael McConnell, director of national intelligence, had told a Senate committee just months before. "We assess that Tehran seeks to develop nuclear weapons and has shown greater interest in drawing out the negotiations rather than reaching an acceptable diplomatic solution," he told the Senate Armed Services Committee the previous February.[41]

Although the NIE report also noted that Iran could reverse the decision to halt its weapons program at any point, and a classified version of it discussed evidence that didn't make it into the public version—that Iran might still have more than a dozen other covert nuclear facilities doing illicit enrichment and weapons development—the report threatened to weaken the case for sanctions against Iran and for military action.[42] US Defense Secretary Robert Gates, who opposed an air strike, nonetheless questioned the report's conclusion. During a congressional hearing to discuss it, he warned that Iran was engaged in suspicious procurement activities that suggested its nuclear plans were much more organized and directed than the NIE suggested. Gates wasn't the only one who disagreed with the NIE conclusion. Privately, German officials told the United States that their own intelligence indicated that Iran still had a weapons program, and Israeli officials also said they had information indicating that although Iran had halted its weapons program in 2003, it had revived it in 2005.[43]

---

41 "McConnell Fears Iran Nukes by 2015," *Washington Times*, February 27, 2007.

42 The *New York Times* wrote, "Rarely, if ever, has a single intelligence report so completely, so suddenly, and so surprisingly altered a foreign policy debate." It noted that the report "will certainly weaken international support for tougher sanctions against Iran, . . . and it will raise questions, again, about the integrity of America's beleaguered intelligence agencies." Steven Lee Myers, "An Assessment Jars a Foreign Policy Debate About Iran," *New York Times*, December 4, 2007.

43 Germany's deputy national security adviser Rolf Nikel told US officials in early 2008 that the NIE report complicated efforts to convince the German public and German companies that sanctions against Iran had merit. US State Department cable, February 2008, published by WikiLeaks at wikileaks.org/cable/2008/02/08BERLIN180.html. See also wikileaks.org/cable/2007/12/07BERLIN2157.html. With regard to the Israeli comments, according to a US State Department cable published by WikiLeaks in May 2009, IDF intelligence chief Maj. Gen.

As the sun set on 2007, Iran had 3,000 centrifuges installed at Natanz and was planning to double that number in the next year. Experts estimated that 3,000 P-1 centrifuges alone could already produce enough low-enriched uranium for a bomb in less than a year, if Iran decided to further enrich it.[44]

It seemed there was nothing anyone could do to halt the enrichment program now without risking a war.

Or was there?

While tensions over the enrichment program approached the breaking point, an alternative plan was being secretly set in motion. As Iranian technicians congratulated themselves over the progress they'd made at Natanz and were making preparations to expand the operation, a digital weapon was silently unleashed on computers at the plant with a clear-cut mission embedded in its code. With hundreds of rapidly spinning centrifuges in its sights, the precision weapon stealthily and decisively made its way straight to its target.

Amos Yadlin made the comments to Congressman Robert Wexler. See wikileaks.cabledrum.net/
cable/2009/05/09TELAVIV. The NIE had other repercussions. A German-Iranian trader named
Mohsen Vanaki was on trial in Germany for smuggling dual-use equipment to Iran. He was charged
in June 2008 under the War Weapons Control and Foreign Trade Acts. But he asserted in his defense
that he couldn't have been supplying equipment for a nuclear weapons program in Iran because
the NIE had said Iran had no such program. All charges against him were dismissed, in large part
because of the 2007 NIE report. Prosecutors appealed, however, and in 2009 the dismissal of charges
was overturned and he was later convicted, in large part based on BND intelligence about suspicious
procurements made by entities associated with Iran's military.
44 International Institute for Strategic Studies, *Iran's Strategic Weapons Programmes: A Net
Assessment* (London: Routledge, 2005), 33.

CHAPTER 6

DIGGING FOR ZERO DAYS

It was a Friday evening in late August, and Liam O'Murchu was celebrating his thirty-third birthday at a swanky rooftop lounge in Venice, California. He'd rented out a section of the open-air, U-shaped bar on top of the Hotel Erwin overlooking the Pacific Ocean, and was tipping back beer and cocktails with his girlfriend, his sister and brother-in-law visiting from Ireland, and a dozen good friends. This being Southern California, a reality-TV crew was filming a couple sitting nearby, going through the awkward motions of a "private" date.

O'Murchu's group had already been at the bar for three hours when Eric Chien showed up around nine p.m. His mind wasn't on partying, though. He was itching to show his friend and colleague an e-mail that had popped up on a security list earlier that day. But he was reluctant to bring it up because he knew once O'Murchu saw it, he wouldn't be able to put it out of his mind. "I'll show you this one thing," Chien told O'Murchu. "But then we're not going to talk about it the rest of the night, OK?" O'Murchu agreed.

Chien pulled out his BlackBerry and brought up the e-mail—a note from a researcher at another antivirus firm hinting that there might be additional zero-day exploits hidden in Stuxnet. O'Murchu looked at Chien. They'd been working on Stuxnet for weeks trying to reverse-engineer its components and had seen a few clues that suggested there might be another zero-day embedded in it, but they hadn't had time to pursue them. The clues were in the missile portion of the code responsible for spreading Stuxnet, but they had been focused on the payload, the part of the code that affected the Siemens software and PLCs.

The e-mail was vague on details, and it wasn't clear from the message whether the other researcher had actually *found* more zero-days in Stuxnet or had simply seen the same clues they had seen. Either way, O'Murchu's competitive spirit was sparked. "That's it," he told Chien. "I'm not drinking any more tonight." The next morning, a Saturday, O'Murchu was back in the office digging through Stuxnet.

The office was deserted, so O'Murchu was left to work without distraction. The Symantec team had already mapped out most of Stuxnet's missile portion before moving to the payload, so now it was just a matter of combing through the code carefully for signs of an exploit. This wasn't as simple as it sounded. Zero-day exploits weren't the sort of thing you found just by opening a malicious file and peering at the code. You had to track each reference the code made to the operating system or to other software applications on the machine to spot any suspicious ways it interacted with them. Was it forcing an application to do something it shouldn't? Jumping security barriers or bypassing system privileges? The missile portion, when reverse-engineered, consisted of thousands of lines of code, each of which had to be examined for suspicious behavior.

Stuxnet's structure wasn't linear, so trying to track what it was doing was doubly difficult. The commands skipped and jumped around, and O'Murchu had to follow their movement at every step.

After about an hour, however, he was pretty sure he'd nailed a second exploit. He searched the archive for any sign that the vulnerability it attacked had been exploited before, but found none. Then he tested the exploit on a machine with the latest Windows software installed, to be certain he wasn't making a mistake. Sure enough, Stuxnet was using a zero-day vulnerability in a Windows keyboard file to gain escalated privileges on the machine.

Zero-day vulnerabilities were valuable commodities and to use two of them at once in a single attack, and risk having them both discovered, seemed an odd waste of resources, O'Murchu thought. But he didn't stop to ponder it. He simply documented his findings and turned back to the code.

Hours later, he thought he spotted yet another exploit—signs that Stuxnet was using a vulnerability in the Windows print-spooler function to spread between machines that shared a printer. Once again, he tested it on a machine and searched the archive for any evidence that it had been exploited before, but found none. The feeling that had made his hair stand on end weeks earlier was beginning to return. He documented his findings and turned back to the code to continue foraging.

By midafternoon, when Chien came into the office to check on him, O'Murchu was bleary-eyed and needed a break. He handed his findings off to Chien, who continued working on the code until evening. They worked on it some more on Sunday and by the end of the weekend, they'd uncovered an astonishing three zero-day exploits. These, plus the .LNK exploit already discovered, made four zero-day exploits in a single attack.[1]

This was crazy, they thought. One zero day was bad enough. Two was overkill. But four? Who did that? And why? You were just burning through valuable zero days at that point. A top-notch zero-day bug and exploit could sell for $50,000 or more on the criminal black market, even twice that amount on the closed-door gray market that sold zero-day exploits to government cyber armies and spies. Either the attackers had an unlimited supply of zero days at their disposal and didn't care if they lost a

---

1 The fourth exploit they uncovered attacked a vulnerability in the Windows task scheduler. This and the Windows keyboard exploits were used to gain Stuxnet higher privileges on a machine. If the user account on a machine had limited privileges that prevented Stuxnet from installing itself or performing any other functions, the two exploits escalated these to system-level or "administrative" privileges that gave Stuxnet permission to do what it wanted without displaying any warnings or asking for an actual administrator's approval.

handful or more, or they were really desperate and had a really good reason to topload their malware with spreading power to make certain it reached its target. Chien and O'Murchu suspected that both might be true.

Chien contacted Microsoft to report the new zero-day exploits they'd found, but discovered that Kaspersky Lab in Russia had already beat them to it. Right after news of Stuxnet had broken, Kaspersky assembled a team of ten analysts to examine the missile portion of the code and within days they had found a second zero-day exploit, followed a week later by the third and fourth. At the time, they had reported the vulnerabilities to Microsoft, which was now working on patches to fix them, but couldn't go public with the news, under the rules of responsible disclosure, until Microsoft patched the software holes.[2]

The four zero-day exploits in Stuxnet were remarkable, but this wasn't the end of the story. During Chien and O'Murchu's weekend marathon with the code, they also discovered four additional ways that Stuxnet spread, without the use of zero-day vulnerabilities, for a total of eight different propagation methods. The attack code had a virtual Swiss Army knife of tools to pry its way into a system and propagate.

The most important of these involved infecting the Step 7 project files that programmers used to program PLCs, and hijacking a username (winccconnect) and password (2WSXcder) that Siemens had hard-coded into its Step 7 software.[3] The Step 7 system used the name and password to gain automatic access to a backend database where they injected code to infect the machine on which the database was stored. The database is a shared system that all the programmers working on a Step 7 project can use. Stuxnet would then infect the machine of any programmer who accessed the database. Both of these infection methods increased the

---

2 Microsoft and Kaspersky Lab began publishing information about the three other zero-day vulnerabilities in mid-September.

3 A hard-coded password is one that the software maker embeds in their code so that the system can do certain things automatically, without the user needing to enter a password. Often, the passwords can't be changed without creating problems for the system. But hard-coded passwords are a security hazard because it means that every system has the same password, and someone can discover the password by reading the code.

likelihood that Stuxnet would reach a PLC the next time the programmer connected his laptop or a USB flash drive to one to program it. The attackers used a vulnerability in an obscure feature of the Step 7 system to infect the Step 7 project files, indicating they had deep knowledge of the system that few others possessed—another sign of the extensive skill that went into the attack.[4]

In addition to these spreading mechanisms, Stuxnet had a peer-to-peer component that let it update old versions of itself when new ones were released. This let them update Stuxnet remotely on machines that weren't directly connected to the internet but were connected to other machines on a local network. To spread an update, Stuxnet installed a file-sharing server and client on each infected machine, and machines that were on the same local network could then contact one another to compare notes about the version of Stuxnet they carried; if one machine had a newer version, it would update the others. To update all the machines on a local network, the attackers would have only had to introduce an update to one of them, and the others would grab it.

It was clear from all the methods Stuxnet used to propagate that the attackers were ruthlessly intent on getting their malware to spread. Yet unlike most malware that used e-mail or malicious websites to spread to thousands of machines at a time, none of Stuxnet's exploits leveraged the internet.[5] Instead, they relied on someone carrying the infection from one

---

4 Chien and O'Murchu learned about the obscure nature of the vulnerability in the Step 7 system after consulting with control system experts like Eric Byres of Tofino Security, who had deep knowledge of the Siemens software. The vulnerability lay in the fact that the files were designed so that programmers could add more than simple data to a Siemens project file. It wasn't a vulnerability per se, but a feature, since Siemens had intentionally included this in the design of its files. But Stuxnet exploited it to slip its .DLL into the files. This alone wasn't sufficient to get Stuxnet to infect a system when a project file was opened, however. Stuxnet also had to modify critical portions of the project file, including configuration data, to make sure the .DLL got loaded to any machine that opened the file.

5 The seventh method Stuxnet used to spread was via network shares—by infecting resources and files that were shared by multiple computers on a local network. The eighth method involved an exploit that targeted a two-year-old Windows vulnerability that Microsoft had already patched. It was a vulnerability that Conficker had used previously in November 2008. Microsoft patched the vulnerability in October 2008 after hackers in China had used it first to spread a Trojan horse.

machine to another via a USB flash drive or, once on a machine, via local network connections. Based on this, it appeared the attackers were targeting systems they knew were not connected to the internet and, given the unprecedented number of zero-day exploits they used to do it, they must have been aiming for a high-value, high-security target.

But this roundabout way of reaching their goal was a messy and imprecise method of attack. It was a bit like infecting one of Osama bin Laden's wives with a deadly virus in the hope that she would have passed it on to the former al-Qaeda leader. The virus was bound to infect others along the way and thereby increase the likelihood of exposing the plot. And, in the end, this is exactly what occurred with Stuxnet. It spread to so many collateral machines that it was only a matter of time before something went wrong and it was caught.

As Chien reviewed the long list of methods and exploits the attackers had used, he realized the collection was far from arbitrary. Each accomplished a different task and overcame different obstacles the attackers needed to achieve their goal. It was as if someone had drafted a shopping list of exploits needed for the attack—something to escalate privileges, something to spread inside a victim's network, something to get the payload to a PLC—then gave someone the task of buying or building them. It was another indication of how much planning and organization had gone into the attack.

Of all the methods and exploits the hackers used, however, the most crucial to the attack were the .LNK exploit and the infection of the Step 7 project files, because these were the ones that were most likely to get Stux-

---

Microsoft issued a rare out-of-band patch for the hole—out-of-band patches are ones released ahead of a company's regular patch schedule when a security hole was serious—after realizing the hole could be easily used to spread a worm. Unfortunately, the makers of Conficker realized this too, and didn't waste time using it to spread their worm the next month. Even though Microsoft had released a patch by then, the Conficker team gambled on the fact that many computer users don't keep current with patches. They won the bet. An estimated one-third of Windows machines remained unpatched, and by April 2009 Conficker had infected millions of them. When Stuxnet was released two months later, its attackers gambled on the same bet. But Stuxnet only used this exploit to spread under certain conditions; it wasn't a primary method of propagation.

net to its final target—the Siemens PLCs. PLC programmers often crafted their commands on workstations that were connected to the internet but not connected to the production network or to PLCs on a plant floor. To transfer commands to a PLC, someone had to transfer them via a laptop connected directly to a PLC with a cable or to carry them on a USB flash drive to a programming machine, called a Field PG—a Windows laptop used in industrial-control settings. The Field PG is not connected to the internet but is connected to the production network and the PLCs. By infecting Step 7 project files and investing Stuxnet with the power to jump the air gap as a USB stowaway, the attackers had essentially turned every engineer into a potential carrier for their weapon.

Once Chien and O'Murchu documented all of the exploits and vulnerabilities that Stuxnet used to spread, they realized there was something else that stood out about them. A number of them had actually been seen before. Although VirusBlokAda believed the .LNK vulnerability had never been exploited before, Microsoft discovered that another attack had used an .LNK exploit in November 2008. It had been used by criminal hackers to install a variant of the Zlob Trojan onto victim machines.[6] Although various antivirus scanners had caught the Trojan at the time it was used, they had failed to spot the zero-day exploit that came with it, leaving the vulnerability open to attack by Stuxnet. The print-spooler exploit had also made a prior appearance—in a Polish security magazine in April 2009. The magazine had published an article about the hole, along with source code for an exploit to attack it.[7] News of the vulnerability never reached Microsoft at the time, however, so that vulnerability also remained un-

---

6 Zlob generated pop-up windows on infected machines that looked like legitimate Microsoft alerts, warning users that their machines were infected and urging them to click a link to download an antivirus program. The antivirus program that got downloaded, however, was a malicious backdoor that allowed the attacker to do various things on infected machines. The .LNK exploit was an ingenious attack, but it wouldn't have been much use to the Zlob gang and other cybercriminals, whose goal was to infect as many machines as possible in a short amount of time. The .LNK exploit spread malware at a slow rate since it was reliant on a USB flash drive being hand-carried from machine to machine. The Zlob gang was better off using an exploit that could infect thousands of machines over the internet.

7 Carsten Kohler, "Print Your Shell," *Hakin9*, April 1, 2009, available at hakin9.org/print-your-shell.

patched. The hard-coded Siemens password also had been exposed before, when someone published it online to a Siemens user forum in April 2008.[8]

Chien and O'Murchu wondered if a team of curators had scouted hacker forums and security sites to collect information about holes and exploits that the Stuxnet attackers could use in their assault or if they had simply purchased the exploits readymade from brokers.

Oddly, of all the exploits Stuxnet used, only the print-spooler exploit appeared in the first version of the attack, the one unleashed in 2009. The rest showed up for the first time in the March 2010 attack, which was the one that spread wildly out of control.[9] The 2009 version of Stuxnet did spread via USB flash drives, but it used a trick that took advantage of the Autorun feature of Windows to do this.[10] As noted previously, the Autorun feature could be turned off to thwart malware. So when the next version of Stuxnet was released in March 2010, the attackers swapped out the code for the Autorun feature and replaced it with the .LNK zero-day exploit.

The authors also added one other important feature to the 2010 versions of Stuxnet—the RealTek certificate used to sign the drivers.[11]

In looking at modifications the attackers made from 2009 to 2010, it appeared to Chien and O'Murchu that the attack had been deliberately

---

8 The password was posted in April 2008 by someone named "Cyber" after another user complained that his Siemens system had stopped working after he changed the hard-coded default password. He couldn't remember the original password to restore it, so "Cyber" posted it online to help him out. The passwords were subsequently deleted from the Siemens forum after someone chastised Cyber for posting them online. But the same passwords were also posted to a Russian-language Siemens forum by someone named "Cyber" and were still there when Stuxnet was discovered, though the page where they were posted has since moved or been deleted. The English-language forum where the password was posted is available at: automation.siemens.com/forum/guests/PostShow.aspx?PostID=16127&16127&Language=en&PageIndex=3.

9 In all three versions of Stuxnet—June 2009 and March and April 2010—the only part of the attack that changed was the missile portion of the code with the spreading mechanisms; the payload targeting the PLCs remained the same.

10 The Autorun trick doesn't count as a zero-day vulnerability since it's a feature of the Windows system, which attackers simply have found to be advantageous for spreading their malware. See pages 9–10, footnotes 7 and 8, for previous discussion of Autorun.

11 The attackers had to add the certificate to the 2010 version of Stuxnet because in late 2009, Microsoft released a new version of its operating system, Windows 7, which, as previously noted on page 11, included a new security feature that prevented drivers from installing unless they were digitally signed with a valid certificate.

altered to become more aggressive over time, beginning conservatively in 2009, then amping it up in 2010 by adding more spreading mechanisms—perhaps in a desperate bid to reach their target more quickly or to reach different machines than they had hit in their first attack. The .LNK exploit used in 2010, for example, was a much more efficient spreading mechanism than the Autorun exploit they had used in 2009.[12] But while it increased the chance that Stuxnet would reach its target, it also increased the risk that it would spread to other machines. Indeed, with this and other exploits added to the March 2010 version, the malware spread to more than 100,000 machines in and outside Iran.[13] None of these collateral infections helped the attackers reach their goal; they only increased their chance of getting caught.[14] They had to have known the risk they were taking in super-sizing Stuxnet's spreading power. But apparently it was a risk they were willing to take.

It was easy, in fact, for the researchers to track the exact paths that Stuxnet took in spreading. Tucked inside every copy of Stuxnet, the researchers found a little gem that helped them trace the course the mal-

---

12 As previously noted, many companies disable Autorun because it's a security risk. The .LNK feature couldn't be disabled in the same way, and because the vulnerability affected every version of Windows since Windows 2000, it made more machines vulnerable to it.

13 There's a caveat regarding the extensive spread of the 2010 version compared to the 2009 version. Chien and O'Murchu examined 3,280 copies of Stuxnet collected from infected machines by various antivirus firms. The June 2009 version of Stuxnet accounted for only 2 percent of these; the rest were from the March and April 2010 versions. The limited number of 2009 samples found is presumed to be due to the fact that this version spread less and infected fewer machines outside of Iran. But it could also be that the 2009 version got replaced on machines by the March 2010 version when it was released. Anytime Stuxnet encountered a machine, it looked to see if an older version of itself was already on the machine and replaced it with the new version. This could have resulted in fewer 2009 samples in the wild for researchers to find. It's just as likely, however, that the limited number of 2009 copies was due to the limited ways in which it could spread.

14 The fact that Stuxnet spread via USB flash drives and local networks instead of through the internet should have made it less likely to spread so widely, yet it did. This probably occurred because some of the companies infected in Iran had satellite offices outside Iran or used contractors who had clients in other countries and spread the infection each time they connected an infected laptop to another client's network or used an infected USB flash drive at multiple sites. After Stuxnet was discovered, the Symantec researchers sifted through their archive for any copies of Stuxnet that might have been caught and flagged as suspicious by their automated reporting system before VirusBlokAda discovered it in June 2010. They found one copy of the March 2010 version of the code on a customer's machine in Australia that had been flagged by their reporting system the month that version of Stuxnet was released. This showed just how far the malware traveled in a short time and how inevitable it was that it was going to eventually get caught.

ware had traveled in trying to reach its goal—a small log file containing data about every machine that it had infected. As the worm slithered its way through machines in search of its target, it logged the IP address and domain name of each of its victims, as well as a timestamp of when the infection occurred based on the machine's internal clock. It stored the data, about 100 bytes in size, in the log file, which grew as the worm passed from machine to machine. Thus, every copy of Stuxnet collected from infected machines contained a history of every computer it had infected up to that point, leaving a trail of digital breadcrumbs that Chien and O'Murchu could trace back to the initial victims. The log had been designed to help the *attackers* track the path Stuxnet took, but they likely hadn't counted on someone else using it for the same purpose.[15]

Chien and O'Murchu examined 3,280 copies of Stuxnet collected from infected machines by various antivirus firms, and based on the data in the log files, it appeared the attackers had launched their offensive against a cluster of five companies in Iran, likely chosen for their ability to provide a gateway for Stuxnet to reach its target. Each of the companies was hit by one or more versions of the malware launched in June 2009 and in March and April 2010. Symantec counted 12,000 infections at these five targets, and from these initial victims Stuxnet then spread to more than 100,000 machines in more than 100 countries.

Symantec has never publicly identified the companies, due to its policy of not naming victims, and has only referred to them as Domain A, B, C, D, and E in public documents. But the names of the victims are in the log files for others to see. They were Foolad Technique, Behpajooh, Kala, Neda Industrial Group, and a company only identified in the file as CGJ, believed to be Control Gostar Jahed. Kala was believed to refer to the same Kala Electric, or Kalaye Electric, that the Iranian opposition group, NCRI, had mentioned in their 2002 press conference as a front company for Iran's uranium enrichment program.

---

15 The attackers could have retrieved the log remotely from an infected system that contacted their command servers.

Although the attack struck some of the companies multiple times, not always the same machines were hit each time, suggesting the attackers may have been looking for better-placed machines each time they unleashed their attack or for ones that offered different routes to the targets to increase the likelihood that they would succeed. Only one of the companies, Behpajooh, was hit in all three attacks, suggesting it may have provided the best route to the targeted machines. This company was also, however, the victim that caused the most collateral damage. It was the only target hit in the March 2010 attack, which was the one that spread out of control. Of 12,000 infections that occurred at these five companies, 69 percent of them could be traced to this single victim.

CHAPTER 7

ZERO-DAY PAYDAYS

Stuxnet's zero-day exploits raised a lot of troubling questions about the burgeoning role of governments in the secret sale and use of such exploits—questions that have yet to be considered by Congress or resolved in public debate, despite evidence that the practice is creating dangerous vulnerabilities for corporations, critical infrastructure, and individual computer users alike.

Although the market for zero-day vulnerabilities and exploits has been around for more than a decade, until recently it was fairly small and lurked in the closed, underground world of hackers and criminals. In the last few years, however, it has gone commercial and exploded as the number of buyers and sellers has ballooned, along with prices, and the once murky trade has become legitimized with the entry of government dollars into the arena to create an unregulated cyberweapons bazaar.

One of the first hints of the free-market commercialization of zero days appeared in December 2005, when a seller named "fearwall" posted a zero-day vulnerability for sale on eBay and sparked fears that legitimate security researchers and bug hunters would soon go the way of mercenaries and sell their skills and wares to the highest bidder instead of handing information about software holes over to vendors to be fixed. Before putting his Windows Excel zero day on the auction block, fearwall did disclose information about the vulnerability to Microsoft, as "responsible" researchers were expected to do, but the software giant was noncommittal about fixing it, and Microsoft didn't have a bounty program at the time that paid researchers for the bugs they disclosed. So fearwall decided to offer his bug to the open market to embarrass the software giant and force it to fix the hole faster. The bidding reached only $60 before eBay yanked the listing. But the aborted sale was a foreshadowing of things to come.

Today the markets for zero-day vulnerabilities and exploits are legion— from the white-market bug bounty programs offered by software makers and website owners themselves to the thriving underground black markets run by criminal hackers to the clandestine gray markets that feed the bottomless demand of law enforcement and intelligence agencies around the world.

The white-market bounty programs offered by Google, Microsoft, and other companies now pay for information about security holes in their software, and have made the companies more responsive about fixing them. Third-party security firms like HP TippingPoint also pay for zero days, which they use to test the security of customer networks and protect them against attacks. TippingPoint discloses the vulnerabilities privately to software vendors so they can be fixed, but patches can take weeks or months to produce, and during that time TippingPoint gets a leg up on competitors by being able to protect customers from attacks that they don't know about yet.

The thriving underground black market that caters to crooks and corporate spies sells not just zero-day vulnerabilities and exploits but also the payloads to weaponize the exploits—Trojan horses, spy kits, and other malicious tools designed to steal online banking credentials and company secrets or amass armies of zombie computers for a botnet. Vulnerabilities sold on this market become known to the public and vendors only after attacks that use them are discovered, something that can take years to occur, as evidenced by the length of time it took researchers to discover the .LNK exploit that Stuxnet, and the Zlob Trojan before it, used.

But the underground criminal sales—troubling as they are—are rapidly being eclipsed by the newest market for zero-day vulnerabilities and exploits, one that critics predict will soon have a more serious effect on security than the criminal market. This is the flourishing gray market of digital arms dealers—defense contractors and private marketeers—whose government customers have driven up the price of zero days and enticed sellers away from the vendor bounty programs where the holes will be fixed and into the arms of people who only want to exploit them.

The market is "gray" only because the buyers and sellers are presumed to be the good guys, acting in the interest of public safety and national security. But one person's national security tool can be another's tool of oppression, and there's no guarantee that a government that buys zero days won't misuse them to spy on political opponents and activists or pass them to another government that will. Even if a government agency is using a zero day for a legitimate national security purpose, vulnerabilities sold on the gray market are not disclosed to vendors for patching, which leaves anyone who doesn't know about them—including other government agencies and critical infrastructure owners in the buyer's own country—open to attack should foreign adversaries or independent hackers discover the same security holes and exploit them.

The sale of exploits is legal and largely unregulated. Though export controls in the United States that govern the sale of conventional software would also prohibit the sale of exploits to countries like Iran and North Korea, exploits don't come with a copyright notice identifying their maker or country of origin, so anyone selling to these markets would not likely be caught.

The price of zero days varies greatly, depending on the rarity of the vulnerability—systems that are more difficult to crack produce fewer holes—as well as the time and difficulty involved in finding a hole and developing an exploit for it, the ubiquity of the software it exploits, and the exclusivity of the sale. An exploit sold exclusively to one customer will naturally bring more than one that's sold to many. Exploits that require more than a single vulnerability to provide the attacker root-level access to a machine also demand a higher price, as do ones that bypass antivirus and other security protections on a system without producing any side effects, such as crashing the browser or the machine or otherwise tipping off the computer owner that something is amiss.

A zero-day exploit for Adobe Reader can go for $5,000 or $30,000, while an exploit for the Mac OS can cost $50,000. But an exploit for Flash or Windows can jump to $100,000 or more because of the programs' ubiquity in the marketplace. An exploit for Apple's iOS can also go for $100,000 because the iPhone is more difficult to crack than competing mobile phones. Browser exploits that attack Firefox, Internet Explorer, and Chrome can sell for anywhere from $60,000 to more than $200,000, depending on their ability to bypass security protections the vendors have put in the software.[1]

Whatever the price on the gray market, however, it far surpasses in most cases what a seller can get from the white-market bounty programs. The Mozilla Foundation pays just $3,000 for bugs found in its Firefox browser and Thunderbird e-mail client, for example, while Microsoft, which was criticized for years for having no bug bounty program, began offering just $11,000 in 2013 for bugs found in the preview release of its new Internet Explorer 11 browser. The company, however, also now offers $100,000 for vulnerabilities that can help an attacker bypass the security protections in its software products, plus an additional $50,000 for a solution to fix it. Google usually pays just $500–$20,000 for bugs found in its Chrome browser and web properties, such as Gmail and YouTube, though it will pay $60,000 for some types of holes found in Chrome during an annual contest it sponsors. But while some vendors are making attempts to compete with the black market, they're still no match, in most cases,

---

1 See Andy Greenberg, "Shopping for Zero-Days: A Price List for Hackers' Secret Software Exploits," *Forbes,* March 23, 2012. Zero-day vulnerabilities have become more challenging to find in recent years as the makers of some of the most targeted software programs have added features to make them more secure. Google and other companies have built so-called sandboxes into their browsers, for example, that erect a protective barrier to contain malicious code and prevent it from spilling out of the browser into the operating system or other applications on a machine. As a result, exploits that allow an attacker to escape a sandbox are valuable.

for the price some governments will pay on the gray market. And Apple and Adobe still offer no bounty programs whatsoever to pay for bugs in software used by millions of people.

The gray market for zero days has been around for about a decade, but only recently has it emerged in its current, robust form. For many years it operated ad-hoc, with sales occurring only quietly in private between security firms and researchers and their government contacts. If someone wanted to sell an exploit but had no government contacts, it was difficult to sniff out a buyer.

Beginning in 2006, for example, one security firm sold several zero-day exploits to a contact at a large US defense firm, according to a former employee who worked there. The zero days, all browser exploits targeting security holes in Safari, Firefox, and Internet Explorer, sold for about $100,000 each. The security firm got $50,000 up front for each sale it made and $10,000 a month thereafter until the price was paid off—payments were spread out to discourage them from reselling the exploits to other buyers or disclosing them to the vendors for patching.

One of the first people to openly admit selling exploits to the government is security researcher Charlie Miller, a former NSA hacker who was recruited by the spy agency in 2000 after earning a PhD in mathematics from the University of Notre Dame. Miller worked for the intelligence agency about five years, initially cracking codes on its behalf before turning his skills to cracking computers—doing reconnaissance scans to map foreign networks and conduct "computer network exploitations against foreign targets," according to his NSA-cleared résumé. CNE in spy-speak means hacking systems and networks to siphon data and intelligence. After leaving the NSA, Miller earned prominence in the security community for hunting zero-day bugs and creating exploits, not all of which he sold to the government. He was the first, with a colleague, to crack the security of the iPhone after its debut in 2007, and he's a four-time winner of Pwn2Own, an annual hacking contest sponsored by HP TippingPoint that pays contestants for zero-day bugs found in specific software targets.

But in 2006, Miller was working for a small security firm, doing a little bug hunting on the side, when he sold a zero-day exploit to a US government contractor for $50,000. He sold the exploit to someone he knew from his days at the NSA, but says he has no idea where it went after the sale or how it was used. The contracts he signed for this and other exploits he sold never stipulated what the buyer could do with them. "I don't know if he did anything good or bad with it; I do know that he worked for the US government," Miller says. "They're buying the intellectual property, you know? They can do whatever they want with it."

Miller caused an uproar in 2007 when he published a paper about the zero-day market and admitted publicly that he sold exploits to the government.[2] He wrote the paper because he wanted people to know the practice existed and to help other researchers navigate the pitfalls of the trade that he'd experienced. At the time, selling exploits was the security industry's dirty little secret. Researchers occasionally discussed the practice among themselves, but no one was willing to talk about it openly. Miller soon learned why. Colleagues in the security community accused him of putting users at risk, and some called for his CISSP (certified information systems security professional) certification to be revoked for violating the industry's code of ethics. "I talked about it . . . I got beat up for it. And I don't talk about it anymore," Miller says.[3]

But to him, it didn't make sense to hand over bugs to vendors for free—only a couple of vendor bounty programs existed at the time, and they paid little for bugs and exploits. It was also a time when vendors were less likely to thank researchers for disclosing a hole than threaten them with a lawsuit or criminal prosecution for probing their system or software to discover it.

Miller abandoned the zero-day trade years ago—he now works on Twitter's security team—but he still sees nothing wrong with selling zero days to the government and gets annoyed when people talk about the eth-

---

2 Charlie Miller, "The Legitimate Vulnerability Market: Inside the Secretive World of 0-Day Exploit Sales," Independent Security Evaluators, May 6, 2007, available at weis2007.econinfosec.org/papers/29.pdf.
3 Author interview with Charlie Miller, September 2011.

ics of it. "No one gets mad that, you know, companies sell the government guns and tanks," he says, noting that while US researchers are selling zero days to their government, Chinese and Russian hackers are doing the same for their governments. It's better for the United States to pay top dollar for exploits, he says, than allow them to get into the hands of enemies.

"I don't think it's earth-shattering that researchers can sell exploits to the government," Miller told me, "but I think people should . . . be aware that it happens. I'm OK with the government doing it out in the open. . . . I don't know why they don't just set up a public program [and say] 'find a zero day, we'll buy it.'"[4]

But in the years since Miller's days on the exploit hunt, the gray-market demand for zero days has mushroomed, as evidenced by the fact that exploits that might have taken months to sell before now do so within days or weeks. A burgeoning ecosystem has emerged to meet the demand—populated by small firms whose primary business is bug hunting as well as by large defense contractors and staffing agencies that now employ teams of professional hackers dedicated to the task of creating exploits for governments. There are also more middlemen willing to broker exploit sales for independent sellers.

One such middleman is a South African security researcher based in Thailand who is known in the security community by his hacker handle "The Grugq." The Grugq brokers exploit sales between his hacker friends and government contacts, pocketing a 15 percent commission per transaction. He only launched his business in 2011, but by 2012 sales were so good, he told a reporter he expected to make $1 million in commissions. A published photo of him taken at a Bangkok bar showed a satchel of cash at his feet, evidently payment from one of his sellers, though he later said the photo was just a joke.[5]

Most of the exploits he sold went to government buyers in the United States and Europe, he told *Forbes*, because they were willing to pay more

---

4 Ibid.
5 Greenberg, "Shopping for Zero-Days: A Price List for Hackers' Secret Software Exploits."

than others. One Apple iOS exploit he sold to a US government contractor went for $250,000, though he later concluded he'd asked too little because the buyer was way too happy with the sale. He attributed his success to the professionalism he put into marketing the exploits and the support he gave to his clients. "You're basically selling commercial software, like anything else," he told *Forbes*. "It needs to be polished and come with documentation."

But the really big trade in exploits these days is not done by middlemen and individual sellers like Miller and The Grugq, but by the security firms and defense contractors who have made the development and sale of exploits for government part of the new military industrial complex.

Although governments still produce their own exploits—the NSA employs teams for this—they also outsource to other firms because the demand for exploits has grown, as has the cost of producing them: two or three years ago, a single vulnerability was sufficient to gain root-level access to a machine. But today, it can take multiple ones to bypass security protections to achieve the same results.

Most of the companies involved in the trade are secretive about their work in this area, not only because it's classified but because they don't want to be targeted by activists who oppose the work or by adversaries who might hack them to steal their exploits. Because zero days can be used for both defending a system and attacking it, many of the companies also hide their offensive activity behind a cover of defensive work. US companies like Endgame Systems, Harris, Raytheon, Northrop Grumman, SAIC, Booz Allen Hamilton, and Lockheed Martin have all been in the exploit game to varying degrees. Companies in Europe include the boutique firms ReVuln in Malta, which creates exploits for industrial control systems, and VUPEN in France, which sells to law enforcement and intelligence agencies. Hacking Team in Italy and the Gamma Group in the UK both sell surveillance tools for law enforcement and intelligence agencies that use zero-day exploits to get installed.

The zero-day work of Endgame Systems, a Georgia-based firm, was a badly kept secret in the security community for years but wasn't widely known outside of the community until 2011, when hackers with the Anonymous collective broke into servers belonging to another firm called HBGary Federal and dumped thousands of its e-mails online, including correspondence with executives at Endgame. The e-mails discussed Endgame's exploit work as well as its efforts "to maintain a very low profile" on the advice of its government customers. The e-mails, which included PowerPoint presentations for prospective Endgame clients, described the company's mission to enhance the "Information Operations capability of the United States intelligence and military organizations." The head of Endgame's board of directors is also the chief executive of In-Q-Tel, the CIA's venture capital firm.

Publicly, Endgame was offering services to protect customers against viruses and botnets, while privately selling vulnerability and exploit packages containing information that could "lead to actionable intelligence for CNA efforts." CNA, or computer network attacks, is military-speak for hacking that manipulates or destroys data or systems or retards or halts the performance of systems. The company launched in 2008 and its business prospects were so rosy that two years later it raised $30 million in venture capital, followed by $23 million in a subsequent round. In 2011, Endgame CEO Christopher Rouland told a local paper in Atlanta that the company's revenue was "more than doubling yearly."[6]

The stolen e-mails described three different packages Endgame offered, called Maui, Cayman, and Corsica. For $2.5 million a year, the Maui package provided buyers with a bundle of twenty-five zero-day exploits. The Cayman package, which cost $1.5 million, provided intelligence about millions of vulnerable machines worldwide already infected with botnet worms like Conficker and other malware. A sample map in the e-mails showed the location of vulnerable computers in the Russian Federation and a list of infected systems in key government offices and critical infrastructure facilities that included the IP address of each machine and

6 Tonya Layman, "Rouland's Tech Security Firm Growing Fast," *Atlanta Business Chronicle*, June 11, 2011.

the operating system it used. The list showed 249 infected machines at the Central Bank of the Russian Federation, and a handful of machines at the Ministry of Finance, the National Reserve Bank, the Novovoronezh Nuclear Power Plant, and the Achinsk Oil Refinery Plant. Endgame collected the data in part by setting up sinkholes to communicate with machines infected with Conficker—when the malware contacted the sinkhole, Endgame collected intelligence about the machine. A similar map for Venezuela showed the location of web servers in that country and the software running on them. Web servers, if breached and poorly configured, can often provide attackers access to back-end systems and databases. The systems on the list included servers for Corporación Andina de Fomento—a development bank that provides financing to eighteen member countries in Latin America, the Caribbean, and Europe—as well as Venezuela's central budget office, the Office of the Presidency, the Ministry of Defense, and the Ministry of Foreign Affairs. After it was hacked, Endgame began telling reporters in 2012 that it was getting out of the exploit business, and in early 2014 it made a formal announcement to this effect.

While Endgame made a concerted effort to hide its exploit business, one company that's positively garrulous about its role in the zero-day trade is VUPEN Security, based in Montpellier, France. VUPEN bills itself as a boutique security firm creating and selling exploits to intelligence agencies and law enforcement for offensive cyber security operations and lawful intercept missions. Originally launched in 2008 to protect government clients from zero-day attacks, the company began creating exploits for offensive operations two years later. In 2011, it earned $1.2 million in revenue, nearly 90 percent of which came from sales outside France. In 2013, it announced that it was opening an office in the United States.

VUPEN's founder and CEO, Chaouki Bekrar, is a bold and cheeky sort who likes to rile critics on Twitter who think supplying exploits to governments is unethical. He also often challenges his secretive competitors to come clean about their own zero-day trade. "We are the only company in the world saying clearly that we are doing this stuff," he says. "There are some companies in the US or in Europe, for example, doing this, but they are doing this undercover. But we have chosen to do it clearly, just because we want to be very transparent."[7]

Where Endgame and others take pains to keep a low profile, Bekrar and his researchers regularly travel the security conference circuit, participating in contests like Pwn2Own, to increase the company's profile. At the CanSecWest conference (an annual computer security conference in Canada) in 2012, where the Pwn2Own competition is held, Bekrar and a team of four of his researchers took first place wearing matching black hoodies with the company's name on the back.

But VUPEN's transparency goes only so far. Bekrar won't discuss his background or answer other personal questions, deflecting attention to his company instead. "I'm just an actor. I want to talk about the movie," he says. But when it comes to the company, he's equally close-mouthed—he won't say how many employees he has, just that the company is small, or reveal their last names.

VUPEN's researchers devote all their time to finding zero-day vulnerabilities and developing exploits—both for already-known vulnerabilities as well as for zero days. Bekrar won't say how many exploits they've sold since they began this part of their business, but says they discover hundreds of zero days a year. "We have zero days for everything," he says. "We have almost everything for every operating system, for every browser, for every application if you want."

How much of Bekrar's boasting is true and how much is strategic marketing is unclear, but whatever the case, his tactics seem to be working. In 2012, several months after his team won the Pwn2Own contest, the NSA purchased a one-year subscription for VUPEN's "Binary Analysis and Exploits (BAE)" service. The contract, released under a public records request, was heavily redacted and didn't reveal the price paid for the subscription. But a business-consulting firm, which named VUPEN entrepreneurial company of the year in 2011, indicated the subscription runs

---

7 This and all quotes from Bekrar in this chapter are from an author interview in March 2012, unless otherwise cited.

about $100,000 a year. According to VUPEN's website, the BAE service provides "highly technical reports for the most critical and significant vulnerabilities to understand their root cause, exploitability techniques, mitigations and both exploit-based and vulnerability-based attack detections."[8]

VUPEN also offers a Threat Protection Program that provides detailed research on exclusive vulnerabilities discovered by its researchers to allow customers "to reduce their exposure to zero-day attacks," according to a company brochure that got leaked to WikiLeaks.[9] Both of these programs are described as if they're meant to help customers defensively protect themselves from zero-day attacks—zero-day exploits can be used to test a system for its vulnerability to an attack—but the information provided in them can also be used to offensively attack other unpatched systems. The company's Threat Protection Package even provides customers with ready-made exploits for attacking the vulnerabilities it reveals. And VUPEN has a third service for law enforcement and intelligence agencies that's clearly designed solely for covertly attacking targeted machines to gain remote access to them. "Law enforcement agencies need the most advanced IT intrusion research and the most reliable attack tools to covertly and remotely gain access to computer systems," Bekrar is quoted saying in the brochure. "Using previously unknown software vulnerabilities and exploits which bypass Antivirus products and modern operating system protections . . . could help investigators to successfully achieve this task."

The intrusion program is restricted to police and intelligence agencies in NATO, ANZUS, and ASEAN, as well as the partner countries of these associations—what Bekrar describes as "a limited number of countries."

"It's very sensitive, so we want to keep the number of customers small," he says. But NATO has twenty-eight member countries, including Romania and Turkey, and another some forty countries are considered its part-

---

8 From a press release titled "VUPEN Gets Entrepreneurial Company of the Year Award in the Vulnerability Research Market," June 1, 2006, available at vupen.com/press/VUPEN_Company_of_the_year_2011.php.
9 The brochure is available at wikileaks.org/spyfiles/files/0/279_VUPEN-THREAD-EXPLOITS.pdf.

ners, including Israel, Belarus, Pakistan, and Russia. Bekrar insists that VUPEN won't sell to all of them, however, just because they're on the lists.

The company sells exploits that attack all the top commercial products from Microsoft, Apple, Adobe, and others, as well as that target enterprise database and server systems made by companies like Oracle. But browser exploits are the most coveted item, and Bekrar says they have exploits for every brand. The company sells only exploits and what Bekrar calls intermediate payloads that allow a customer to burrow into a network. It's the customer's job to weaponize the exploit with a final payload.

After Stuxnet was discovered, VUPEN also turned its attention to industrial control systems when customers began inquiring about exploits for them. Stuxnet's exploits, which he said his team analyzed after the attack was exposed, were admirable. "The vulnerabilities themselves were really nice, and the exploit to take advantage of them was nicer," he says. "They were not very easy to exploit. . . ." But to seriously develop attacks for industrial control systems requires access to special hardware and facilities for testing, and Bekrar says, "We don't have such things and we don't want to have such things."

Subscribers to their exploit service have access to a portal, where they can shop a menu of existing zero days, or special-order exploits for a specific operating system or application. Exploits are priced at four levels, according to the brochure. Subscribers purchase a set number of credits, which can be applied to the purchase of exploits worth 1, 2, 3, or 4 credits. Each exploit comes with a description of the software it targets and an indication of how reliable the exploit is. Customers can also obtain real-time alerts any time a new vulnerability is discovered and an exploit is available. VUPEN monitors announcements from Microsoft and other vendors to see when a vulnerability one of their exploits attacks is discovered or patched, and alerts customers that the bug and exploit have been burned—sometimes with an announcement through Twitter.

Bekrar says his company doesn't offer exclusivity on exploits but sells the same exploits to multiple buyers. The more an exploit is used, however, the more likely it will be caught, which would make it less attractive to an agency like the NSA, where stealth and secrecy are priorities. Bekrar insists that VUPEN works with only a limited number of governments, and says customers don't use the exploits "in massive operations," so there is "almost no chance" they will be widely deployed.

Bekrar, like Miller, has little sympathy for people who criticize the sale of exploits and has said in the past that software vendors created this government market for exploits by initially refusing to pay researchers for vulnerabilities they discovered, then refusing to pay top dollar, leaving them little choice but to turn to other buyers willing to compensate them for their work. He also insists, however, that he's not in the exploit trade for the money. "We are not businessmen, we don't care about sales. We mainly care about security, about ethics," he said.

At the Pwn2Own contest, when Google offered to pay $60,000 for an exploit and information about a vulnerability the VUPEN team used against Google's Chrome browser, Bekrar refused to hand over the information.[10] He joked that he might consider it if Google offered $1 million. But later in private he said even for $1 million, he wouldn't hand over the exploit, preferring to keep it for his customers. Asked if VUPEN's customers had such money to pay for an exploit, he laughed and said, "No, no, no, no. Never. . . . They don't have the budget."

But he insisted his reasons for supplying to governments went deeper than money: "We mainly work with governments who are facing national security issues . . . we help them in protecting their democracies and protecting lives. . . . It's like any surveillance method. The government needs to know if something bad is being prepared and to know what people are doing, to protect national security. So there are many ways to use the exploits for national security and to save lives."

---

10 VUPEN had already won $60,000 from HT Tipping Point for the contest, but Google was offering an additional $60,000 on top of that to obtain information about the hole in order to fix it. The Pwn2Own contest generally requires contestants to hand over the exploit and information about a hole so that it can be fixed, but not for exploits that bypass a browser's security sandbox, which is what VUPEN said its exploit did. The Google staffer accused VUPEN of showboating at the expense of users. "We're trying to get information out of somebody so that we can fix it . . . [Without that information] it's not about protecting users anymore, it's about showing off. It's good for stroking egos, but aside from that it doesn't make the web safer," a Google staffer told me.

But critics argue that companies like VUPEN have no way of knowing where their exploits will end up or how they will be used, such as for domestic spying on innocent citizens. Bekrar acknowledges that VUPEN's customer agreement doesn't explicitly prohibit a government buyer from using VUPEN exploits to spy on its citizens. "But we say that the exploits must be used in an ethical way," he says.

Bekrar says they can't spell it out more specifically in the contract, because the legal agreements need to be general to cover all possible cases of unethical use. "For us it's clear," he said. "You have to use exploits in respect of ethics, in respect of international regulations and national laws and you cannot use exploits in massive operations." But ethics, of course, are in the mind of the beholder, and Bekrar acknowledges that he has no way to control how customers interpret ethical injunctions. "My only way, at my side, to control this, is to control to which country I sell. And we only sell to democratic countries."

Christopher Soghoian of the American Civil Liberties Union is one of VUPEN's biggest critics. He calls exploit sellers like VUPEN "modern-day merchants of death" and "cowboys," who chase government dollars to supply the tools and bullets that make oppressive surveillance and cyber-warfare possible—putting everyone at risk in the process.[11] He acknowledges that governments would make and use their own zero days whether or not companies like VUPEN sold them, but says the free-market sellers are a "ticking bomb" because there's no control over their trade.

"As soon as one of these weaponized zero-days sold to governments is obtained by a 'bad guy' and used to attack critical US infrastructure, the shit will hit the fan," Soghoian told an audience of computer professionals at a conference in 2011. "It's not a matter of if, but when. . . . What if a low-paid, corrupt police officer sells a copy of one of these weaponized exploits to organized crime or terrorists? What if Anonymous hacks into

---

11 Ryan Naraine, "0-Day Exploit Middlemen Are Cowboys, Ticking Bomb," ZDNet.com, February 16, 2012, available at zdnet.com/blog/security/0-day-exploit-middlemen-are-cowboys-ticking-bomb/10294.

a law enforcement agency's network and steals one of these weaponized exploits?"[12]

In 2013, initial steps were taken to try to regulate the sale of zero days and other cyberweapons. The Wassenaar Arrangement—an arms-control organization composed of forty-one countries, including the United States, the UK, Russia, and Germany—announced that it was for the first time classifying software and hardware products that can be used for hacking and surveillance and that "may be detrimental to international and regional security and stability" as dual-use products. The dual-use designation is used to restrict materials and technology (such as maraging steel used in centrifuges) that can be used for military ends as well as peaceful ones. Although the organization's declarations are not legally binding, member states are expected to implement requirements for export licenses in their countries and cooperate with one another in controlling sales of dual-use products.[13] Germany, a Wassenaar member, already has a law that effectively prohibits the sale of exploits as well as the practice of giving them away for free, something that security researchers do regularly among themselves to test systems and improve security. Lawmakers in the United States with the Senate Armed Services Committee introduced legislation in 2013 that calls on the president to establish a policy "to control the proliferation of cyberweapons through unilateral and cooperative export controls, law enforcement activities, financial means, diplomatic engagement, and such other means as the President considers appropriate." But it's unclear exactly how such controls would work, since zero days and other digital weapons are much more difficult to monitor than conventional weapons, and such controls requiring export licenses for the foreign sale of exploits and the screening of buyers can increase the cost for legitimate sellers, but not all sellers are interested in legitimacy.

Furthermore, these kinds of controls are meant to keep exploits only

---

12 Ibid.
13 "The Wassenaar Arrangement on Export Controls for Conventional Arms and Dual-Use Goods and Technologies," Public Statement 2013 Plenary Meeting, available at wassenaar.org/ publicdocuments/2013/WA%20Plenary%20Public%20Statement%202013.pdf.

out of the hands of criminals and rogue actors, such as terrorists. They're not meant at all to curb government use of them for law enforcement or national security purposes. The thriving gray market for zero days makes it clear that law enforcement and spy agencies are anxious to get their hands on exploits like the ones that Stuxnet used—and are willing to pay generously for the privilege. That frenzied demand for zero days is only likely to grow, and with it, the number of state-sponsored programs that use them.

CHAPTER 8

THE PAYLOAD

Nico Falliere was hunched over his desk on the eighth floor of the forty-story Tour Egée, a triangular glass-and-concrete building in the La Défense business district of Paris. Outside, a grim forest of office towers rose in front of his window, obscuring his view of the pigeons and summer tourists ambling toward the steps of La Grande Arche. But Falliere wasn't focused on the view. He was focused intently on making his first foray into Stuxnet's complicated payload.

It was early in August 2010, a mere two weeks into the Symantec team's analysis of Stuxnet, before Chien and O'Murchu discovered the unprecedented number of zero days that were hiding in the worm. During these first two weeks, Falliere had been working with O'Murchu to analyze the malware's large Windows .DLL, but he knew Stuxnet's real secrets lay in its payload, and he was anxious to get at them.

He had just returned from lunch with friends when he began digging through the payload files, separating each one out and trying to understand its format and structure. He noticed that one of them was a .DLL file with a familiar name. The Symantec researchers had by this point obtained copies of the Siemens Step 7 software, so Falliere scrolled through the Step 7 program files installed on his test system. It didn't take long to find what he was looking for—a Siemens Step 7 .DLL that had the same name as the Stuxnet file. Hmm, he thought, that's interesting.

He quickly determined that anytime Stuxnet found itself on a computer with the Siemens Step 7 or WinCC software installed, it unpacked its .DLL file with the matching name from inside its larger Windows .DLL and decrypted it.

Falliere used the key embedded in the malware to decrypt the .DLL and found that it contained all of the same functionality as the legitimate Step 7 .DLL. But it also contained some suspicious code that included commands like "write" and "read." Falliere had seen enough malware in his career to know exactly what he was looking at—Stuxnet's Step 7 .DLL was acting as a rootkit, lurking on the system silently, waiting to hijack, or hook, these functions anytime the system attempted to read or write code blocks to or from the targeted PLCs. Similar to the rootkit in the missile portion of Stuxnet, this one was hooking the read function to hide something that Sutxnet was doing to the PLCs. It was the first time, as far as he knew, that anyone had created a rootkit for an industrial control system. It was another first in the growing list of Stuxnet firsts.

Falliere couldn't tell if Stuxnet's rogue .DLL was hooking the read function to simply monitor the PLCs passively and gather intelligence about their operations, or if it had more sinister aims in mind. But the fact that it was also intercepting the "write" function suggested it was probably the latter and was attempting to halt the operation of the PLCs or change their operation in some way. He glanced at his watch and noted that it was around five a.m. in California—too early to call Chien—so he decided to keep digging.

He continued for several more hours, and when he had all the pieces of the puzzle he needed—it was exactly what he'd suspected. Stuxnet was indeed intercepting commands passing from the Siemens .DLL to the PLCs and replacing them with its own. He couldn't say for sure what it was instructing the PLC to do—he couldn't find the code blocks that Stuxnet injected into the PLC—but he was pretty sure it wasn't good. By now it was nine a.m. in California, so he picked up the phone and called Chien.

Normally the two of them spoke once a week to exchange a quick update about whatever Falliere was working on; the calls were efficient and to-the-point and lasted no more than a few minutes. But this time Falliere recounted everything he had found in detail. Chien listened intently, amazed at what he heard. The attack kept getting more and more complex. Every corner they turned with Stuxnet they found a new surprise.

Chien agreed that Falliere should drop everything to find the code blocks that Stuxnet injected into the PLC. They also decided Falliere should make a brief announcement on their blog about the PLC rootkit. The rest of the information they would keep under wraps, for the time being, until Falliere could determine the nature of what Stuxnet was injecting into the PLC.

That night on the Métro on his way home from work, Falliere was charged with nervous energy. For four years he'd been deconstructing viruses and worms and had seen so many malicious programs during that time that it was hard to get excited about them anymore. But this one was different. An attack on a PLC was unprecedented and had the potential to usher in an entirely new breed of malicious attacks.

Despite his excitement, he knew the road ahead was filled with hurdles. The Siemens .DLL that Stuxnet replaced was huge, and the structure of the Step 7 software and the PLCs it controlled was largely undocumented. Falliere and Chien were completely in the dark about how the system worked, and the technical challenges of deciphering the payload were going to be formidable. What's more, there was no guarantee they'd even crack it. There were so many things Falliere didn't know at this point. But one thing he did know was that he was in for a long and exhausting ride.

FALLIERE WAS TWENTY-EIGHT, with the dark, Gallic looks of someone who seemed like he'd be more at home DJing trance music in an underground Paris nightclub than poring over reams of printed computer code during a commute on the Métro. In reality, he was fairly shy and reserved, and sifting through dense computer code was in fact a much bigger draw to him than spending sweaty nights in a throbbing club.

Falliere was a master reverse-engineer who specialized in deep-dive analysis of malicious code. Reverse-engineering is a bit of a dark art that involves taking the binary language of ones and zeroes that a computer can read and translating it back to a programming language that humans can read. It requires a lot of intense focus and skill, particularly with code as complex as Stuxnet. But Falliere didn't mind. The more complicated the code, the more satisfying it was when he finally cracked it.

He first honed his skills as a teenager in France breaking "crackme" files—code games that programmers wrote for one another to test their reverse-engineering skills. Coders would write small programs coated in an encrypted shell, and reverse-engineers would have to crack it open and bypass other protections to unearth the secret message hidden inside, then send it back to the author to prove that they had solved it. Viruses and worms were just another type of crackme file in one sense, though some were more sophisticated than others. The only difference now was that Falliere got paid to crack them.

Falliere was born and raised near Toulouse in southern France, home of the Airbus aerospace corporation and a center for satellite technology. In a region dominated by engineers, aeronautical and otherwise, it seemed natural that Falliere would be drawn to technology. But his early influences actually veered toward the mechanical. His father was an automobile mechanic who owned and operated his own garage. Falliere's introduction to computers in high school, however, led him in a different direction—to study computer science at the National Institute for Applied Sciences in France. The spread of the prolific Code Red worm in 2001, which struck more than 700,000 machines, got him interested in computer security. While still in college, he wrote several security articles for a small French technical magazine, as well as a paper for SecurityFocus, a security website that Symantec owned.[1] In late 2005 while doing his master's program in computer science, he was told he needed a six-month internship under his belt to complete it. So he reached out to his contacts at SecurityFocus, who referred him to Chien. The timing couldn't have been more fortuitous. Symantec was still in the midst of its Dublin hiring spree, and Chien was desperate to find experienced reverse-engineers. He told Falliere that rather than a six-month internship at Symantec he could offer him a full-time job instead. "How much do you want to make?" he asked Falliere.

"I don't need any money," Falliere told him. "Just an internship."

"Are you crazy?" Chien replied. "I'll send you an offer in an e-mail. Just accept it."

A few weeks later, Falliere was settled in Dublin. He adjusted to his new life fairly quickly, but after two years of constant plane rides back to France to see his girlfriend, he asked for a transfer to Paris, where Symantec had a sales and marketing office. He turned out to be the only technical person in the office, which left him feeling isolated at times, but also helped focus him on his work.

His desk, in an office shared with two colleagues, was an orchestrated mess of technical papers and books scattered around a test machine that he used to run malware and a laptop containing the debugger software that he used to analyze code. A cylinder-shaped Rubik's puzzle was the only personal item on the desk, which he fingered like worry beads whenever he butted up against an unwieldy patch of code that resisted cracking.

Though Falliere was a whiz at reverse-engineering, he was actually doing very little of it when Stuxnet came along. Over time, he'd become Symantec's de-facto tool guy, whipping together programs and tools to make deciphering malware more efficient for other analysts. The job snuck up on him over time. He began by tweaking forensic tools for himself that he found clunky and inefficient, then began doing it for colleagues as well, even creating new tools after they began submitting requests. Eventually, he was spending more time working on tools than deciphering code. He

---

1 Symantec acquired SecurityFocus in 2002.

only jumped on the occasional malware threat if Chien made a special request, which he did in the case of Stuxnet.

FALLIERE BEGAN HIS analysis of the payload by studying the Siemens Step 7 software. The Step 7 software that Stuxnet attacked was Siemens's proprietary application for programming its S7 line of PLCs. It ran on top of the Windows operating system and allowed programmers to write and compile commands, or blocks of code, for the company's PLCs. The system wasn't complete without the Simatic WinCC program, a visualization tool used for monitoring the PLCs and the processes they controlled. PLCs, connected to monitoring stations via a facility's production network, were in a constant state of chatter with the machines, sending frequent status reports and updates to give operators a real-time view of whatever equipment and operations the PLC controlled. The Siemens .DLL was central to both the Step 7 and WinCC programs, serving as middleman to create commands for the PLCs or receive status reports from them. That's where Stuxnet's rogue .DLL came in. It did everything the real .DLL was designed to do, and more.

To understand how the doppelgänger .DLL worked, Falliere had to first understand how the Step 7 system and the legitimate .DLL worked. He searched online for experts to consult, and even thought about reaching out to Siemens for help, but he didn't know whom to call there. The Step 7 .DLL was just one in a galaxy of .DLLs the Siemens software used, and to locate the two or three programmers behind the code who knew it well enough to help would take just as long as it would take for him to figure it out on his own. And in the end, there was a certain amount of pride to be had in cracking it himself.

To reverse the .DLL files—the original and the doppelgänger—Falliere opened them in a disassembler, a tool designed for translating binary code into assembly language, which was one step back from binary. The disassembler allowed him to add notations and comments to the code or rearrange sections to make it easier to read. He worked on small bits of code at a time, labeling each with a description of the function it performed as he went along.

As researchers typically did when examining complex malware like this, Falliere combined static analysis (viewing the code on-screen in a disassembler/debugger) with dynamic analysis (observing it in action on a test system, using the debugger to stop and start the action so he could match specific parts of the code with the effect it was having on the test machine). The process could be excruciatingly slow under the best of circumstances, since it required jumping back and forth between the two machines, but it was all the more difficult with Stuxnet due to its size and complexity.

It took two weeks of documenting every action the .DLL took before Falliere finally confirmed what he'd suspected all along, that Stuxnet was kidnapping the Siemens .DLL and putting the doppelgänger in its place to hijack the system. It did this by changing the name of the Siemens .DLL from s7otbxdx.DLL to s7otbxsx.DLL and installing the rogue .DLL with the original's name in its place, essentially stealing its identity. Then when the system called up the Siemens .DLL to perform any action, the malicious .DLL answered instead.

Once the rogue .DLL was in place, what it did was quite remarkable.

Whenever an engineer tried to send commands to a PLC, Stuxnet made sure its own malicious command code got sent and executed instead. But it didn't just overwrite the original commands in a simple swap. Stuxnet increased the size of the code block and slipped its malicious code in at the front end. Then to make sure its malicious commands got activated instead of the legitimate ones, Stuxnet also hooked a core block of code on the PLC that was responsible for reading and executing commands. A lot of knowledge and skill were required to inject the code seamlessly in this way without "bricking" the PLCs (that is, causing them to seize up or become nonfunctional), but the attackers pulled it off beautifully.

The second part of the attack was even more ingenious. Before Stuxnet's malicious commands went into action, the malware sat patiently on the PLC for about two weeks, sometimes longer, recording legitimate operations as the controller sent status reports back to monitoring stations. Then when Stuxnet's malicious commands leapt into action, the malware replayed the recorded data back to operators to blind them to anything amiss on the machines—like a Hollywood heist film where the thieves insert a looped video clip into surveillance camera feeds. While Stuxnet sabotaged the PLC, it also disabled automated digital alarms to prevent safety systems from kicking in and halting whatever process the PLC was controlling if it sensed the equipment was entering a danger zone. Stuxnet did this by altering blocks of code known as OB35 that were part of the PLC's safety system. These were used to monitor critical operations, such as the speed of a turbine the PLC was controlling. The blocks were generated every 100 milliseconds by the PLC so that safety systems could kick in quickly if a turbine began spinning out of control or something else went wrong, allowing the system or an operator to set off a kill switch and initiate a shutdown. But with Stuxnet modifying the data the safety system relied on, the system was blind to dangerous conditions and never had a chance to act.[2]

The attack didn't stop there, however. If programmers noticed something amiss with a turbine or other equipment controlled by the PLC and

---

2 There was very little whimsy in Stuxnet or anything that seemed superfluous. But in the part of the code responsible for intercepting the OB35 blocks, the attackers had placed a "magic marker" (a value placed in code that signifies a condition or triggers an action) that seemed like a bit of an inside joke—0xDEADF007. The marker was the hexadecimal representation of a number. When Stuxnet checked conditions on the system it was sabotaging to determine when it should start disabling the safety system, a magic marker was produced to indicate when conditions were right to disable the system. The attackers could have chosen any random number—1234—but chose one that when written in hexadecimal produced a word and numbers—DEADF007. It wasn't uncommon for programmers to use whimsical values in their code to spell words in hexadecimal. For example, the first four bytes of Java class files translate to "0xCAFEBABE" in hexadecimal. 0xDEADBEEF is another hexadecimal value that in hacker-speak refers to a software crash. So Chien wondered if 0xDEADF007 in Stuxnet might actually mean "dead fool"—a derogatory way to indicate when the safety system was no longer functional—or "dead foot." Dead foot is an expression used by airplane pilots to refer to an engine failure, "Dead foot, dead engine" being the maxim to help pilots realize quickly in a stressful situation that when a foot pedal is dead it means an engine is out—the pilot essentially has no control of the engine. Similarly "DEADF007" in Stuxnet signaled the point at which operators in Iran lost control of their PLCs while Stuxnet was sabotaging them, preventing both the safety system from initiating its own automatic shutdown or operators from stepping in to do an emergency manual shutdown. It made Chien wonder if one or more of Stuxnet's authors were pilots.

tried to view the command blocks on the PLC to see if it had been mispro-grammed, Stuxnet intervened and prevented them from seeing the rogue code. It did this by intercepting any requests to read the code blocks on the PLC and serving up sanitized versions of them instead, minus the mali-cious commands. If a troubleshooting engineer tried to reprogram the de-vice by overwriting old blocks of code on the PLC with new ones, Stuxnet intervened and infected the new code with its malicious commands too. A programmer could reprogram the PLC a hundred times, and Stuxnet would swap out the clean code for its modified commands every time.

Falliere was stunned by the attack's complexity—and by what it im-plied. It was suddenly clear that Stuxnet wasn't trying to siphon data out of the PLC to spy on its operations, as everyone had originally believed. The fact that it was injecting commands into the PLC and trying to hide that it was doing so while at the same time disabling alarms was evidence that it was designed not for espionage but for sabotage.

But this wasn't a simple denial-of-service attack either. The attackers weren't trying to sabotage the PLC by shutting it down—the PLC re-mained fully functional throughout the attack—they were trying to physi-cally destroy whatever process or device was on the other end of the PLC. It was the first time Falliere had seen digital code used not to alter or steal data but to physically alter or destroy something on the other end of it.

It was a plot straight out of a Hollywood blockbuster film. A Bruce Wil-lis blockbuster, to be exact. Three years earlier, *Live Free or Die Hard* had imagined such a destructive scenario, albeit with the typical Hollywood flair for bluster and creative license. In the film, a group of cyberterrorists, led by a disgruntled former government worker, launch coordinated cyber-attacks to cripple the stock market, transportation networks, and power grids, all to distract authorities from their real aim—siphoning millions of dollars from government coffers. Chaos ensues, along with the requisite *Die Hard* explosions.

But Hollywood scenarios like this had long been dismissed by com-puter security pros as pure fantasy. A hacker might shut down a critical system or two, but blow something up? It seemed improbable. Even most of the explosions in *Die Hard* owed more to physical attacks than to cyber ones. Yet here was evidence in Stuxnet that such a scenario might be possible. It was leaps and bounds beyond anything Falliere had seen before or had expected to find in this code.

For all of its size and success, Symantec was in the end just a nerdy company, in the business of protecting customers. For fifteen years the adversaries they had battled had been joy-riding hackers and cybercriminals or, more recently, nation-state spies hunting corporate and government secrets. All of them were formidable opponents to varying degrees, but none were bent on causing physical destruction. Over the years, malware had gone through a gradual evolution. In the early days, the motivations of malware writers remained pretty much the same. Though some programs were more disruptive than others, the primary goal of virus writers in the 1990s was to achieve glory and fame, and a typical virus payload included shout-outs to the hacker's slacker friends. Things changed as e-commerce took hold and hacking grew into a criminal enterprise. The goal wasn't to gain attention anymore but to remain stealthy in a system for as long as possible to steal credit card numbers and bank account credentials. More recently, hacking had evolved into a high-stakes espionage game where nation-state spies drilled deep into networks to remain there for months or years while silently siphoning national secrets and other sensitive data.

But Stuxnet went far beyond any of these. It wasn't an evolution in malware but a revolution. Everything Falliere and his colleagues had examined before, even the biggest threats that targeted credit card processors and Defense Department secrets, seemed minor in comparison. Stuxnet thrust them into an entirely new battlefield where the stakes were much higher than anything they had dealt with before.

There had long been a story floating around that suggested something like this might have occurred before, but the tale has never been substantiated. According to the story, in 1982 the CIA hatched a plot to install a logic bomb in software controlling a Russian gas pipeline in order to sabotage it. When the code kicked in, it caused the valves on the pipeline to malfunction. The result was an explosive fireball so fierce and large that it was caught by the eyes of orbiting satellites.[3]

Back in Culver City, Chien wondered if there had been unexplained explosions in Iran that could be attributed to Stuxnet. When he searched the news reports, he was startled to find a number of them that had occurred in recent weeks.[4] Toward the end of July, a pipeline carrying natural gas from Iran to Turkey had exploded outside the Turkish town of Dogubayazit, several miles from the Iranian border. The blast, which shattered windows of nearby buildings, left a raging blaze that took hours to extinguish.[5]

Another explosion occurred outside the Iranian city of Tabriz, where a 1,600-mile-long pipeline delivered gas from Iran to Ankara. Yet a third explosion ripped through a state-run petrochemical plant on Kharg Island in the Persian Gulf and killed four people.[6] Weeks later, a fourth gas explosion occurred at the Pardis petrochemical plant in Asalouyeh, killing five people and injuring three.[7] It occurred just a week after Iranian president Mahmoud Ahmadinejad had visited the plant.

The explosions didn't all go unexplained. Kurdish rebels claimed responsibility for the ones at Dogubayazit and Tabriz, and the Iranian news agency, IRNA, attributed the Kharg Island fire to high-pressure buildup in a central boiler.[8] The explosion at Pardis was blamed on a leak of ethane that ignited after workers began welding a pipeline. But what if one or more of the explosions had actually been caused by Stuxnet? Chien wondered.

---

3 For more on the story of the alleged pipeline sabotage, see pages 197–99.
4 Con Coughlin, "Who's Blowing up Iran's Gas Pipelines?" *The Telegraph*, August 18, 2010, available at blogs.telegraph.co.uk/news/concoughlin/100050959/whos-blowing-up-irans-gas -pipelines.
5 Agence France-Presse, "Suspected Kurd Rebels Blow up Iran–Turkey Gas Pipeline," July 21, 2010, available at institutkurde.org/en/info/latest/suspected-kurd-rebels-blow-up-iran-turkey-gas -pipeline-2372.html.
6 "Petrochemical Factory Blast Kills 4 in Iran," Associated Press, July 25, 2010, available at gainesville.com/article/20100725/news/100729673.
7 "Explosion in Petrochemical Complex in Asalouyeh Kills 5," Tabnak News Agency, August 4, 2010, available at tabnak.ir/en/news/180.
8 Ivan Watso and Yesim Comert, "Kurdish Rebel Group Claims Responsibility for Gas Pipeline Blast," CNNWorld, July 21, 2010, available at articles.cnn.com/2010-07-21/world/turkey.pipeline .blast_1_pkk-kurdistan-workers-party-ethnic-kurdish-minority?_s=PM:WORLD.

This was much more than anyone on the team had bargained for when they first began deconstructing Stuxnet weeks earlier. If Stuxnet was doing what Chien and his colleagues thought it was doing, then this was the first documented case of cyberwarfare.

Chien, O'Murchu, and Falliere convened on the phone to discuss their options. They still didn't know what exactly Stuxnet was doing to the PLC or even the identity of its target, but they knew they had to reveal what they'd learned about its payload so far. So on August 17, 2010, they went public with the news that Stuxnet wasn't an espionage tool as everyone had believed but a digital weapon designed for sabotage. "Previously, we reported that Stuxnet can steal code . . . and also hide itself using a classic Windows rootkit," Falliere wrote in his typical understated tone, "but unfortunately it can also do much more."[9]

To illustrate Stuxnet's destructive capability, they referenced the 1982 attack on the Siberian pipeline. Their words had been carefully parsed by the company's PR team, but there was no denying the shocking nature of what they implied. As soon as the post went public, they waited on edge for the community's response. But instead of the dramatic reaction they thought they would get, all they got in return was, in Chien's words, "silence like crickets."

Chien was confused by the lack of response. After all, they were talking about digital code that was capable of blowing things up. They had assumed, at the very least, that once they published their findings, other researchers would publish their own research on Stuxnet. That was the way malware research worked—whenever new attack code was uncovered, teams of competing researchers at different firms worked to decipher the code simultaneously, each one racing to be the first to publish their results. As soon as one team published, the others quickly weighed in to deliver

9 Nicolas Falliere, "Stuxnet Introduces the First Known Rootkit for Industrial Control Systems," Symantec blog, August 6, 2010, available at symantec.com/connect/blogs/stuxnet-introduces-first-known-rootkit-industrial-control-systems. Note that the date on the blog post is August 6, but that's the date the post was first published with news of the PLC rootkit. They updated it when they added the news that Stuxnet was bent on sabotage.

their own findings. If multiple groups arrived at the same results, the duplicate work served as an informal peer-review process to validate all of their findings. The silence that greeted their post about Stuxnet, then, was unusual and disconcerting—Chien began to wonder if they were the only team examining the payload or if anyone else even cared about it.

For a brief moment, he questioned their decision to devote so much time to the code. Had everyone else seen something that made them dismiss it as insignificant, something that Chien and his team had completely missed? But then he reviewed everything they had discovered in the past few weeks. There was no possible way they could have been wrong about the code, he concluded—either about Stuxnet's importance or its aggressive intentions.

As for continuing their research, there was no question anymore that they had to press on. If anything, their work on the code seemed more urgent than before. They had just announced to the world that Stuxnet was a digital weapon designed for physical destruction. But they still hadn't identified the malware's target. Having made a public declaration about the code's destructive aim, they worried that the attackers might suddenly feel pressure to accelerate the mission and destroy their target. That is, if they hadn't already done so.

And apparently, they weren't the only ones concerned about the possibility of things blowing up. Five days after they published their announcement, the steady stream of traffic still coming into their sinkhole from Stuxnet-infected machines in Iran suddenly went dark. It seemed that someone in the Islamic Republic had taken note of their news. To prevent the attackers or anyone else from remotely accessing the infected machines and doing some damage, someone in Iran had finally got wise and given the order to sever all outbound connections from machines in that country to Stuxnet's two command-and-control domains.

CHAPTER 9

INDUSTRIAL CONTROLS
OUT OF CONTROL

Fifty miles outside Idaho Falls, Idaho, on a vast desert prairie owned by the Department of Energy's Idaho National Lab, a handful of engineers shivered against the cold as they paced around a generator the size of a small bus parked on a slab of concrete. It was March 4, 2007, and the workers were making final safety checks for a groundbreaking test they were about to conduct.

About a mile away at the lab's visitor's center, a group of officials from Washington, DC, as well as executives from the power industry and NERC, the North American Electric Reliability Corporation, gathered in a theater warming their hands around cups of steaming coffee as they waited for a live feed of the demo to begin.

In 2010, when the Symantec researchers discovered that Stuxnet was designed to sabotage Siemens PLCs, they believed it was the first documented case in which digital code had been used to physically destroy equipment. But three years earlier, on this Idaho plain, the Aurora Generator Test had demonstrated the viability of such an attack.

It was around eleven thirty a.m. that March day when a worker back in Idaho Falls got the signal to launch a stream of vicious code against the target. As the generator's 5,000-horsepower diesel engine roared over speakers in the lab's small theater, the spectators stared intently at a screen searching for signs of the code's effects. At first, there were none. But then they heard a loud snap, like a heavy chain slapping against a metal drum, and the steel behemoth rattled briefly as if shaken awake. Several seconds passed and they heard another snap—this time the generator lurched and shuddered more violently as if jolted by a defibrillator. Bolts and bits of rubber grommet ejected from its bowels toward the camera, making the observers wince. About fifteen seconds passed before another loud snap sent the machine lurching again. This time, after the vibrations subsided, the generator spit out a puff of white smoke. Then suddenly, *bam!* the machine heaved again before coming to a final rest. After a lengthy pause, when it seemed the beast might have survived the assault, a plume of angry black smoke billowed from its chambers.

Only three minutes had elapsed since the test began, but that was all it took to reduce the colossal machine to a smoldering, lifeless mess of metal and smoke. When it was all done, there was no applause in the theater, just stunned silence. To rock a piece of equipment the size of a tank should have required exceptional force. Yet all it had taken in this case was twenty-one lines of malicious code.

The test had been exhaustively planned and modeled for weeks, yet the force and violence of the attack still took its engineers by surprise—"a moment of incredible vividness," Michael Assante, one of the architects of the test, said.[1] It was one thing to simulate an attack against a small motor perched atop a table, but quite another to watch a twenty-seven-ton machine bounce like a child's toy and fly apart.

The test provided certified proof that a saboteur didn't need physical access to destroy critical equipment at a power plant but could achieve the same result remotely with just a piece of well-crafted code. Three years

---

1 Author interview with Assante, September 2011.

later, when Stuxnet was found on machines in Iran, no one who worked on the Aurora project was surprised that a digital attack could cause physical destruction. They were only surprised that it had taken so long for such an attack to show up.

WHEN THE SYMANTEC researchers discovered in August 2010 that Stuxnet was designed for physical sabotage of Siemens PLCs, they weren't the only ones who had no idea what a PLC was. Few people in the world had ever heard of the devices—this, despite the fact that PLCs are the components that regulate some of the most critical facilities and processes in the world.

PLCs are used with a variety of automated control systems that include the better-known SCADA system (Supervisory Control and Data Acquisition) as well as distributed control systems and others that keep the generators, turbines, and boilers at power plants running smoothly.[2] The systems also control the pumps that transmit raw sewage to treatment plants and prevent water reservoirs from overflowing, and they open and close the valves in gas pipelines to prevent pressure buildups that can cause deadly ruptures and explosions, such as the one that killed eight people and destroyed thirty-eight homes in San Bruno, California, in 2010.

There are less obvious, but no less critical, uses for control systems as well. They control the robots on car assembly lines and dole out and mix the proper portion of ingredients at chemical and pharmaceutical plants.

---

2 SCADA systems are generally used where the systems being managed are geographically dispersed over large areas—such as in pipelines, railway systems, and water and electrical distribution. Distributed control systems, on the other hand, are best for when operators need extensive and complex control in confined facilities like refineries and water-treatment and power-generation plants, although power plants also use SCADA systems to monitor remote substations in the field. SCADA systems consist of an operator's station, a communications network, and a remote terminal unit, or RTU, in the field. The RTUs, which are similar to PLCs, send data back through the network to the operator's monitoring station. The operator's station generally runs on Windows—with all of its inherent vulnerabilities—and the field devices use specialized operating systems, which generally have little security built into them.

They're used by food and beverage makers to set and monitor temperatures for safely cooking and pasteurizing food to kill deadly bacteria. They help maintain consistent temperatures in the furnaces and kilns where glass, fiberglass, and steel are made to ensure the integrity of skyscrapers, cars, and airplanes. They also control traffic lights, open and close cell doors at high-security federal prisons, and raise and lower bridges on highways and waterways. And they help route commuter trains and freight trains and prevent them from crashing. On a smaller scale, they control the elevators in high-rise buildings and the heating and air conditioning in hospitals, schools, and offices. In short, control systems are the critical components that keep industries and infrastructures around the world functioning properly. They need to be reliable and secure. Yet, as Stuxnet clearly showed, they are anything but.

And now with that code available in the wild for anyone to study and copy, the digital weapon can serve as a blueprint to design other attacks targeting vulnerable control systems in the United States and elsewhere—to manipulate valves in a gas pipeline, for example, or to release sewage into waterways, or possibly even to take out generators at a power plant. It wouldn't necessarily require the resources of a wealthy nation to pull off such attacks. With most of the core research and development already done by Stuxnet's creators to expose the vulnerabilities in these systems, the bar has been lowered for other attackers, state and nonstate players alike, to get in the game. From anarchic hacker groups like Anonymous and LulzSec to extortionists looking to hold the controls of a power plant hostage to hackers-for-hire working for terrorist groups, the door is now open for a variety of attackers who never have to venture beyond their borders, or even their bedrooms, to launch an assault. And although Stuxnet was a surgical attack targeting specific machines while leaving others untouched, not all attacks would be so targeted or skilled, raising the possibility of assaults that create widespread disruption or damage—whether intentionally or not.

Attackers wouldn't need to design a sophisticated worm like Stuxnet, either. An ordinary run-of-the-mill virus or worm can have detrimental effects as well.[3] In 2003, train-signaling systems on the East Coast went dark after computers belonging to CSX Corporation in Florida got infected with the Sobig virus. CSX operates rail systems for passenger and freight trains in twenty-three states, and as a result of the signals going out, trains running between Pennsylvania and South Carolina and in the DC Beltway had to be halted.[4] Similarly, the Slammer worm took out the safety monitoring system and process control network at the Davis-Besse nuclear power plant in Ohio for about five hours that same year.[5]

On a scale of one to ten measuring the preparedness of US critical infrastructure to withstand a destructive cyberassault, one being least prepared and ten being most prepared, NSA Director Gen. Keith Alexander told a Senate committee in 2013 that the nation is at three, due in part to the lack of security with control systems.[6]

"We've been working on offensive cyber capabilities for more than a decade in the Department of Defense," Jim Lewis of the Center for Strategic and International Studies has said. "But . . . I think people . . . just don't realize that behind the scenes, there's this new kind of vulnerability that really puts a lot of things at risk."[7]

In truth, the problems with control systems are not new; Stuxnet just

---

3 Industrial control system incidents are tracked in the RISI database (Repository of Industrial Security Incidents), which began recording incidents in 2001 but fell dormant between 2006 and 2009. The subscription database is maintained by the Security Incidents Organization and can be found at securityincidents.org.

4 Marty Niland, "Computer Virus Brings Down Train Signals," Associated Press, August 20, 2003, available at informationweek.com/news/13100807.

5 The worm arrived via the corporate network of the utility company that operated the plant, and spread from the plant's business network to the control network. Luckily, the plant had been offline for nearly a year due to other issues, so no harm was done. Plant operators also said they had manual controls that would have served as backup with the automated ones down. See Kevin Poulsen, "Slammer Worm Crashed Ohio Nuke Plant Network," SecurityFocus, August 19, 2003, available at securityfocus.com/news/6767/.

6 "Cybersecurity: Preparing for and Responding to the Enduring Threat," Speech to the Senate Committee on Appropriations, June 12, 2013, available at hsdl.org/?view&did=739096.

7 Lewis was speaking on the Diane Rehm radio show, broadcast by WAMU in Southern California, on June 4, 2012. Interview available at thedianerehmshow.org/shows/2012-06-04/growing-threat-cyberwarfare.

exposed them for the first time to the public. But some control-systems experts had known about them for years.

PLCs WERE FIRST developed in the 1960s, when computer hackers and viruses were still the stuff of science fiction.[8] They were designed for the automotive industry to replace hardwired relay logic systems that controlled the assembly lines on factory floors. With hardwired relay systems, the only way to make an adjustment to a line was to send an electrician to physically rewire the relays. PLCs made it easy to update the systems with just a few hundred lines of code, though technicians still had to update the systems in person, traveling out to devices in the field to upload the commands from a tape cartridge.

As the use of digital control systems grew in the '90s, operators pressured vendors to provide them with the ability to log into systems remotely via dial-up modem. Hackers were by then becoming legion, but operators still weren't concerned about the security of their systems, because control systems ran on standalone networks, using custom protocols to communicate and having proprietary software that was incompatible with other programs and systems. You couldn't just plug any computer into a control system and communicate with it. And even if you did have a system that could talk to the machines, the universe of people who understood how control systems worked and had the ability to manipulate them was small.

All of this began to change in the late '90s, however. Congress passed environmental laws requiring companies to monitor and control their factory emissions, and the Federal Energy Regulatory Commission began to require access to electricity transmission systems to monitor their output and distribution. Suddenly compliance officers and corporate execu-

---

8 Gregory Benford, a physicist, is credited with one of the first mentions of a computer virus in a story he wrote in 1969 called "The Scarred Man," which was published in the May 1970 issue of *Venture* magazine. The notion of digital worms originated in John Brunner's 1975 science-fiction book *The Shockwave Rider*, which featured a digital tapeworm that slithered from machine to machine.

tives demanded access to data and systems that were previously accessible only to plant operators. Out went proprietary operating systems that no one could communicate with or understand, and in came control systems that ran on commercial operating systems, such as Windows and Linux, making it easy for other computers on a company's corporate network to connect and communicate with them. The switch to Windows, however, meant that control systems were now vulnerable to the same viruses and worms that plagued personal PCs. And as the systems became increasingly connected to the internet, or to dial-up modems to make them remotely accessible to operators, they also became increasingly vulnerable to remote attack from hackers.

In March 1997, a teenage hacker in Massachusetts who went by the name "Jester" gave a small preview of what could occur when he dialed into the Bell Atlantic computer system via modem and knocked out systems that managed phone and radio communications for the air traffic control tower at Worcester Airport, as well as phone service for six hundred homes in a nearby town. Communications for the airport's security and fire departments were down for six hours, as was the system pilots used to activate the runway lights. Air traffic controllers had to use cell phones and battery-powered radios to direct planes during the outage.[9] No accidents occurred, but an air traffic control manager told CNN, "We dodged a bullet that day."[10]

That same year, the specially convened Marsh Commission published a report examining the vulnerability of critical infrastructure systems to attack—both physical and digital. The commission had been charged with investigating the matter after Timothy McVeigh blew up a federal building in Oklahoma City in 1995 and took out a number of key data and communication centers in the process. The commissioners warned of the increasing perils created from connecting critical systems for oil, gas, and electricity to the internet. "The capability to do harm . . . is growing

9 "Teen Hacker Pleads Guilty to Crippling Mass. Airport," *Boston Globe*, March 19, 1998.
10 "Teen Hacker Faces Federal Charges," CNN, March 18, 1998, available at edition.cnn.com/TECH/computing/9803/18/juvenile.hacker/index.html.

at an alarming rate; and we have little defense against it," they wrote. The right commands sent over a network to a power-generating station's control computer, they wrote, "could be just as devastating as a backpack full of explosives. . . . We should attend to our critical foundations before we are confronted with a crisis, not after. Waiting for disaster would prove as expensive as it would be irresponsible."[11]

A second report released the same year by the White House National Security Telecommunications Advisory Committee warned that the nation's power grid and the utilities feeding it were pockmarked with security holes that made them vulnerable to attack. "An electronic intruder . . . could dial into an unprotected port and reset the breaker to a higher level of tolerance than the device being protected by the breaker can withstand," investigators wrote, anticipating the Aurora Generator Test a decade before it occurred. "By doing this, it would be possible to physically destroy a given piece of equipment within a substation."[12]

Despite these early warnings, there were no signs yet that anyone was interested in conducting such attacks. That is until 2000, when a former worker sabotaged the pumps at a water treatment plant in Australia, in what is considered to be the first publicly reported case of an intentional control-system hack.

MAROOCHY SHIRE ON Queensland's Sunshine Coast is the kind of place made for picture postcards, with a lush rain forest, rugged volcanic peak, and azure coastal waters bordered by white sandy beaches. But in early 2000, the shire's beauty took an ugly turn when, over the course of four months, a hacker caused more than 750,000 gallons of raw sewage to spill from a number of wells and pour into public waterways.

---

11 "Critical Foundations: Protecting America's Infrastructures," President's Commission on Critical Infrastructure Protection, October 1997. The report is available at https://www.fas.org/sgp/library/pccip.pdf.
12 "Electric Power Risk Assessment," National Security Telecommunications Advisory Committee, Information Assurance Task Force, available at solarstorms.org/ElectricAssessment.html.

At first it was just a small amount of sewage spilling from a well at the Hyatt Regency Hotel into a lagoon on the five-star resort's PGA golf course. But after workers cleaned it up, the well overflowed again and again. The worst spills occurred, however, in Pacific Paradise, a suburb along the Maroochy River. Here several hundred thousand gallons of sewage poured into a tidal canal, endangering the health of children playing in backyards abutting the canal, and into the Maroochy River itself, where it killed off fish and other marine life.

The problems began on New Year's Eve 1999, after Maroochy Water Services installed a new digital management system. The treatment plant's control system had been installed in stages by Hunter WaterTech, a contract firm, and was just nearing completion when settings for the pump stations responsible for moving sewage to the treatment plant began to mysteriously change. Pumps would turn off or continue to run in defiance of operator instructions, and the two-way radio network used to broadcast instructions to pump stations would become clogged with traffic, preventing operators from communicating with the stations. Alarms that should have sounded when things went awry didn't.[13]

The pumps were controlled by two central computers, using proprietary Hunter WaterTech software, which communicated with a remote terminal unit at each pump station via two-way radio signals. Signals got transmitted from the computers to the RTUs, or between the RTUs, via repeater stations in the field that operated on nonpublic frequencies. Only someone on the central computers or within range of a repeater station, using Hunter WaterTech proprietary software and the proper communication protocols, could send commands to the pumping stations. Hunter WaterTech initially suspected an outside hacker was behind the attacks, but the water district had no intrusion-detection tools or logging system

---

13 Information about the Maroochy Shire case comes from an author interview conducted August 2012 with Robert Stringfellow, a water district engineer who helped investigate the case, as well as from redacted court documents and a police report written by forensic examiner Peter Kingsley. Some details from the court documents were first published by Joe Weiss in his book *Protecting Industrial Control Systems from Electronic Threats* (New York: Momentum Press, 2010).

in place to detect a breach. But even after they installed these systems they were still unable to detect a breach.

The attacks continued on and off for weeks and reached a peak one night in March when more than two-dozen incidents occurred. Investigators finally concluded it must be a rogue insider sending malicious commands in the field via two-way radio signals.[14] They zeroed in on a former contractor named Vitek Boden, a forty-nine-year-old engineer who had worked for Hunter WaterTech until his contract expired in December, around the time the first water pump failed. Boden had subsequently sought a full-time job with the water district but was turned down in January—which coincided with when the bulk of the problems began.

Sure enough, when police caught up with Boden one night in April after alarm systems at four pump stations were disabled, they found a laptop in his car with Hunter WaterTech's proprietary software installed and a two-way radio set to the nonpublic frequency the water district used to communicate with pumping stations. They also found an RTU Boden had apparently used to send out the bogus commands.[15]

Boden's case was the first cyberattack against a critical infrastructure system to come to light, but it likely wasn't the first to occur. Others no doubt had simply gone undetected or unreported.[16] In the wake of the

---

14 Between March 14 and April 23 about ninety incidents occurred. A worker traced some of the activity to the RTU at pump station 14, where the malicious radio signals seemed to originate. He knew it was easy to alter the address of an RTU simply by flipping certain switches on the device, so he concluded the intruder must be using a rogue RTU that had its switches set to 14 to send out malicious commands as if they were coming from the real pump station 14. To set a trap, he changed the address for pump station 14 to 3. If an intruder *was* sending spoofed messages, he wouldn't know the address had changed and would continue sending his messages under the old address. That's exactly what occurred one night when a flood of malicious traffic sailed across the network from pump station 14 aimed at crashing the central computer. Investigators concluded, then, that the attacker must be an insider with knowledge of the Maroochy system and access to Hunter WaterTech software and equipment.

15 Boden was convicted and sentenced in October 2001 to two years in prison. He later appealed, at which point his conviction on two of the charges was set aside, but his conviction on other charges remained, as well as his sentence.

16 A survey of utilities conducted by the Electronic Power Research Institute in 1996 found that only 25 percent of respondents reported using any intrusion detection methods. The survey, the EPRI Summer 1996 Electronic Information Security Survey, and the statistic are referenced at solarstorms.org/ElectricAssessment.html.

Maroochy incident, workers from other utilities told investigators that they would never have pursued criminal charges against Boden as Maroochy had done, in order to keep the matter quiet.[17]

The case should have been a wake-up call to control-system operators around the world, but many dismissed it because it involved an inside attacker who had extensive knowledge of the Maroochy Shire system and access to the specialized equipment needed to conduct the attack. No outsider could have done what Boden did, they argued, ignoring a number of security problems with Maroochy's control-system network that outsiders could have exploited to achieve similar attacks. Peter Kingsley, one of the investigators on the case, later warned attendees at a control-system conference that although the Maroochy hack had been an inside job, breaches from outsiders were by no means impossible. "Some utilities believe they're protected because they themselves can't find an unauthorized way to access their systems," he said. "But hackers don't restrict themselves to ordinary techniques."[18]

Kingsley's words seemed quaint in 2002 because there were still few signs that outsiders were interested in hacking critical infrastructure systems. And in the absence of any major disaster, the security of control systems simply wasn't a concern.

It was around this time that Joe Weiss became an evangelist for control-system security.

Weiss is a lean and energetic sixty-four-year-old who works out of his home in Cupertino, California, the heart of Silicon Valley, and is used to thinking about catastrophic scenarios. He lives just five miles from

---

17 Maroochy Water Services had little choice but to involve law enforcement in the case, because the spillages were so public and threatened public safety. The incidents also brought heavy scrutiny from Australia's environmental protection agency and from regional government officials who demanded an explanation for why they occurred.

18 Kingsley was speaking at the AusCERT2002 conference in Australia. In a report examining the Maroochy case in 2008, eight years after it occurred, the authors concluded that some of the issues raised by the incident were just beginning to be addressed by companies, while "some are unresolved with no solution in sight." See Marshall Abrams and Joe Weiss, "Malicious Control System Cyber Security Attack Case Study–Maroochy Water Services, Australia," February 23, 2008, available at csrc.nist.gov/groups/SMA/fisma/ics/documents/Maroochy-Water-Services-Case-Study_report.pdf.

California's notorious San Andreas Fault and the seventy-year-old Stevens Creek Dam. When the Loma Prieta earthquake struck the area in 1989, chimneys toppled, streetlights and phones died for several days, and shockwaves in the swimming pool at nearby DeAnza College ejected polo players from the water and onto the pavement like beached seals.

Weiss first became aware of the security problems with control systems in 1999. A nuclear engineer by training, he was working for the Electric Power Research Institute when the Y2K issue arose. Armageddon warnings in the press predicted dystopian meltdowns when computer clocks struck midnight on New Year's Eve because of a programming error that failed to anticipate the millennial rollover to triple zeroes on January 1, 2000. Weiss began to wonder: if such a minor thing as a change of date could threaten to bring control systems to a halt, what would more serious issues do? More important, if Y2K could accidentally cause huge problems, what might an intentional attack from hackers do?

Dozens of security conferences held around the world each year focused on general computer security, but none of them addressed control systems. So Weiss began attending them to learn what security guidelines the control-system community should adopt. But the more conferences he attended, the more worried he got. When network administrators talked about using encryption and authentication to prevent unauthorized users from accessing their systems, Weiss realized that control systems had none of the standard protections that normal computer networks used. When security experts asked him what brand of firewall control-system operators at energy plants used or how often they reviewed their network logs for evidence of intruders, Weiss had to reply, "We don't have firewalls. No network logs, either."[19] And when he began to ask control-system makers about the security of their products, he got blank stares in response. They told him no one had ever asked about security before.

Then two planes struck the Twin Towers in September 2001 and not

---

19 This and other quotes from Weiss in this chapter come from an author interview, June 2012.

long afterward, authorities uncovered suspicious patterns of searches on government websites in California. The searchers appeared to be exploring digital systems used to manage utilities and government offices in the San Francisco region. The activity, which appeared to originate from IP addresses in Saudi Arabia, Indonesia, and Pakistan, showed a particular interest in emergency phone systems, power and water plants, and gas facilities.[20] Other searches focused on programming controls for fire-dispatch systems and pipelines.

The following year, US forces in Kabul seized a computer in an al-Qaeda office and found models of a dam on it along with engineering software that could be used to simulate its failure.[21] That same year, the CIA issued a Directorate of Intelligence Memorandum stating that al-Qaeda had "far more interest" in cyberterrorism than previously believed and had begun to contemplate hiring hackers.

There were signs that others might be interested in US critical infrastructure too.[22] In 2001, hackers broke into servers at the California Independent System Operator, or Cal-ISO, a nonprofit corporation that manages the transmission system for moving electricity throughout most of the state. The attackers got in through two unprotected servers and remained undetected for two weeks until workers noticed problems with their machines.[23] Cal-ISO officials insisted the breach posed no threat to the grid, but unnamed sources told the *Los Angeles Times* that the hackers were caught just as they were trying to access "key parts of the system" that would have allowed them to cause serious disruptions in electrical service. One person called it a near "catastrophic breach." The attack appeared to

---

20 Barton Gellman, "Cyber-Attacks by Al Qaeda Feared," *Washington Post*, June 27, 2002.
21 Ibid.
22 "Critical infrastructure" in the United States is broadly defined by the government as any facility or system that falls into one of sixteen categories that include: agriculture and food, banking and finance, chemical, commercial facilities, critical manufacturing, dams, defense industrial base, drinking-water and water-treatment systems, emergency services, energy, government facilities, information technology, nuclear reactors and waste, public health and health care, telecommunications, and transportation. See dhs.gov/critical-infrastructure-sectors.
23 Dan Morain, "Hackers Victimize Cal-ISO," *Los Angeles Times*, June 9, 2001.

originate from China, and came in the midst of a tense political standoff between China and the United States after a US spy plane collided in mid-air with a Chinese fighter jet over the South China Sea.

In response to growing concerns about critical infrastructure, and in particular the security of the nation's power grids, the Department of Energy launched a National SCADA Test Bed program in 2003 at the Idaho National Lab (INL). The goal was to work with the makers of control systems to evaluate their equipment for security vulnerabilities, and was an initiative that ultimately led to the 2007 Aurora Generator Test.[24]

There are 2,800 power plants in the United States and 300,000 sites producing oil and natural gas.[25] Another 170,000 facilities form the public water system in the United States, which includes reservoirs, dams, wells, treatment facilities, pumping stations, and pipelines.[26] But 85 percent of these and other critical infrastructure facilities are in the hands of the private sector, which means that aside from a few government-regulated industries—such as the nuclear power industry—the government can do little to force companies to secure their systems. The government, however, could at least try to convince the makers of control systems to improve the security of their products. Under the test-bed program, the government would conduct the tests as long as the vendors agreed to fix any vulnerabilities uncovered by them.[27]

Around the same time, DHS also launched a site-assessment program

---

24 A previous SCADA testing program had launched at Sandia National Laboratory in 1998, but didn't involve vendors. INL is the Department of Energy's lead lab for nuclear energy research and runs the largest test reactor in the world. The Atomic Energy Commission took over the land in Idaho after World War II to build a nuclear research lab. Over the years, the lab's work expanded to include research on the electric grid and, after the Bush administration released its National Strategy to Secure Cyberspace in February 2003, the security of industrial control systems. That strategy called for the Department of Energy and the Department of Homeland Security (DHS) to partner with private industry to address the security of control systems.

25 Department of Homeland Security, "The National Strategy for the Physical Protection of Critical Infrastructures and Key Assets" (report, The White House, February 2003), 9. Available at dhs.gov/xlibrary/assets/Physical_Strategy.pdf.

26 Ibid., 39.

27 One problematic loophole in the test program, however, is that the reports vendors receive describing the vulnerabilities found in their systems are covered by a nondisclosure agreement and the vendors are not required to tell customers about the vulnerabilities found in their systems.

through its Industrial Control System Cyber Emergency Response Team (ICS-CERT) to evaluate the security configuration of critical infrastructure equipment and networks already installed at facilities. Between 2002 and 2009, the team conducted more than 100 site assessments across multiple industries—oil and natural gas, chemical, and water—and found more than 38,000 vulnerabilities. These included critical systems that were accessible over the internet, default vendor passwords that operators had never bothered to change or hard-coded passwords that couldn't be changed, outdated software patches, and a lack of standard protections such as firewalls and intrusion-detection systems.

But despite the best efforts of the test-bed and site-assessment researchers, they were battling decades of industry inertia—vendors took months and years to patch vulnerabilities that government researchers found in their systems, and owners of critical infrastructure were only willing to make cosmetic changes to their systems and networks, resisting more extensive ones.

Weiss, who worked as a liaison with INL to help develop its test-bed program, got fed up with the inertia and launched a conference to educate critical-infrastructure operators about the dangerous security problems with their systems. In 2004, he resorted to scare tactics by demonstrating a remote attack to show them what could be done. The role of hacker was played by Jason Larsen, a researcher at INL, who demonstrated an attack against a substation in Idaho Falls from a computer at Sandia National Laboratory in New Mexico. Exploiting a recently discovered vulnerability in server software, Larsen bypassed several layers of firewalls to hack a PLC controlling the substation and release his payload in several stages. The first stage opened and closed a breaker. The second stage opened all of the breakers at once. The third stage opened all of the breakers but manipulated data sent to operator screens to make it appear that the breakers were closed.

"I call it my 'wet pants' demo," Weiss says. "It was a phenomenal success."

Weiss followed the demo a few years later with another one and then another, each time enlisting different security experts to demonstrate different modes of attack. The only problem was, they were ahead of their time. Each time engineers would leave his conference fired up with ideas about improving the security of their networks, they would run up against executives back home who balked at the cost of re-architecting and securing the systems. Why spend money on security, they argued, when none of their competitors were doing it and no one was attacking them?

But what Weiss and the test lab couldn't achieve in a decade, Stuxnet achieved in a matter of months. The digital weapon shone a public spotlight on serious vulnerabilities in the nation's industrial control systems for the first time, and critical equipment that for so long had remained obscure and unknown to most of the world now caught the attention of researchers and hackers, forcing vendors and critical-infrastructure owners to finally take note as well.

THE NEWS IN August 2010 that Stuxnet was sabotaging Siemens PLCs caught the interest of a twenty-five-year-old computer security researcher in Austin, Texas, named Dillon Beresford. Beresford, like most people, had never heard of PLCs and was curious to see how vulnerable they might be. So he bought several Siemens PLCs online and spent two months examining and testing them in the bedroom of his small apartment. It took just a few weeks to uncover multiple vulnerabilities that he could use in an attack.

He discovered, for example, that none of the communication that passed between a programmer's machine and the PLCs was encrypted, so any hacker who broke into the network could see and copy commands as they were transmitted to the PLCs, then later play them back to a PLC to control and stop it at will. This would not have been possible had the PLCs rejected unauthorized computers from sending them commands, but Beresford found that the PLCs were promiscuous computers that would talk to any machine that spoke their protocol language. They also didn't require that commands sent to them be digitally signed with a certificate to prove that they came from a trustworthy source.

Although there was an authentication packet, or password of sorts, that passed between a Step 7 machine and the PLC, Beresford was able to decode the password in less than three hours. He also found that he could simply capture the authentication packet as it passed from a Step 7 machine to the PLC and replay it in the same way he replayed commands, eliminating the need to decode the password at all. Once he had control of a PLC, he could also issue a command to change the password to lock out legitimate users.[28]

Beresford found other vulnerabilities as well, including a back door that Siemens programmers had left in the firmware of their PLCs—firmware is the basic software that is resident on hardware devices to make them work. Vendors often place global, hard-coded passwords in their systems to access them remotely to provide troubleshooting for customers—like an OnStar feature for control systems. But backdoors that allow vendors to slip in also let attackers in.[29] The username and password for opening the Siemens back door was the same for every system—"*basisk*"—and was hard-coded into the firmware for anyone who examined it to see. Using this back door, an attacker could delete files from the PLC, reprogram it, or issue commands to sabotage whatever operations the PLC controlled.[30]

Beresford reported his findings to ICS-CERT, which worked with Siemens to get the vulnerabilities fixed. But not all of them could be. Some, like the transmission of unencrypted commands and the lack of strong

---

28 Kim Zetter, "Hard-Coded Password and Other Security Holes Found in Siemens Control Systems," Wired.com, August 3, 2011, available at wired.com/2011/08/siemens-hardcoded -password.

29 Joe Weiss estimates that more than half of all control systems have a back door embedded in them by the vendor.

30 Beresford also found one more surprise—an "Easter egg" that a Siemens programmer had hidden in the firmware. Easter eggs are inside jokes that coders bury in their programs for users to find. Often they can be seen only if a user types a specific sequence of keys or accesses an obscure part of the program. In Siemens's case, the Easter egg consisted of an animated image of dancing chimpanzees that appeared on-screen with a German proverb. Translated loosely the proverb said, "All work and no play makes Jack a dull boy." Though the Easter egg wasn't malicious, it raised serious concerns about Siemens's security. If a programmer had slipped the joke past the company's internal code reviewers, what else might have slipped by them?

authentication, were fundamental design issues, not programming bugs, which required Siemens to upgrade the firmware on its systems to fix them or, in some cases, re-architect them. And these weren't just problems for Siemens PLCs; they were fundamental design issues that many control systems had, a legacy of their pre-internet days, when the devices were built for isolated networks and didn't need to withstand attacks from outsiders.

Beresford's findings defied longstanding assertions by vendors and critical-infrastructure owners that their systems were secure because only someone with extensive knowledge of PLCs and experience working with the systems could attack them. With $20,000 worth of used equipment purchased online and two months working in his spare time, Beresford had found more than a dozen vulnerabilities and learned enough about the systems to compromise them.

Since Beresford's findings, other researchers have uncovered additional vulnerabilities in Siemens and other control systems. According to a database of control-system vulnerabilities managed by Wurldtech Security, a maker of systems for protecting critical infrastructure, about 1,000 vulnerabilities have been found in control systems and control-system protocols since 2008. Most of them would simply allow an attacker to prevent operators from monitoring their system, but many of them would also allow an attacker to hijack the system.[31]

In 2011, a security firm hired by a Southern California utility to evaluate the security of controllers at its substations found multiple vulnerabili-

---

31 In 2013, two researchers found problems with a popular protocol used by control centers to communicate with PLCs and RTUs installed at substations. An intruder who couldn't gain direct access to the control-center machine via the internet could compromise the communication device at a remote substation—either by accessing it physically or hacking into the wireless radio network it uses to communicate with the control center—and exploit a vulnerability in the protocol to send malicious commands to the control center. In this way an attacker could either crash the control-center machine or use it to distribute malicious commands to all of the substations with which that machine communicates, potentially taking out dozens or even hundreds of substations at a time, depending on the size of the utility. See Kim Zetter, "Researchers Uncover Holes That Open Power Stations to Hacking," Wired.com, October 16, 2013, available at wired.com/2013/10/ics.

ties that would allow an attacker to control its equipment. "We've never looked at a device like this before, and we were able to find this in the first day," Kurt Stammberger, vice president of Mocana said. "These were big, major problems, and problems frankly that have been known about for at least a year and a half, but the utility had no clue."[32]

The security problems with control systems are exacerbated by the fact that the systems don't get replaced for years and don't get patched on a regular basis the way general computers do. The life-span of a standard desktop PC is three to five years, after which companies upgrade to new models. But the life-span of a control system can be two decades. And even when a system is replaced, new models have to communicate with legacy systems, so they often contain many of the same vulnerabilities as the old ones.

As for patching, some control systems run on outdated versions of Windows that are no longer supported by Microsoft, meaning that if any new vulnerabilities are discovered in the software, they will never get patched by the vendor. But even when patches are available, patching is done infrequently on control systems because operators are wary of buggy patches that might crash their systems and because they can't easily take critical systems—and the processes they control—out of service for the several hours it can take to install patches or do other security maintenance.[33]

All of these problems are compounded by a growing trend among vendors to package safety systems with their control systems. Safety systems used to be hardwired analog systems configured separately from control systems so that any problems with the control system wouldn't interfere with the safety system's ability to shut down equipment in an emergency.

---

32 Jordan Robertson, "Science Fiction–Style Sabotage a Fear in New Hacks," Associated Press, October 23, 2011, available at news-yahoo.com/science-fiction-style-sabotage-fear-hacks-120704517 .html.

33 In 2003, according to Joe Weiss, when the SQL Slammer worm hit the internet, one control-system supplier warned its customers not to install a patch released by Microsoft to combat the worm, because the patch would shut down their system.

But many vendors are now building the safety system into their control system, making it easier to disable them both in a single attack.[34]

Many of the vulnerabilities in control systems could be mitigated if the systems ran on standalone networks that were "air-gapped"—that is, never connected to the internet or connected to other systems that are connected to the internet. But this isn't always the case.

In 2012, a researcher in the UK found more than 10,000 control systems that were connected to the internet—including ones belonging to water-treatment and power plants, dams, bridges, and train stations—using a specialized search engine called Shodan that can locate devices like VoIP phones, SmartTVs, and control systems that are connected to the internet.[35]

In 2011 a hacker named pr0f accessed the controls for a water plant in South Houston after finding the city's Siemens control system online. Although the system was password-protected, it used a three-character password that was easily guessed. "I'm sorry this ain't a tale of advanced persistent threats and stuff," pr0f told a reporter at the time, "but frankly most compromises I've seen have been a result of gross stupidity, not incredible technical skill on the part of the attacker."[36] Once in the SCADA system, pr0f took screenshots showing the layout of water tanks and digital controls, though he didn't sabotage the system. "I don't really like mind-

---

34 Safety systems at nuclear plants, luckily, are still controlled by analog means, according to Joe Weiss, and the horror of a core meltdown being caused by a cyber incident is very low for existing nuclear plants. But that could change, since designs for next-generation plants include digital, networked systems, he says, that could make it easier to attack such plants.

35 Kim Zetter, "10K Reasons to Worry About Critical Infrastructure," Wired.com, January 24, 2012, available at wired.com/2012/01/10000-control-systems-online. Researcher Eireann Leverett was unable to determine how many of the control systems were working systems as opposed to demo systems, and couldn't tell how many of them were critical systems as opposed to simply an office heating system at a plant. But he did identify control systems for water facilities in Ireland and sewage facilities in California among them, and even controls for a heating system can sometimes be leveraged by attackers to access other parts of a network. And only 17 percent of the 10,000 systems he found required authorization to connect to them. In some cases, the owners weren't even aware their systems were accessible online.

36 Paul F. Roberts, "Hacker Says Texas Town Used Three Character Password to Secure Internet Facing SCADA System," Threatpost blog, November 20, 2011, available at threatpost .com/blogs/hacker-says-texas-town-used-three-character-password-secure-internet-facing-scada -system-11201/75914.

less vandalism. It's stupid and silly," he wrote in a post he published online. "On the other hand, so is connecting interfaces to your SCADA machinery to the internet."[37]

Many SCADA field devices, if not connected directly to the public internet, are accessible via modem and are secured only with default passwords. Switches and breakers for the power grid, for example, are often set up this way with default passwords so that workers who need to access them in an emergency will remember the password. For the same reason, control systems aren't generally designed to lock someone out after several failed password attempts—a standard security feature in many IT systems to prevent someone from brute-forcing a password with multiple guesses—because no one wants a control system to lock out an operator who mistypes a password a few times in a state of panic. In 2011, a test team led by security researcher Marc Maiffret penetrated the remote-access system for a Southern California water plant and was able to take control of equipment the facility used for adding chemicals to drinking water. They took control of the system in just a day, and Maiffret said it would have taken just a couple of additional steps to dump chemicals into the water to make it potentially undrinkable.[38]

Making critical systems remotely accessible from the internet creates obvious security risks. But if Stuxnet proved anything, it's that an attacker doesn't need remote access to attack a system—instead, an autonomous worm can be delivered via USB flash drive or via the project files that engineers use to program PLCs. In 2012, Telvent Canada, a maker of control software used in the smart grid, was hacked by intruders linked to the Chinese military, who accessed project files for the SCADA system the company produced—a system installed in oil and gas pipelines in the United States as well as in water systems. Telvent used the project files to manage the systems of customers. Though the company never indicated whether the attackers modified the project files, the breach demonstrated

---

37 His statements appeared on the Pastebin site on November 18, 2011. See Pastebin.com/Wx90L Lum.
38 Ken Dilanian, "Virtual War a Real Threat," *Los Angeles Times*, March 28, 2011.

how easily an attacker might target oil and gas pipelines by infecting the project files of a company like Telvent.[39]

Direct computer network intrusions aren't the only concern when it comes to critical infrastructure, however. There are documented cases involving electromagnetic pulses interfering with SCADA systems and field devices. In November 1999, the radar system from a US Navy ship conducting exercises twenty-five miles off the coast of San Diego interrupted the wireless networks of SCADA systems at local water and electric utilities. The disturbance prevented workers from opening and closing valves in a pipeline, forcing them to dispatch technicians to remote locations to manually activate the valves and prevent water from overflowing reservoirs. Electromagnetic pulse (EMP) disturbances were also responsible for a gas explosion that occurred near the Dutch naval port of Den Helder in the late '80s when a naval radar system caused the SCADA system for a natural gas pipeline to open and close a valve.[40]

OVER THE YEARS, numerous Doomsday scenarios have explored the possible consequences of a massive cyberattack.[41] But to date, no such attack has occurred, and unintentional events involving control systems have far outnumbered intentional ones.

But one need only look at accidental industrial disasters to see the extent of damage a cyberattack *could* wreak, since often the consequences of

---

39 Kim Zetter, "Chinese Military Linked to Hacks of More Than 100 Companies," Wired.com, February 19, 2013, available at wired.com/2013/02/chinese-army-linked-to-hacks. For more information on the specifics of the Telvent hack, see also Kim Zetter, "Maker of Smart-Grid Control Software Hacked," Wired.com, September 26, 2012, available at wired.com/2012/09/scada-vendor -telvent-hacked.

40 "Report of the Commission to Assess the Threat to the United States from Electromagnetic Pulse (EMP) Attack," April 2008, available at empcommission.org/docs/A2473-EMP_Commission -7MB.pdf. See also page 201, footnote 25 for a description of an intentional electromagnetic pulse attack plan.

41 A 1996 RAND study titled "The Day After . . . in Cyberspace" was one of the first to imagine the consequences of a multipronged attack that targeted planes, trains, phone systems, and ATMs on a number of continents. See Robert H. Anderson and Anthony C. Hearn, "An Exploration of Cyberspace Security R&D Investment Strategies for DARPA: The Day After . . . in Cyberspace II," RAND, 1996, available at rand.org/pubs/monograph_reports/MR797.html.

an industrial accident can be replicated for an intentional attack. A smart hacker could simply study the causes and effects of an accidental disaster reported in the news and use them to design an attack that would achieve the same destructive results.

The NSA's Keith Alexander has cited the catastrophic accident that occurred at the Sayano-Shushenskaya hydroelectric plant in southern Siberia as an example of what could occur in an attack.[42] The thirty-year-old dam, the sixth largest in the world, was eight hundred feet high and spanned about half a mile across a picturesque gorge on the Yenisei River, before it collapsed in 2009, killing seventy-five people.

Just after midnight on August 17, a 940-ton turbine in the dam's power-generation plant was hit with a sudden surge of water pressure that knocked it off its bolts and caused it to shoot in the air. As a geyser of water flooded the engine room from the shaft where the turbine had been, it caused massive damage to more than half a dozen other turbines, triggering multiple explosions and causing the roof to cave in.

The catastrophe was attributed in part to a fire at the Bratsk power station some five hundred miles away that caused the energy output from Bratsk to drop. This forced the turbines at Sayano-Shushenskaya to pick up the load. But one of those turbines was already at the end of its life and had been vibrating dangerously on and off for a while. A new control system had been installed months earlier to stabilize the machine, but vibrations from the added workload proved to be too much. The turbine sheared off the bolts holding it down and became unmoored. Surveillance images showed workers scrambling over equipment to flee the site. In addition to killing seventy-five workers and flooding the surrounding community, the plant spilled 100 tons of oil into the Yenisei River and killed 4,000 tons of trout in local fisheries. Experts calculated that repairs would take four years and cost $1.3 billion.[43]

---

42 Bill Gertz, "Computer-Based Attacks Emerge as Threat of Future, General Says," *Washington Times*, September 13, 2011.
43 Joe P. Hasler, "Investigating Russia's Biggest Dam Explosion: What Went Wrong," *Popular Mechanics*, February 2, 2010.

The June 1999 pipeline explosion in Washington state also presented a blueprint for hackers to follow. In that case, a 16-inch-diameter pipeline belonging to the Olympic Pipe Line Company in Bellingham ruptured and spewed more than 237,000 gallons of gasoline into a creek in What-com Falls Park. Gas poured out of the pipe for ninety minutes before it ignited into a fireball that stretched 1.5 miles downstream, killing two ten-year-old boys and a teen and injuring eight others. Although multiple issues contributed to the disaster, including improperly configured valves and a backhoe that weakened part of the pipe, an unresponsive control system also played a role. "[I]f the SCADA system computers had remained responsive to the commands of the Olympic controllers," investigators found, "the controller operating the accident pipeline probably would have been able to initiate actions that would have prevented the pressure increase that ruptured the pipeline."[44]

It took operators more than an hour to register the leak, and by then residents were already calling 911 to report a strong smell of petroleum in the creek. Although the gas leak wasn't caused by hackers, investigators found a number of security problems with Olympic's system that made it vulnerable to attack. For example, the company had set up remote dial-in access for its SCADA control system that was secured only with a user-name and password, and its business and SCADA networks were interconnected. Although they were connected by a bridge that provided some security from a casual intruder, the connection lacked a robust firewall as well as virus protection or access monitoring, raising the possibility that a determined attacker could break into the business network from the internet, then jump to the critical SCADA network.

The natural-gas pipeline explosion in San Bruno, California, in 2010 was another worst-case scenario that served as a cautionary tale. The explosion occurred after maintenance on an uninterrupted power supply

---

44 "Pipeline Rupture and Subsequent Fire in Bellingham, Washington June 10, 1999," published by the National Transportation Safety Board, 2002, available at ntsb.gov/doclib/reports/2002/PAR0202.pdf.

unit, or UPS, caused electricity to the SCADA system to go out. A control valve on the pipeline was programmed to fall open automatically if the SCADA system lost power; as a result, gas poured into the pipeline unimpeded, causing pressure to build in the aging structure until it burst. Since the SCADA system had lost power, operators couldn't see what was happening in the pipeline.[45]

Then there was the collapse of a dike in Missouri in December 2005. The disaster began when sensors on the dam wall became detached from their mounts and failed to detect when the dam's 1.5 billion-gallon reservoir was full. As pumps continued to feed water to the reservoir, a "failsafe" shutdown system also failed to work.[46] The overflow began around 5:10 a.m. and within six minutes a 60-foot section of the parapet wall gave way. More than a billion gallons of water poured down Proffit Mountain, sweeping up rocks and trees in its massive embrace before entering Johnson's Shut-Ins State Park and washing away the park superintendent's home—with him and his family still in it—and depositing them a quarter of a mile away.[47] No one was seriously injured, but cars on a nearby highway were also swept up in the torrent, and a campground at the park was flooded. Luckily, because it was winter, the campsite was empty.

Railway accidents also provide blueprints for digital attacks. The systems that operate passenger trains combine multiple, often interconnected components that provide possible avenues for attack: access-control systems to keep nonticketed pedestrians out of stations, credit-card processing systems, digital advertising systems, lighting management, and

45 "Pacific Gas and Electric Company Natural Gas Transmission Pipeline Rupture and Fire," National Transportation Safety Board, September 9, 2010, available at ntsb.gov/investigations/summary/PAR1101.html.
46 J. David Rogers and Conor M. Watkins, "Overview of the Taum Sauk Pumped Storage Power Plant Upper Reservoir Failure, Reynolds County, MO," presented at the 6th International Conference on Case Histories in Geotechnical Engineering, Arlington, VA, August 11–16, 2008, available at web.mst.edu/~rogersda/dams/2_43_rogers.pdf.
47 Emitt C. Witt III, "December 14th, 2005 Taum Sauk Dam Failure at Johnson's Shut-Ins Park in Southeast Missouri," National Oceanic and Atmospheric Administration, available at crh.noaa.gov/lsx/?n=12_14_2005.

closed-circuit TVs, not to mention the more critical systems for fire and emergency response, crossings and signals control, and the operation of the trains themselves. In the past, these systems were separate and did not communicate with one another except through wires. But today the systems are increasingly digital and interconnected, including systems that communicate via radio signals and transmit unencrypted commands in the clear. Although rail systems have redundancies and fail-safe mechanisms to prevent accidents from occurring, when many systems are interconnected, it creates the opportunity for misconfigurations that could allow someone to access the safety systems and undermine them.

On June 22, 2009, a passenger train in the DC Metro system collided during the afternoon rush hour with another train stopped on the tracks, killing one of the operators and eight passengers, and injuring eighty others. Malfunctioning sensors on the track had failed to detect the presence of the stopped train and communicate that to the moving train. Although the latter train was equipped with anti-collision sensors that should have triggered its brakes when it got within 1,200 feet of the other cars, that system had failed too, and for some reason the operator never applied the manual brakes. A decade earlier, communication relays on the same Metro system had sent incorrect instructions to trains on several occasions—one time telling a train to travel 45 miles per hour on a section of track with a 15 mile per hour speed limit.[48]

These incidents were all accidental, but in Poland in 2008 a fourteen-year-old boy in Łódź caused several trains to derail when he used the infrared port of a modified TV remote control to hijack the railway's signaling system and switch the tram tracks. Four trams derailed, and twelve people were injured.[49]

---

48 Lyndsey Layton, "Metro Crash: Experts Suspect System Failure, Operator Error in Red Line Accident," *Washington Post*, June 23, 2009.
49 Graeme Baker, "Schoolboy Hacks into City's Tram System," *Telegraph*, January 11, 2008.

ALTHOUGH THERE ARE many different ways to attack critical infrastructure, one of the most effective is to go after the power grid, since electricity is at the core of all critical infrastructure. Cut the power for a prolonged period, and the list of critical services and facilities affected is long—commuter trains and traffic lights; banks and stock exchanges; schools and military installations; refrigerators controlling the temperature of food and blood supplies; respirators, heart monitors, and other vital equipment in hospitals; runway lights and air traffic control systems at airports. Emergency generators would kick in at some critical facilities, but generators aren't a viable solution for a prolonged outage, and in the case of nuclear power plants, a switch to generator power triggers an automatic, gradual shutdown of the plant, per regulations.

One way to target electricity is to go after the smart meters electric utilities have been installing in US homes and businesses by the thousands, thanks in part to a $3 billion government smart-grid program, which has accelerated the push of smart meters without first ensuring that the technology is secure.

One of the main problems security researchers have found with the system is that smart meters have a remote-disconnect feature that allows utility companies to initiate or cut off power to a building without having to send a technician. But by using this feature an attacker could seize control of the meters to disconnect power to thousands of customers in a way that would not be easily recoverable. In 2009, a researcher named Mike Davis developed a worm that did just this.

Davis was hired by a utility in the Pacific Northwest to examine the security of smart meters the company planned to roll out to customers. As with the Siemens PLCs that Beresford examined, Davis found that the smart meters were promiscuous and would communicate with any other smart meters in their vicinity as long as they used the same communication protocol. They would even accept firmware updates from other meters. All an attacker needed to update the firmware on a meter was a network encryption key. But since all the meters the company planned to install had the same network key embedded in their firmware, an attacker only had to compromise one meter to extract the key and use it to deliver malicious updates to other meters. "Once we had control of one device, we had pretty much everything we needed," Davis said. "That was the case across a bunch of meters that we had looked at from different vendors."[50]

The meters communicated with one another via radio and were always in listening mode to detect other meters nearby. Some meters could communicate with one another from miles away. The ones Davis examined had a reach of about 400 feet, a little longer than the length of a football field—which was more than enough to propagate a malicious update between neighboring houses that would shut off the electricity and spread the worm to additional meters. Davis didn't even need to compromise an existing meter at a house to get the infection going; he could simply buy his own meter of the same brand—as long as it spoke the same protocol—and load it with malware and the necessary encryption key, then place it in the vicinity of a metered house. "Because of the radio, it's going to get picked up automatically [by other meters around it]," Davis says. Once the update was complete, the victim meter would restart with the new firmware in place and automatically begin spreading its update to other meters within range, setting off a chain reaction. Operators wouldn't know anything had changed with the meters until power started dropping out in neighborhoods.

Normally the vendor's meters got upgraded remotely through a utility company's central network, or via a technician in the field who used a special dongle connected to a laptop to communicate wirelessly with the meters. So when Davis and his team told the vendor they could write software that propagated automatically from one meter to another without using the central computer or a dongle, the vendor scoffed and said the meters didn't have the ability to initiate a firmware update to other meters. "They told us . . . that wasn't part of their feature set," Davis recalls. "We said we know, we added the feature [to our malicious firmware update]." The

---

50 From author interview, August 2012.

vendor still didn't believe a worm would have much effect, so Davis wrote a program to simulate an infection in a residential neighborhood of Seattle that in a day spread to about 20,000 smart meters.[51] "We had pretty much full compromise by the end of the twenty-four-hour cycle," he says. The infection spread one meter at a time, but a real-world attack would move much more quickly since an attacker could send out a plague of firmware updates from multiple patient zeros located strategically throughout a city.

The vendor scoffed at Davis's simulation, too, saying a worm would take two to four minutes to update each meter's firmware, and in that time, technicians would spot the outage before too many customers lost electricity and send out a remote firmware update to turn the power back on to them.

That's when Davis delivered his final blow and told the vendor that his malicious software didn't just turn the power off, it also deleted the firmware update feature on the meters so they couldn't be updated again to restore power. Technicians would have to replace the meter at each house or take them back to the lab and flash their chips with new firmware. "That actually seemed to get their attention more than anything," he says. "We were able to prove the point that this could get out of hand well before they would be able to figure out what's going on."

Since conducting the simulation, Davis has seen vendors improve their meters. Some vendors now use multiple network keys on their meters, assigning a different key for different neighborhoods to limit the damage an attacker could do with a single key. But the remote disconnect is still a problem with most smart meters, since an attacker who breaches a utility's central server could do what Davis's worm did, but in a much simpler way. "Were [the remote disconnect] not in there, none of this would really be all that much of an issue," Davis says. "In my opinion, if it's got the remote disconnect relay in it, whether it's enabled or not . . . it's a real big, ugly issue."

---

51 A YouTube video of the simulation can be seen online at: youtube.com/watch?v=kc_ijB7VPd8. Or see links to Davis's presentation slides and two other smart meter simulations at ioactive.com/ services_grid_research.html.

Going after smart meters is an effective way to cut electricity. But an even more effective and widespread attack would be to take out generators that feed the grid or the transmission systems that deliver electricity to customers. Defense Secretary Leon Panetta said at his confirmation hearing in June 2011 that the next Pearl Harbor the nation experiences could very well be a cyberattack that cripples the grid.

The North American power grid is large and complex and actually consists of three large regional grids—known as the Eastern, Western, and Texas Interconnections. The grids are composed of more than 450,000 miles of high-voltage transmission lines owned and operated by about three thousand utilities. Because power is traded on energy markets, it sometimes gets routed long distances between and within states to fulfill demand, such as by Cal-ISO, the entity that was hacked in 2001. Although the existence of many independent systems means that an attack on one utility or substation will have a limited effect, their interconnectedness means that a coordinated and strategic attack on a number of systems could cause cascading blackouts that are difficult to fix and plunge users into darkness for weeks.[52]

For example, circuit breakers that monitor distribution lines are designed to sense a dangerous surge on the lines and open to disconnect them from the grid to prevent them from being damaged. When one breaker trips, however, the power from that line gets redirected to other lines. If those lines reach capacity, their breakers will also trip, creating a blackout. But a well-crafted attack could trip the breakers on some lines while manipulating the settings on others to prevent them from tripping, causing the lines to overheat when they exceed capacity.

When distribution lines overheat, it causes them to sag or melt. Sagging lines were the cause of the 2003 Northeast blackout that cut power to

---

52 NERC has cyber security regulations that utilities are supposed to follow, but they apply only to bulk electric systems (defined as facilities and systems that operate at or above 100 kilovolts) and compliance doesn't guarantee a system won't get hacked. Security is an evolving condition, not a static one, and can change anytime new equipment is installed or configurations are changed.

50 million people in eight states and parts of Canada. Although a digital attack wasn't the cause of the outage, a software bug thwarted early detection and prevention of the cascade.

The problem began in Ohio when sagging power lines tangled with trees, but it was exacerbated by the fact that the emergency alert system at FirstEnergy's control center in Akron failed to register faults in the system, leaving operators ignorant about deteriorating conditions. About two and a half hours before the blackout occurred, industrial customers and even other power plants were calling FirstEnergy to report low voltages and tripping transmission lines—indications that major problems were brewing in the grid. But because FirstEnergy operators didn't see any sign of trouble on their control screens, they assumed the problem lay elsewhere. "[American Electric Power] must have lost some major stuff," one First-Energy operator told a caller, pointing the finger at another utility.[53] It wasn't until the lights in FirstEnergy's own control room went dark that operators realized the problem was with their own system. They eventually traced the glitch in the alert system to a software bug. "[The bug] had never evidenced itself until that day," a FirstEnergy spokesman later said. "This fault was so deeply embedded, it took them weeks of poring through millions of lines of code and data to find it."[54]

An even more destructive attack than targeting distribution lines, however, would be to target equipment at substations that feed electricity to those lines. The grid consists of more than 15,000 nodes, or substations, divided into three types—generator substations that create power, transmission substations that transfer it between power lines, and distribution substations that deliver it to consumers. The majority of these are transmission substations, which are responsible for "stepping up" the voltage to

53 US-Canada Power System Outage Task Force, "Final Report on the August 14th Blackout in the United States and Canada," April 2004, available at https://reports.energy.gov/BlackoutFinal-Web .pdf.
54 Kevin Poulsen, "Software Bug Contributed to Blackout," SecurityFocus.com, February 11, 2004, available at securityfocus.com/news/8016.

transmit it long distances and then "stepping down" the voltage before it gets distributed to end users. A recent study by the Federal Energy Regulatory Commission found that an attack that took out just nine critical substations—four in the Eastern grid, three in the Western grid, and two in the Texas grid—could cause a national power outage for weeks, possibly months, creating panic and leading to loss of life.[55]

The good news is that because grid systems are owned and operated by different utilities, they use different equipment and configurations, thwarting a one-size-fits-all attack and making a single widespread attack on energy systems difficult to pull off. But regional attacks and blackouts are not out of the reach of average hackers. And an attack that also destroyed industrial-sized generators at power-generation plants would make recovery more difficult. This was precisely the point of the Aurora Generator Test.

NAMED AFTER THE Roman goddess who was mother to the four winds, the test had its origins in the cascading Northeast blackout of 2003. That blackout lasted for only two days, but it got people thinking about the possibility of remote attacks against power-generation plants that might not be so recoverable. Mike Assante was in charge of pulling a team together to test the hypothesis.

While a naval intelligence officer in 2001, Assante had been assigned to work at the FBI's new National Infrastructure Protection Center in Washington, DC, to research the risks posed by cyberattacks against energy infrastructures. After a year, he left the Navy to take a job with American Electric Power (AEP) in Ohio, one of the largest electric utilities in the country. AEP wanted help developing an infrastructure protection program, and it was during this time that Assante began to think about attacks that might cause physical destruction to the grid.

---

55 Rebecca Smith, "U.S. Risks National Blackout from Small-Scale Attack," *Wall Street Journal*, March 12, 2004.

While at AEP, Assante was struck by a *Washington Post* story about the Idaho National Lab's SCADA test-bed program, in which workers there terrified the chairman of the Federal Energy Regulatory Commission with a simulation showing him how easily a hacker could destroy a utility's turbine by shutting down the mechanism responsible for lubricating the machine. Without oil greasing the moving metal parts, the turbine seized up and tore itself apart.[56] The chairman's reaction to the demo was visceral. "I wished I'd had a diaper on," he told the *Post* after the test.[57]

Assante visited the INL lab for himself and was impressed with the group of experts the lab had recruited for its program. In addition to control-system engineers, the lab had hired a group of code warriors fresh out of high school and college who knew how to hack them. They cut through the control-system networks with little resistance, exploiting weaknesses that were invisible to the engineers who had worked on them for years. The lab also had its own substations and mini-grid—a seven-mile section of redundant grid that researchers could isolate from the public grid—to run live tests. Assante was so intrigued by the possibilities for conducting real security research on the grid—not just simulated tests—that he quit his job at AEP in 2005 and took a position with the lab.

Once there, Assante and his colleagues began to consider scenarios for how equipment might be destroyed. Until then, most of the cyber concern around the security of the grid had been focused on someone getting into a power network to open breakers and create an outage. A power outage, however, could be resolved fairly quickly by resetting the breakers. But what about an attack that defeated or bypassed security and safety systems to physically destroy a generator that couldn't be easily fixed?

They decided to get at the generator by focusing the attack on protective relays—safety devices that monitor changes in the grid and are

---

56 The scenario was similar to a real-life incident that occurred at a Coors bottling plant in 2004 when an employee mistakenly changed the settings on a system responsible for greasing the bearings on a bottling line. Instead of greasing the bearings every twenty minutes he set it to grease them every eight hours, and eventually the bottling line seized up.

57 Justin Blum, "Hackers Target US Power Grid," *Washington Post*, March 11, 2005.

responsible for tripping breakers if conditions enter a danger zone that could harm transmission lines. Disabled protective relays played a role in a large outage in February 2008, when nearly 600,000 people in Florida lost power after a field engineer with Florida Power and Light turned off the protective relays at a substation while investigating a malfunctioning switch.[58] When a fault occurred on the line that he was examining, there was nothing to keep it from radiating out. The result was a cascading outage that spread to thirty-eight substations, including one that fed electricity to a nuclear plant, causing the plant to go into automatic shutdown.

But protective relays don't just trigger breakers on transmission lines, they also disconnect generators and other equipment from the grid if conditions grow dangerous. The power grid operates at 60 Hz—or sixty cycles a second—and devices connected to it have to be in sync or they can be damaged. Plug something into the grid when it's out of sync and it creates torque that can destroy the equipment. When a generator connects to the grid, the load from the grid pushes back, like the gravitational force that pushes against a car climbing a hill. But when a breaker opens up and disconnects the generator from the grid, the still-running generator speeds up in the absence of any load pushing against it. Within just 10 milliseconds, the generator will be out of sync with the grid. If the breaker then closes, bringing the generator back onto the grid while the two are out of sync, the effect is similar to a car hitting a brick wall. The generator expends too much energy that has nowhere to go, and once it hits the slower grid, the force of that energy slams back against it. It's a well-known phenomenon that has been the cause of accidents in the past.

So the question Assante's team posed for their test was simple: If protective relays were supposed to prevent equipment from being damaged, what if they could be subverted to aid the equipment's destruction? Designing such an attack turned out to be only slightly more complicated

---

58 Florida Power and Light, "FPL Announces Preliminary Findings of Outage Investigation," February 29, 2008, available at fpl.com/news/2008/022908.shtml.

than the question. The hack involved writing malicious code to change the settings of the digital relays so that the breaker for a generator opened and closed in rapid succession, causing the equipment to disconnect from the grid quickly and repeatedly and then reconnect when it was out of sync. Without the protection of the relays, there was nothing to prevent the generator from destroying itself. "This is what made it so damn insidious," says Joe Weiss. "The thing that was supposed to stop an attack like this from happening was the thing they used to conduct the attack." By abruptly opening and closing the protective circuit, the relay went from "providing maximum protection to inflicting maximum damage," the DHS later wrote in a report about the test.[59]

For their victim, they chose a Wärtsilä generator that had been retired from the oil fields in Alaska and was purchased through a broker for one-third of its $1 million price tag brand-new.[60]

The attack lasted three minutes but could have achieved its aim in just fifteen seconds. The researchers had built in pauses to the attack to give engineers time to assess the damage and check safety systems at each stage. Each time the circuit breaker closed on the out-of-sync generator, connecting it back to the grid, the machine jumped and vibrated from the force of its own energy hitting back, until eventually the coupling between the diesel engine and the generator broke.[61]

Workers in the operations center who monitored the grid for anomalies

---

59 From an undated DHS slide presentation obtained through a FOIA request made by the author. The slide presentation is titled "Control Systems Vulnerability—Aurora."

60 The figure comes from a cost assessment developed for the Aurora test and released by DHS in the author's FOIA request.

61 As an example of what can happen when the coupling on a turbine is damaged, in 2011, a steam turbine generator at a power plant in Iran exploded in Iranshahr and was attributed to a coupling failure. The explosion was so forceful that investigators couldn't even *find* the power turbine after the accident. Couplings need to be inspected regularly for signs of wear and need to be lubricated to maintain operations and prevent accidents. The plant in Iranshahr had three oil burners in the room where the generator was installed, which likely exacerbated the explosion when it occurred. The explosion could indeed have been the result of badly maintained coupling or faulty installation, but there were some at the time who thought it might have been the result of sabotage on par with the Aurora attack.

and weren't told of the attack before it occurred never noticed anything amiss on their monitors. The safety system that was designed to ride out little spikes and valleys that normally occurred on the grid also never registered the destructive interruption. "We could do the attack, essentially open and close a breaker so quickly that the safety systems didn't see it," said Perry Pederson, who headed DHS's control-system security program at the time and oversaw the test.[62]

Replacing a twenty-seven-ton generator that was destroyed in this way wouldn't be trivial, but it was doable. But there were 800-megawatt generators at large power plants and other facilities that would take months or a year to replace, since generators that size are often built to order overseas. Not all generators powering the grid would be susceptible to this attack in the same way—it would depend on how the power on that part of the grid is balanced. But the same thing could happen with critical equipment, powering things other than the grid, that isn't easily replaced. A substation powering a bank of pumps responsible for delivering drinking water to a major metropolitan area, for example, would cause major disruptions if taken out of commission. "I don't know what would happen to a big 50,000 horsepower pump, but I could imagine it would be just as bad as a generator," Pederson said.[63]

Since the Aurora test took place in 2007, there have been other demonstrations of destructive cyberattacks. In a 2009 report on *60 Minutes*, researchers at Sandia National Lab showed how they could cause components at an oil refinery to overheat by simply changing the settings of a heating element and disabling the recirculation pumps that helped regulate the temperature.[64]

STUXNET AND THE Maroochy Shire incident aside, there have been no really destructive digital attacks recorded in the world to date. Experts

---

62 Author interview, August 2012.
63 Ibid.
64 *60 Minutes*, "Cyber War: Sabotaging the System," original air date November 6, 2009, CBS.

have offered a number of possible reasons for why this is the case—such attacks are more difficult to pull off than the evidence presented here seems to indicate, and those who possess the skills and resources to conduct them have simply lacked the motivation to take action thus far, while others who have the will to launch such an attack don't yet have the way.

One thing, however, seems certain: given the varied and extensive possibilities for conducting such attacks, and the proof of concept provided by Stuxnet, it is only a matter of time until the lure of the digital assault becomes too irresistible for someone to pass up.

CHAPTER 10

PRECISION WEAPON

R alph Langner sat in his Hamburg office and watched as his two engineers fed a stream of artful lies to the Stuxnet code they had installed on their test machine. Langner, an expert in the arcane field of industrial-control-system security, had been working with his colleagues for days to identify and re-create the precise conditions under which the stubborn code would release its payload to their PLC, but it was proving to be more difficult than they'd expected.

Days earlier, Langner's team had set up a computer with the Siemens Step 7 software installed and connected it to a Siemens PLC they happened to have on hand. They also installed a network analyzer to watch data as it passed between the Step 7 machine and the PLC. Unlike the Symantec researchers, Langner and his team worked with PLCs all the time and knew exactly what kind of traffic should pass between the Step 7 machine and the PLC; as a result, they assumed it would be easy to spot any anomalies in the communication. But when they initially infected their Step 7 system with Stuxnet, nothing happened. Stuxnet, they discovered, as others had before, was on the hunt for two *specific* models of Siemens PLC—the S7-315 and S7-417—and they didn't have either of these models on hand.

So they installed a Windows debugger on their test machine to observe the steps Stuxnet took before releasing its payload and devised a way to trick the code into thinking it had found its target. Stuxnet ran through a long checklist pertaining to the target's configuration, each seemingly more specific than the last. Langner and his colleagues didn't know what exactly was on the checklist, but they didn't need to know. As Stuxnet queried their system for each item on the list, they fed it a series of manufactured responses, until they landed on the answers Stuxnet wanted to hear. It was a crude, brute-force method of attack that took several days of trial and error. But when they finally got the right combination of answers and ran the code through its paces one last time, they saw exactly what the Symantec researchers had described: Stuxnet injected a series of rogue code blocks into their PLC. "That's it," Langner recalls thinking. "We got the little motherfucker."[1]

They only noticed the rogue code going into the PLC because the blocks of code were slightly larger than they should have been. Before infecting their Step 7 system with the malware, they had transferred blocks of code to the PLC and captured them with the analysis tool to record their basic size and characteristics. After infecting the machine with Stuxnet, they transferred the same blocks of code again and saw that they had suddenly grown.

They couldn't yet see what the Stuxnet code was doing to the PLC, but the injection itself was big news. It was way beyond anything they'd ever warned customers about and way beyond anything they expected to see in the first known attack against a PLC.

WHEN SYMANTEC HAD revealed on August 17 that Stuxnet was bent on sabotaging PLCs, it might have seemed to Chien and Falliere that no one was listening. But six thousand miles away, Langner was sitting in his small office in a leafy suburb of Germany, reading Symantec's words with

---

1 All quotes from Langner come from interviews conducted with him in 2010, 2011, and 2012.

great interest. Langner had been warning industrial clients for years that one day someone would devise a digital attack to sabotage their control systems and now, it appeared, the day had finally arrived.

Langner was the owner of a three-man boutique firm that specialized in the security of industrial control systems. It was the only thing his company did. He had no interest in general computer security and couldn't care less about announcements warning of the latest viruses and worms infecting PCs. Even zero-day exploits held no allure for him. So when Stuxnet first made headlines in the technology press and became the subject of extensive chatter on security forums, he paid it little notice. But when Symantec wrote that Stuxnet was sabotaging Siemens PLCs, Langner was immediately intrigued.

Symantec didn't reveal what Stuxnet was doing to the PLCs, only that it was injecting code into the so-called ladder logic of the PLC—whether that meant bringing the PLC to its knees, or worse, the antivirus firm didn't say.[2] But it struck Langner that thousands of Siemens customers, including many of his own clients, were now facing a potential killer virus and were waiting anxiously for Siemens or Symantec to tell them what exactly Stuxnet was doing to their PLCs. But, oddly, after making their startling announcement, the Symantec researchers had gone quiet.

Langner suspected the researchers had hit a wall, due to their lack of expertise with PLCs and industrial control systems. But curiously, Siemens had also gone silent. This was strange, Langner thought. It was, after all, Siemens controllers that were being attacked; the company had an obligation to analyze the malevolent code and tell customers what it might be doing to their systems. But after a couple of brief announcements the German company had made in July, it had gone mum.[3]

---

2 "Ladder logic" is a generic term to describe the structure of commands used to code a control system. The name comes from the ladderlike structure of the programming, which lays out each process in a step-by-step, sequential fashion.

3 In its initial announcement, Siemens said it had assembled a team of experts to evaluate Stuxnet and would begin alerting customers to their potential risk of infection from it. The company later said that less than two dozen of its customers were infected with Stuxnet. The company's second announcement had to do with the hard-coded database password in the Siemens software that Stuxnet used to spread. Siemens warned customers against changing the password at the risk of

Langner was incensed. Although Stuxnet appeared to be targeting only Siemens Step 7 machines, no one really knew what the malicious code was capable of doing or if it might be laced with bugs that could damage other PLCs. And there was one more important concern: the vulnerability that let Stuxnet inject its malicious code into the ladder logic of a Siemens PLC also existed in other controllers.[4] Samples of Stuxnet were already available for download on the internet; any random hacker, criminal extortionist, or terrorist group could study the code and use it as a blueprint to devise a more wide-scale and destructive attack against other models of PLCs.

This made the silence of two other parties even more perplexing—the CERT-Bund, Germany's national computer emergency response team; and ICS-CERT in the United States. Both organizations were tasked with helping to secure critical infrastructure systems in their respective countries, but neither party had said much about Stuxnet. There was no talk in an ICS-CERT alert about injecting ladder logic into the Siemens PLCs, or even any mention of sabotaging them. There was also nothing at all about the dangers that Stuxnet presented for future attacks.[5] The silence of German authorities was even stranger, since Siemens controllers were installed in almost every German plant or factory Langner could name.

Langner talked it over with his two longtime engineers, Ralf Rosen and Andreas Timm. None of them had any experience reverse-engineering viruses or worms, but if no one else was going to tell them what Stuxnet was doing to the Siemens PLCs, then they would have to take it apart themselves. It would mean days of doing pro bono work squeezed in

---

disrupting critical functions in their systems. "We will be publishing customer guidance shortly, but it won't include advice to change default settings as that could impact plant operations," a spokesman said a week after Stuxnet was exposed. See Robert McMillan, "After Worm, Siemens Says Don't Change Passwords," PCWorld.com, July 19, 2010.

4 The vulnerability is partly due to the fact that the Siemens system lacked authentication, which allowed rogue ladder logic to be sent to the PLC. If the system had required the code to be digitally signed, the PLC would not have accepted it.

5 See ICS-CERT Advisory ICSA-10-201-01C, "USB Malware Targeting Siemens Control Software," August 2, 2010, with subsequent updates available at ics-cert.us-cert/gov/advisories/ICSA-10-201-01C; and ICS-CERT Advisory ICSA-10-238-01B, "Stuxnet Malware Mitigation," September 15, 2010, available at ics-cert.us-cert/gov/advisories/ICSA-10-238-01B.

between other assignments from paying customers, but they concluded they didn't have a choice.

Langner and his colleagues made an odd but effective team. In a profession sometimes characterized by frumpy, pale, and ponytailed engineers, Langner, a vigorous fifty-two-year-old with short dark hair minus any gray, sported crisp business suits and finely crafted leather shoes. He had piercing blue eyes in a vacation-tanned face and the trim, toned frame of a seasoned mountaineer—the by-product of ski excursions in the Alps and rugged hikes in the hills. If Langner's dapper appearance didn't set him apart from the pack, his brusque and bold manner did. He had a reputation for being an outspoken maverick, and often made provocative statements that riled his colleagues in the control-system community. For years he had railed about security problems with the systems, but his blunt, confrontational manner often put off the very people who most needed to listen. Rosen and Timm, by contrast, were both graybeard engineers in their forties who had a more relaxed approach to dress and fitness and took a quieter, more backseat role to Langner's conspicuous one.

Although the three of them seemed in many ways mismatched, there was probably no better team suited to the task of examining Stuxnet. Timm had worked for Langner as a control-system expert for at least a decade, and Rosen for three years longer than that. During that time, they'd amassed extensive knowledge about industrial control systems in general, and Siemens controllers in particular. Siemens, in fact, was a longtime customer. The company bought software products from Langner's firm, and he and his engineers sometimes trained Siemens employees on their own systems. There were probably only a handful of Siemens employees who knew the Siemens systems better than they did.

Langner's path to ICS security had been a circuitous one, however. He was a certified psychologist by training, something seemingly far removed from the world of control systems. But it was his psychology background that actually led to his present career. In the 1970s, while studying psychology and artificial intelligence at the Free University of Berlin, he began writing software to do statistical analysis of data collected from experiments. He also wrote a program that modeled human decision-making patterns to arrive at psychiatric diagnoses.

But it was a driver program he wrote to connect his home computer to the university's mainframe that ended up launching his ICS career. In college, Langner owned an early-generation PC that lacked the computational power needed to conduct statistical analysis. Whenever he wanted to crunch data collected from one of his experiments, he had to travel to the campus and plug his computer into the college mainframes. Langner hated the commute to campus, so he studied the protocols needed to communicate with the servers remotely and wrote a driver program that let him dial in via modem from home.

It wasn't much of a stretch when, after graduating college, he launched a software-consulting firm, using his driver program as the basis for the business. It was considered a breakthrough product at the time, and it wasn't long before control-system engineers began seeking it out to communicate with their sensors and controllers in the field. The methods they had been using at the time often dropped data during transmission, and Langner's driver proved to be very reliable.

In 1997, Rosen joined the firm to design custom systems for clients who wanted to connect desktop computers to their Siemens PLCs. As he and Langner studied the Siemens protocols and PLCs to make the connections work, they were surprised to find a host of security problems with the systems—the same flaws other researchers would find more than a decade later. They were also surprised to learn that owners and operators of industrial control systems were completely oblivious to these gaps in security and had therefore done nothing to protect their systems from attack. Instead of layered or segmented networks where critical systems were gated off from everyday business computers, they had flat network architectures that provided access to PLCs from any machine on the network. They also had systems that were directly connected to the internet, with no firewalls or passwords in place to keep intruders out, or they used default and hard-coded passwords that never got changed.

Langner and his team launched a consulting business to help clients rebuild their networks more securely. But the concept of control-system security turned out to be a hard sell. For years, the ICS community had been largely immune to the deluge of malware and hacker attacks that had pummeled the general IT community, and as a result, most in the community didn't think they were at risk. Langner warned customers that eventually they would pay for their complacency and often demonstrated for them how an attacker with little skill could knock their operations offline. But few did anything to address the problem. "Nobody wanted to listen," Langner says, "except for some very few companies who invested in control-system security."

Now, a decade later, Stuxnet was the bellwether Langner had warned about. But even he was surprised by the strength and furor of the attack when it finally arrived. He had imagined a number of scenarios over the years for how hackers would attack PLCs once the security vulnerabilities in them became publicly known; but none of them involved rogue ladder logic injected into the PLC. Computer attacks typically evolved over time and developed incrementally. Hackers first pulled off simple attacks that required the least amount of effort and skill to succeed, and security firms and software makers responded with fixes to stop them. The attackers then found alternative paths into systems, until the defenders defeated these as well. Each round of attack got progressively more sophisticated, as defenses to defeat them did too. Similarly, in the case of control systems, Langner had expected hackers would start out with simple denial-of-service attacks—sending a stop command to a PLC to halt whatever process it controlled—then escalate to logic bombs and other simple techniques to alter settings. But Stuxnet bypassed the rudimentary stages of development and jumped straight into one of the most sophisticated attacks someone could devise against a PLC.

Of everything that Langner saw in the code, it was the man-in-the-middle attack against the safety system and operator monitoring stations that really blew his mind. The way Stuxnet smoothly disabled the former and deviously recorded the normal operations of the PLC to play them back to operators during the attack was astounding to him—the digital equivalent of a six-ton circus elephant performing a one-legged handstand. It was a level of grace and finesse he'd never seen or even considered possible.

It was also the most aggressive scenario he could imagine, because once an attacker disabled the logic responsible for feeding important data to a safety system, it was only a matter of time before someone got seriously injured or killed. Disable the safety system and sensors at a chemical plant or gas refinery, and you could release poisonous gas or flammable liquids without anyone knowing until it was too late. Stuxnet's authors might not have intended to injure or kill anyone with their attack, but copycat hackers who learned from Stuxnet's techniques might not be so careful.

Langner estimated there were maybe a few dozen people in the world who had the level of Siemens control-system knowledge needed to design this kind of attack, and three of them were sitting in his office. But even they could not have pulled it off with the sophistication the attackers did.

THREE WEEKS INTO their examination of Stuxnet, Langner walked into the conference room where he and his colleagues had been gathering each morning to discuss their progress on the code. Rosen and Timm looked him over, amused. Ordinarily he was crisply dressed and alert. But today he looked scruffy and haggard after a sleepless night bent over a computer doing research online. He'd been following one trail after another, chasing lead after lead down a rabbit hole trying to figure out what Stuxnet was attacking until finally he grasped hold of a tail and pulled. When he retrieved his hand he was surprised at what he'd found. "I know what this is about," he blurted to his colleagues. "This is about taking down Iran's nuclear program. This is about taking out Bushehr."

Bushehr, as noted previously, was the nuclear power plant in southwest Iran that had been under construction on and off for several decades. It had gone through many delays and cancellations over the years and had finally been scheduled to begin operation that month. But shortly before it was about to launch, officials announced another delay. Since the delay coincided with the discovery of Stuxnet, it seemed logical to Langner that a cyberattack might be at play.[6]

Rosen and Timm stared at him in disbelief. No one was dumb enough to take out a nuclear power plant, Rosen thought. Wouldn't they risk releasing radioactive material? And why use an unreliable worm to do the job when they could more reliably damage it with a bomb? But as Langner connected the dots, his crazy theory actually began to make sense to them.

For nearly a month now, since they had first observed the malicious code Stuxnet injected into their PLC, Langner and his team had been searching Stuxnet's blocks of code for clues about the facilities they might be attacking. The configuration of the systems Stuxnet targeted could reveal as much if not more about the code's intentions than the code itself. If they could learn what kinds of devices the PLCs controlled, and whether they were configured in any distinct ways, they could narrow the range of possible targets.

They labored for several weeks to decipher the blocks, working out of the small office suite they occupied on the upper floor of a two-story building. The quiet, residential street where they worked was dense with trees and was a sharp contrast to Symantec's modern glass complex. Instead of multiple stories lined with cubicles, they had one open room where Timm and Rosen worked, a meeting room for clients, and office space for Langner and his assistant.

Each morning they gathered to review the progress they had made, then worked on the code the rest of the day, hashing out theories during lunch in the conference room and over dinner at nearby restaurants. In between, they responded to customer-support calls. But when clients called to offer them new work, Langner turned them all down, so intent were they on cracking Stuxnet. It's not as though they could afford to reject the paid work. They didn't have anything near the corporate resources Symantec had, and no outside client was bankrolling their research. Instead,

---

6 A couple of weeks later, Iranian officials denied that Stuxnet was the cause and instead attributed the delay to a leak in a pool near the reactor.

Langner had to pay for their time and labor out of the company's profits. But none of them were complaining. They all knew that Stuxnet was the job of a lifetime. "We understood this is the biggest story in malware ever," Langner recalls. "It was absolutely fantastic work. It was the best work that I have ever done and I'm sure I can't do any better."

After weeks of painstaking analysis, they reached a startling conclusion. Stuxnet wasn't just attacking two specific models of Siemens PLCs, it was attacking a specific facility where the PLCs were used. Stuxnet was a military-grade precision weapon aimed at a single target. It wasn't searching for just any S7-315 and S7-417 PLC it could find: the PLCs had to be configured in a very precise way. Embedded in the attack code was a detailed dossier describing the precise technical configuration of the PLCs it sought. Every plant that used industrial control systems had custom configurations to varying degrees; even companies within the same industry used configurations that were specific to their needs. But the configuration Stuxnet was looking for was so precise that it was likely to be found in only a single facility in Iran or, if more than one, then facilities configured exactly the same, to control an identical process. Any system that didn't have this exact configuration would remain unharmed; Stuxnet would simply shut itself down and move on to the next system in search of its target.

The idea that someone had put so much money and effort into a weapon attacking a single target left Langner dumbfounded. It could mean only one thing—the target had to be extraordinarily important. Now they just had to figure out what it was.

Most of the steps involved in analyzing code are systematic and highly technical—isolate the components, decrypt the code, reverse-engineer it. But mapping digital code to a real-world environment is more art than science. The three of them tossed around a number of hypotheses about what they thought the target might be, then sifted through the code for evidence to support them. Meanwhile, Langner reached out to colleagues in various industries to quiz them about the configuration of their PLCs to see if he could find a match. But after a number of days, they still had little success isolating Stuxnet's target. Finally Langner decided to step back from the technical details and approach the problem from a different angle, searching news articles and other sources for clues. After several late nights spent surfing the web he finally arrived at his theory of Bushehr.

Langner's suspicions about the plant were first roused when he recalled a photo he had seen online the previous year, purportedly taken during a press tour at Bushehr. The image showed a computer screen with a pop-up message indicating that a license for the Siemens WinCC software on the machine had expired. It seemed proof to Langner that Siemens software was being used at the plant.[7] Contacts in the control-system community confirmed for Langner that Siemens S7-417 PLCs were installed at Bushehr. Further research revealed that the Russian firm responsible for installing equipment at the plant also used Siemens PLCs in other facilities it equipped—including a plant in Bulgaria supposedly modeled after Bushehr. The Bulgarian plant had a steam turbine operated by Siemens controllers, Langner learned, which reminded him of the Aurora Generator Test conducted by the Idaho National Lab three years earlier. That test had provided proof that malicious code could destroy a turbine.

As the three of them sat in the conference room with Langner making his case, Rosen and Timm found themselves nodding reluctantly in agreement with his theory. They knew there were very few targets in the world that justified the amount of work that had gone into Stuxnet. But if Langner was right and Bushehr was the target, and physical sabotage was its goal, then Stuxnet was essentially an act of war.

And if Stuxnet was an act of war, then what kind of response would its discovery elicit from Iran once news of this got out? Whoever had launched Stuxnet might have done so to avert an all-out war with Iran— but its exposure now could very well lead to one.

---

7 The screenshot, taken by a UPI photographer, includes a caption identifying it as a computer screen at Bushehr and says the image was snapped in February 2009. Some critics have disputed the accuracy of the caption, saying the image appears to show a water-treatment facility and not Bushehr, but water-treatment facilities are generally part of nuclear plant operations, which would explain how both could be true. The image can be seen at upi.com/News_Photos/Features?The -Nuclear-Issue-in-Iran/1581/2/.

After speaking with Rosen and Timm, Langner was certain he was on the right track, but just to be sure that Iran's nuclear program was indeed the target, he called up a client who had extensive knowledge of nuclear plants. The client worked for Enrichment Technology Company, a top European maker of uranium enrichment equipment, formerly known as Urenco—the company whose early generation centrifuge designs Pakistan's A. Q. Khan had stolen and sold to Iran. If it wasn't a turbine that Stuxnet was targeting, Langner thought, perhaps it was the centrifuges being used to enrich uranium for Bushehr. (Langner believed, mistakenly, that centrifuges for enriching uranium were housed at Bushehr.)

"I have one question for you," Langner said to his friend over the phone. "Is it possible to destroy a centrifuge just by manipulating the controller code?"

There was a pause on the other end before his friend replied.

"I can't tell you that, Ralph. It's classified information," he said. But then he added, "You know, centrifuges for uranium enrichment are not just used by us in Germany and the Netherlands. They're also used in other countries."

"Yes, I know," Langner replied. "For example, in Iran. That's exactly why I've called you. Because we're analyzing Stuxnet."

"I'm sorry," the man responded firmly. "I can't tell you anything about centrifuges; it's all classified."

That was enough for Langner. He told Rosen and Timm that they had to go public with the news immediately. If Bushehr was the target, then someone should be able to confirm it once they did. Stuxnet and its target were like a key and lock. There was just one lock in the world that the key would open, and once they published details about the key's design, anyone with a lock should be able to see if their facility matched.

On September 13, 2010, nearly a month after Symantec's revelation that Stuxnet was sabotaging PLCs, Langner published a brief blog post under the title "Hack of the Century." In it, he asserted that Stuxnet was a directed attack "against a specific control-system installation," and left it at that. But three days later he followed up with additional information. "With the forensics we now have it is evident and provable that Stuxnet is a directed sabotage attack involving heavy insider knowledge," he wrote. "Here is what everybody needs to know right now."[8]

What followed was a technical roadmap detailing the precise steps Stuxnet took to intercept and inject its commands into the Siemens PLC to sabotage it. "This is not some hacker sitting in the basement of his parents' house," Langner wrote. These were sophisticated nation-state actors with very specific knowledge of the system they were attacking. He described in broad terms how the malware injected its rogue code into the PLC to hijack some unknown critical process, then laid out his thoughts about Bushehr, carefully labeling them as speculation. There were still a lot of unknowns, but the forensic evidence in the code, he asserted, would ultimately point them not only to the exact system Stuxnet attacked but also possibly to the attackers themselves.

With these few words, the jig was finally up for Stuxnet's creators. A cyberweapon that had taken years and perhaps millions of dollars to plan and develop had been completely exposed and undone in a matter of weeks by an obscure antivirus firm in Belarus, a handful of researchers in California who knew nothing about centrifuges and PLCs, and a brash-talking German and his band of engineers.

But now that Stuxnet's secret was out, Langner began to have the same concerns that Chien had had about how the attackers might respond. Stuxnet was near useless to the attackers once its true purpose was exposed. They must have anticipated that their code would eventually be caught and that once it was they would have a narrow window of opportunity to complete their mission. Would they now, in a last-ditch effort to achieve their aim, take one final and drastic step? Langner believed they would. "We can expect that something will blow up soon," he wrote in his

---

8 "Stuxnet logbook, Sept 16, 2010, 1200 hours MESZ," available at langner.com/en/2010/09/16/stuxnet-logbook-sep-16-2010-1200-hours-mesz.

post. "Something big." He signed off with a singular warning: "Welcome to cyberwar."

Accompanying the post was a picture of the three "Stuxnet busters" snapped in front of a whiteboard in their office, Langner dressed in a crisp, white shirt and unbuttoned suit vest, and Rosen and Timm behind him, the latter, in a cheeky nod to the covert nature of Stuxnet, sporting a pair of black shades.

Once he'd written his post Langner sent a press release to several top media outlets and waited for an explosion of headlines to hit. But to his dismay, nothing happened. Like Symantec's disclosure before, the revelation was met with deafening silence. "Everyone must think I'm nuts," he remembers thinking.

At least one person didn't think so, however. Frank Rieger, chief technology officer for a German security firm called GSMK, read Langner's speculation about Bushehr and agreed that Stuxnet was likely built for sabotaging Iran's nuclear program. But he suspected Natanz, several hundred miles north of Bushehr, was the more likely target.[9] The Natanz plant, unlike Bushehr, was already operational and had been since 2007. Also unlike Bushehr, it was actually filled with thousands of rapidly spinning centrifuges, making it a rich target for anyone wanting to cripple Iran's nuclear program with a digital attack. Rieger detailed his thoughts in a blog post and in an article for a German newspaper.[10] In both, he referenced an earlier Reuters piece, published right around the time Stuxnet was unleashed in 2009, describing a "decade-old cyberwarfare project" launched by Israel against Iran's nuclear program. The article quoted a US

9 The article appeared in the German newspaper *Frankfurter Allgemeine Zeitung* on September 22, 2010. The article is in German, but he describes its content in English in the blog post published on his website, available at frank.geekheim.de/?p=1189.

10 At the time he speculated about Bushehr, Langner wasn't aware that the nuclear reactor plant didn't have centrifuges. Once that became clear, he continued to think that Bushehr was the target, but thought the equipment Stuxnet was attacking was a turbine or generator at the plant. It was only later when more information came out about the exact devices Stuxnet was targeting that he concluded that Natanz was in fact a match for Stuxnet, not Bushehr.

source speculating that "malicious software" could be used to comman-
deer or crash controls at an enrichment plant.[11]

But there was another reason to suspect that Natanz was Stuxnet's target. On July 16, 2009, three weeks after the 2009 version of Stuxnet was
released, WikiLeaks founder Julian Assange posted a cryptic note to his
website about a possible accident at Natanz. An anonymous source claiming to be associated with Iran's nuclear program had told Assange that a
"serious" nuclear accident had recently occurred at the plant.[12] WikiLeaks
usually published only documents on its site, not tips from anonymous
sources, but Assange broke protocol, he said, because he had reason to believe the source was credible. He linked to a BBC story published that day,
which announced the resignation of Gholam Reza Aghazadeh, the head
of Iran's Atomic Energy Organization, who had relinquished his position
twenty days earlier for unknown reasons.[13] The time frame seemed to
align with when the 2009 version of Stuxnet was released.

Whether or not Aghazadeh's resignation was related to an accident
at Natanz, Rieger's "Natanz theory" got attention and at last catapulted
Stuxnet into the limelight. The mainstream US media, which had largely
ignored Stuxnet until this point, picked up on his speculations and began
reporting on the story themselves. For nearly a decade, Natanz had been
the focus of mounting political tension over repeated efforts to halt the

---

11 Dan Williams, "Wary of Naked Force, Israelis Eye Cyberwar on Iran," July 7, 2009, available at
reuters.com/article/2009/07/07/us-israel-iran-cyberwar-analysis-idUSTRES663EC20090707.
12 The WikiLeaks post can be seen at mirror.wikileaks.info/wiki/Serious_nuclear_accident_may_
lay_behind_Iranian_nuke_chief%27s_mystery_resignation/.
13 The story was published at: news.bbc.co.uk/2/hi/8153775.dtm. Although it's possible
Aghazadeh's resignation was related to something that occurred at Natanz in late June 2009, it was
just as likely related to politics. In addition to being head of Iran's Atomic Energy Organization,
Aghazadeh was Iran's vice president. He resigned both positions simultaneously, two weeks after
Iran's hotly contested presidential elections on June 12, 2009. Aghazadeh had aligned himself with
President Ahmadinejad's political challenger, Mir-Hossein Mousavi, and there was speculation that
vehement protests over the legitimacy of the election results made it impossible for Aghazadeh to
retain his government positions once Ahmadinejad's victory was sanctioned. There's also a problem
of timing, which doesn't quite align with the June 2009 version of Stuxnet. According to the BBC
report, Aghazadeh resigned sometime around June 26. But the June 2009 version of Stuxnet was
unleashed June 22, and once it found itself on the right PLC, it took thirteen days for the sabotage
to begin. So unless an earlier version of Stuxnet or something else caused an accident at Natanz, the
timing didn't match Aghazadeh's resignation.

enrichment program there. Now it seemed a sophisticated digital weapon, the likes of which had never been seen before, had been part of those plans. Suddenly the story of Stuxnet was sexy and full of intrigue. Where previously it was just a dry technical tale of interest only to the technology press, now it had the aura of mystery and underworld spy games, all played out against the backdrop of a high-stakes nuclear showdown.

Shortly after Langner published his first post about Stuxnet, he contacted Joe Weiss in the United States to discuss what he and his team had found. Langner and Weiss shared the same confrontational style that didn't always endear them to peers in the control-system community. They'd both been on the same side of the battle for years, trying to convince ICS owners that their systems were vulnerable to attack. People in the community tended to sigh at the mention of either man's name, but no one doubted their commitment. Langner was scheduled to speak at Weiss's upcoming ICS conference in Maryland on another topic and asked if he could talk about Stuxnet instead. "I don't know whether to tell you yes or hell yes," Weiss replied.

Langner was on a flight to the conference the next week. Advance buzz about his talk guaranteed that the conference room would be full. Langner had teased on his blog that he would reveal full details of his team's research at the gathering, so the audience was primed and eager for what he had to say, especially after two presentations about Stuxnet given by Siemens and someone from DHS, respectively, turned out to be devoid of any substance.

Weiss had allotted forty-five minutes for Langner's talk, but it took up an hour and a half instead. No one complained, though. More than 100 attendees from the water, chemical, and electric industries hung on Langner's words. "All of us were sitting with our mouths open while he was talking," Weiss recalls.[14] Langner was among that rare breed of tech guys—a skilled and charismatic orator who was adept at delivering dry technical details with humor and flair. But what he said that day was more

14 Author interview, September 2010.

than entertaining, it shocked everyone in the room. Slowly, it dawned on the owners of industrial control systems that if another more widely targeted attack were unleashed on PLCs tomorrow, the control-system community would have no way to stop or even detect it. There were ways to tell if a Windows desktop PC or laptop was compromised, but with the stealth techniques that Stuxnet used, there would be no way to tell if a PLC was infected. There was no such thing as antivirus software for PLCs and no easy way to know if a controller had rogue code installed if it used the same kind of subterfuge that Stuxnet had used. The only way to detect an attack was at the Windows stage before it reached the PLC. But Stuxnet had shown the folly of even that defense, since no antivirus scanner had caught it before it reached the PLCs. Operators would never be able to detect a warhead until it was too late.

Langner suspected it would take just six months for the first copycat attacks to appear. They wouldn't be exact replicas of Stuxnet, or as sophisticated in design, he told attendees, but then they wouldn't need to be. It wasn't just high-value targets like Natanz that were at risk of attack; Stuxnet had put every vulnerable facility potentially in the crosshairs. And while Stuxnet's authors had skillfully designed their attack to avoid collateral damage on machines that weren't its target, subsequent attacks might not be as carefully crafted or controlled. A criminal group bent on extorting a power plant by seizing control of its PLCs wouldn't care if their malicious code damaged the plant or spread to other control systems as well.

Following the conference, Langner spent the weekend in Washington, DC, to meet with Melissa Hathaway, the former national cybersecurity coordinator for the White House, to brief her on what his team had found. Hathaway immediately understood the potential for blowback against US critical infrastructure as well as the problem of digital weapons proliferation the world would now face—a problem, she later told the *New York Times*, no country was prepared to deal with. "We have about 90 days to fix this," she told the paper, "before some [copycat] hacker begins using it."[15]

---

15 John Markoff, "A Silent Attack, but Not a Subtle One," *New York Times*, September 26, 2010.

That weekend while Langner was still in DC, Iranian officials revealed for the first time that computers at Bushehr had indeed been hit by Stuxnet. They made no mention of Natanz, however, and the details about the attack on Bushehr made it doubtful that Stuxnet's payload had even deployed there. Mahmoud Jafari, a project manager for the plant, told reporters that only the personal computers of some of the plant's workers got hit by the attack, not the plant's production systems. "All computer programs in the plant are working normally and have not crashed due to Stuxnet," he said.[16] Reza Taghipour, an official with the Ministry of Communications and Information Technology, also insisted that damage from the worm was minor and that the malware had been "more or less" contained.[17] The reports of limited damage weren't surprising, given Stuxnet's selectiveness in unleashing its destructive payload. It had likely spread to Bushehr's Windows machines, then simply shut itself down after failing to find the PLCs it was seeking.[18]

Amidst the comments from Iran, however, there was one odd detail that stood out. Mahmoud Jafari said in one of his interviews that *five* versions of Stuxnet had been found in Iran.[19] Symantec and other antivirus researchers had uncovered only three.

---

16 Laurent Maillard, "Iran Denies Nuclear Plant Computers Hit by Worm," Agence France-Presse, September 26, 2010, available at iranfocus.com/en/index.php?option=com_content&view=article&id=21820.

17 David E. Sanger, "Iran Fights Malware Attacking Computers," *New York Times*, September 25, 2010.

18 Six months later, a report from the Iranian Passive Defense Organization, a military organization chaired by Revolutionary Guard General Gholam-Reza Jalali, which is responsible for defending Iran's nuclear facilities, contradicted these statements. It stated that Stuxnet had so thoroughly infected computers at Bushehr that work at the plant had to be halted indefinitely. The report claimed that if Bushehr went online, the worm would "bring the generators and electrical power grid of the country to a sudden halt." There were plenty of reasons to doubt the report's conclusions, however, since it contained a number of exaggerations about Stuxnet's known capabilities—such as the claim that the worm could "destroy system hardware step-by-step"—and the fact that the configuration Stuxnet was seeking didn't match what one would find at the nuclear power plant. All of this suggested that Iran might be using Stuxnet as an excuse to explain delays at Bushehr. But there was also the possibility that a different digital attack—a modified version of Stuxnet—might have been released separately against Bushehr. See Ken Timmerman, "Computer Worm Wreaking Havoc on Iran's Nuclear Capabilities," Newsmax, April 27, 2011, available at newsmax.com/KenTimmerman/iran-natanz-nuclear-stuxnet/2011/04/27/id/394327.

19 Maillard, "Iran Denies Nuclear Plant Computers Hit by Worm."

Although it was possible Jafari was mistaken, the revelation raised the intriguing possibility that at least two other versions of Stuxnet had been unleashed in the wild. And if two other versions of the code existed, they might contain additional clues about Stuxnet and its authors. Unfortunately, however, there was little chance that Western researchers would ever see them, since Iranian officials were unlikely to provide copies of the code to anyone outside of Iran.[20]

Following his presentation at Weiss's conference and his meeting with Hathaway, Langner needed downtime to make sense of all that had occurred over the previous weeks. That weekend he walked to the National Mall and sat for hours on the steps of the Lincoln Memorial staring at the reflecting pool while tourists around him snapped photos. He thought about the reports from ICS-CERT and Siemens and their silence about the ladder-logic injections in Stuxnet and the risks to critical infrastructure posed by copycat attacks. Then there was the mind-boggling silence from the public and Congress, who seemed to have little concern about the Pandora's box Stuxnet had opened in legitimizing the use of cyberweapons to resolve political disputes. Neither did they seem alarmed about the digital arms race Stuxnet had launched that would be impossible to curb. It was as if, Langner thought, no one wanted to discuss these things for fear that it would raise questions about who was behind the attack.

Langner decided that if everyone else was going to be silent, then he

---

20 There were other statements made by officials that, if true, suggested that other versions of Stuxnet existed. Mahmoud Liayi, head of the information technology council at the Ministry of Industries, told reporters that when Stuxnet got activated, "the industrial automation systems start[ed] transmitting data about production lines" to an outside destination. Gen. Gholam-Reza Jalali had stated at a press conference in 2011 that the worm was discovered communicating with systems in Israel and Texas. There, data about infected machines was processed by the worm's architects, who then engineered plots to attack the nuclear program. (See "Iran Military Official: Israel, US Behind Stuxnet Computer Worm," Associated Press, April 16, 2011, available at haaretz. com/news/world/iran-military-official-israel-u-s-behind-stuxnet-computer-worm-1.356287.) But the three versions of Stuxnet that were discovered communicated with command servers in Denmark and Malaysia. This doesn't discount that another version was somehow traced to Texas or that a spy tool that preceded Stuxnet might have been traced to Texas. But although the NSA does in fact have an elite hacking team based in the Lone Star state, it seems unlikely that they would have made a mistake that allowed the worm or a spy tool to be traced to them.

should go public with more information about the code. So once he returned to Germany, he published additional blog posts laying out the technical details that he had previously disclosed only behind the closed doors of Weiss's conference room. As soon as the posts were up, the blog was besieged with traffic from around the world, including, noticeably, from US government and military domains. Langner hoped that, with Stuxnet's importance now clearly established, other security firms would pick up the baton where he and his team had left off. Despite everything they had learned so far, there was still a lot more work to be done. They had only discovered that Stuxnet was bent on sabotaging a single facility, a facility that was likely Natanz—but they still didn't know what it was doing to the plant. That information was still buried in the code.

Over the next three weeks, he and his colleagues worked on a couple of projects from paying clients to make up for the income they had lost while analyzing Stuxnet. But when no new information came out about the code from Symantec or anyone else, Langner decided they should pick up where they had left off.

"Guys," he said to Rosen and Timm, "I think we need to reopen the case."

CONTRARY TO LANGNER'S belief that the US government was ignoring Stuxnet or missing important details about it, there were elements of the government that *were* paying attention—albeit behind a veil of secrecy. In fact, a group of DHS analysts had completed most of their own examination of Stuxnet within a couple of days after it was exposed in July and knew even before Symantec and Langner did that Stuxnet was sabotaging PLCs.

Stuxnet first made its way to the watch floor of the Department of Homeland Security's National Cybersecurity and Communications Integration Center, or NCCIC, in Arlington, Virginia, on the morning of July 15, 2010, at the same time that security researchers around the globe were getting their first look at the code. The files came in from CERT-Bund, after Siemens had contacted the Computer Emergency Response Team, to report a malicious attack that was targeting its PLCs.

NCCIC, or N-Kick as it's commonly pronounced, was just nine months old and was part of the government's new mission control for monitoring and coordinating responses to cyber threats against critical infrastructure and civilian government systems. When the files arrived, Sean McGurk, director of the center, was ironically in the midst of planning for the government's upcoming Cyber Storm III exercise, a biennial three-day drill that would simulate digital attacks against US critical infrastructure. It was to be the twenty-four-hour watch center's first real test of its coordinating abilities since the facility had opened. But the real threat of Stuxnet quickly took priority over plans for the faux attack.

The windowless watch floor was an alphabet soup of three-letter agencies, with intelligence analysts from the CIA and NSA sitting next to law enforcement agents from the FBI and Secret Service and computer security experts from US-CERT and ICS-CERT. Liaisons from all the top telecoms and other critical-infrastructure industries were there as well.

McGurk sent a copy of Stuxnet to ICS-CERT's lab in Idaho Falls, where analysts determined that the attack code unleashed its payload only on specific models of Siemens PLCs. Two years earlier, the lab's test-bed program had conducted a vulnerability assessment of the same Step 7 software that Stuxnet was attacking, but the PLC they had used for the tests had been returned to Siemens. Now they had to request that Siemens send another one before they could watch Stuxnet deliver its payload. It took about three weeks for the PLC to arrive, and when it did, a group of Siemens engineers accompanied it.

In the meantime, the researchers in Idaho reverse-engineered the payload code while analysts on the watch floor back in Virginia pored over the missile portion, documenting each of its functions in an extensive flow chart. Within two days, McGurk says, they had catalogued some 4,000 functions in the code—more than most commercial software packages contained—and had also uncovered the four zero-day exploits that Symantec and Kaspersky would later find.

ICS-CERT released an advisory on July 20 announcing to control-system owners that malware targeting the Siemens Step 7 system had been found. But the advisory provided very few details about its operation, saying only that the "full capabilities of the malware and intent . . . are not yet known." A subsequent advisory provided a few more details about the zero-day exploits Stuxnet used, plus information about how to detect and remove the malicious code, but said little about what the attack was designed to do and made no mention at all of sabotage.[21] McGurk says it was the government's job to help critical-infrastructure owners detect and remove Stuxnet, not to provide extensive analysis of the malware.[22]

A few days after the group's analysis was complete, McGurk had a conference call with several government agencies and private-industry representatives to review what they had found. In most discussions about malware and vulnerabilities, there were always a few critics in the group who downplayed the vulnerability's importance or claimed that a piece of malicious code was nothing new. Sometimes other federal agencies were the naysayers; sometimes it was the owners and operators of critical infrastructure or the vendor that made the control system that was being discussed. But as McGurk laid out the details of Stuxnet there was only silence on the phone. "Everyone had that 'oh shit' moment all at the same time," he says.[23]

Oddly, the source of Stuxnet never came up, either during the call or on the NCCIC watch floor. McGurk says that when the code first arrived, intelligence analysts from various agencies on the floor searched their classified data sources for any information or reports related to the worm, but

---

21 ICS-CERT Advisory ICSA-10-201-01, "USB Malware Targeting Siemens Control Software" and ICS-CERT Advisory ICSA-10-238-01B, "Stuxnet Malware Mitigation."

22 The ICS-CERT advisories did provide a link to Symantec's website for additional information about the code, but didn't specify what readers would find there.

23 All quotes from McGurk from author interview, September 2012.

came up with nothing. He also says no one on the watch floor wondered out loud if the worm had been spawned by the United States. An outsider might question why no one on the watch floor turned to the CIA or NSA analysts sitting in the room to ask with a wink, "Is this one of yours?" But McGurk insists this never occurred to them because attribution wasn't the watch floor's concern. Their mission was to uncover an attack code's capabilities and determine the best way for US networks to defend against it.

"At first when you look at [malware] . . . your assumption is that it's not friendly fire. You don't think the sniper on the roof is one of your guys shooting at you," he says. "It could turn out to be . . . But in the heat of it, at the very beginning, you're not overly concerned, nor do you naturally default to [that.]"

But very quickly, Stuxnet became "an item of high interest" in Washington. Over the next few weeks and months, McGurk gave briefings to a number of high-level groups—to DHS secretary Janet Napolitano, to John Brennan and other members of the White House National Security staff, to the Senate and House intelligence committees, the DoD, and the Defense Intelligence Agency. He even went to Fort Meade to brief Gen. Keith Alexander, director of US Cyber Command and the NSA—the very entities that many in the security community suspected were behind the attack.

At Fort Meade, a dozen senior military, government, and intelligence leaders sat listening to McGurk as he described what his team had found, but the question of whether the United States was behind the attack never came up. They asked McGurk if Stuxnet was directed against US control systems and how many US systems were vulnerable to the malicious code.[24] They were also curious to know if McGurk's team could tell who the intended target was. And finally they asked if there was anything in

_____

24 The Siemens Step 7 system, it turned out, made up less than 10 percent of the US control-system market. Analysts at NCCIC determined this by consulting a database used by research firms that provides statistics on the market penetration of various products—including the number of industrial control systems made by specific vendors that had been sold in the United States. They determined that most of the US Step 7 systems were being used in manufacturing facilities, though there were also some Step 7 systems used in agriculture and water treatment and power plants.

the code that gave away its source. McGurk told them no, there were no clues revealing who was behind the attack. There weren't even any familiar "footprints" in the code that matched the modus operandi of known hacker groups or nation-state spies.

McGurk maintains that never, either in classified briefings or in open testimony with lawmakers, did anyone ask him the question that was on everyone else's mind. "I don't think, even jokingly, did someone say in a formal briefing, 'Hey did we do this?' Because that's just not the way those interactions occur. I'm sure there was speculation elsewhere, but it wasn't done at our level."

McGurk says he also never got the impression from anyone he briefed that Stuxnet was a homemade job. "When I was in a room, regardless of who the audience was, whether it was senior intelligence folks—and I mean *senior* intelligence folks—I never got the impression that this was all smoke-and-mirrors for them," he says. "The same thing inside the Department of Homeland Security, when I was briefing up to the secretariat level. Never did I get the impression that, you know, they already knew this . . . and they were just hoping that I would go away."

Nor did anyone suggest to McGurk that he should pull his team off of Stuxnet either. "No one said hey, cease and desist, leave it alone, don't go there," he says. "We were actually getting a lot of cooperation from all of those organizations . . . assisting with the analysis and assisting with the understanding of what type of threat this actually posed."

But even if officials in Washington weren't openly asking the obvious question, there was little doubt among experts and observers that the United States was behind the attack—either alone or with Israel—and it seemed only a matter of time before the details behind the attack got out.

Ralph Langner's assertion that Stuxnet was a precision weapon aimed at Iran's nuclear program must have caused a lot of consternation and panic in the halls of the White House and the Pentagon, as a plot that had been meticulously planned and executed over a number of years was slowly unraveling before their eyes.

CHAPTER 11

A DIGITAL PLOT IS HATCHED

The halls of the White House may have been troubled over Stuxnet in 2010 after it was discovered, but in May 2008, optimism reigned among those who knew about the covert program, as the plot behind the digital weapon was unfolding exactly as planned.

At the time, the US presidential campaign was in full swing as candidates Barack Obama and John McCain were battling it out for the lead in the polls. President Bush was just beginning the final lap of his presidency when, during a visit to Israel to mark that country's sixtieth anniversary, he was confronted with a bold request. The Israelis wanted US support and endorsement for an air strike to take out the uranium enrichment plant at Natanz.

The Israelis had been gunning for an air strike since at least 2003, when IAEA inspectors got their first look at Natanz and found highly enriched uranium particles in environmental samples taken from the plant. Talk of an air strike died down for a while after Iranian officials agreed to suspend their enrichment activities in 2003 and 2004, but returned in 2006 when Iran withdrew from the suspension agreement and proceeded to install the first centrifuges in one of the underground halls at the plant.

Now, with 3,000 centrifuges already in place and spinning, and the number expected to double soon, talk of a strike was growing louder than ever before.

Israel wasn't the only one urging an attack. Behind closed doors, its Arab neighbors were just as adamant about halting Iran's nuclear program, according to secret government cables released by WikiLeaks. "We are all terrified," Egyptian President Hosni Mubarak told US diplomats at one point.[1] Saudi Arabia's King Abdullah privately urged the United States to do them all a favor where Iran and Ahmadinejad were concerned and "cut off the head of the snake."[2] A nuclear-armed Iran threatened the peace of the entire region, not just Israel, Mohammad bin Zayed, crown prince of Abu Dhabi said. If Iran got the bomb, "all hell will break loose," he said, warning that Egypt, Saudi Arabia, Syria, and Turkey would all seek nuclear weapons to maintain parity.[3] There were hawks within the Bush administration who supported an air strike as well—the "bomber boys," as Bush called them. Vice President Dick Cheney, who had supported Israel's attack on Syria the previous year, was among them.[4]

But Bush opposed an air strike. "I think it's absolutely absurd that people suspect I am trying to find a pretext to attack Iran," he said in 2007.[5] Even if he did support a strike, he would have had difficulty drumming up widespread backing for one. A November 2007 Gallup poll showed that 73 percent of Americans preferred sanctions and diplomacy to an air strike against Iran, and the National Intelligence Estimate, released that year, asserted that Iran was not actively developing nuclear weapons, which also undermined support for an air strike.

Israel had, of course, been in this position before, seeking US support

---

1 *Spiegel* staff, "Cables Show Arab Leaders Fear a Nuclear Iran," *Der Spiegel*, December 1, 2010.
2 US State Department cable, from CDA Michael Gfoeller, April 20, 2008, available at nytimes.com/interactive/2010/11/28/world/20101128-cables-viewer.html#report/iran-08RIYADH649.
3 "Cables Show Arab Leaders Fear a Nuclear Iran," *Der Spiegel*.
4 Jeffrey Goldberg, "The Point of No Return," *The Atlantic Monthly*, September 2010.
5 Catherine Collins and Douglas Frantz, *Fallout: The True Story of the CIA's Secret War on Nuclear Trafficking* (New York: Free Press, 2011), 212.

for a strike—in 1981 when it took out Iraq's Osirak reactor, and again in 2007 when it bombed the suspected nuclear reactor in Syria.[6] Israeli intelligence agents had obtained crucial information about the latter facility in 2006 when they tailed a senior Syrian official to London and installed a Trojan horse on his laptop after he unwisely left it behind in his hotel room one day. The malware siphoned dozens of documents from the computer, including blueprints and photos showing construction of the Al Kibar complex, which the Israelis believed was a nuclear reactor the Syrians were building to develop weapons. They won US support to attack the site after providing evidence that North Korea was helping Syria build it.[7]

Late in the evening on September 5, 2007, Operation Orchard commenced when Israeli military jets departed from a base in Northern Israel and headed west toward the sea before suddenly banking east. They flew low as they crossed the border into Syria and took out a radar station near the Turkish border using electronic attacks and precision bombs. About twenty minutes later, they unloaded their cargo onto the Al Kibar complex before safely returning home without incident. Syrian president Bashar al-Assad downplayed the strike, saying the Israelis hit nothing but an empty military building. "There's no people in it, there's no army, there's nothing in it," he said.[8] But US intelligence determined that the reactor had been just weeks away from being operational before the Israelis took it out.[9]

Now the Israelis wanted to do the same in Iran. They believed an air strike would set Iran's nuclear program back at least three years. But an

---

6 In June 1991 when then–Defense Secretary Cheney visited Israel, he reportedly gave Israeli Maj. Gen. David Ivry a satellite image of the Osirak reactor taken after it was obliterated. Cheney annotated the image: "For General Ivry, with thanks and appreciation for the outstanding job he did on the Iraqi Nuclear Program in 1981, which made our job much easier in Desert Storm." See Douglas Frantz and Catherine Collins, *The Nuclear Jihadist: The True Story of the Man Who Sold the World's Most Dangerous Secrets* (New York: Free Press, 2007), 190.

7 Erich Follath and Holger Stark, "The Story of 'Operation Orchard': How Israel Destroyed Syria's Al Kibar Nuclear Reactor," *Der Spiegel*, November 2, 2009. For information about the electronic warfare used to take out the radar station, see David A. Fulghum, "U.S. Watches Israeli Raid, Provides Advice," *Aviation Week*, November 21, 2007.

8 Julian Borger, "Israeli Airstrike Hit Military Site, Syria Confirms," *Guardian*, October 1, 2007.

9 David Albright notes that when fully operational, the reactor could have produced enough plutonium for a nuclear weapon every one to two years. David Albright, *Peddling Peril: How the Secret Nuclear Trade Arms America's Enemies* (New York: Free Press, 2010), 3.

attack on Iran carried many more complications and risks than the attacks on Syria and Iraq. In both of those cases, the Israelis had targeted a single, aboveground facility that was not heavily fortified, and in the case of Syria, the target was close enough to home that pilots could make their strike quickly and return before the Syrians had time to respond. A strike against Iran, however, would require refueling and a flight through large swaths of Arab airspace. And, instead of a single target, the planes would have to strike at least half a dozen sites dispersed throughout the country—the enrichment plant at Natanz and the uranium conversion plant at Esfahan being just two of them—some of which were underground. Iran had learned from the Israeli attack on Iraq decades earlier that the key to preserving its nuclear program was to disperse facilities around the country, and US officials had "little confidence" that Israel even knew the location of all the facilities it needed to strike to cripple the program.[10] Israel's national security adviser Giora Eiland even admitted as much when he told a US congressional delegation in 2006, "We don't know all the sites and we don't know what we don't know."[11]

In his State of the Union address in January 2002, President Bush had identified Iran as part of the "axis of evil," along with Iraq and North Korea, that threatened the peace of the world. The United States, he said, would not permit "the world's most dangerous regimes" to "threaten us with the world's most destructive weapons."[12] They were strong words. But in the intervening years—years filled with the difficulties of prosecuting a war in Iraq—Bush had softened his stance. US Defense Secretary Robert M. Gates was convinced an attack on Iran would not only fail but would have wide-ranging repercussions on US troops in Iraq and Afghanistan. It might also trigger terrorist retaliation against Israel from pro-Iran groups in Lebanon and the Gaza Strip and disrupt oil prices, sending economic

---

10 Tim Shipman, "U.S. Pentagon Doubts Israeli Intelligence Over Iran's Nuclear Program," *Telegraph*, July 5, 2008.

11 US State Department cable, "Israeli NSA Eiland on Iranian Nuclear Threat," April 26, 2006, published by WikiLeaks at http://wikileaks.org/cable/2006/04/06TELAVIV1643.html.

12 Erich Follath and Holger Stark, "The Birth of a Bomb: A History of Iran's Nuclear Ambitions," *Der Spiegel*, June 17, 2010.

shockwaves around the world. Most important, instead of curbing Iran's nuclear ambitions, it could set Iran on an even more determined course to nuclear weapons and cause officials to kick IAEA inspectors out of the country, taking their nuclear activities even further underground and out of sight.

For all of these reasons and more, Bush rejected Israel's push for an air strike, but not without an alternative strategy to take its place.[13]

Two years earlier, Bush's advisers had offered him what seemed like an even better solution to the problem with Iran, possibly even a brilliant one. And in the spring of 2008, while he was touring Israel for the last time as president, it looked like they might actually pull it off.

IT'S NOT CLEAR exactly when the first planning and development on Stuxnet began, but sometime in 2006, after Iran withdrew from its suspension agreement, US military and intelligence officials reportedly brought the proposal for the cyber operation, later dubbed "Olympic Games," to the president. Bush had been weighing his options for a while. With two protracted and complex wars already being fought in Iraq and Afghanistan, he had already decided he wanted no part in a third battle in the Middle East. On-the-ground covert attacks that physically sabotaged Iran's nuclear sites also were ruled out, since they, too, would likely spark a war.[14]

So his advisers proffered a third option—a digital bunker buster that, if designed and executed carefully, could achieve some of the same results as its kinetic counterparts, without all of the risks and consequences of those other attacks.

The military and intelligence communities had been preparing for an attack like this for nearly a decade and had engaged in smaller cyber opera-

---

13 David E. Sanger, "U.S. Rejected Aid for Israeli Raid on Iranian Nuclear Site," *New York Times,* January 10, 2009.
14 David E. Sanger, "Iran Moves to Shelter Its Nuclear Fuel Program," *New York Times,* September 1, 2011.

tions before, but nothing at the scale they were proposing now. Most previous operations were simply spy missions carried out with digital tools or digital operations conducted as adjuncts to conventional warfare—cyber activities meant to simply assist troops on the battlefield, not take their place.[15]

This innovative new plan, however, called for a digital attack against the centrifuges and computer systems at Natanz to physically sabotage Iran's uranium enrichment efforts. The requirements and restrictions for such an operation were extensive. It had to be a surgical strike capable of homing in on the specific machines the United States wanted to attack while leaving other systems unharmed. The code had to bypass internal security systems so that it could do its dirty deed undetected for months. And it had to cause enough damage for the results to have meaningful effects, without drawing attention to itself.

But if the attack succeeded, the potential payoff was huge. If a cyberstrike could destroy some of Iran's IR-1 centrifuges or otherwise slow the country's rapid race to nuclear breakout, it would relieve some of the pressure on diplomatic efforts and give the IAEA and intelligence agencies more time to gather evidence about Iran's nuclear aspirations. It would also get the Israelis off their backs for a while. Israeli officials had accused the United States of dragging its feet on Iran; a digital attack on the nuclear program would prove that the United States wasn't just sitting idly by, waiting for sanctions and diplomacy to succeed.

More important, if centrifuges were destroyed and uranium gas was wasted in the process, it would deplete Iran's already dwindling supply of precious materials for the nuclear program. Experts estimated that Iran had only enough materials to build 12,000 to 15,000 centrifuges; if an attack could force Iran to waste a few thousand of the devices, it would cut sharply into that supply. If luck was on their side, it could also create a political rift in the Iranian regime. There was already pressure on Ahmadinejad and his supporters to achieve progress in the nuclear program; if a

---

15 See chapter 12 for more on the history of the US government's cyberwarfare capabilities.

covert attack thwarted their efforts and set the program back a few years, it could very well sow dissension within the regime.

The advantages of a cyberattack over other forms of attack were many. A digital bomb could achieve some of the same effects as a kinetic weapon without putting the lives of pilots at risk. It could also achieve them covertly in a way a physical bomb could never do, by silently damaging a system over weeks and months without being detected. The Iranians would eventually see the effects of the digital sabotage, but if done well, they would never know its cause, leaving them to wonder if the problem was a material defect, a programming error, or something else. Even if the Iranians discovered the malware, a digital attack done properly left no fingerprints to be traced back to its source. This plausible deniability was key, since the United States was trying to prevent a war, not start one.

There were other benefits to a digital attack. Air strikes had obvious disadvantages when it came to bombing facilities buried deep underground, as Natanz and other Iranian facilities were.[16] But a digital attack could slip past air-defense systems and electrified fences to burrow effortlessly into infrastructure deep underground that was otherwise unreachable by air and other means. It could also take out centrifuges not just in known facilities but in *unknown* ones. You couldn't bomb a plant you didn't know about, but you could possibly cyberbomb it. If Iran had other secret enrichment plants distributed throughout the country that used the same equipment and configuration as Natanz, a digital weapon planted in

---

16 In mid-2007, Western satellites spotted evidence of a possible tunnel being built into a mountain adjacent to Natanz, possibly to sequester materials and equipment from an anticipated attack on the plant. The NCRI reported that Iran was in fact constructing secret tunnels in more than a dozen locations around the country to protect missile and nuclear installations from potential attack. Israel had secured an agreement to obtain a new generation of bunker-busting bombs from the United States—said to be ten times more powerful than the previous generation and capable of breaking through cement and penetrating deep underground. But the new bombs weren't expected to be ready until 2009 or 2010 and there was no guarantee they would work against Natanz. See David Albright and Paul Brannan, "New Tunnel Construction at Mountain Adjacent to the Natanz Enrichment Complex," ISIS, July 9, 2007, available at isis-online.org/uploads/isis-reports/documents/IranNatanzTunnels.pdf. See also William Broad, "Iran Shielding Its Nuclear Efforts in Maze of Tunnels," *New York Times*, January 5, 2010.

the computers of the contractors who serviced them all could spread from known facilities to unknown ones.

Digital sabotage, albeit on a far less sophisticated level, wasn't without precedent. In the 1980s, the CIA, the DoD, and the FBI had run a joint operation to sabotage software and hardware headed to the Soviet Union. It began after Lt. Col. Vladimir Ippolitovich Vetrov, a forty-eight-year-old official in the Line X division of the KGB's Technology Directorate, began leaking intelligence to the French about a decade-long Soviet operation to steal technology from the West.

Vetrov leaked about three thousand documents, dubbed the "Farewell Dossier" by the French, detailing a long list of technologies the Soviets had already pilfered from the West as well as a wish list of items still to be procured. When the wish list made its way to Dr. Gus Weiss, an economics adviser to Reagan's National Security Council, he proposed a shrewd plan to then-CIA director William Casey. The CIA would let the Soviets continue to obtain the technology they wanted—but with the spy agency slipping modified designs and blueprints into the mix to misdirect their scientific efforts toward money-wasting ventures. He also proposed modifying products and components before they reached the Iron Curtain so that they would pass any quality-assurance tests the Soviets might subject them to, then fail at a later date. The plan was a veritable win-win because even if the Soviets discovered the counterintelligence operation, they would forever be suspicious of any information or technology later acquired from the West, never certain how or if it had been altered or when it might malfunction. It would be a "rarity in the world of espionage," Weiss later wrote in an internal CIA newsletter describing the scheme: "an operation that would succeed even if compromised."[17]

Under the scheme, "contrived computer chips found their way into

17 The newsletter was later declassified. See Gus Weiss, "The Farewell Dossier: Strategic Deception and Economic Warfare in the Cold War," in *Studies in Intelligence*, 1996, available at https://www .cia.gov/library/center-for-the-study-of-intelligence/csi-publications/csi-studies/studies/96unclass/ farewell.htm.

Soviet military equipment, flawed turbines were installed on a gas pipe-line, and defective plans disrupted the output of chemical plants and a tractor factory," Weiss wrote. Additionally, the Soviets were fed mislead-ing information about stealth and tactical aircraft as well as Western space defense programs. The Soviet Space Shuttle was also built on "a rejected NASA design" that had been slipped to the Soviets, Weiss revealed.[18]

The Farewell operation was never discovered, according to Weiss, but Vetrov was not so lucky. He was imprisoned in 1982 after stabbing his mistress, a married KGB colleague, and was exposed as a double agent—though the CIA's sabotage efforts remained a secret.[19] In 1986, the CIA shuttered the operation.

Weiss, who is now dead, never specified the effects of the contrived computer chips and other defective parts that were slipped into the Soviet supply chain, but in 2004, Thomas C. Reed, who worked with Weiss on the National Security Council, wrote a book that briefly mentioned the Farewell Dossier and attributed a 1982 Siberian pipeline explosion to the CIA scheme—the same pipeline explosion that Symantec referenced in its blog post about Stuxnet. According to Reed, one of the items on the Line X shopping list was software for controlling the pumps, valves, and turbines on the Trans-Siberian Pipeline, which was being built to carry natural gas from the Urengoi gas fields in Siberia to countries in Europe. When the CIA learned the Soviets were trying to obtain the software from a company in Canada, the agency, in cooperation with the firm, embed-

18 According to Weiss, the CIA also launched a misinformation campaign around a laser weapons technology to convince the Soviets that the unproven technology was something they should pursue. When the CIA found Soviet documents discussing the technology, the agency arranged for renowned physicists to plant stories about it in *Nature* and another reputable publication to create buzz about it as if it were a promising discovery. Then they abruptly halted publication of information on the matter, to make the Soviets think the technology had strategic importance and that conversations about it had been stifled. Weiss said the Soviets must have taken the bait because years later, when the Soviet Union collapsed, evidence was found that the Soviets had been pursuing research on the laser technology.

19 The complete story of Vetrov's life and the Farewell Dossier is recounted in Sergei Kostin and Eric Raynaud, *Farewell: The Greatest Spy Story of the Twentieth Century*. The book, published in French in 2009, was translated into English by Catherine Cauvin-Higgins and published in 2011 by Amazon Crossing. The book was made into a French film released in 2009 titled *L'affaire Farewell*.

ded a logic bomb in the code. The code was designed to reset pump speeds and valve settings on the pipeline to "produce pressures far beyond those acceptable to the pipeline joints and welds," Reed wrote.[20] The software "ran the pipeline beautifully—for a while," he noted. But then at some predetermined point it caused the pumps and valves to go haywire, creating a gas-pressure buildup so immense it set off a three-kiloton explosion—the "most monumental non-nuclear explosion and fire ever seen from space," according to Reed.

There are many who believe the story of the exploding pipeline is apocryphal; a former KGB official has denied the tale and believes Reed and Weiss confused their facts.[21] Regardless, the Farewell Dossier operation did exist and served as inspiration for later sabotage schemes focused on Iran's nuclear program.

One such operation occurred after the CIA infiltrated A. Q. Khan's nuclear supply network around 2000 and began inserting doctored parts

---

20 Thomas C. Reed, *At the Abyss: An Insider's History of the Cold War* (New York: Presidio Press, 2004), 268–69.

21 Reed's account of the pipeline explosion, the first to be published, has taken on a life of its own and been re-reported many times as fact, though no reporters have been able to substantiate it. There are reasons to doubt the story. According to Reed, the explosion was captured by US infrared satellites and caused a stir among members of the National Security Council at the time, who were trying to determine whether the Soviets had detonated an atomic device in Siberia when Weiss told them not to worry about it. Weiss never explained why they shouldn't worry about it, but twenty years later when Reed was writing his book, Weiss told him the cause of the explosion they had been concerned about was CIA sabotage. But Vasily Pchelintsev, the former head of the KGB in the region where Reed said the explosion occurred has said it never happened, and that Weiss may have conflated his memory of the Farewell Dossier incident with an explosion that occurred in April 1982 in a different region. But that explosion, Pchelintsev said, was caused by shifting pipes that moved when snow melted, not by CIA sabotage. See Anatoly Medetsky, "KGB Veteran Denies CIA Caused '82 Blast," *Moscow Times*, March 18, 2004.

Asked if he believed Weiss's account of the pipeline, Reed told me in a phone interview in October 2010, "I don't really know if it happened. . . . Clearly the whole Dossier episode happened. The agency had a very major campaign to adjust the tech of stuff that was being sent off to the Russians." He said he does recall that an explosion occurred at the time he was on the NSC. "I remembered there was a great event that puzzled the intelligence community." But whether that was in fact a pipeline explosion, "that was thirty years ago," he said, acknowledging that both his and Weiss's memories may have been altered in the ensuing years. "I have respect for Russian historians who say there was no explosion in connection with Dossier. . . . So it could be there was an explosion, but it was not a result of a Trojan horse. . . . Whether it was true or not I do not know." It may be too much to hope, however, that any future retellings of the pipeline tale will be done with the appropriate caveats.

into components headed to Iran and Libya—where Khan had also begun peddling his illicit nuclear services. A weapons expert at Los Alamos National Laboratory worked with the CIA to alter a series of vacuum pumps so that they would malfunction at random intervals. As with the operation against the Soviets, the plan was to sabotage the parts so subtly that they would work fine for a little while before breaking down in such a way that it would be difficult to spot a pattern or pinpoint the problem.

Of seven pumps the CIA compromised, six of them went to Libya; but the seventh one ended up in Iran. IAEA inspectors later stumbled across it by chance when they visited Natanz.[22] The Iranians apparently didn't know the pump had been altered.

They did, however, discover another sabotage operation that occurred in 2006. This one involved UPSes—uninterruptible power supplies—obtained from Turkey. UPSes help regulate the flow of electricity and are important to the operation of centrifuges, which require reliable and consistent energy to spin for long periods of time at uniform speeds. If the electrical current wavers, the centrifuges will speed up and slow down, sabotaging the enrichment process and even throwing the centrifuges themselves off balance.

The Khan network evidently purchased the devices from two businessmen in Turkey and secretly shipped them to Iran and Libya.[23] But in early 2006, when Iran attempted to enrich its first batch of uranium in a small cascade at the pilot plant at Natanz, things went terribly wrong. The cascade ran fine for about ten days, but then the sabotage kicked in and all of the centrifuges had to be replaced. No one said anything about it at the time. But a year later, during a televised interview, the head of Iran's Atomic Energy Organization described what had occurred. Technicians

---

22 When IAEA inspectors saw the pump at Natanz, it stood out for them because a sticker was affixed to it identifying it as property of the Los Alamos National Lab, which they thought was odd. When the IAEA investigated, the agency found that the serial number on the pump was consecutive with the serial numbers of pumps they had seen in Libya, indicating the pumps had all come from the same batch. The inspectors traced the order for the pumps to the US lab. No one was ever able to figure out how the Los Alamos sticker got onto the pump at Natanz, or why the Iranians weren't suspicious of it. See Collins and Frantz, *Fallout*, 138.
23 Frantz and Collins, *Nuclear Jihadist*, 238.

had installed 50 centrifuges in the cascade, he explained, but one night "all 50 had exploded." The UPS controlling the electricity "had not acted properly," he said, and created a surge. "Later we found out that the UPS we had imported through Turkey had been manipulated." He also said that after the incident occurred they began checking all imported instruments before using them.[24]

There have been other known plans to alter parts and components for Iran's nuclear program, but at least one was aborted, while others failed to work as planned.[25] What Bush's advisers were proposing in 2006, however, promised to take the black art of sabotage to a whole new level.

What they proposed was a stand-alone surgical strike involving code that could operate independently once unleashed, that had the intelligence to know when it had found its target and would only release its payload when conditions were right, that also disguised its existence by carefully monitoring attempts to detect it, and that had the ability to destroy physical equipment not through bold, explosive strokes but through subtle, prolonged ones.

Some officials in the Bush administration were skeptical that such an attack could work, likening it to an untried science experiment.[26] But the planners weren't expecting miracles from the operation. They didn't expect to destroy Iran's uranium enrichment program altogether, just to set it back and buy some time. And even if the operation were discovered and the Iranians learned that their computers had been infiltrated, it would still be a win-win situation, as Weiss had pointed with the Farewell Dossier, since it would succeed in sowing doubt and paranoia among the Iranians.

---

24 Gholam Reza Aghazadeh interview, January 2007, with *Ayande-ye* (New Future). The interview itself is not online, but it's referenced in Sheila MacVicar and Farhan Bokhari, "Assessing Iran's Nuclear Program," CBS News, April 4, 2007, available at cbsnews.com/news/assessing-irans-nuclear-program.

25 One ill-conceived plan conjured by the Mossad and the CIA, as described in James Risen's *State of War*, involved using an electromagnetic pulse to fry computers used in Iran's nuclear facilities. Spies planned to smuggle equipment into Iran that would deliver the electromagnetic pulse to power transmission lines outside the facilities. The CIA dropped the plan, however, after realizing that the equipment was far too big to truck into Iran and position stealthily. Risen, *State of War: The Secret History of the CIA and the Bush Administration* (New York: Free Press), 208–9.

26 Sanger, "U.S. Rejected Aid for Israeli Raid."

Even if technicians wiped their machines clean and reprogrammed them, they could never be certain that the systems wouldn't be infected again or that their enemies wouldn't try a different tack. They would always be on guard for any signs of trouble, and if something did go wrong, they would never know for certain if the cause had been a material defect or enemy sabotage. They'd also be much more wary of any equipment procured outside of Iran for fear that it might have already been compromised.

The daring and sophisticated scheme, which combined both covert and clandestine activities, was reportedly conceived by US Strategic Command—the Defense Department division that operates and oversees the country's nuclear weapons—with Gen. James Cartwright as one of its architects.[27] A former senior U.S. official described General Cartwright as the concept man, while former NSA Director Keith Alexander was responsible for executing the plan. "Cartwright's role was describing the art of the possible, having a view or a vision," the official told the *Washington Post*. But Alexander had the "technical know-how and carried out the actual activity."[28] The code was then developed by an elite team of programmers at the NSA, at least initially. Later versions reportedly combined code from the NSA with code from the Israeli Defense Force's Unit 8200—Israel's version of the NSA. Once the code was designed, however, it would have been handed off to the CIA to oversee delivery to its destination, since only the CIA has legal authority to conduct covert operations.

The technical challenges of the operation were daunting, but there were legal issues to work out as well, since they were proposing to attack

---

27 *Clandestine* operations involve secret activity that isn't meant to be detected or noticed, such as surveillance and intelligence collection activities to uncover information about a target that might be later attacked. *Covert* activity, however, is meant to be noticed, since it's intended to influence conditions—political, economic, or military—although the party responsible for the activity is hidden, such as the CIA. The Stuxnet operation involved both clandestine and covert activity. The clandestine activity involved the initial reconnaissance to gather intelligence about the plant. But the planting of malicious code in a control system to send centrifuges spinning off their axis was covert since it was meant to be noticed while hiding the hand behind it.

28 Ellen Nakashima and Joby Warrick. "Stuxnet Was Work of U.S. and Israeli Experts, Officials Say," *Washington Post*, June 2, 2012.

another country's infrastructure outside of a declaration of war. Covert action requires a legal document known as a Presidential Finding to authorize it, as well as notification to Congress. And before Bush signed off on the operation, there would have been extensive review to consider the risks involved.[29]

Luckily, sabotaging the centrifuges in a cascade carried no risk of a nuclear accident. Uranium hexafluoride gas was destructive to lungs and kidneys if inhaled in sufficient quantities, but an entire cascade contained only tens of grams of gas, which would dissipate quickly once released into the air.

But if there was no risk of a nuclear incident to consider, there were still other consequences to weigh, including the risk of bricking the computers at Natanz if the code contained an error or a bug that was incompatible with the systems, thereby tipping off the Iranians to the attack and ruining the operation. There was also the risk of retaliation if Iran discovered that the United States was behind the attack, as well as the risk of blowback if someone altered the code and used it against American critical infrastructure.

Perhaps the biggest consideration of all was the risk of tipping off Iran and other enemies to US cyber capabilities. The problem with using a cyberweapon, says one former CIA agent, is that "once it's out there, it's like using your stealth fighter for the first time—you've rung that bell and you can't pretend that the stealth fighter doesn't exist anymore. So the question is, which air battle do you really want to use that stealth fighter for?"[30]

Was the operation against Iran worth exposing this new capability? And what about losing the moral high ground if it became known that the United States was behind the attack? A digital assault that destroyed another country's critical infrastructure—and Iran would no doubt claim

---

29 Sanger, "U.S. Rejected Aid for Israeli Raid."
30 Author interview, 2012.

that the centrifuges *were* critical infrastructure—was essentially an act of war. It would be very hard for the United States to point an accusing finger at any nation that used digital attacks thereafter.

It's unclear how much advance research and work had already been done by the time Bush's advisers proposed their plan in 2006. But once he gave the go-ahead for the covert operation to advance, it reportedly took just eight months to finalize the scheme.[31]

It was an ingenious plot that proceeded exactly as planned.

Until suddenly it didn't.

---

31 David E. Sanger, *Confront and Conceal: Obama's Secret Wars and Surprising Use of American Power* (New York: Crown, 2012), 193.

CHAPTER 12

A NEW FIGHTING DOMAIN

B y the time Bush's advisers floated the idea of a precision digital weapon aimed at sabotaging Iran's centrifuges to him, plans for developing such capabilities had already been in the works for a decade, born out of the realization that the military's own networks were vulnerable to enemy attack.

Academics and military experts had been pondering the concept of cyberwarfare and the potential for digital weaponry even longer than that. As early as 1970, the Defense Science Board had examined the potential military advantages of subverting computer networks to render them unreliable or useless in what was then known as information warfare. Few operations were computerized at the time, however, and the internet didn't exist, so the theoretical possibilities had to wait for reality to catch up.

It finally did in the '90s, around the same time the term "cyberwar" was coined in a seminal 1993 RAND article titled "Cyberwar Is Coming!": "We anticipate that cyberwar may be to the 21st century what *blitzkrieg* was to the 20th century," John Arquilla and his coauthor wrote at the time.[1] Arquilla, now a professor at the Naval Postgraduate School in

---

1 John Arquilla and David Ronfeldt, "Cyberwar Is Coming!" published by RAND in 1993 and reprinted as chapter 2 in Arquilla and Ronfeldt's book *In Athena's Camp: Preparing for Conflict in the Information Age* (RAND, 1997).

California and a military consultant, recognized the potential for digital attacks during the first Gulf War when the United States used a special radar system to spot moving targets in Iraq and realized it could easily have been thwarted if the Iraqis found a way to disrupt it. It struck Arquilla that the computerized technologies that made a modern army strong also made it potentially very weak. "What made that thought even more chilling was the notion that this power existed in the hands of a few hackers," he later said, not just in the hands of government armies. And the disruptive power of these peripheral groups was "growing by leaps and bounds."[2]

The military already had its first taste of their capabilities in the 1980s, when a German named Markus Hess, who was reportedly recruited by the KGB, hacked into hundreds of military systems and research facilities, such as Lawrence Berkeley National Laboratory, in search of intelligence about satellites and the Star Wars defense system.[3] Other scares followed. In 1990 in the run-up to the first Gulf War, Dutch teens broke into nearly three-dozen US military computers seeking information about Patriot missiles, nuclear weapons, and the operation against Iraq. Officials feared the teens planned to sell the intelligence to Iraq. Then in 1994, a sixteen-year-old British hacker, mentored by a twenty-one-year-old in Wales, breached US Air Force systems and used them to hack into a South Korean nuclear research institute, as well as attacking one hundred other victims. With the breach appearing to come from US military computers, it became clear that the potential consequences of such intrusions weren't limited to intelligence theft. The United States was engaged in delicate nuclear negotiations with North Korea at the time, and the military feared that if the hackers had targeted a facility in North Korea instead, they could have brought the two nations to the brink of battle.[4]

---

2 He was speaking to PBS *Frontline* in 2003 for its show "CyberWar!" Interview available at pbs
.org/wgbh/pages/frontline/shows/cyberwar/interviews/arquilla.html.
3 The operation was thwarted by a system administrator named Cliff Stoll, who stumbled upon
the intrusion while investigating the source of a seventy-five-cent billing discrepancy. Stoll recounts
the story in his now-classic book *The Cuckoo's Egg: Tracking a Spy Through a Maze of Computer
Espionage* (New York: Doubleday, 1989).
4 Jonathan Ungoed-Thomas, "How Datastream Cowboy Took U.S. to the Brink of War,"
Toronto Star, January 1, 1998.

But connectivity was a double-edged sword. If US systems were vulnerable to attack, so were the systems of adversaries. Although the United States didn't have the capabilities to pull off such attacks yet, the wheels were being set in motion.

The Air Force was the first to take steps in this direction in 1993, when it transformed its Electronic Warfare Center into the Air Force Information Warfare Center and established, two years later, the 609 Information Warfare Squadron—the military's first cybercombat unit.[5] Located at Shaw Air Force Base in South Carolina, its job was to combine offensive and defensive cyber operations in support of combat commands.[6] Offensive operations were largely still academic at this point, so the unit focused mostly on defensive tactics. But the military quickly learned that there were advantages to having defensive and offensive operations intertwined, because in defending its own networks against enemy attack it gained the intelligence and skills needed to hack back. In 1996, the squadron organized a red team/blue team exercise to test the unit's offensive and defensive skills, and within two hours the red team had seized full control of the blue team's Air Tasking Order System.

In 1997 the military conducted a more organized exercise to measure its defensive capabilities against enemy network attacks. The exercise, dubbed "Eligible Receiver," pitted a red team of NSA hackers against the networks of the US Pacific Command in Hawaii. The team was prohibited from using inside knowledge to conduct the attack or anything but off-the-shelf tools that were available to ordinary hackers. When the attack began, they launched their offensive through a commercial dial-up internet account and barreled straight into the military's networks with little resistance. The system administrators in Hawaii, who had no advance knowledge of the exercise, spotted only two of the multiple intrusions the

---

5 Information warfare didn't just involve offensive and defensive cyber operations, it also included psychological operations, electronic warfare, and physical destruction of information targets.
6 A thirty-nine-page book recounts the history of the 609th. A copy of the book, titled *609 IWS: A Brief History Oct. 1995–June 1999*, was obtained under a FOIA request and is available at securitycritics.org/wp-content/uploads/2006/03/hist-609.pdf.

attackers made over the course of ninety days, but even then they thought nothing of the breaches because they resembled the kind of ordinary traffic that administrators expected to see on the network. It wasn't unlike the attack on Pearl Harbor in 1941, when an alert operator at the Opana Radar Site on the island of Oahu spotted inbound aircraft heading toward the island but didn't raise an alarm because his superiors believed they were friendlies.

The red-team hackers dropped marker files onto the systems to plant a virtual flag, proving they were there, and also created a number of simulated attacks showing how they could have seized control of power and communications networks in Oahu, Los Angeles, Chicago, and Washington, DC. Had they wanted to, they could have seized control of a system used to command hundreds of thousands of troops or set up "rolling blackouts and other activities that would cause social unrest," according to Lt. Gen. John H. Campbell, a now-retired Air Force general who headed the Pentagon's information operations at one time. The exercise "scared the hell out of a lot of folks," Campbell later said, "because the implications of what this team had been able to do were pretty far-reaching."[7]

Afterward, when military leaders were briefed about the exercise, they assumed the red team had used classified tools and techniques for the attack and were surprised to learn that the NSA had used the same techniques any teenage hacker would use.

The next year, in fact, a group of teenagers broke into military networks using the same kinds of low-level techniques, in a case dubbed Operation Solar Sunrise. The intruders, who pilfered sensitive data across five hundred systems, turned out to be two California teens on a digital joyride, egged on by an Israeli hacker named Ehud Tenenbaum. At the time, the DoD was prosecuting two military campaigns, in Bosnia and

---

7 John "Soup" Campbell speaking as part of a panel titled "Lessons from Our Cyber Past: The First Military Cyber Units," at the Atlantic Council, March 5, 2012. Campbell was the first commander of the Joint Task Force-Computer Network Defense in December 1998 and later was principal adviser to the CIA director on military issues. A transcript of the panel discussion can be found at atlanticcouncil.org/news/transcripts/transcript-lessons-from-our-cyber-past-the-first-military-cyber -units.

Herzegovina and in Iraq. The intrusion, to military leaders, looked a lot like what enemy attackers would do if they were trying to gain a battlefield advantage. Deputy Defense Secretary John Hamre, in fact, thought the attacks "might be the first shots of a genuine cyber war, perhaps by Iraq."[8] It was a real-life *War Games* moment that underscored the difficulty of distinguishing a nation-state attack from teenagers testing their limits. "Everything we learned in Eligible Receiver, we relearned in Solar Sunrise," Hamre later said of the intrusion. "There's nothing like a real-world experience to bring the lessons home."[9]

The real lesson, though, came afterward when Hamre called a meeting to discuss the intrusion and looked around a room filled with two-dozen people to ask, "Who's in charge? Who's responsible for protecting us?" and learned that when it came to cyberattacks, no one apparently was in charge. The shock of this realization led to the creation of the Joint Task Force–Computer Network Defense (JTF-CND) in December 1998, the first military group charged with figuring out how to defend the military's networks.[10]

The task force, led by Campbell, was a motley group composed of a couple of Air Force and Navy fighter pilots, a Marine officer, some Airborne Rangers, a submarine pilot, intelligence staff, and a few contractors. One officer described them as "some guys in flight jackets . . . [and] a bunch of civilians with no ties."[11] Only a few of them were geeks who knew their way around a network. Initially they had no office and no support staff and had to work out of temporary trailers in a parking lot. But eventually the group grew to more than 150 people.

8 Bradley Graham, "U.S. Studies a New Threat: Cyber Attack," *Washington Post*, May 24, 1998.
9 Ibid.
10 Some of the information about the first task force and the history of the military's cyber activities comes from a March 2012 interview with Jason Healey, head of the Cyber Statecraft Initiative at the Atlantic Council in Washington, DC, and an original member of the military's first cyber taskforce. Healey also recounts some of the history of cyber conflict in a book he edited, which is one of the first to examine it. See *A Fierce Domain: Conflict in Cyberspace, 1986 to 2012* (Cyber Conflict Studies Association, 2013).
11 Maj. Gen. James D. Bryan, founding commander of the JTF-Computer Network Operations, speaking on the panel "Lessons from Our Cyber Past: The First Military Cyber Units."

Their mission was to develop doctrines and methods for defending DoD networks against attack, but before they got started, they had two questions for the military brass: Should they develop a NORAD-type structure to defend civilian critical infrastructure as well? And what about offense? "All of us wanted to get into the attack mode," recalls Marcus Sachs, an Army engineer and one of the task force's initial members. "Everyone was thinking about the potential for launching digital bullets. . . . We wanted to go down that road and kind of flush out what would it mean for us to be offensive."[12]

It was the era of hacker conferences like Def Con and HOPE, two confabs held in Las Vegas and New York that became popular forums for hackers and researchers to talk about security holes and hacking tools.[13] The FBI and intelligence agencies were already lurking undercover at Def Con each year, so Sachs decided to attend as well and had his eyes opened to the possibilities of what the military might do. But the task force was told to slow down, that the military wasn't ready for offensive operations yet. "The legal questions hadn't been worked out," Sachs explains.

There was another reason for caution, however. A cyberweapon was the "type of weapon that you fire and it doesn't die. Somebody can pick it up and fire it right back at you," Sachs says. "That was a very strong motivator to not do this."

What Sachs didn't know at the time was that the previous year, the secretary of defense had already given the NSA authority to begin developing computer network attack (CNA) techniques, a task the spy agency embraced as an extension of its existing electronic warfare duties, which included jamming enemy radar systems and taking out communication channels.[14] The NSA believed its technical geniuses could play a critical role on the emerging digital battlefield as well.

---

12 This and other quotes from Sachs come from author interview, March 2012.
13 "HOPE" stands for Hackers on Planet Earth.
14 Electronic warfare, which dates to World War I, involves the use of electromagnetic and directed energy to control the electromagnetic spectrum to retard enemy systems. Computer network attacks, by contrast, are defined as operations designed to disrupt, deny, degrade, or destroy information

The advantages of digital combat over kinetic warfare were clear, the NSA wrote in an internal newsletter in 1997.[15] In an age of televised warfare, when images of body bags brought the stark realities of war back to the homefront, cyberwarfare offered an antiseptic alternative that the public could more easily embrace. But there were other advantages too, the report noted: the low cost of entry to conduct such campaigns; a "flexible base of deployment," where being "in range" of a target wasn't a necessity; and a diverse and ever-expanding set of targets as more and more critical systems became computerized.

The spy agency, in fact, was already contemplating, a decade before Stuxnet, the offensive opportunities presented by the world's growing reliance on computerized control systems in critical infrastructure. Another article in the same newsletter proposed building a road map to track the technologies that were already on the shelves, as well as those that were still "a twinkle in some engineer's eye," in order to develop attack capabilities against them.[16] The newsletter also suggested compiling a list of public hacking tools already available for use—viruses, worms, logic bombs, Trojan horses, and back doors. These powerful tools "if effectively executed," the author noted, "[could be] extremely destructive to any society's information infrastructure."[17] That included, however, US infrastructure. "So . . . before you get too excited about this 'target-rich environment,'" the newsletter cautioned the agency's would-be cyberwarriors, "remember, General Custer was in a target-rich environment too!"[18]

---

resident on computers and computer networks, or the computers or networks themselves, according to Department of Defense Directive 3600.1.

15 Author redacted, "IO, IO, It's Off to Work We Go," *Cryptolog: The Journal of Technical Health* (Spring 1997): 9. *Cryptolog* is an internal classified quarterly newsletter produced by and for NSA employees that includes everything from book reviews to employee profiles to technical articles about topics of interest. In 2013, the agency declassified issues published between 1974 and 1999 and released them publicly, though parts of them are still redacted. The archive is available at nsa.gov/public_info/declass/cryptologs.shtml.

16 Author redacted, "Thoughts on a Knowledge Base to Support Information Operations in the Next Millennium," *Cryptolog: The Journal of Technical Health* (Spring 1997): 32.

17 William B. Black Jr., "Thinking Out Loud About Cyberspace," *Cryptolog: The Journal of Technical Health* (Spring 1997): 4.

18 Author redacted, "IO, IO, It's Off to Work We Go."

Despite obvious interest in pursuing digital attacks, however, the legal issues continued to confound. In the spring of 1999, as NATO forces were raining bombs onto Yugoslavia, the Air Force Association convened a closed-door symposium in Texas to ponder the capabilities of what was still referred to as "information warfare." Gen. John Jumper, commander of US Air Forces in Europe, told the gathering that while information warfare conjured images of seizing an enemy's "sacred infrastructure," the military was not there yet. Cyberweapons were still largely laboratory fare, and the only information warfare being waged at that point was between the lawyers, policymakers, and military leaders in Washington who were still arguing over the value and legality of network attacks.[19] Jumper told the gathering, "I picture myself around that same targeting table where you have the fighter pilot, the bomber pilot, the special operations people and the information warriors. As you go down the target list, each one takes a turn raising his or her hand saying, 'I can take that target.' When you get to the info warrior, the info warrior says, 'I can take the target, but first I have to go back to Washington and get a [presidential] finding."[20]

Something began to change in 2000, however, when the Pentagon's network defense task force was suddenly told to add offensive operations to its mission and to develop a doctrine for their use. The change in focus also led to a name change. Instead of Joint Task Force–Computer Network Defense, they were now to be called Joint Task Force–Computer Network Operations. The change was subtle to avoid attracting attention, Sachs says, but internally it signaled the military's readiness to begin seriously planning offensive operations.

The questions the task force now had to ponder were many. Was an offensive network attack a military action or a covert operation? What

---

19 William M. Arkin, "A Mouse that Roars?" *Washington Post*, June 7, 1999.

20 In 1999, the DoD's Office of the General Counsel examined a range of existing treaties and international laws and concluded there was no international legal principle or corpus that clearly addressed the kind of cyber operations the military proposed conducting. Department of Defense Office of the General Counsel, *An Assessment of International Legal Issues in Information Operations*, published May 1999, available at au.af.mil/au/awc/awcgate/dod-io-legal/dod-lo-legal.pdf.

were the parameters for conducting such attacks? Taking out computerized communication systems seemed like an obvious mission for an offensive operation, but what about sabotaging the computer controls of a
weapons system to misdirect its aim or cause it to misfire?[21] And who
should be responsible for conducting such operations? Until then, if the
Air Force needed an enemy's radar system taken out, it worked jointly with
the NSA's electronic warfare team. But the NSA was an intelligence out-
fit whose primary job was intercepting communications. Taking out the
computers that controlled an artillery system seemed more the territory of
combat units.

With the addition of the offensive mission to the task force, Maj. Gen.
James D. Bryan became the task force's new commander. But Deputy
Defense Secretary Hamre made it clear that defense was still the group's
priority, and that offensive operations were to be mere accessories to conventional military operations, not a replacement for them.

That is, until the terrorist attacks on 9/11, which Bryan recalled,
"changed the dynamics for us." Offensive operations suddenly took on
more importance, and for the first time, the group began to approach offensive cyberattacks the way they approached kinetic ones—as a means of
taking out targets, not just exploiting computers for intelligence-gathering
purposes or to retard their performance. "We actually went out into the
combatant commands and asked them for their target list," he later recalled. "And we actually went through the drill of weighting them and
analyzing them and prioritizing them on a global scale."[22]

US offensive operations advanced further in 2003 when the Pentagon
prepared a secret "Information Operations Roadmap" aimed at turning

21 As an example of how reliant weapons systems are on software, during Operation Desert Storm
in 1991, a Patriot missile defense system installed in Dhahran, Saudi Arabia, failed to intercept
incoming Scud missiles because of a software problem in the control system that caused it to look for
incoming Scuds in the wrong place. The Scud attack killed twenty-eight US soldiers. See "Software
Problem Led to System Failure at Dhahran, Saudi Arabia," US Government Accountability Office,
February 4, 1992, available at gao.gov/products/IMTEC-92-26.
22 Bryan, "Lessons from Our Cyber Past."

information warfare into a core military competency on par with air, ground, maritime, and special operations.[23] The classified report, released with redactions a few years later, noted that a comprehensive process was already under way to evaluate the capabilities of cyberweapons and spy tools and develop a policy for their use. The latter included trying to determine what level of data or systems manipulation constituted an attack or use of force and what qualified as mere intelligence gathering. What actions could be legally undertaken in self-defense, and what level of attribution was needed before the United States could attack back? Also, could the United States use "unwitting hosts" to launch an attack—that is, transit through or control another system to attack an adversary—if the unwitting host faced retribution as a result?

In 2004, to accommodate this increased focus on offensive operations, the Defense Department split its offensive and defensive cyber operations into two divisions, a move that signaled for many the beginning of the militarization of cyberspace. The defensive division became known as Joint Task Force–Global Network Operations, while the offensive division was called the Joint Functional Component Command–Network Warfare. The latter was housed at Fort Meade, home of the NSA, but placed under the US Strategic Command and the leadership of Marine Corps Gen. James E. Cartwright. But the following year, some say, is when the "cult of offense" really began—when Gen. Keith Alexander took over as director of the NSA from Gen. Michael Hayden, and the focus on developing cyberweapons for warfare ramped up. It was during this period that Operation Olympic Games and Stuxnet were hatched.

Six years later, in May 2010, as Stuxnet was spreading wildly on computers around the world and was about to be exposed, the Pentagon recombined its defensive and offensive cyber operations under the newly formed US Cyber Command. The new division was still part of the US Strategic Command but was under the command of NSA director Alex-

---

23 "The Information Operations Roadmap," dated October 30, 2003, is a seventy-four-page report that was declassified in 2006, though the pages dealing with computer network attacks are heavily redacted. The document is available at http://information-retrieval.info/docs/DoD-IO.html.

ander, giving the spy leader unprecedented authority over both intelligence operations and cyber military ones. Three months after the US Cyber Command was formed, the Pentagon formally recognized cyberspace as the "fifth domain" of warfare after air, land, sea, and space.

This was all just formal recognition, however, of activity that had already been occurring in varying degrees for a decade. Due to the classified nature of offensive operations, however, the public has only had minor hints of these activities as they have leaked out over the years.

In the late '90s in Kosovo, for example, NATO forces may have used certain cyber techniques "to distort the images that the Serbian integrated air defense systems were generating," according to John Arquilla, who worked for US Strategic Command at the time.[24] President Clinton also reportedly approved a covert cyber operation to target the financial assets of Yugoslavian president Slobodan Milošević in European banks, though there are conflicting reports about whether the operation actually occurred.[25] In 2003, when a similar cyberattack was proposed to freeze the financial assets of Saddam Hussein, however, it was nixed by the secretary of the US Treasury out of concern that an attack like this could have cascading effects on other financial accounts in the Middle East, Europe, and the United States.[26]

In 2007, the US reportedly assisted Israel with a cyberattack that accompanied its bombing of the Al Kibar complex in Syria by providing

---

24 Arquilla *Frontline* "CyberWar!" interview. A *Washington Post* story indicates that attacks on computers controlling air-defense systems in Kosovo were launched from electronic-jamming aircraft rather than over computer networks from ground-based keyboards. Bradley Graham, "Military Grappling with Rules for Cyber," *Washington Post*, November 8, 1999.

25 James Risen, "Crisis in the Balkans: Subversion; Covert Plan Said to Take Aim at Milosevic's Hold on Power," *New York Times*, June 18, 1999. A *Washington Post* story says the plan never came to fruition. "We went through the drill of figuring out how we would do some of these cyber things if we were to do them," one senior military officer told the paper. "But we never went ahead with any." Graham, "Military Grappling with Rules for Cyber."

26 John Markoff and H. Sanker, "Halted '03 Iraq Plan Illustrates US Fear of Cyberwar Risk," *New York Times*, August 1, 2009. According to Richard Clarke, it was the secretary of treasury who vetoed it. See Richard Clarke and Robert Knake, *Cyber War: The Next Threat to National Security and What to Do About It* (New York: Ecco, 2010), 202–3. In general, nations have observed an unspoken agreement against manipulating financial systems and accounts out of concern over the destabilizing effect this could have on global markets and economies.

intelligence about potential vulnerabilities in the Syrian defense systems. As previously noted, before Israeli pilots reached the facility, they took out a Syrian radar station near the Turkish border using a combination of electronic jamming and precision bombs. But the Israelis also reportedly hacked Syria's air-defense system using on-board technology for an "air-to-ground electronic attack" and then further penetrated the system through computer-to-computer links, according to US intelligence analysts.[27] A recent report from the US Government Accountability Office describes air-to-ground attacks as useful for reaching "otherwise inaccessible networks" that can't be reached through a wired connection.[28]

In 2011, during the civilian uprising in Libya, there had also been talk of using cyberattacks to sever that country's military communications links and prevent early-warning systems from detecting the arrival of NATO warplanes. The plan was nixed, however, because there wasn't enough time to prepare the attack. The need for a longer lead time is one of the primary drawbacks of digital operations—designing an attack that won't cascade to nontargeted civilian systems requires advance reconnaissance and planning, making opportunistic attacks difficult.[29]

More recently, leaks from former NSA systems administrator Edward Snowden have provided some of the most extensive views yet of the government's shadowy cyber operations in its asymmetric war on terror. The documents describe NSA elite hacker forces at Fort Meade and at regional centers in Georgia, Texas, Colorado, and Hawaii, who provide US Cyber Command with the attack tools and techniques it needs for counterterrorism operations. But the government cyberwarriors have also worked with the FBI and CIA on digital spy operations, including assisting the CIA in tracking targets for its drone assassination campaign.

---

27 David A. Fulghum, Robert Wall, and Amy Butler, "Israel Shows Electronic Prowess," *Aviation Week,* November 25, 2007. The article is no longer available on the *Aviation Week* website but has been preserved in full at warsclerotic.wordpress.com/2010/09/28/israel-shows-electronic-prowess.
28 "Electronic Warfare: DOD Actions Needed to Strengthen Management and Oversight," published by the US Government Accountability Office, July 2012.
29 Eric Shmitt and Thom Shanker, "US Debated Cyberwarfare in Attack Plan on Libya," *New York Times,* October 17, 2011.

To track Hassan Ghul, an associate of Osama bin Laden who was killed in a drone strike in 2012, the NSA deployed "an arsenal of cyber-espionage tools" to seize control of laptops, siphon audio files, and track radio transmissions—all to determine where Ghul might "bed down" at night, according to Snowden documents obtained by the *Washington Post*.[30] And since 2001, the NSA has also penetrated a vast array of systems used by al-Qaeda associates in Yemen, Africa, and elsewhere to collect intelligence it can't otherwise obtain through bulk-data collection programs from internet companies like Google and Yahoo or from taps of undersea cables and internet nodes.

Terrorism suspects aren't the NSA's only targets, however. Operations against nation-state adversaries have exploded in recent years as well. In 2011, the NSA mounted 231 offensive cyber operations against other countries, according to the documents, three-fourths of which focused on "top-priority" targets like Iran, Russia, China, and North Korea. Under a $652-million clandestine program code named GENIE, the NSA, CIA, and special military operatives have planted covert digital bugs in tens of thousands of computers, routers, and firewalls around the world to conduct computer network exploitation, or CNE. Some are planted remotely, but others require physical access to install through so-called interdiction— the CIA or FBI intercepts shipments of hardware from manufacturers and retailers in order to plant malware in them or install doctored chips before they reach the customer. The bugs or implants operate as "sleeper cells" that can then be turned on and off remotely to initiate spying at will.[31] Most of the implants are created by the NSA's Tailored Access Operations Division (TAO) and given code names like UNITEDDRAKE and VALIDATOR. They're designed to open a back door through which NSA hackers can remotely explore the infected systems, and anything else connected to them, and install additional tools to extract vast amounts of data

---

30 Greg Miller, Julie Tate, and Barton Gellman, "Documents Reveal NSA's Extensive Involvement in Targeted Killing Program," *Washington Post*, October 16, 2013.
31 Barton Gellman and Ellen Nakashima, "U.S. Spy Agencies Mounted 231 Offensive Cyber-Operations in 2011, Documents Show," *Washington Post*, August 30, 2013.

from them. The implants are said to be planted in such a way that they can survive on systems undetected for years, lasting through software and equipment upgrades that normally would eradicate them.[32] In 2008, the NSA had 22,252 implants installed on systems around the world. By 2011, the number had ballooned to 68,975, and in 2013, the agency expected to have 85,000 implants installed, with plans to expand this to millions. But the embarrassment of riches provided by so many implants has created a problem for the NSA. With so many implants lurking on systems around the world, the spy agency has been unable in the past to take advantage of all the machines under its control. In 2011, for example, NSA spies were only able to make full use of 10 percent of the machines they had compromised, according to one Snowden document. To remedy this, the agency planned to automate the process with a new system code named TURBINE, said to be capable of managing millions of implants simultaneously.[33]

All of these operations, however—from Kosovo to Syria to Libya, and the ones exposed in the Snowden documents—have focused on stealing or distorting data or using cyber methods to help deliver physical bombs to a target. None involved a digital attack as *replacement* for a conventional bomb. This is what made Stuxnet so fundamentally different and new.

Stuxnet stands alone as the only known cyberattack to have caused

---

32 The NSA accomplishes this by installing the implant in the BIOS of machines as well as in the master boot record—core parts of the hard drive that don't get wiped when software on the computer gets upgraded or erased. See "Interactive Graphic: The NSA's Spy Catalog," *Spiegel Online*, available at spiegel.de/international/world/a-941262.html.

33 In one case, the NSA and the UK spy agency Government Communications Headquarters, or GCHQ, used a sophisticated method called Quantum Insert to hack the machines of Belgian telecom workers to gain access to the telecom's network and to a router the company used for processing the traffic of mobile phone users. The elaborate attack involved using high-speed servers the NSA had set up at key internet switching points to intercept the surfing traffic of system administrators who worked for the telecom. The spy agencies first collected extensive intelligence on the workers—their e-mail addresses, IP addresses, and possible surfing habits—then the high-speed servers watched for requests from the employees' machines for specific web pages, such as the victim's own LinkedIn profile page. When the victim tried to access the LinkedIn page, the server would intercept the request before it reached LinkedIn and would feed a fake LinkedIn page to the victim that injected malware into his machine. Once on the system administrator's machine, the spy agencies could then use his credentials to gain access to other parts of the telecom network to subvert the router.

physical destruction to a system. But there are hints that the United States has been preparing for others. In October 2012, President Obama ordered senior national security and intelligence officials to produce a list of foreign targets—"systems, processes and infrastructures"—for possible cyberattack, according to a top-secret Presidential Directive leaked by Snowden.[34] Whether the United States actually intends to attack them or just wants to have plans in place in case a situation arises is unclear. But such operations, the directive noted, could provide "unique and unconventional" opportunities "to advance US national objectives around the world with little or no warning to the adversary or target and with potential effects ranging from subtle to severely damaging."

The surge in offensive operations and the planning for them has been matched by an equal surge in the demand for skilled hackers and attack tools needed by the NSA to conduct these operations. Although most of the implants used by the NSA are designed in-house by the agency's TAO division, the NSA also budgeted $25.1 million in 2013 for "covert purchases of software vulnerabilities" from private vendors—that is, the boutique firms and large defense contractors who compose the new industrial war complex that feeds the zero-day gray market.[35] This trend in government outsourcing of offensive cyber operations is visible in the job announcements that have sprung up from defense contractors in recent years seeking, for example, Windows "attack developers" or someone skilled at "analyzing software for vulnerabilities and developing exploit code." One listing for defense contractor Northrop Grumman boldly described an "exciting and fast-paced Research and Development project" for an "Offensive Cyberspace Operation (OCO)," leaving little ambiguity about the nature of the work. Others are more subtle about their intentions, such as a listing for Booz Allen Hamilton, the contractor Snowden worked for while at the NSA, seeking a "Target Digital Network Analyst" to develop

---

34 Glenn Greenwald and Ewen MacAskill, "Obama Orders US to Draw up Overseas Target List for Cyber-Attacks," *Guardian*, June 7, 2013. The eighteen-page Presidential Policy Directive 20 was issued in October 2012, and refers to offensive cyberattacks as Offensive Cyber Effects Operations.
35 Gellman and Nakashima, "US Spy Agencies Mounted 231 Offensive Cyber-Operations."

exploits "for personal computer and mobile device operating systems, including Android, BlackBerry, iPhone and iPad." Many of the job listings
cite both CND (computer network defense) and CNA (computer network
attack) among the skills and expertise sought, underscoring the double
duty that vulnerability and exploit research can perform in both making
systems secure and attacking them.

Who are the people filling these jobs? Sometimes they're people like
Charlie Miller, the mathematician mentioned in chapter 7 who was recruited by the NSA for code and computer cracking. And sometimes
they're former hackers, wanted by law enforcement as much for breaking into US government systems as they are coveted by spy agencies for
their ability to do the same against an adversary. A shortage of highly
skilled candidates in the professional ranks who can fill the demand for
elite cyberwarriors has led the military and intelligence agencies to recruit
at hacker conferences like Def Con, where they may have to forgive a
hacker's past transgressions or lower their expectations about office attire
and body piercings to attract the choicest candidates. One code warrior
employed by a government contractor told an interviewer that he worried
that his history hacking US government systems would preclude him from
working with the feds, but the staffing company that hired him "didn't
seem to care that I had hacked our own government years ago or that I
smoked pot."[36]

He described a bit of the work he did as part of a team of five thousand
who labored out of an unmarked building in a nondescript office park in
Virginia. Workers were prohibited from bringing mobile phones or other
electronics into the building or even leaving them in their car.

As soon as he was hired, the company gave him a list of software
programs they wanted him to hack, and he quickly found basic security
holes in all of them. His group, he said, had a huge repository of zero-day

---

36 Roger A. Grimes, "In His Own Words: Confessions of a Cyber Warrior," *InfoWorld*, July 9,
2013.

vulnerabilities at their disposal—"tens of thousands of ready-to-use bugs" in software applications and operating systems for any given attack. "Literally, if you can name the software or the controller, we have ways to exploit it," he said. Patched holes didn't worry them, because for every vulnerability a vendor fixed, they had others to replace it. "We are the new army," he said. "You may not like what the army does, but you still want an army."[37]

This expansion in government bug-hunting operations highlights an important issue that got little consideration when the DoD task force was first developing its offensive doctrine a decade ago, and that even today has received little public attention and no debate at all in Congress—that is, the ethical and security issues around stockpiling zero-day vulnerabilities and exploits in the service of offensive operations. In amassing zero-day exploits for the government to use in attacks, instead of passing the information about holes to vendors to be fixed, the government has put critical-infrastructure owners and computer users in the United States at risk of attack from criminal hackers, corporate spies, and foreign intelligence agencies who no doubt will discover and use the same vulnerabilities for their own operations.

As noted previously, when researchers uncover vulnerabilities, they generally disclose them to the public or privately to the vendor in question so that patches can be distributed to computer users. But when military and intelligence agencies need a zero-day vulnerability for offensive operations, the last thing they want to do is have it patched. Instead, they keep fingers crossed that no one else will discover and disclose it before they've finished exploiting it. "If you've built a whole operational capability based on the existence of that vulnerability, man, you've just lost a system that you may have invested millions of dollars and thousands of man hours in creating," Andy Pennington, a cybersecurity consultant for K2Share said at a conference in 2011. Pennington is a former weapons-systems officer in the Air Force whose job before retiring in 1999 was to review new

---

37 Ibid.

cyberspace technologies and engineer next-generation weapons for the Air Force.[38] "You are not going to hire teams of researchers to go out and find a vulnerability and then put it on the web for everybody to see if you're trying to develop [an attack for it]," he later said in an interview.[39] "We're putting millions of dollars into identifying vulnerabilities so that we can use them and keep our tactical advantage."

But it's a government model that relies on keeping everyone vulnerable so that a targeted few can be attacked—the equivalent of withholding a vaccination from an entire population so that a select few can be infected with a virus.

Odds are that while Stuxnet was exploiting four zero-day vulnerabilities to attack systems in Iran, a hacker or nation-state cyberwarrior from another country was exploiting them too. "It's pretty naïve to believe that with a newly discovered zero-day, you are the only one in the world that's discovered it," Howard Schmidt, former cybersecurity coordinator for the White House and former executive with Microsoft, has said. "Whether it's another government, a researcher or someone else who sells exploits, you may have it by yourself for a few hours or for a few days, but you sure are not going to have it alone for long."[40]

Certainly the .LNK vulnerability that Stuxnet used was already known by the Zlob banking gang in 2008, two years before Stuxnet used it. Information about the print-spooler vulnerability was also in the public domain for others to discover and use.[41] Who knows how long the other zero days Stuxnet used might have been known and used by others in different attacks? In 2007, Immunity, a security firm in Florida, determined that the average zero-day exploit survived in the wild 348 days before being discovered on systems. The ones with the longest life-span could

38 Pennington was speaking at the Industrial Control System-Joint Working Group conference in 2011. The conference is sponsored by the Department of Homeland Security.

39 Author interview, November 2011.

40 Joseph Menn, "Special Report: US Cyberwar Strategy Stokes Fear of Blowback," Reuters, May 10, 2013, available at reuters.com/article/2013/05/10/us-usa-cyberweapons-specialreport -idUSBRE9490EL20130510.

41 See chapter 6 for previous mention of how these two vulnerabilities had already been discovered by others before Stuxnet's authors used them in their attack.

live in hiding for nearly three years.[42] Today the situation isn't much different, with the average life-span of a zero day now ten months, and others lurking in systems undiscovered for as long as two and a half years.[43]

Shortly after he took office in 2009, President Obama announced that cybersecurity in general and securing the nation's critical infrastructure in particular were top priorities for his administration. But withholding information about vulnerabilities in US systems so that they can be exploited in foreign ones creates a schism in the government that pits agencies that hoard and exploit zero days against those, like the Department of Homeland Security, that are supposed to help secure and protect US critical infrastructure and government systems.

In his remarks at the 2011 conference, Andy Pennington acknowledged that there were "competing interests" in government when it came to the vulnerability issue, but he said when the government found vulnerabilities it wanted to exploit, it used "coordinated vulnerability disclosure"—a kind of limited disclosure—to "facilitate the defense of the United States" in a way that still allowed the government to retain the ability to attack. He said the DoD worked "very closely with Microsoft on the enterprise side," as well as with the makers of control systems, to let them know about vulnerabilities found in their systems. "But I would like to stress again that the objective is to handle this . . . so that we can sustain operations," he said. To that end, you would want to be "very deliberate [in] how you disclose it and how it's fixed."[44] Though he didn't elaborate on what limited disclosure involved, others have suggested it's about providing information about vulnerabilities to DoD administrators—so they can take steps to protect military systems from being attacked—while still withholding it from the vendor and the public, to prevent adversaries from learning

---

42 Summer Lemon, "Average Zero-Day Bug Has 348-Day Lifespan, Exec Says," IDG News Service, July 9, 2007, available at computerworld.com/s/article/9026598/Average_zero_day_bug_has_348_day_lifespan_exec_says.
43 Robert Lemos, "Zero-Day Attacks Long-Lived, Presage Mass Exploitation," Dark Reading, October 18, 2012, available at darkreading.com/vulnerabilities—threats/zero-day-attacks-long-lived-presage-mass-exploitation/d/d-id/1138557. The research was conducted by Symantec.
44 Pennington, Industrial Control Systems–Joint Working Group Conference, 2011.

about them. Microsoft also reportedly gives the government and private companies advance notice when it learns of new security holes found in its software, to help the government take steps to protect its systems before a patch is available. But this can equally serve as a handy tipoff to the NSA to retire any exploits already being used to attack that vulnerability—before Microsoft discloses it publicly—or, conversely, to quickly exploit machines using the vulnerability before it gets patched.[45]

Greg Schaffer, former assistant secretary of Homeland Security, told NPR that DHS, which helps protect the government's nonmilitary systems, does occasionally get assistance "from the organizations that work on the offensive mission," though he didn't indicate if this meant sharing information with DHS about vulnerabilities so they could be patched.[46] But "whether they bring their work [to us] is something they have to decide," he said. "That is not something that we worry about."

Another DHS official, however, says he can't recall having "ever seen a vulnerability come to us from DoD in a disclosure. . . . We would like to have as many vulnerabilities disclosed and coordinated as possible to give us the best defensive posture." But while it was frustrating not to get such disclosures, he recognized that it was "the nature of the beast" if the government was to still retain its ability to attack adversaries, and he didn't see any way to resolve it.[47]

Though information about vulnerabilities might not get passed from the offensive side to the defensive side to be fixed, there were in fact times when vulnerabilities uncovered by the defensive side got passed to the offensive side. This might occur, for example, to make sure that a vulnerability in a control system already being exploited by the NSA or other agencies wasn't disclosed and patched too soon. A former DHS official said that this "vulnerabilities equities process" for control systems, as it's

45 Michael Riley, "U.S. Agencies Said to Swap Data with Thousands of Firms," Bloomberg, June 14, 2013, available at bloomberg.com/news/2013-06-14/u-s-agencies-said-to-swap-data-with-thousands-of-firms.html.
46 Tom Gjelten, "Stuxnet Raises 'Blowback' Risk in Cyberwar," *Morning Edition*, NPR, November 2, 2011, available at npr.org/2011/11/02/141908180/stuxnet-raises-blowback-risk-in-cyberwar.
47 Author interview, 2012.

called, began some time after the Aurora Generator Test was conducted in 2007. Since then, vulnerabilities that government researchers find in other control systems get vetted by an equities panel to make sure their disclosure won't harm ongoing operations. "If someone is using it . . . under their authorities for a legitimate purpose . . . well, we'd have to balance the necessity of disclosing it based on the value of leaving it open for a while," the former official said.

The equities process in government has a long tradition. In World War II, for example, when the British cracked Germany's Enigma code and discovered that Allied convoys were being targeted by the Germans, they had to weigh the benefits of redirecting convoys away from attack— and thus risk tipping off the Germans that their code had been cracked— against the cost of sacrificing a convoy to continue exploiting a critical intelligence source.

The US equities process involves a central committee composed of representatives from multiple departments and agencies—DoD, Justice Department, State Department, Homeland Security, the White House, and the intelligence community—and is patterned after one developed by the Committee on Foreign Investment in the United States, known as the CFIUS process, which weighs the national security implications of foreign investments in the United States.

In the case of software vulnerabilities, if government researchers discover a security hole in a PLC that is commonly used, for example, they submit the finding to the committee to see if anyone has an equity interest in it. "Everyone has a say in the likelihood of impacts to companies or systems [from the vulnerability being disclosed or not]," the official said. "It's all done via e-mail on a classified network, and everyone comes back and says yea or nay. And if there's a yea, then we discuss it. If everything is nay, then we just go on our normal responsible vulnerability disclosure process."

Asked if DHS ever passed information about vulnerabilities to the offensive side so that they could specifically be exploited, he said no. But he acknowledged that the very act of discussing vulnerabilities with the equities committee might inadvertently provide members with ideas about new vulnerabilities to exploit. While he says he never heard anyone on the committee tell an industrial control system representative not to publicly disclose a vulnerability so they could exploit it, he acknowledged that they probably wouldn't be so overt about it. "They would probably just silently take notes, and we may never ever know [if they developed an exploit for] it," he said.

CHAPTER 13

DIGITAL WARHEADS

Liam O'Murchu was growing tired and bored. He'd been sitting at his desk for two hours diligently plugging virtual hardware components, piece after piece, into a Step 7 emulator, making a last-ditch effort to identify what Stuxnet was attacking, but he was having no luck.

It was early October, weeks after Ralph Langner had identified Stuxnet as a precision weapon aimed at a single target, and both teams—in Hamburg and California—were now working independently, without the other knowing it, to identify the digital weapon's target.

One of the things the Symantec researchers discovered was that right before Stuxnet unleashed its destructive payload on a 315 PLC, it searched the PLC for three "magic values"—combinations of numbers and letters embedded in the data blocks of the PLC itself. When Stuxnet encountered a 315 PLC, it rifled through these blocks in search of the magic values 2C CB 00 01, 7050h, and 9500h—and knew it had reached its target when it found all three.

Eric Chien had done a Google search on the values but found nothing that made sense in the context of Stuxnet. The researchers suspected the first one was some kind of part or serial number for a hardware component that got plugged into the PLC, so O'Murchu had set up a simulated Step 7

PLC environment to try to determine its identity. The Step 7 system included an emulator feature for building a virtual PLC network to test different hardware configurations before building the real network in a plant. The emulator featured a long list of hardware components that engineers could virtually plug into the configuration one at a time simply by clicking on a name from the menu. Each time an engineer selected an item from the list, an ID number for the component popped up on the screen. O'Murchu was hoping the mysterious 2C CB 00 01 was among them. But for two hours he'd been systematically plugging in one device after another and still hadn't found a match after trying more than a hundred components. It was beginning to feel like an exercise in futility, until, that is, he reached a cluster of Profibus and Profinet cards on the list—devices that transmitted data between PLCs and the components they controlled. O'Murchu clicked on a Profibus CP 342-5 card and, just like that, the value popped up.

The Profibus card was just one half of the puzzle, however. He still didn't know what devices the PLC controlled. Encouraged by this bit of success, however, he quickly plugged in the rest of the components on the list, but neither of the other magic values appeared. It didn't matter. They'd made a big leap with this new finding anyway. They now knew that Stuxnet was looking for a system with six of these network cards attached, and they knew it was only a matter of time before they solved the rest of the configuration mystery.

THREE MONTHS INTO the discovery of Stuxnet, the rest of the world now knew about the mysterious code that had evidently targeted Iran. Yet speculation that it had specifically targeted the uranium enrichment program at Natanz remained just that—speculation. Symantec's engineers were about to find the proof they needed in the code. But first, they needed a crash course in PLCs.

Discovering that Stuxnet was sabotaging the Siemens PLCs had certainly been a big breakthrough for Falliere and his colleagues. But Langner had been right that they had hit a wall in their research and were stymied by the PLCs. "We quickly knew that we knew nothing," Chien says.[1]

If that weren't enough, in discovering that Stuxnet was injecting malicious code into the PLCs, Falliere had also discovered that Stuxnet didn't have just one payload, but *two*. Stuxnet sent out dual warheads to attack the PLCs, like special ops commandos. One targeted the Siemens S7-315 PLC; the other homed in on the S7-417.

Just a few kilobytes of malicious code got injected into each PLC, but cracking that code was the key to solving Stuxnet's biggest puzzle. There was just one problem. The code was written in a format and language that Falliere didn't understand. Stuxnet's missile portion was written in C and C++ and compiled into Intel x86 assembly—the most common and widely known computer assembly language. But the digital warheads used an obscure programming language, unique to the Siemens PLCs, called STL.[2] To program Siemens PLCs, engineers wrote their commands in STL, then converted them into MC7, an assembly language, before compiling that into binary that the PLCs could read. All of this meant that even if Falliere succeeded in reversing the ones and zeros of the binary back to STL, he still would have no idea what it said. It was a bit like unscrambling the coded message of the CIA's famous *Kryptos* sculpture only to find that the unencrypted message was written in Greek. In Symantec's August 17 announcement, they had put out a call for anyone with knowledge of PLCs and STL to contact them, but they got no response.

They wouldn't have needed to seek help from the public if Siemens had been able to assist them, but unfortunately that turned out not to be the case. Chien contacted the company early in their analysis and throughout the months that they worked on Stuxnet. But whenever he sent the German firm questions about how the Step 7 system worked, Siemens took days or weeks to respond. Usually by then the Symantec researchers had

---

1 This and all quotes from Chien are from author interviews in 2010 and 2011.
2 "STL" stands for Statement List programming language.

discovered the answer on their own and had prepared a new set of questions for Siemens to answer.[3]

There was also another group of people who could have helped them out. Langner and his team excelled in the very areas that confounded Symantec. It would have been the perfect marriage of skills—Symantec with its expertise in Windows systems and reverse-engineering malicious code, and Langner's team with their extensive knowledge of the Siemens software and PLCs. But any hopes of collaboration were quickly dashed after a brief e-mail exchange between the two groups, followed by a couple of blog posts, led to misunderstandings and bad feelings on both sides. It was a communication lapse that might have been easily resolved with a quick phone call, but neither side was motivated to make it.

In the absence of any help, the Symantec researchers did the only thing they could do—they bought a handful of books about STL online and proceeded to teach themselves how the code worked. The best way to reverse-engineer STL code, they reasoned, was to learn how to write it.

Each day on the Métro during his morning and evening commutes, Falliere pored over the books trying to make sense of the code. He made little progress for days until he discovered an open-source tool online that someone had created to program Siemens PLCs as a freeware alternative to

---

3 Chien had no idea why Siemens wasn't more responsive. It was possible the company didn't consider the issue an urgent one, since only about a dozen Siemens customers reported being infected by Stuxnet. It was also possible Siemens wasn't used to dealing with in-depth questions about its software. The Symantec researchers weren't asking questions that could be answered easily by product reps; they were fundamental engineering questions about how the Siemens code worked. This required the company to track down programmers who'd worked on the Step 7 system. But it's also possible that Siemens was relatively quiet on Stuxnet because the company didn't want to stir up discussions about its business in Iran. The company had recently found itself in hot water after a shipment of its controllers was seized in Dubai on its way to Iran for the uranium enrichment program. Another shipment of Siemens turbo processors was intercepted in Hamburg by export authorities as it was on its way to Iran. Both of these shipments violated European Union export controls prohibiting the sale of dual-use equipment to Iran without a permit. Siemens claimed it didn't know the shipments were headed to Iran, but the incidents eventually forced the company's CEO to announce in January 2010 that Siemens would not initiate any new business with Iran after mid-2010. When Stuxnet was discovered in Iran a few months later, Siemens's relative silence about the code may have been in part an effort to not stir up a discussion about how its controllers got to be at the uranium enrichment plant in the first place. There were Siemens workers who urged the company to take a more active role in examining Stuxnet, but they were silenced. Siemens in effect wanted the issue to go away and had hoped that Symantec and other researchers would give up.

the Step 7 software. Falliere studied the tool to see how STL code looked when it was compiled into MC7 and then used this as a road map to take Stuxnet's MC7 code in reverse.

It took weeks of picking through the code to get it all reversed, and, when he finally did, the few kilobytes of binary that Stuxnet injected into the PLCs had ballooned into more than 4,000 lines of instructions for the 315 attack and more than 13,000 lines for the 417 attack. It was too large and unwieldy for Falliere to read in this format, not to mention too complicated for him to follow. So he decided to translate it into something resembling C code to give himself fewer and simpler commands to read. All of this only provided him with a static reading of the code, however; without a PLC, he still couldn't see the attack in action. So he wrote a small program to simulate a PLC on his Windows machine and unleashed the code on that. Between this and a static reading of the reversed code, he was finally able to piece the attack together.

One of the first things that struck him about the attack was that it unfolded in six stages that repeated over weeks and months. Once the attack was done, it recycled itself and began again. This meant that rather than launching a single blow that caused catastrophic failure, as the researchers originally believed Stuxnet was designed to do, the attackers were going for subtle sabotage that extended over time. This, combined with the man-in-the-middle attack that concealed the sabotage from operators as it occurred, would have made it hard for anyone to detect and pinpoint the source of problems. The attackers, Falliere realized, had expected to go undetected for months, and indeed they had.

The first part of the attack, a reconnaissance stage, lasted about thirteen days, during which Stuxnet sat silently on the PLC recording normal operations in order to loop that data back to operators when the sabotage began. Stuxnet recorded data at least once a minute and only progressed to the next stage after recording data at least 1.1 million times.

Once enough data was recorded, a two-hour countdown commenced. Then when the count reached zero, the sabotage began. It lasted just fifteen minutes, however, and once it was done, normal operations on the

PLC and the devices it controlled resumed. Then, after a five-hour interval passed, the entire sequence began again, with Stuxnet this time waiting about twenty-six days to strike, and recording twice the amount of data it recorded the first time. And when the sabotage kicked in this time, it lasted fifty minutes instead of fifteen. As before, once the sabotage was done, operations returned to normal for another twenty-six days, and the whole cycle repeated again. Each time the sabotage occurred thereafter, it alternated between fifteen minutes and fifty minutes in length, though the reconnaissance stage remained twenty-six days.

Falliere had no idea why the length of the sabotage changed or what the difference was between the two sequences. Without knowing what devices were being attacked, he had no way of knowing the nature of the assault. It was a bit like watching tracer bullets fly through the night sky without having any idea what they would hit.

THE FINAL BREAK in the Stuxnet puzzle came in early November when a Dutch programmer named Rob Hulsebos, an expert on the Profibus protocol, sent Chien an e-mail. He was responding—albeit belatedly—to a second call for help the Symantec researchers had posted on their blog, asking anyone with knowledge of Profibus cards and critical infrastructure to contact them. Hulsebos's e-mail contained just two paragraphs, most of it information about Profibus that Chien already knew, but one sentence stood out. Hulsebos wrote that every peripheral device connected to a Profibus network card had a unique ID assigned to it by Profibus. Each ID was about 2 bytes in size, or 16 bits, Hulsebos wrote.

Chien recalled that the two mystery values they were trying to crack— 7050h and 9500h—were exactly 16 bits each.

He walked over to O'Murchu's cubicle and showed him the e-mail on his BlackBerry. As Chien watched anxiously over his shoulder, O'Murchu did a Google search on Profibus device IDs and got a series of links for product brochures. Chien pointed to one, a PDF listing devices commonly used with Profibus network cards. O'Murchu opened the file, and alongside the name of each device on the list was the unique Profibus ID the e-mail had described. O'Murchu scrolled down the list until he reached the bottom, and there it was—one of the magic values that they (and Stuxnet) were seeking—9500h. According to the manual, the ID corresponded to a brand of frequency converter made by a company in Finland. Chien dug around on the site for information about the other ID but couldn't find anything. So he wrote an e-mail to Profibus asking the company to identify the 7050h. He didn't expect a response and was surprised when he got a reply indicating it was a frequency converter made by a company in Iran.

Frequency converters are power supplies that control the electric current fed to motors and rotors to modulate their speed. Increase the frequency of the drive and the speed of the motor increases. The 9500h ID was for a frequency converter made by a company named Vacon in Finland; the 7050h ID was an unspecified model of converter made by a company named Fararo Paya in Iran. O'Murchu suspected the Fararo Paya converters were an Iranian knock-off of the Finnish one.[4] If this was the case, there was likely no other facility outside of Iran that used the converters from Fararo Paya.

They downloaded everything they could find about frequency converters, including a dozen manuals for various brands. None of them were manuals for the Vacon and Fararo Paya converters, but some of them listed commands for controlling the converters that were identical across different brands of devices. One of the STL commands Falliere had pulled from the Stuxnet code was "47F and 1," and sure enough, when they looked in one of the manuals they found these words: "To start the frequency converter, send down the word 47F and set the value to 1." O'Murchu's fingers hovered above the keyboard as he read the line aloud. He couldn't believe it. For four months they'd been struggling to solve the mystery of what Stuxnet was attacking, working nights and weekends to understand

---

4 Because Iran had been the victim of sabotage in 2006 when parts purchased from Turkey for its nuclear program were reportedly sabotaged (see page 200), Iranian officials may have decided they needed to manufacture their own frequency converters to avoid saboteurs who were targeting the supply chain and manipulating ones they bought abroad.

what it was doing, and now with a couple of simple Google searches they had found their answer. It was as exhilarating and gratifying as it was anticlimactic.

It was the end of the day and the two of them were exhausted, so they sent a quick e-mail to Falliere letting him know what they'd found, along with a few of the PDF manuals showing the commands. "Take a look at these and see if you find anything in here that works," Chien told Falliere.

When Falliere awoke that morning and saw the e-mail, he raced to the office. He pulled out a list of all the configuration data and commands he'd extracted from Stuxnet and sifted through them side-by-side with the manuals. It didn't take long before he found matches for all of them. He'd already suspected that Stuxnet might be changing the frequency of something on the other end of the PLC—the attack code contained numbers like 10640, which he suspected was 1,064 Hz expressed in deciHertz. Now the new information confirmed it.

He used the manuals to translate all of Stuxnet's commands and within an hour or two had a complete blueprint of the attack, which he sent to O'Murchu and Chien.

Before Stuxnet began its assault on the S7-315 PLC, it made sure the system was using frequency converters made by Vacon and Fararo Paya, and that the converters were operating at a frequency somewhere between 807 Hz and 1,210 Hz. Stuxnet was looking for a plant that had up to 186 of the converters installed, all of them operating above 800 Hz. Frequency converters were used in a number of varied applications, but converters that operated at 600 Hz or higher had limited use—so limited, in fact, that when Chien did a search online he discovered they were regulated for export in the United States by the Nuclear Regulatory Commission. There could be no doubt about it now. Stuxnet was targeting a nuclear facility. Langner had gone out on a limb asserting that Stuxnet was targeting Iran's nuclear program, but now they had evidence in the code to back it up.

Chien was stunned by how beautifully everything now fell into place.

They had struggled for months to decipher the code, achieving their progress in increments of inches rather than miles, worried that they would never reach the end of the road. Now in hindsight, it all seemed so elegant and complete. With the final details resolved, Falliere laid out a step-by-step description of the attack from start to finish.

Once Stuxnet found a Step 7 machine, it unpacked its Step 7 .DLL doppelgänger and kidnapped the Siemens .DLL to take its place. Then it waited patiently for a programmer to launch the Step 7 program to read or create code blocks for an S7-315 PLC. Stuxnet then injected its malicious code into the blocks and waited until the programmer connected his laptop to a PLC or copied the commands to a USB flash drive to transfer them to a PLC. It could take days or weeks for the malicious commands to land on a PLC, but once they did, the attack unfolded without resistance.

After the initial reconnaissance stage recording data for thirteen days, Stuxnet first increased the frequency of the converters to 1,410 Hz for fifteen minutes, then reduced it to 1,064 Hz, presumably the normal operating frequency, for about twenty-six days. Once Stuxnet recorded all of the data it needed to record during these three weeks, it dropped the frequency drastically to 2 Hz for fifty minutes, before restoring it to 1,064 Hz again. After another twenty-six days, the attack began again. Each time the sabotage commenced, the man-in-the-middle attack fed false frequency readings back to the operators and safety system to keep them blind to what was happening.

SYMANTEC AT LAST knew exactly what Stuxnet was doing to the S7-315 PLC. But the attack targeting the S7-417 PLC remained a mystery. The two digital weapons arrived with the same missile but operated completely independent of each other.

The S7-417 was Siemens's high-end PLC, which came with 30 megabytes of RAM and a price tag of more than $10,000 compared to about $500 for the S7-315. As if to match its higher status, the attack targeting this PLC was also much larger, with many more blocks of code—40 blocks of code compared to 15 blocks for the 315 attack—some of which got generated on the fly based on conditions Stuxnet found on the system it was attacking.

The 417 attack code was also far more complex, both in terms of the steps that got executed and the conditions under which the attack was unleashed. In addition, it had bizarre constructs that made it a huge pain to reverse-engineer. There were pointers leading to pointers leading to pointers, which made it difficult to follow the sequence of events in the code. The difference in structure between the two attacks made it appear as if the codes had been created by completely different teams using different tools.

The attackers had obviously put a lot of thought and effort into the 417 code, so Falliere was perplexed when he discovered that it didn't work—that in fact the attackers had intentionally disabled it. In part of the code responsible for fingerprinting the 417 PLC to see if its configuration matched the target configuration Stuxnet was seeking, the attackers had inserted an exception—a programming trick that involved introducing an intentional error into the code to abort a mission before it began. What's more, there was no sign the attack had ever been active. Stuxnet needed to generate a crucial block of code on the fly to make the attack work, but the code that was supposed to create that block was incomplete.

It wasn't clear if the attackers had disabled the code because it was still a work in progress or if it had been completed at one point and later disabled for a different reason. Falliere recalled the recent news story quoting an Iranian official saying that *five* versions of Stuxnet were found in Iran.[5] Symantec and other researchers had seen only three versions of Stuxnet so far. But was there, perhaps, another version of Stuxnet in the wild that contained a complete version of the 417 attack?

Based on clues Falliere and his colleagues had found in the three versions of Stuxnet discovered so far, it seemed there might in fact be another version out in the wild. The version numbers of the three variants, for example, were out of sequence. The attackers themselves had numbered

---

5 See page 183.

them—the June 2009 variant was version 1.001, while the March and April 2010 variants were 1.100 and 1.101. Gaps in the numbers suggested that other variants had at least been developed—including a 1.00 version that pre-dated all three of the ones already identified—even if they were never released in the wild.

Whatever the 417 code was attacking, it was different from the 315 attack. Unlike the 315 attack, the 417 code targeted a system that consisted of 984 devices configured into six groups of 164. And during the attack, only 110 of the 164 devices in each group got sabotaged. Unfortunately, the 417 code contained no magic values to help the Symantec team identify what it attacked—like the ones that helped identify the frequency converters. Langner and his team, who analyzed the 417 code at the same time Symantec did, surmised that the 417 code might be targeting the cascade itself, not the individual centrifuges, perhaps the pipes and valves that controlled the flow of gas in and out of the cascades. But without more details in the code to offer definitive proof, neither Langner nor Symantec could say for sure what the 417 attack was doing. After months of work and extensive progress in other regards, they all had to resign themselves to the fact that they had reached another dead end—it seemed that Stuxnet was determined to hold on to at least one of its mysteries.

In the absence of a clear understanding of the 417 attack code, the Symantec researchers decided to publish what they *did* know—which were the final details of the 315 assault.

So on November 12, 2010, exactly four months after VirusBlokAda had first announced its discovery of the Stuxnet code, Symantec published a blog post announcing that Stuxnet was attacking a very unique configuration of specific frequency converters. "Stuxnet's requirement for particular frequency converter drives and operating characteristics focuses the number of possible speculated targets to a limited set of possibilities," Chien wrote in the Symantec team's typically cryptic and cautious style.[6]

---

6 Eric Chien, "Stuxnet: A Breakthrough," Symantec blog, November 12, 2010, available at symantec.com/connect/blogs/stuxnet-breakthrough.

He never mentioned the Iranian nuclear program by name, or even centrifuges, but the message behind his words was clear.

Four days after Symantec published its post, technicians at Natanz brought all of the spinning centrifuges at the plant to a complete halt. For six days, until November 22, all enrichment activity at the facility stopped. Iranian officials offered no explanation for the sudden freeze, but the Symantec researchers suspected administrators at the plant were tearing apart the computers for any lingering traces of Stuxnet. Although information about the worm had been in the public domain for months, the revelations until now hadn't been specific about what devices Stuxnet attacked or how it conducted its operation, and Stuxnet had been meticulously crafted to make it hard for anyone to find its malicious code on the PLCs or to trace the sabotage to its source. Symantec's latest report, however, provided all the evidence operators needed to connect the problems they were having at Natanz to the digital weapon. Although antivirus firms had long ago released signatures to detect Stuxnet's files, they could only detect the ones on Windows machines—not the rogue code that Stuxnet injected into the PLCs. And since Stuxnet was like an octopus with many tentacles to help it spread, technicians at Natanz would have had to wipe and restore every machine at the plant to completely disinfect the stubborn code from their systems.

It was clear now that Stuxnet's days were finally over. Not only would it no longer be able to mess with the centrifuges at Natanz, but any future problems with systems at the plant would immediately spark suspicion that malicious code was the cause. It would be much more difficult to pull off a similar stealth attack in the future without scrutiny quickly focusing on the control systems.

With nearly all the mysteries of Stuxnet now resolved, the Symantec researchers focused on tidying up some loose ends and finalizing their lengthy dossier about the code before turning their attention to other things.

But a week after the halted centrifuges at Natanz resumed their operation, the story of Stuxnet took a darker and more sinister turn, suggesting that efforts to thwart the enrichment program weren't yet done. If the use of malicious code was no longer a viable option, other means to halt the program were still at the attackers' disposal.

THE RUSH-HOUR TRAFFIC on Artesh Boulevard in northern Tehran was particularly congested the morning of November 29, 2010, when Majid Shahriari, a slim forty-year-old professor of nuclear physics maneuvered his Peugeot sedan through the bumper-to-bumper gridlock on his way to work. It was only seven forty-five on that Monday morning, but a layer of smog already hovered in the air as Shahriari inched his way toward Shahid Beheshti University, where he was a lecturer. With him in the car were his wife, also a nuclear physics professor and mother of two, and a bodyguard.

As the sedan approached a busy intersection, assailants on a motorcycle suddenly pulled alongside Shahriari's vehicle and brazenly slapped a "sticky" bomb to the driver's-side door. Seconds after they zipped away, the bomb exploded, shattering the car's rear window and leaving the driver's-side door a twisted mess of molten metal. Shahriari was instantly killed; his wife and bodyguard were injured, though spared. A small pit in the asphalt next to the car testified to the force of the blast.[7]

Not long after, in another part of the city, Fereydoon Abbasi, a fifty-two-year-old expert in nuclear isotope separation, was also making his way through traffic toward the same destination, when, out of the corner of his eye, he spotted a motorcycle approaching. A second later he heard the distinctive sound of something being attached to his door. Abbasi was a member of Iran's Revolutionary Guard, so his defensive instincts were more honed than Shahriari's. He quickly leapt from the car and pulled his wife from her seat. Although the two were injured when the bomb exploded, both of them survived the attack.

---

7 "Iranian Nuclear Scientist Killed in Motorbike Attack," BBC, November 29, 2010, available at bbc.co.uk/news/world-middle-east-11860928.

News reports indicated the two scientists were targeted for their prominent roles in Iran's nuclear program. "They're bad people," an unnamed US official said afterward, "and the work they do is exactly what you need to design a bomb."[8]

Shahriari was an expert in neutron transport—essential to creating nuclear chain reactions for reactors and bombs—and Western news reports claimed that only political appointees ranked higher than Shahriari in Iran's nuclear program. Iran's nuclear chief, Ali Akbar Salehi, told reporters that he had been working on a "major project" for Iran's Atomic Energy Organization (AEOI), but didn't elaborate.[9]

Abbasi was even more important to the program. He was one of only a few specialists in Iran who had expertise in separating uranium isotopes, a core part of the uranium enrichment process. He was also on the UN Security Council's sanctions list for his role as a senior scientific adviser to Iran's Ministry of Defense and for his close working relationship with Mohsen Fakhrizadeh-Mahabadi, an officer in the Iranian Revolutionary Guard. If Iran did indeed have a nuclear weapons program, Fakhrizadeh-Mahabadi was believed to be its architect.

President Ahmadinejad wasted no time laying blame for the attacks on "the Zionist regime and Western governments."[10] Saeed Jalili, general secretary of Iran's Supreme National Security Council, called the attacks an act of desperation by powerless enemies.[11] "When the enemy sees no other option, he resorts to the methods of terror," he said. "This is not a sign of strength, but of weakness."[12] After his recovery, Abbasi was appointed head of the AEOI, as if to assert Iran's determination to achieve

---

8 William Yong and Robert F. Worth, "Bombings Hit Atomic Experts in Iran Streets," *New York Times*, November 29, 2010.

9 Ibid.

10 Ibid.

11 Dieter Bednarz and Ronen Bergman, "Israel's Shadowy War on Iran: Mossad Zeros in on Tehran's Nuclear Program," *Spiegel Online*, January 17, 2011, available at spiegel.de/international/world/israel-s-shadowy-war-on-iran-mossad-zeros-in-on-tehran-s-nuclear-program-a-739883.html.

12 "Iran's Chief Nuclear Negotiator: 'We Have to Be Constantly on Guard,' *Der Spiegel*, January 18, 2011.

its nuclear goals despite enemy plots against it. Abbasi was said to keep a photo of Shahriari in his office to remind him of that resolve.[13]

But the two attacks on busy streets in broad daylight had their desired effect and sent a message to anyone involved in Iran's nuclear program that no one was safe or beyond the reach of assassins. Other Iranian scientists reportedly called in sick to work for several days after the bombings to avoid the fate of their colleagues.[14]

In response to the accusations from Ahmadinejad, the US State Department offered only a brief statement. "All I can say is we decry acts of terrorism wherever they occur and beyond that, we do not have any information on what happened," spokesman Philip J. Crowley said.[15] Israel declined to respond, at least directly. Instead, on the day of the attacks, Israeli prime minister Benjamin Netanyahu announced the retirement of Mossad chief Meir Dagan after eight years of service as the spy agency's leader. The timing of the announcement seemed to suggest that the attacks on the scientists and on the centrifuges at Natanz were part of Da-

---

13 Shahriari and Abassi were not the first Iranian scientists targeted. In 2007, Ardeshire Hassanpour, a nuclear physicist working at the uranium conversion plant at Esfahan died under mysterious circumstances, though his death was reported as an industrial accident. Then, ten months before Shahriari's death, a colleague of his, Massoud Alimohammadi, was killed in a car bombing attack. Iran accused the Mossad of masterminding the attack on Alimohammadi, but questions arose later when news reports revealed he was not a nuclear scientist at all but a quantum field theorist. In December that year, a twenty-six-year-old kickboxer named Majid Jamali Fashi was arrested for the crime and later told a bizarre story on Iranian TV of having been recruited and trained by the Mossad, after visiting Turkey in 2007. He said he was paid $30,000 up front for the assassination and promised $20,000 more after the attack. Iranian news agencies reported that Fashi was executed by hanging in May 2012. In a 2014 interview, Alimohammadi's widow said that her husband had indeed been secretly working on Iran's nuclear program. See Scott Peterson, "Covert War Against Iran's Nuclear Scientists: A Widow Remembers," *Christian Science Monitor*, July 17, 2014.

14 As a further intimidation tactic, an Iranian official revealed in a 2014 interview that the Mossad had once ordered a bouquet of flowers to be sent from an Iranian florist to the family of an Iranian nuclear engineer with a card expressing condolences over his death. The engineer was still alive and well, however. The spy agency, he said, also created videos of fake Iranian news broadcasts showing the images of murdered Iranian scientists and sent the videos to the still-living scientists as a warning. See "How West Infiltrated Iran's Nuclear Program, Ex-Top Nuclear Official Explains," *Iran's View*, March 28, 2014, www.iransview.com/west-infiltrated-irans-nuclear-program-ex-top -nuclear-official-explains/1451.

15 Yong and Worth, "Bombings Hit Atomic Experts in Iran Streets."

gan's swan song. Dagan was known to favor assassination as a political weapon.[16] Upon his appointment as head of Mossad in 2002, then–Prime Minister Ariel Sharon crudely praised him for his skill at separating Arabs from their heads.

The day of the assaults on the scientists, President Ahmadinejad seemed to tie the attacks to Stuxnet and provide what appeared to be the first official confirmation that the digital weapon had struck Natanz. As he condemned Israel and the West for the bombing attacks, he also blamed them for a virus attack that he said had been unleashed on Iran's nuclear program a year earlier. The virus had been embedded in software "installed in electronic parts," he said, and had damaged some of Iran's centrifuges. But he downplayed the effects of the attack, saying the worm had created problems for only "a limited number of our centrifuges," before workers discovered and immobilized it.[17] Though he didn't identify the digital attack by name or the facility where the centrifuges were damaged, it seemed clear to everyone that he was referring to Stuxnet and Natanz.

When news of the attacks on the scientists reached Ralph Langner in Germany, his stomach dropped. He wondered if his team's work exposing Stuxnet had pushed the attackers to take even more drastic measures than he'd expected them to take once their digital attack was exposed. It underscored for him the reality that their work on Stuxnet had placed them in the midst of a very dark and bloody business.

Symantec's researchers were no less shaken by the news. During the months they had worked on Stuxnet, black humor and paranoia had hung in the air, a by-product of the uncertainty about who was behind the attack or what they were capable of doing. O'Murchu began hearing strange clicking sounds on his phone, making him think it was tapped, and one Friday afternoon as he left the office to go home, he joked to Chien and Falliere that if he turned up dead over the weekend, he wanted them to know in advance that he wasn't suicidal. Chien for his part had begun

---

16 Dagan was reportedly pushed out by Prime Minister Netanyahu and Defense Minister Ehud Barak because he opposed an air strike against Iran.
17 Yong and Worth, "Bombings Hit Atomic Experts in Iran Streets."

glancing around his neighborhood each morning when he left the house to see if anyone was watching him. He never seriously believed he was in danger, though, and the day that news of the attacks on the scientists broke, he joked to O'Murchu that if motorcyclists ever approached his car, he'd take out the driver with a quick swerve of his wheels. But when he drove away from work that day and stopped at the first traffic light, he was momentarily startled when he saw a motorcyclist pull up behind in his rearview mirror.

None of them really thought assassins would target them for their work on Stuxnet, but it was clear that the dynamics of virus hunting had changed with Stuxnet, and that going forward companies like theirs would be forced to make new risk calculations about the information they exposed.

At various points in their work on Stuxnet, they had indeed debated at times whether to withhold information they uncovered or to release it anonymously. In the end, although they did withhold some of the details they found—such as the identity of Stuxnet's five initial victims—they decided in favor of disclosure, believing that the more information they released, the better it would be for everyone to defend against Stuxnet and any copycat attacks. There was just one thing, they concluded, that would have merited censorship, and that was the identity of the attackers. But in the end this was a moot point, since they never did uncover definitive proof of who was behind the attack.

In fact, they also never found incontrovertible proof that Stuxnet targeted Natanz. Although the information about the frequency converters added a major piece to the Stuxnet puzzle, they found no evidence that the specific configuration Stuxnet targeted existed at Natanz. It took David Albright and his colleagues at the Institute for Science and International Security to provide the last bit of evidence.

SYMANTEC PUBLISHED ITS last report on the frequency converters in mid-November, but it wasn't until two weeks later that Albright made the final connection. It happened one day in December when he was sitting in a meeting with his staff at ISIS, along with a handful of centrifuge experts they had invited to their office to discuss Iran's nuclear program, and the group began puzzling over a mystery that had been bothering them for more than a year.

ISIS had published the satellite images of Natanz back in 2002 to pressure Iran into letting UN inspectors examine the enrichment plant, and Albright and his staff had been following Iran's nuclear progress ever since, sometimes gleaning information from government sources but mostly gathering it from the quarterly reports the IAEA published about its inspections. The latter reports were the only inside view that most Iran-watchers had of Natanz.

For eighteen months, Albright and his staff had been scratching their heads over fluctuating numbers that appeared in the reports. Every three months, the inspectors listed the number of centrifuges and cascades the Iranians had installed at Natanz, as well as the number of centrifuges that were actually enriching gas, as opposed to the ones that were just sitting in cascades empty. They also reported the amount of gas Iranian technicians fed into the centrifuges and the amount of enriched gas the centrifuges produced from this.

For most of 2007 and 2008 all of these numbers had risen fairly steadily with occasional glitches. But in mid- to late 2009, the numbers began to noticeably change. The amount of enriched gas being produced by the centrifuges suddenly dropped, and centrifuges that were once spinning in eleven out of eighteen cascades in one of the rooms at Natanz were eventually disconnected. There was no indication in the reports about why this occurred, though it was clear that something was wrong.

Albright and his colleagues had puzzled over the changes for many months, considering the data from various angles: perhaps the problems were due to poorly manufactured components or inferior materials, or perhaps the technicians had simply installed the pipes and valves in the cascades incorrectly, causing gas to leak out of them. None of the explanations, however, seemed to account for all of the changes they had seen in the reports. Now in December 2010 as they sat with their guests discussing the anomalies, someone mentioned Stuxnet and Symantec's recent report about the frequency converters. Albright hadn't read the report, but knew that Iran used frequency converters made by Vacon, the Finnish company mentioned by Symantec, and that it had also purchased converters in the past from Turkey and Germany. But he had never heard of Fararo Paya converters before. This was significant: he and his staff closely followed Iran's procurement and manufacturing activities for the nuclear program and weren't aware that Iran was making its own converters. If Iran was using such converters at Natanz, then the attackers had knowledge of the enrichment program that even some of its closest watchers didn't possess.

When the meeting was over and he went back to his desk, Albright pulled up the report from Symantec to examine it carefully. He also found a report that Langner had written about the disabled 417 attack code. He spent the next couple of weeks sifting through the technical details of the attacks and even contacted Chien for explanations about some of the things he didn't understand. As he and Chien were talking one day, something struck him that he hadn't noticed before. Each time Stuxnet completed a round of sabotage on the frequency converters, it reset their frequency to 1,064 Hz. The number leapt out at him. Albright knew that centrifuge motors had different optimal frequencies for operating, depending on the model of the centrifuge and the materials from which it was made. And the optimal frequency for the IR-1 centrifuges at Natanz was exactly 1,064 Hz.

What's more, the 1,064 Hz frequency was very specific to IR-1 centrifuges. No other centrifuge had this nominal frequency, and there was no country outside of Iran that used them. (Although the IR-1s were based on the P-1 centrifuge design that Pakistan had used during the early years of its enrichment program, Pakistan had since moved on to more advanced designs, which operated at different frequencies.)

The optimal frequency for the IR-1s wasn't widely known, however. Albright knew it only because a government source had told him in 2008. But even though the optimal frequency was 1,064 Hz, the source told him that Iran actually operated its centrifuges at a slightly lower frequency, which Albright and his staff learned was 1,007 Hz, due to their tendency to break at higher speeds. Albright thought about the discrepancy for a minute. Either the Stuxnet attackers weren't aware that Iran had made this change, or Iran had reduced the frequency of its centrifuges some time after the attackers had already written their code.

But this wasn't the only detail that stood out to Albright. He also noticed that when Stuxnet conducted its attack, it increased the frequency of the converters to 1,410 Hz for fifteen minutes, which was nearly the maximum frequency an IR-1 rotor could withstand before it would begin to break from stress.

Then he looked at what Symantec and Langner had written about the 417 attack code. Although what they knew about the attack was still pretty sketchy, they knew it targeted devices that were configured into six arrays of 164 devices each. Centrifuges at Natanz, Albright knew, were installed 164 to a cascade, suggesting the 417 attack had targeted six cascades containing 984 centrifuges.

Chien also told Albright that instead of changing frequencies like the 315 attack, the 417 attack sequence appeared to simply be turning devices on or off. Albright and his colleagues ran down the list of components in a uranium enrichment plant that might fit this scenario, and the only one that made sense to them was valves.

Centrifuges at Natanz each had three valves that controlled the movement of gas in and out of them, plus auxiliary valves that controlled the movement of gas in and out of the cascade and between rows of centrifuges in a cascade. Albright and his staff ran through various scenarios to determine what would happen if certain valves were opened or closed with malicious intent for extended periods of time, and in each scenario the outcome was likely damaged or destroyed centrifuges.

It was clear to Albright that they had finally found the answer to the puzzling numbers they had seen in the IAEA reports. In statements made to the press, Ahmadinejad had insisted that the damage done to centrifuges by the virus sent by the West was limited. But to Albright, the numbers that appeared in IAEA reports around the time that Iran said the virus had struck appeared to indicate that at least 1,000 centrifuges might have been damaged or replaced during that period.

Albright published a paper discussing his thoughts that appeared to resolve the Natanz question once and for all. Then, shortly after he did, the *New York Times* came out with a story that seemed to resolve Stuxnet's most enduring mystery—who had created and launched it. The story surprised no one in its findings. The paper reported that Stuxnet was a joint operation between Israel and the United States, with a little bit of assistance, witting or otherwise, from the Germans and the British.[18]

According to the story, which relied on anonymous sources, the worm had been written by US and Israeli coders and tested at Israel's Dimona complex in the Negev Desert—the site that developed Israel's own illicit nuclear weapons program in the 1960s. Dimona was enlisted to set up a test-bed of Siemens controllers and centrifuges, which were identical to the IR-1s at Natanz, to measure the effectiveness of the worm at destroying the spinning devices. But a US lab also played a role in the tests. In 2004, the Oak Ridge National Laboratory in Tennessee had obtained some P-1 centrifuges, the type that Iran's IR-1s were modeled on, and the British, who were partners in the Urenco consortium that had created the original centrifuge designs, may have played a role. When testing was completed, the United States and Israel worked together to target the machines in Iran.

When asked about the role the United States might have played in Stuxnet, Gary Samore, Obama's chief adviser on weapons of mass destruction and arms control, simply smiled at a *Times* reporter and said, "I'm glad to hear they are having troubles with their centrifuge machines, and the US and its allies are doing everything we can to make it more complicated."[19]

The news of US involvement in developing and releasing the digital weapon should have created a stir in Washington and in other government

18 William J. Broad, John Markoff, and David E. Sanger, "Israeli Test on Worm Called Crucial in Iran Nuclear Delay," *New York Times*, January 15, 2011.
19 Ibid.

circles beyond. But it was largely met with silence, despite the fact that it raised a number of troubling questions—not only about the risks it created for US critical infrastructures that were vulnerable to the same kind of attack, but about the ethical and legal considerations of unleashing a destructive digital attack that was essentially an act of war. Ralph Langner had been right in signing off his original post about Stuxnet the way he did. With confirmation, albeit unofficial, that Israel and the United States were behind the attack, the world had now formally entered the age of cyberwarfare.

CHAPTER 14

SON OF STUXNET

As spring arrived in 2011, the story of Stuxnet seemed to be winding down. Symantec had resolved the mystery of the devices the digital weapon attacked, Albright had made the final connection between Stuxnet and the centrifuges at Natanz, and although the US government still hadn't made a formal admission of responsibility for the attack, the *New York Times* had confirmed what everyone suspected—that the United States and Israel were behind it.

Symantec, for its part, was ready to move on. The researchers had spent half a year tearing apart the code and had produced a seventy-page dossier of all their findings. They were relieved to finally be done with it. But they hadn't put the project aside for long when startling new evidence emerged in Europe—evidence suggesting that Stuxnet was just one in an arsenal of tools the attackers had used against Iran and other targets.

BOLDIZSÁR BENCSÁTH TOOK a bite from his sandwich and stared at his computer screen. The software he was trying to install on his machine was taking forever to load, and he still had a dozen things to do before the Fall 2011 semester began at the Budapest University of Technology and

Economics, where he taught computer science. Despite the long to-do list, however, he was feeling happy and relaxed. It was the first day of September and was one of those perfect, late-summer afternoons when the warm air and clear skies made you forget that cold autumn weather was lurking around the corner.

Bencsáth, known to his friends as Boldi, was sitting at his desk in the university's Laboratory of Cryptography and System Security, aka CrySyS Lab, when the telephone interrupted his lunch. It was Jóska Bartos, CEO of a company for which the lab sometimes did consulting work.[1]

"Boldi, do you have time to do something for us?" Bartos asked.

"Is this related to what we talked about before?" Bencsáth said, referring to a previous discussion they'd had about testing new services the company planned to offer customers.

"No, something else," Bartos said. "Can you come now? It's important. But don't tell anyone where you're going."

Bencsáth wolfed down the rest of his lunch and told his colleagues in the lab that he had a "red alert" and had to go. "Don't ask," he said as he ran out the door.

A while later, he was at Bartos's office, where a triage team had been assembled to address the problem they wanted to discuss. "We think we've been hacked," Bartos said.

They'd found a suspicious file on a developer's machine that had been created late at night when no one was working. The file was encrypted and compressed so they had no idea what was inside, but they suspected it was data the attackers had copied from the machine and planned to retrieve later. A search of the company's network found a few more machines that had been infected as well. The triage team felt confident they had contained the attack but wanted Bencsáth's help determining how the intruders had broken in and what they were after. The company had

---

1 Jóska Bartos is a pseudonym. The company asked Bencsáth not to disclose its identity or the identities of people working for it. The description of these events comes from an interview with Bencsáth except where otherwise noted.

all the right protections in place—firewalls, antivirus, intrusion-detection and -prevention systems—and still the attackers got in.

Bencsáth was a teacher, not a malware hunter, and had never done such forensic work before. At the CrySyS Lab, where he was one of four advisers working with a handful of grad students, he did academic research for the European Union and occasional hands-on consulting work for other clients, but the latter was mostly run-of-the-mill cleanup work— mopping up and restoring systems after random virus infections. He'd never investigated a targeted hack before, let alone one that was still live, and was thrilled to have the chance. The only catch was, he couldn't tell anyone what he was doing. Bartos's company depended on the trust of customers, and if word got out that the company had been hacked, they could lose clients.

The triage team had taken mirror images of the infected hard drives, so they and Bencsáth spent the rest of the afternoon poring over the images in search of anything suspicious. By the end of the day, they'd found what they were looking for—a combination keystroke logger/infostealer that was designed to record passwords and other keystrokes on infected machines, as well as steal documents and take screenshots. It also catalogued any devices or systems that were connected to the machines so the attackers could build a blueprint of the company's network architecture. The malware didn't immediately siphon the stolen data from infected machines but instead stored it on the machines in a temporary file, like the one the triage team had found. The file grew fatter each time the infostealer sucked up data, until at some point the attackers would reach out to the machine to retrieve it from a command-and-control server in India.[2]

---

2 They uploaded the keylogger to VirusTotal, a free online virus tool that researchers use to detect malicious files, to see if it was known malware. VirusTotal aggregates nearly four dozen antivirus engines from multiple companies to detect malicious files. Two scanners flagged the file as suspicious, but it was unclear if it was a known keylogger or something new. It was flagged by BitDefender and AVIRA scanners. Technically it was also detected by F-Secure and G-DATA, but only because both of these scanners use BitDefender's engine. VirusTotal is sometimes used by attackers to test their malware before unleashing it to make sure virus engines won't detect it. But the fact that this keylogger was flagged by two of the engines suggests the attackers either hadn't

By now it was the end of the day, so Bencsáth took the mirror images and the company's system logs with him, after they had been scrubbed of any sensitive customer data, and over the next few days scoured them for more malicious files, all the while being coy to his colleagues back at the lab about what he was doing. The triage team worked in parallel, and after several more days they had uncovered three additional suspicious files—including a kernel-mode driver, and another driver that was found on some infected systems but not others.

When Bencsáth examined the kernel driver, his heart quickened—it was signed with a valid digital certificate from a company in Taiwan. Wait a minute, he thought. Stuxnet used a driver that was signed with a certificate from a company in Taiwan. That one came from RealTek Semiconductor, but this certificate belonged to a different company, C-Media Electronics. The driver had been signed with the certificate in August 2009, around the same time Stuxnet had been unleashed on machines in Iran.

Could the two attacks be related? he wondered. He mulled it over for a minute, but then dismissed it. Anyone could have stolen C-Media's signing key and certificate, he reasoned, not just the attackers behind Stuxnet.

Then a member of the triage team noticed something else about the driver that seemed familiar—the way it injected code into a certain process on infected machines. "I know only one other attack that does this," he told Bencsáth. He didn't have to say the name; Bencsáth knew he was talking about Stuxnet. But Bencsáth dismissed this connection too, since he was pretty sure the technique wasn't unique to Stuxnet.

Twice more over the next few days, Bencsáth and the triage team found something in the attack code that reminded them of Stuxnet. But each time they convinced themselves it was just a coincidence. There was just no way lightning would strike twice, they reasoned. Besides, there was no sign that this new attack was targeting PLCs.

---

bothered to test it against these two scanners before unleashing it or they weren't expecting their victims to be using the two engines.

After working on the project for a week, Bencsáth began wondering if anyone else had been infected with the files, so he decided to see if he could smoke out other victims, or the attackers themselves, with a sly test. On September 8, he posted hashes for the malicious files on his personal website, boldi.phishing.hu, along with a cryptic note: "Looking for friends [or] foes of 9749d38ae9b9ddd8ab50aad679ee87ec to speak about. You know what I mean. You know why." His site, an odd compendium of fish recipes and culinary reviews of canned fish (the domain name, phishing, was a pun on the computer security term for malicious e-mail), was the perfect cover for posting the covert message, since the only way someone would find the hashes was if they specifically did a Google search looking for them—either another victim who found the same files on their machine and was searching the internet for information about them, or the attackers themselves, who might want to see if any victims had found the files and were discussing them online. If someone did visit his site in search of the hashes, Bencsáth would be able to see their IP address.

Unfortunately, he got no nibbles on his bait, so he deleted the hashes after a few days.

By now the fall semester had begun, and Bencsáth got busy with other things. He had classes to teach and office hours with students to keep. He also had a research paper to deliver at a conference in Dubrovnik. But through it all, the attack nagged at him in the back of his mind. When he returned to Budapest after the conference, he and the triage team decided to compare the code of one of the drivers they had found on their machines with one of the drivers that had been used with Stuxnet—just to settle once and for all that the two attacks weren't related. When they put the codes into a hexadecimal (hex) editor to examine them side-by-side, however, they got a big surprise. The only difference between them was the digital certificates used to sign them.

Bencsáth immediately called Bartos, the company's CEO, and told him he needed to bring the other members of the CrySyS Lab onto the investigation. This wasn't a simple hack anymore; it looked like it might be a nation-state attack with national-security implications. Bartos agreed, but only on condition that Bencsáth not reveal the company's name to any of his colleagues. The only people aside from Bencsáth who knew the company had been hacked was the local government Computer Emergency Response Team, and they had been notified only because of the nature of the company's business.[3]

Bencsáth made plans to tell his colleagues the following Monday. Over the weekend, he collected all the technical literature he could find on Stuxnet—including the lengthy dossier Symantec had prepared—and reread it to refresh his memory. When he reached the part discussing the encryption routines that Stuxnet used to conceal its code, he pulled up the encryption routines for the new attack and got another surprise. They were nearly identical. The new attack code even used one of the same decryption keys that Stuxnet used.[4]

Then he examined the six kernel hooks the new code used—specific functions on the machine that the malware hooked or hijacked to pull off its attack—and compared them to the functions hooked by other known malicious attacks. He found some that hooked two or three of the same functions, but none that hooked all six. He sifted through the Stuxnet literature to examine what Stuxnet hooked, and there it was—the digital weapon hooked all six of the same functions. There was no doubt in his mind now that the two attacks were related.

It didn't mean the codes were written by the same people, but it was clear the creators of the new code had developed their attack from the same source code and framework that had been used to develop Stuxnet. Stuxnet had sabotaged Iran's uranium enrichment program but who knew what this new attack was doing and how many systems it had infected?

Bencsáth dashed off an e-mail to Bartos telling him what he'd found. Until now they'd been working at a leisurely pace, looking at the code

---

3 Confirmation of the nature of the company's business did not come from Bencsáth or his lab but was gleaned from other sources who were familiar with the breach and the victim.
4 The inoculation value that Stuxnet had used—0x19790509 (which Symantec had interpreted to be a date—May 9, 1979)—also showed up in this new attack code. In Stuxnet it had been used to prevent the worm from infecting machines that had this value in their registry, but here it was part of the encryption.

whenever they had time. But now he realized they needed to determine what the attack was doing quickly and get the information out to the public before anyone could stop them. After Symantec had published its research on Stuxnet, there were some who wondered why the US government had never tried to thwart them. Bencsáth worried that this time someone would try to intervene.

The next day he told his colleagues, Levente Buttyán and Gábor Pék, about the attack. The three of them knew they weren't equipped to do a thorough analysis of the files on their own—none of them had ever done malware analysis like this before and had little experience using the debugging tools needed to reverse-engineer it. But they knew they had to do enough analysis to convince other, more experienced, researchers to look at it. The CrySyS Lab, like VirusBlokAda, was hardly a familiar name in the computer security world, and they needed solid evidence to connect the attack to Stuxnet or no one else would agree to examine it.

They set a deadline ten days away and decided to focus only on the parts of the attack that were similar to Stuxnet. But to their surprise, there were more similarities than they expected. At the end of the ten days, they had a sixty-page report. Bartos gave Bencsáth permission to share it with Symantec, but only on condition that if they went public with the report, the CrySyS Lab would not be named in it. Bartos worried that if anyone knew the lab was in Hungary, it wouldn't take long to identify the victim.

They sent the report to the government CERT, to Chien and his team at Symantec, and to a few others—Péter Szőr, a Hungarian researcher at McAfee; someone at VeriSign, because VeriSign would need to revoke the digital certificate the malware used; and to a researcher at Microsoft.[5] Bencsáth's heart was pounding as he clicked Send to e-mail the report. "I was really excited," he says. "You throw down something from the hill, and you don't know what type of avalanche there will be [as a result]."

---

5 The Microsoft researcher, Tareq Saade, was on the list because the government CERT had already sent Microsoft a copy of the keylogger file after it was discovered, so Bencsáth thought Microsoft should see the CrySyS Lab report as well.

WHEN CHIEN AWOKE on October 14, a Friday, he immediately reached for his BlackBerry to check his e-mail. The subject line of one message caught his eye. It read simply, "important malware," and came with an attachment. It had been sent by two computer scientists at an obscure university lab in Hungary, who wrote in stilted English that they'd discovered a new attack that bore "strong similarities" to Stuxnet. They dubbed it "Duqu" (dew queue)—because temporary files the malware created on infected machines all had names that began with ~DQ—and were certain it would "open a new chapter in the story of Stuxnet."

"As we don't really have experience with this sort of incidents yet [*sic*], we are uncertain about the next steps that we should make," they wrote. "We are ready to collaborate with others, including you, by providing access to the malware and participating in its further analysis."

Chien forwarded the e-mail to the rest of the incident-response team at Symantec and sent a text message to O'Murchu telling him to read it as soon as he woke up. Then he headed to the office feeling cautiously excited.

Over the past year, Chien had grown wary of people contacting him with false alarms about new Stuxnet sightings. Working for an antivirus firm, he was already used to friends and neighbors appealing to his expertise whenever they thought their computers were infected with a virus. But after his team's work on Stuxnet got widely publicized, random strangers began contacting him too, insisting that the government was spying on them with Stuxnet. One guy even sent an envelope stuffed with fifty pages of printed-out screenshots and network traffic logs that he'd highlighted in yellow. On one, he'd circled the URL of a website he'd visited that contained the letters "en/us"—proof that the US government was watching his computer, he said.[6] Another correspondent, a female cookbook author,

---

6 The "en/us" letters in the URL merely indicated that the man had visited a site that was localized for English-speaking readers in the United States.

sent Chien a few e-mails via Hushmail—an anonymous encrypted e-mail service used by activists and criminals to hide their identity. When Chien ignored the e-mails, she tracked down his phone number and left a message. She, too, was certain someone was spying on her with Stuxnet, she said, because every time she went to the library and inserted a USB flash drive into a computer there, her home computer later got infected with a virus from the same USB flash drive.

Despite Chien's cynicism about every new Stuxnet claim that crossed his desk, he only had to read the first two pages of the report from Hungary before he knew that this one was different. "This is Stuxnet," he said with certainty.

Despite their lack of experience analyzing malicious code, the Hungarians had produced an impressive report, although they apologized that "many questions and issues remain unanswered or unaddressed." They had included snippets of decompiled code showing Duqu's likeness to Stuxnet and produced a side-by-side checklist highlighting more than a dozen ways the two attacks were the same or similar. There was no attack against PLCs in this code—in fact, there was no real payload at all, unless you considered the keylogger a payload. But the fingerprints of Stuxnet's creators were all over it. Duqu was either written by the same team that was behind Stuxnet or, at the very least, by people with access to the same source code and tools.

Chien e-mailed Bencsáth to let him know they'd received the report, then waited anxiously for O'Murchu to arrive, feeling a mix of emotions. They had long hoped that they or someone else would uncover additional clues to help them resolve their remaining questions about Stuxnet. And Duqu looked like it might provide some of the answers they were seeking. But their analysis of Stuxnet had required months of work, including nights and weekends, and he feared the new code might exact the same amount of time and energy.

———

O'MURCHU WAS STILL half-asleep when he saw Chien's text message that morning, but his grogginess quickly dispersed when he opened the attachment and read the report. There was nothing like staring down the barrel of a suspected cyberweapon to clear the fog in your mind. "I've got to get to the office," he told his girlfriend as he threw on some clothes and dashed out the door.

As he drove to work, he tried to wrap his mind around what he'd just seen and couldn't believe the Stuxnet gang was still active. After all the media attention and finger pointing at Israel and the United States, he thought for sure the attackers would have laid low for a while to let things cool off. At the very least he thought they would have altered their methods and code a little to make sure that any attack they unleashed hereafter couldn't be traced back to them if found. But judging by the report from Hungary, it appeared they hadn't bothered to alter their signature moves at all. They really had balls, he thought. They were determined to do whatever they had to do and didn't care who knew it was them. Either that, or they were already so invested in using the Duqu code that they were loath to replace it even after Stuxnet had been caught.

When O'Murchu got to the office, Chien and their colleagues were already buzzing about the new attack. They contacted Falliere, who had by now relocated from Paris to the States and was now working out of Symantec's office in Northern California. They downloaded the binary files for Duqu that the Hungarians had sent and worked on the code throughout the day and the weekend. They were happy to discover that Duqu was much smaller than Stuxnet had been and consisted of just a few files that were fairly easy to decipher. By Monday, they knew pretty much everything there was to know about the code.

Duqu was essentially a remote-access Trojan, or RAT, which operated as a simple back door to give the attackers a persistent foothold on infected machines. Once the back door was installed, however, Duqu contacted a command-and-control server, from which the attackers could download additional modules to give their attack code more functionality, such as the keystroke logger/infostealer the Hungarians had found on one of their systems.

As for Duqu's intent, it was pretty clear it wasn't a saboteur like Stuxnet, but an espionage tool. Whereas Stuxnet was a black ops mission bent on destruction, Duqu appeared to be the forward scout, sent out to collect intelligence for future assaults. Symantec suspected it was the precursor to another Stuxnet-like attack. Duqu's life-span was limited, however; a kill date in the code forced it to self-destruct after thirty-six days, deleting all traces of itself from an infected machine.[7]

All of this seemed fairly straightforward, but as they examined Duqu's files, they stumbled across a surprise that seemed to connect it to another mystery attack that had been puzzling them for months. Six months earlier, officials in Iran had announced that computers there had been struck by a second digital attack in the wake of Stuxnet. The announcement came months after Iranian officials had finally acknowledged that computers controlling centrifuges in Iran had been attacked. Although the Iranians had never identified the specific virus that struck the centrifuges, they gave this new attack the name "Stars." Gholam-Reza Jalali, commander of Iran's Civil Defense Organization, didn't say why they called it Stars, nor did he provide much information about the attack other than to say it was aimed at stealing data. He also said it was likely "to be mistaken [on computers] for executable files of the government," suggesting the malware may have arrived in a phishing attack, with a malicious file attached that masqueraded as a document from a government source.[8]

Symantec and other security researchers didn't know what to make of the report at the time, since Iran didn't release any samples of the malware for outside researchers to examine. The fact that no one else in the world

---

7 Researchers eventually uncovered multiple versions of Duqu, with varying removal times. In some cases it removed itself after 30 days, in other versions it was 36 days. In at least one case, the researchers found a version that lasted 120 days before deletion.

8 Dugald McConnel, "Iranian Official: New Computer Worm Discovered," CNN, April 27, 2011. Available at cnn.com/2011/TECH/web/04/26/iran_computer_worm.

had reported infections from "Stars" led some researchers to dismiss the report, believing that Iran had either fabricated the story to accuse the West of launching more cyberattacks or had simply mistaken a run-of-the-mill virus with a nation-state attack.

But something they found in Duqu suggested it might be Stars. When Duqu's attackers sent their keylogger to infected machines, they embedded it in a .JPEG file—an ordinary image file—to slip it through firewalls unnoticed. The content of most of the image in that file had been deleted so the keylogger code could be tucked inside. As a result, only an inch or so of the image appeared on-screen when O'Murchu opened the file—it consisted of just a few words of white text printed on a dark background. The words were cut off so only their top half was visible, but it was still possible to make them out: "Interacting Galaxy System NGC 6745." A Google search on the words revealed the entire picture—a March 1996 image produced from the Hubble Space Telescope. The striking image depicted a thick cluster of luminous blue and white stars enveloped in a gossamer veil of golden matter and gases—the aftermath, a caption revealed, of two galaxies "colliding" after a small galaxy of stars grazed the top of a larger one. Was it possible that Duqu was the mysterious "Stars" that struck Iran?[9] It seemed to Symantec and the CrySyS Lab that it was.

Symantec wanted to go public with the news of Duqu, but before the researchers could do so, they worked with Bencsáth to scrub the sample files and CrySyS report of anything that might identify the victim or the lab.[10] On October 18, the Symantec team published the anonymized

---

9 After news of Duqu broke, someone on Twitter who identified himself as an Iranian malware researcher in Virginia published a tweet saying that according to investigations by Iran's CERT, "#Duqu is upgraded version of #Stars malware." He deleted the tweet very quickly after posting it, however, and not long afterward also deleted his entire Twitter account. It's unclear if there was any significance to the image of the galaxies in Duqu or if the attackers had just chosen a random picture, but Bencsáth thought it might have been used as a secret signal to identify Duqu as "friendly fire." Sometimes various intelligence branches of the same government will target the same computers. If the United States or Israel was behind Duqu, the image might have been a signal to "friendlies" who came across the keylogger on an infected machine—in the course of trying to hack it themselves—that the machine was already infected by a compatriot.

10 Some criticized Symantec's decision to go public so quickly. A more strategic approach would have been to remain quiet while gathering more intelligence about the attack—for example, asking

CrySyS report, as well as their own analysis of Duqu, identifying the victim only as "an organization based in Europe" and the CrySyS Lab as a "research lab with strong international connections."[11]

Within an hour after the announcement broke, Bencsáth got the first hit to his personal website from someone searching for the hashes he'd posted weeks earlier. Although he'd deleted them from his site, Google cache had preserved his post, and online security forums were buzzing with questions about the deleted message. The next day he got more than four hundred hits to his domain as word spread quickly that this strange Hungarian site about canned fish was somehow connected to Duqu. There was no contact information for Bencsáth on the site, but it didn't take long for someone to look up the registration for the site's domain and find his name. From there it took only a simple Google search to connect him to the CrySyS Lab.

It was futile to hide the lab's identity at this point, so on October 21, Bencsáth published a brief statement on the lab's website, acknowledging their role in discovering Duqu, and urged everyone to stop speculating about the victim's identity. It was too late for this, however. Word was already spreading that Duqu's victim was a certificate authority in Europe after Péter Ször, the McAfee researcher who had received Bencsáth's original report, wrote a blog post titled "The Day of the Golden Jackal" saying that Duqu was targeting certificate authorities and advising CAs to check their systems to make sure they hadn't been infected. Since the Cry-

---

companies hosting the command-and-control servers for a mirror image of the servers to see what the attackers were doing on them—before signaling to the attackers that they had been caught. It was an ongoing tension that existed between investigative and forensic needs and the needs of customers, who would want to know quickly if they had been infected so they could shore up their network against other attacks and determine if the intruders had stolen anything. But the CrySyS Lab had already sent its report to someone at McAfee, a competing antivirus firm, who might go public with the news or inadvertently tip off the attackers that they'd been caught. There were other drawbacks to waiting to go public. Without widening the net of people who knew about the malware, it would be difficult to obtain other samples of Duqu that could tell them more about the attack. The malware was very targeted, infecting only a small number of victims, and every file related to Duqu that they could collect from victims gave them a little more information about the attack.

11 Symantec's Duqu report is available at symantec.com/content/en/us/enterprise/media/security_response/whitepapers/w32_duqu_the_precursor_to_the_next_stuxnet.pdf.

SyS Lab was in Hungary, people assumed the victim was too. And since there were only a few certificate authorities in that country—NetLock and Microsec e-Szigno being the primary ones—it didn't take long for a few researchers to zero in on NetLock as the victim, though none of them went public with the news.[12]

The implications were alarming. Certificate authorities are at the core of the trust relationship that makes the internet function. They issue the certificates that governments, financial institutions, and companies use to sign their software and websites, providing users with assurance that they are downloading a legitimate program made by Microsoft or entering their account login credentials at a legitimate website operated by Bank of America or Gmail. Attacking such an authority would allow the attackers to issue themselves legitimate certificates in the name of any company and use it to sign malware. It went a step beyond Stuxnet's tactic of compromising individual companies like RealTek, JMicron, and C-Media. If Duqu was the work of the United States or Israel, it meant that a NATO country or ally had compromised a fundamental part of the trusted infrastructure that made transactions on the internet possible, all for the sake of advancing a covert campaign. If the United States was behind the attack, it also meant that while one branch of the government was touting the importance of securing critical infrastructure at home and developing acceptable norms of behavior for the internet, another was busy compromising critical systems belonging to a NATO ally that were important for the security of the internet, and establishing questionable norms of behavior that others would copy. But because the identity of the victim was never disclosed at the time Duqu was exposed, the public was denied an opportunity to debate these issues.

Despite the omission of this important detail, when the news of Duqu broke, it elicited a far different response from the security community than Stuxnet had. Research teams that had sat on the bleachers while Symantec

---

12 I was able to confirm the identity of the victim as NetLock from several sources not associated with the CrySyS Lab.

had worked for months to deconstruct Stuxnet's payload quickly jumped on Duqu's code to examine it—in part because it was less complex than Stuxnet and didn't have a PLC payload, but also because they had seen what sitting on the sidelines got them. Stuxnet had signaled the dawn of a new era, and many researchers had chosen to sit it out.[13]

One security firm that was determined not to be left behind this time was Kaspersky Lab in Russia. The Kaspersky researchers hadn't sat idly when Stuxnet was discovered; they had put in extensive work to deconstruct the Windows portion of the attack and had been the first private researchers to discover additional zero days in Stuxnet and report them to Microsoft. But beyond its menagerie of exploits, they hadn't considered Stuxnet a particularly interesting threat. The unfamiliar PLC code was a barrier to examining the payload, and ultimately they had determined there was little to be gained from deciphering it. So once they'd completed their analysis of the missile portion, they had moved on. But they weren't going to make that mistake again.

COSTIN RAIU, DIRECTOR of Kaspersky's Global Research and Analysis Team, was in Beijing when news of Duqu broke, preparing to board an early-morning flight to Hong Kong for a meeting. His first thought was to call his colleagues back in Moscow, but they were still asleep. So before boarding his plane, he quickly downloaded the Duqu files Symantec made available to researchers and examined them during his flight.

As soon as he landed in Hong Kong, he contacted Alexander Gostev in Moscow, a young, highly skilled reverse-engineer and the company's chief malware researcher. Symantec and the CrySyS Lab had examined

---

13 It wasn't just security companies that responded differently this time. The government did as well. For some reason, during the many months the Symantec researchers had been analyzing Stuxnet and publishing pleas for help from PLC experts, ICS-CERT had remained distant, even though its analysts possessed the exact PLC expertise Symantec sought. A DHS official later acknowledged in an author interview that the department made a mistake in not reaching out to Symantec. This time around, ICS-CERT handled it differently and contacted Symantec to compare notes about its own findings about Duqu.

the Duqu files thoroughly, but Raiu and Gostev suspected there was much more intelligence to be gleaned from the threat, and they were right.

It was clear to them immediately that Duqu was the work of master programmers. The code was remarkably different from other spyware that crossed their desks—Raiu likened it to the difference between Vincent Van Gogh's *Starry Night* and an art-school student's amateur rendition of a star-filled night. The master brushstrokes and genius in the code were evident to the practiced eye.

Raiu was a thirty-three-year-old Romanian who worked for Kaspersky out of a tiny office in Bucharest with one other researcher and a handful of marketing folks. He had dark, close-cropped, graying hair and a maturity and wisdom that belied his age. The latter made him a natural mentor to younger members of his research team. He also had a calm, Buddha-like demeanor that served him well under pressure when they were juggling multiple complex projects at a time. It was a quality that would prove invaluable over the many months that followed as his team's research into the Stuxnet-Duqu gang intensified and they began to draw the attention of intelligence agencies.

Raiu had joined the company in 2000 at the age of twenty-three, when it had just a few dozen employees. He was hired to work on its Prague project, the name the company gave the next-generation antivirus engine it was building.

Growing up in Communist Romania, Raiu's passion hadn't been computers but chemistry. He was fascinated by the combustible reaction of certain chemicals when mixed and by the fundamental knowledge that chemistry imparted about the nature and structure of the world. But when one of his experiments nearly blew up his parents' apartment, they bought him a locally made PC clone to steer him toward less lethal pursuits. It wasn't long before he'd taught himself programming and, while still a teenager, designed an antivirus engine from scratch called RAV.

His work on RAV began when his high school network got infested with a virus the school's antivirus scanner didn't detect. Raiu spent a night writing signatures and crafting a detection tool for it. Over time, he added more code and features, and eventually began distributing it for free under the name MSCAN. When word of his creation got out, a Romanian entrepreneur hired him to work for his company, GeCAD Software, which began marketing his program under the name RAV, for Romanian Anti-Virus. It quickly became the company's top-selling product, reliably beating out competitors in test after test, which drew the attention of Microsoft. In 2003, the software giant acquired RAV from GeCAD, but by then Raiu had already jumped ship to work for Kaspersky.[14]

Kaspersky Lab was relatively unknown at the time in the United States, where Symantec and McAfee dominated the antivirus market. As a Russian firm, Kaspersky faced a battle of mistrust in the West—particularly since founder Eugene Kaspersky had been schooled in a KGB-backed institute and had served in Russia's military intelligence. But the company slowly made a name for itself in eastern Europe and elsewhere, particularly in the Middle East, where the United States and US firms faced a similar battle of mistrust.

Raiu began with Kaspersky as a programmer, but in 2004 when the company launched a research team to investigate and reverse-engineer malware, Raiu joined the group. In 2010, he became its director, overseeing research teams on several continents. Now, with the discovery of Duqu, several of these teams went into action.

The technical work was led by Gostev, a whippet-thin analyst with short, light brown hair and a slight stoop that was suggestive of all the hours he spent bent in concentration over a computer. As he and his colleagues picked through the code, they were struck by a number of things.

One particularly interesting part was the component the attackers used to download additional payload modules to a victim's machine to siphon data. Unlike every other Duqu and Stuxnet module, this one was written not in C or C++ but in a language Gostev and Raiu had never seen

---

14 Microsoft's Security Essentials program is based on Raiu's RAV antivirus engine.

before. They tried for weeks to identify it and even consulted experts on programming languages, but still couldn't figure it out. So they put out a call for help on their blog and were finally able to conclude, piecing bits of clues together, that the attackers had employed a rarely used custom dialect of C, along with special extensions to contort the code and make it small and portable.[15] It was a programming style common to commercial software programs produced a decade ago, but not to modern-day pro- grams, and certainly not to malware. It was clear these weren't hot-shot coders using the latest techniques, but old-school programmers who were cautious and conservative. Sometimes C++ could produce compiled code that was unpredictable and executed in unintentional ways. So the attack- ers had chosen C instead, Raiu surmised, to give them the greatest control over their malicious code, then modified it during compilation to make it more compact and easy to deliver to victims.[16]

Their constraints on Duqu extended to its spreading mechanisms. In this regard Duqu was as tightly controlled as Stuxnet had been uncon- trolled. The attack didn't appear to have any zero-day exploits to help it spread, and it also couldn't spread autonomously as Stuxnet did. Instead, once on a machine, it would infect other machines only if the attackers manually sent instructions from their command server to do so.[17] Duqu

---

15 The attackers used a custom object-oriented C dialect known as OO-C.

16 While this component displayed masterful skills, there were other parts that were less masterful. The implementation of encryption, for example, was weak. Duqu was built like an elegant Chinese box with multiple layers of encryption to obfuscate its components and thwart detection. But the way the attackers implemented it was poorly done. One part had an encrypted configuration block that held a key to decrypt a registry; inside the registry was another key to decrypt Duqu's main .DLL file. The design was supposed to make it hard for anyone who got hold of the .DLL to decrypt it without first obtaining the other two keys. But the programmers had undermined their security by making the keys for the registry and the .DLL identical and making the key for the configuration block 0. Once someone unlocked the configuration block, he already had the key to decrypt the main .DLL, bypassing the need for a separate registry key. Stuxnet, by contrast, had used different keys for each stage of encryption. The encryption algorithm used in Stuxnet was also a four-round cipher, while Duqu used a weaker one-round cipher. Clearly different but related teams had designed Duqu and Stuxnet, but even though both teams had strong and advanced methods of encryption at their disposal, the Duqu team hadn't bothered to use them.

17 To accomplish this, they had to first seize control of the administrative account on an infected machine, then set up a task instructing the malware to spread via network shares.

was also much stealthier in communicating with its command servers than Stuxnet had been.[18] The communication was encrypted with a strong encryption algorithm known as AES, to prevent anyone from reading it, and was also tucked inside a .JPEG image file to help conceal it. And unlike Stuxnet, which struck more than 100,000 machines, researchers would eventually uncover only about three dozen Duqu infections.[19]

The victims were scattered among various countries and ranged from military targets to manufacturers of industrial equipment, such as pipes and valves. All of them appeared to have been carefully targeted for their "strategic assets"—products they produced or services they rendered.[20] Not surprisingly, many of the victims Kaspersky uncovered had a connection to Iran; either they had an office in the Islamic Republic or they had some kind of trade relationship with Iran. The only victim so far that didn't appear to have a connection to Iran was the company in Hungary that discovered the attack.

Based on information gleaned from log files provided by some of the victims, the attackers appeared to be particularly interested in swiping AutoCAD files—especially ones related to industrial control systems used in various industries in Iran. AutoCAD, which stands for computer-aided design, is software used for drafting 2D and 3D architectural blueprints and designing computer boards and consumer products; but it's also used for mapping the layout of computer networks and the machinery on plant floors. The latter would come in handy for someone planning to bomb a factory or launch a digital attack like Stuxnet.

---

18 Team Duqu also stored some of the scripts for controlling the operation at other locations, rather than on the command servers, so that anyone who seized control of these front-end servers couldn't seize and examine the scripts to determine what Duqu was doing.

19 There may have been more victims over the years, but these were the only ones uncovered after Duqu was discovered. Symantec found victims in eight countries—one each in France, India, the Netherlands, Switzerland, Sudan, Vietnam, and Ukraine, and at least two in Iran. Kaspersky found eleven more infections in Iran, three in Europe, and four in Sudan. Other antivirus vendors found victims in Austria, Indonesia, and the UK.

20 Kelly Jackson Higgins, "Same Toolkit Spawned Stuxnet, Duqu, and Other Campaigns," Dark Reading, January 3, 2012, available at darkreading.com/advanced-threats/167901091/security/attacks-breaches/232301225/same-toolkit-spawned-stuxnet-duqu-and-other-campaigns.html.

The attackers were systematic in how they approached their victims, compiling new attack files for each target and setting up separate command servers throughout Europe and Asia so that only two or three infected machines reported to a single server. This segmentation no doubt helped them track different operations and sets of victims, but it also ensured that if any outsider got access to one of the servers, their view of the operation would be very limited. The servers, in fact, turned out to be proxy machines—way stations for the attackers to redirect stolen data to other machines—to further prevent anyone from seeing the entire operation or tracking stolen data back to the attackers. Data from the victim in Hungary, for example, was first sent to a server in India before being redirected to one in the Philippines, where it was sent somewhere else. Data from victims in Iran went to a server in Vietnam before going to Germany and somewhere beyond. The researchers tried to follow the trail, but after hitting three different proxies in a row each time, they figured they'd never reach the end of the trail, and gave up.

With help from some of the companies that hosted the servers, however, Kaspersky obtained mirror images of five of the machines, including one in Vietnam that controlled infections in Iran. They discovered that on October 20, two days after Symantec had gone public with news of Duqu, the attackers had conducted a massive cleanup operation in a panicked attempt to scrub data from the servers. Why it took them two days to respond to the news was unclear.[21] But in their haste to eliminate evidence, they left behind traces of logs that provided Kaspersky with clues about their activity.[22] The logs showed, for example, that the attackers had

---

21 If Israel was behind Duqu, the delay might have had something to do with the fact that October 18, the date Symantec published its report, fell during the Sukkot holiday in Israel, which ran from October 13 to 19 that year. Sukkot commemorates the forty years the Israelites spent in the Sinai desert after escaping slavery in Egypt. In Israel, the first day of the festival was a work holiday. Although the remaining six days were not mandatory holidays, many Israelis took them off anyway since schools were closed. Sukkot would have concluded on the nineteenth, with workers back to work on the twentieth—including, presumably, Duqu's server team.

22 They left behind other traces as well. The night before stories about Duqu broke, the attackers had changed Duqu's encryption keys and recompiled their Duqu files with the new keys before pushing out the new files to infected machines. The attackers likely intended for the new version of Duqu to replace older versions on infected systems, but they didn't count on a quirk in the

signed into one of the command servers in Germany in November 2009, two years before Duqu was discovered. This suggested that Duqu was likely in the wild for at least that long. Perhaps, the Kaspersky researchers posited, Duqu was really a *precursor* to Stuxnet, not a successor to it, as Symantec assumed. It wouldn't be long before they found the evidence to support this.

IT WAS INITIALLY unclear to anyone how Duqu infected machines. Stuxnet had used the .LNK exploit embedded on USB flash drives to drop its malicious cargo. But the CrySyS Lab had found no dropper on machines at Bartos's company and no zero-day exploits, either. After Symantec published its paper about Duqu, however, Chien asked Bencsáth to have the Hungarian victim search their systems again for anything suspicious that occurred around August 11, the date the infection occurred. That's when they found an e-mail that had come in then with a Word document attached to it. The attachment was 700k in size—much larger than any documents the company usually received—which drew their attention. Sure enough, when the CrySyS team opened the e-mail on a test system in their lab, Duqu's malicious files dropped onto it.[23]

Given that the attack code had gone undetected until now, the CrySyS guys suspected a zero-day exploit was at play. Bencsáth sent the dropper to the Symantec team, who determined that it was indeed exploiting a zero-day buffer-overflow vulnerability in the TrueType font-parsing en-

---

Windows operating system that caused traces of the older version to remain, which researchers later found when their antivirus products scanned the systems. The attackers may have changed the encryption keys because they sensed the malware had been discovered and were trying to outrun detection. But if they suspected they had been caught, they didn't seem to comprehend the degree to which their mission was about to be exposed, because they also released an update to extend the malware's life-span beyond thirty-six days, as if they fully expected to continue their operation for a while undisturbed. Once the news broke and they understood that their entire operation was toast, however, they had initiated the cleanup operation to wipe all the data from their servers.

23 The dropper didn't immediately install its malicious cargo. Instead it waited until the computer was idle at least ten minutes before springing into action. The date on the computer also had to be within an eight-day window in August or Duqu wouldn't install its files, further evidence of the amount of caution and control the attackers maintained over their code.

gine for Windows. The font-parsing engine was responsible for rendering fonts on-screen. When font code for a character appeared in a Word document, the engine consulted the proper font file to determine how the character should look. But in this case when the engine tried to read the font code, a vulnerability in the parsing engine triggered the exploit instead.

The exploit was quite "badass," in the words of one researcher, because a normal exploit attacking a buffer-overflow vulnerability generally got hackers only user-level access to a machine, which meant they needed a second vulnerability and exploit to get them administrative-level privileges to install their malicious code undeterred.[24] But this exploit cut through layers of protection to let them install and execute malicious code at the kernel level of the machine without interference. Buffer-overflow vulnerabilities that could be exploited at the kernel level are rare and difficult to exploit without causing the machine to crash, but the Duqu exploit worked flawlessly. It was several orders of magnitude more sophisticated than the .LNK exploit Stuxnet had used. The .LNK exploit had been copied by cybercriminals in no time after Stuxnet was exposed in July 2010, but this one would take months before anyone would successfully replicate it.[25]

The exploit was notable in itself, but the attackers had also embedded a couple of Easter eggs in their code—perhaps to taunt victims. The name they gave the fake font that executed their attack was Dexter Regular, and in the copyright notice for the fake font they wrote—"Copyright © 2003 Showtime Inc. All rights reserved. Dexter Regular."[26]

---

24 A blogger for the Finnish antivirus firm F-Secure called it "one badass exploit." November 2, 2011, "Duqu Attack's Installer Discovered," available at f-secure.com/weblog/archives/00002263.html.

25 Researchers saw signs of cybercriminals trying, but failing, to replicate the Duqu exploit in June 2012, eight months after Symantec published information about the vulnerability. They finally succeeded in October 2012, after which Kaspersky saw a spike in attacks using copycat versions of the exploit in December 2012. Microsoft had patched the vulnerability in December 2011, however, so attackers could use the exploit only against unpatched machines.

26 The Kaspersky researchers found something else they thought might be an Easter egg in the code. A decryption key in one version of the Duqu driver had a value—0xAE240682—that also appeared to be a date: June 24, 1982. When Raiu looked it up it turned out to be the day a famous event in aviation history occurred—the date British Airways Flight 09 hit a volcanic ash cloud en

It was clear they were referencing the popular TV show *Dexter*, which was then airing on the Showtime network. But the show didn't begin airing until October 1, 2006, which made the 2003 copyright date seem odd. It was unclear if the Easter egg had any meaning or if it was just a joke. But the reference did appear to have one parallel to Stuxnet. The Showtime series focused on Dexter Morgan, a forensic scientist and vigilante killer who only murdered criminals, making him a killer with a moral code—a murderer who killed for the sake of the greater societal good. At least that's how Dexter saw it. Arguably, it was also the way the United States and Israel might have viewed the cyberattack on Iran, or the attacks on Iran's nuclear scientists—as a means to a greater good.[27]

The font name and copyright date offered a bit of distraction for the researchers, but the more notable part of the dropper was its compilation date—February 21, 2008—providing a clue about how long Duqu might have been around. Not long after this dropper was found, Kaspersky got

---

route from London to New Zealand. The plane had just taken off after a stopover in Malaysia when gritty ash spewing from Mount Galunggung choked all four of the 747's engines, leaving it dead in the air. The pilots attempted to glide it to a landing, and as the plane descended from 37,000 to 12,000 feet, oxygen masks dropped from the ceiling. That's when the British captain, Eric Moody, made one of the most famous understatements in the history of aviation. "Ladies and gentlemen," he told the passengers, "this is your captain speaking. We have a small problem. All four of the engines have stopped. We are doing our damnedest to get them going again. I trust you are not in too much distress." (See "When Volcanic Ash Stopped a Jumbo at 37,000ft," BBC, April 15, 2010. Available at news.bbc.co.uk/2/hi/uk_news/magazine/8622099.stm.) The pilots managed to restart the engines after about fifteen minutes and land in Jakarta. Was it a coincidence that this seemed to be the second aviation reference after the DEADF007 reference in Stuxnet? Or were the attackers just playing with researchers now and dropping little Easter eggs in the code to keep them guessing? Or was the value in the code simply a random number with no significance?

27 Kaspersky's Costin Raiu bought all past episodes of the Dexter show to see if there was some reason the attackers referenced it in Duqu. Only one episode seemed remotely relevant. In it, Dexter's sister, Debra, received a marriage proposal from Det. Joey Quinn. During a discussion about the proposal with her brother, he mused that if she were to marry Quinn, her initials would be DQ.

Raiu did see one other episode that reminded him of Duqu. To confuse investigators who were hot on the serial killer's trail, Dexter crafted a thirty-page manifesto littered with biblical references to distract them. While the investigators wasted time sifting through the meaningless document for clues, Dexter continued his killing spree. The parallels weren't lost on Raiu, who pondered the hours he'd wasted watching the TV show for clues about Duqu.

its hands on a second one, found on a machine in Sudan, that had been compiled even earlier.[28]

Sudan had close military ties to Iran—it received $12 million worth of arms from Iran between 2004 and 2006—and was a vocal supporter of Iran's nuclear program. In 2006, Iran had publicly vowed to share its nuclear expertise with Sudan. Sudan was also a target of UN sanctions. Duqu's victim in Sudan was a trade services firm that had been infected in April 2011, four months before the infection in Hungary. The malicious code arrived via a phishing attack using the same Dexter zero-day exploit that was used in Hungary. The malicious e-mail, purporting to come from a marketing manager named B. Jason, came from a computer in South Korea, though the machine had likely been hacked to send the missive.[29] "Dear Sir," the e-mail read, "I found the details of your company on your website, and would like to establish business cooperation with your company. In the attached file, please see a list of requests." The attached document contained a handful of survey questions as well as an image of a green Earth with plants sprouting from its top. When the victim opened the attachment, the Dexter exploit sprang into action and deposited its illicit cargo onto the victim's machine.

The dropper that installed Duqu in this case had been compiled in August 2007, which further confirmed that Duqu had been around for years before its discovery in Hungary. This wasn't the only evidence supporting that early timeline, however. The researchers also found evidence that Duqu's infostealer file had existed years earlier as well. They only stumbled upon this clue because of a mistake the attackers had made.

When Duqu's self-destruct mechanism kicked in after thirty-six days, it was supposed to erase all traces of itself from infected machines so a victim would never know he had been hit. But the Kaspersky team discovered that when Duqu removed itself, it forgot to delete some of the tem-

---

28 The dropper file, a driver, tried to pass itself off as a graphics driver from Intel, and was responsible for loading the Duqu back door onto a victim's machine.

29 There were two attempts to infect the victim, first on April 17, 2011, which got blocked by the victim's Outlook spam filter, and then on April 21, which succeeded.

porary files it created on machines to store the data it stole. One of these files, left behind on a machine in Iran, had been created on the machine on November 28, 2008.

Kaspersky and Symantec had always suspected that prior to Stuxnet's assault on the centrifuges in Iran, the attackers had used an espionage tool to collect intelligence about the configuration of the Siemens PLCs. The information could have come from a mole, but now it seemed more likely that a digital spy like Duqu had been used.

It seemed plausible that the Stuxnet attackers might also have used Duqu to steal the digital signing keys and certificates from RealTek and JMicron, since this was the tool they had used against the certificate authority in Hungary.

If Duqu had indeed been in the wild infecting systems undetected since 2007, or longer, its sudden discovery in Hungary in 2011 seemed strange. Why now? Raiu wondered. He concluded that it must have been a case of hubris and a bad choice of target. After remaining stealthy for so long, the attackers grew confident that they'd never get caught. They likely considered Stuxnet's discovery the previous year an anomaly that occurred only because the digital weapon had spread too far. But Duqu was carefully controlled and its targets handpicked, which made its discovery less likely. Except, in Hungary, the attackers finally picked the wrong target. The Hungarian certificate authority was much more security conscious than the trading companies and manufacturers Duqu had previously hit. And this was Team Duqu's failing.[30]

Though Stuxnet and Duqu shared some of the same code and

---

30 At the time it was hacked, the Hungarian company would have been doubly alert for a breach because of two other—seemingly unrelated—assaults on certificate authorities that had occurred in the previous months. In March of that year, someone breached the account of a partner company that worked with Comodo Group, a certificate authority based out of New Jersey and the UK. The hacker, who used an IP address in Iran, parlayed the access to issue himself eight fraudulent certificates for mail.google.com, login.yahoo.com, and six other domains that would allow him to impersonate these sites in a man-in-the-middle attack. Four months later, a Dutch certificate authority named DigiNotar was also hacked. The intruders in this case generated more than 200 fraudulent digital certificates for top domains owned by Google, Yahoo, and Mozilla, as well as for the websites of the Mossad, MI6, and the CIA. These intrusions put other certificate authorities on guard, and the company in Hungary had likely stepped up inspection of its network as a result.

techniques, Raiu and his team ultimately concluded that they had been built by separate teams from the same base platform, a platform they dubbed "Tilde-d"—because both Stuxnet and Duqu used files with names that began with ~D.[31]

In fact, Kaspersky discovered evidence that an arsenal of tools might have been built from the same platform, not just Stuxnet and Duqu. They found at least six drivers that shared characteristics and appeared to have been built on the Tilde-d platform. Two of them had been used in the known Stuxnet attacks, and a third one was the driver that had been used with Duqu.[32] But they also found three "phantom drivers" that were discovered by themselves, without any Stuxnet or Duqu files with them, making it difficult to determine if they had been used with either of these attacks or with different attacks altogether. All three of the drivers used algorithms and keys that were the same as or similar to those that the Stuxnet and Duqu drivers used, making it clear they were connected to the Tilde-d team.

The first of these was the driver that had been found in July 2010 by the Slovakian antivirus firm ESET and was signed with the JMicron certificate.[33] Because the driver was found days after the news of Stuxnet broke, everyone assumed it was related to Stuxnet, though it was not found on any system infected with Stuxnet. The driver was a hybrid of the Stuxnet and Duqu drivers, using code that was nearly identical to the Stuxnet driver and some of the same functions and techniques that the Duqu driver used. But it also used a seven-round cipher for its encryption

---

31 Duqu's keylogger/infostealer created file names that began with ~DQ, but other parts of the malware created files whose names began with ~DO and ~DF. Stuxnet also created temporary files whose names began with ~D.

32 Multiple versions of the Duqu driver showed up on infected machines, each time bearing a different name. Each version appeared to contain the same code, however, and was compiled the same day. Notably, one variant of the Duqu driver that was found on the machines in Hungary was unsigned and tried to pass itself off as a product of JMicron—the Taiwanese company whose certificate was used to sign a driver that was found by ESET in July 2010 and was believed to have been associated with Stuxnet. In the "properties" description of the driver, the attackers had indicated that it was a JMicron Volume Snapshot Driver. It was yet another detail that connected Duqu and Stuxnet.

33 The driver file name was jmidebs.sys.

routine instead of the four-round cipher that Stuxnet's driver used, making it more complex. This made Raiu and Gostev suspect it was designed for a different variant of Stuxnet or different malware altogether.

The second phantom driver was discovered when someone submitted it to VirusTotal.[34] It was compiled on January 20, 2008. It also had a seven-round cipher, suggesting that it and the JMicron driver might have been created for use with the same attack—perhaps with a different version of Stuxnet or something else altogether.

The third mystery driver was also submitted to VirusTotal, from an IP address in China on May 17, 2011, months before Duqu infected the Hungarian machines in August.[35] This driver used a four-round cipher like the Stuxnet drivers and an identical encryption key; it was also compiled the same day the Stuxnet drivers were compiled and was signed with the RealTek certificate that had been used to sign Stuxnet's drivers, though it was signed March 18, 2010, instead of January 25, 2010, the date the Stuxnet drivers were signed. March 18 was just weeks before the attackers unleashed their April 2010 variant of Stuxnet, but for some reason they didn't use this driver with that assault. Instead, they reused the driver from the June 2009 attack. This suggested that the third phantom driver might have been prepared for a different attack.

The burning questions for Gostev and Raiu, of course, were what attacks were the phantom drivers created for and who were their victims? Were they evidence that other undetected Stuxnet attacks had occurred prior to June 2009 or after April 2010?

It seemed the story of Stuxnet was still incomplete.

---

34 The name of this driver was rndismpc.sys.
35 The name of this driver was rtniczw.sys.

CHAPTER 15

FLAME

By the Spring of 2012, the team at Kaspersky had completed their analysis of Duqu and its servers, but they were sure there was more to the story than had so far been exposed. Even they, however, could not have imagined the discovery they were about to make: that Stuxnet—a program that awed with its boldness and destructive potential—was just an offshoot of a cyberspying operation that was orders of magnitude larger than this single digital weapon.

THE REVELATIONS BEGAN that April, when a virus began running wild on computers at the Iranian Oil Ministry and the Iranian National Oil Company, wiping out the hard drive of every system it touched. The damage was systematic and complete, destroying gigabytes of data at a time. First, the malware eliminated documents and data files, then it went after system files, zapping core parts of the hard drive to cause them to crash and burn.

It was unclear how many computers were affected, but there were rumors that the destruction had begun on some computers as early as December. No one noticed the trend initially, until it spread and became impossible to ignore. It also was not clear how long the virus had lurked on machines before it turned destructive, but each time it did, the destruction began around the twentieth day of the month. Iranian officials dubbed it "Wiper" and pointed to the United States and Israel as the source. They insisted, however, that the attack caused no lasting damage, because all of the deleted data had been backed up.

When Raiu and the Kaspersky team got hold of a mirror image of one of the erased hard drives from Iran, it was filled with gibberish. Not only were all of the documents and critical system files gone, any sign of the Wiper malware was erased from the disk too. But one important clue remained—a single reference inside the registry key to a temporary file named ~DF78.tmp that had been created on the system at some point before the destruction began. The file itself was now gone, but its name lingered on, a ghost betraying its former presence. The ~D prefix in its name was a familiar signifier to the researchers by now. It was the same distinctive naming convention that Duqu had used for the temporary files it created on infected machines, as well as the naming convention that Stuxnet used for some of its files.

Had Duqu, or some other program written by the same team, been on the machine before Wiper erased it?[1] Was Wiper a creation of the same team behind Duqu?

Raiu and his team programmed Kaspersky's antivirus tools to search for the ~DF78.tmp file—and for good measure, to flag any other temporary file that had a name that began with ~D. They got a number of hits on machines in various countries, but the majority of them showed up on machines in Iran. When they obtained a copy of one of the files—this one named ~DEB93D.tmp—they discovered it was a log for a "sniffer" component that recorded passwords as they flitted across the infected

---

1 Another clue uncovered from the ravaged system also seemed to point to the attackers behind Stuxnet and Duqu. The clue indicated that the first thing Wiper did when it landed on a system was hunt down and obliterate any file that had a .PNF extension. Raiu recalled that the payload file in Stuxnet as well as some of its other files all had .PNF extensions. Duqu also had files with a .PNF extension, an extension that was rarely used in malicious tools.

machine's local network. With a little digging, they also found a module that appeared to be responsible for creating the sniffer log.[2] It turned out to be one of their most significant finds.

The module didn't resemble Stuxnet or Duqu and didn't appear to be Wiper, either—it contained no code for erasing the hard drive of infected machines. They searched their archive to see if anything resembling it had come through their automated reporting system in the past, and to their surprise, module after module popped up, as if they'd just been sitting in the archive waiting to be discovered. They found twenty different files in all, each with odd names like Euphoria, Munch, Limbo, Frog, and Snack. The files all appeared to be plug-ins or components for a related attack.

What intrigued them most, however, was that one of the files had come in through their system in October 2010 and was tagged by the system as a Stuxnet file. At the time, this hadn't made sense to them because when they had examined the file, it didn't look anything like Stuxnet. But now when they examined it again they discovered what the two had in common—both files contained a zero-day exploit that they and Symantec had overlooked when they examined Stuxnet two years earlier.

The exploit had been embedded in a part of Stuxnet called Resource 207, which appeared only in the June 2009 version of the attack code, not the 2010 versions—which explained why they had overlooked it before. Most of the Stuxnet files Kaspersky and Symantec examined had come from the 2010 attacks. Very few samples of the 2009 variant had ever been found on infected machines.

Resource 207 contained the code that Stuxnet 2009 used to trick the Autorun feature in Windows machines to spread itself via USB flash drives. But it also contained this overlooked exploit that was now in the new attack code. The exploit gave the attackers escalated privileges on infected machines by exploiting a buffer-overflow vulnerability in the wallpaper feature of Windows. The vulnerability had been a zero day when the attackers created the exploit in February 2009, but by the time they released

---

2 The log also contained the internal computer names of systems in Iran that had been infected.

Stuxnet four months later that June, Microsoft had patched the hole.[3] When it came time to release the next version of Stuxnet in March 2010, the attackers had eliminated this exploit, along with the Autorun code, and replaced it with the .LNK exploit and two other privilege-escalation exploits that were still zero days at the time.

The discovery of the wallpaper exploit meant that instead of four zero-day exploits—which was already an impressive record—Stuxnet had actually used five zero-day exploits during its lifetime. More important, though, the link between Stuxnet and this new attack provided further evidence that Stuxnet was part of a suite of malicious tools created by the same team.

KASPERSKY'S ALEX GOSTEV and his team divvied up the twenty modules they had found for this new attack and went to work reverse-engineering them to see how they were connected. They worked day and night, fueled by caffeine and the excitement of knowing they had just uncovered another tool in the Stuxnet arsenal.

At the end of three weeks, they had a digital spy kit on their hands that was larger than anything they had seen before. They dubbed it "Flame," after the name of one of the main modules in the attack.[4]

Stuxnet had tipped the scales at 500 kilobytes when compressed, but Flame was at least 20 megabytes with all of its components combined, and consisted of more than 650,000 lines of code. It also had astounding complexity to match its girth. They estimated it would have taken a team of half a dozen programmers at least three years to code it all, and it would

---

3 Microsoft patched it on June 9, about two weeks before the June version of Stuxnet was released on June 22, 2009.

4 With regard to whether Flame was connected to Wiper, there was some confusion between the two attacks after the Kaspersky researchers uncovered a Flame module that was named *Viper*. But the job of this module was to transmit stolen data to a command server, not to wipe the hard drive of infected machines. Its existence, though, raised questions initially about whether the Wiper malware the Iranians found was actually a component of Flame. It didn't help that some Iranian reports identified Wiper as Viper, due to a transliteration error from Persian to English. But in the end, Kaspersky found no direct connection between Wiper and Flame.

take the entire Kaspersky team years more to completely decipher it. Instead, they settled for deciphering just enough of the code to understand it.

The Kaspersky team had seen a lot of digital spy tools over the years—many of them believed to be nation-state tools from China—but this one rewrote the book. If James Bond's Q Branch had a digital armory, Flame would have been part of it. It came with a cornucopia of spy gadgetry aimed at collecting intelligence from victims in a multitude of ways. Among them was one module that siphoned documents from infected machines, and another that recorded keystrokes and captured screenshots every fifteen to sixty seconds. A third module surreptitiously engaged an infected computer's internal microphone to eavesdrop on conversations in its vicinity. A fourth module used the computer's Bluetooth function to swipe data from any discoverable smartphones and other Bluetooth-enabled devices in the area.

Flame appeared to be a multipurpose espionage tool created to meet every need, depending on the mission. Not every victim got the full Flame treatment, though. Each component was installed as needed. A 6 MB starter kit got loaded onto many infected machines first, which included a back door through which the attackers could install new spy modules from their command server at will.[5]

The infrastructure set up to support Flame was also massive and like nothing the researchers had seen before. They found at least eighty domains operating as command servers in Germany, the Netherlands, Switzerland, and elsewhere through which the attackers controlled infected machines and collected siphoned documents from them.[6] The attackers had likely set up so many domains in order to manage different operations and groups of victims separately.

---

5 Most of the machines that were infected had the 6 MB version installed on them. But they also found a smaller starter kit that was about 900 KB with no extra modules included with it and that may have been used to infect machines over slow network connections, since the 6 MB module would take forever to install remotely in countries with slow and unreliable internet connections.
6 The malware's configuration file contained a list of five static domains—among them traffic -spot.biz, dailynewsupdater.com, and bannezone.in—as well as another list that could be altered at random whenever the attackers added new command servers.

They used various fake identities to register the domains—Ivan Blix, Paolo Calzaretta, Traian Lucescu—and purchased some of them with pre-paid credit cards so they couldn't be traced. The Kaspersky researchers got traffic for about thirty of the domains redirected to a sinkhole that they controlled, and as soon as it was set up, infected machines in Iran and around the world began calling in. Stolen files intended for the attackers also poured in, though the files were encrypted so the researchers weren't able to see what the attackers were stealing.

After adding signatures for Flame to Kaspersky's antivirus tools, infections showed up on several hundred machines. Iran, no surprise, was at the top of the list. At least 189 machines were infected there. But there were also 98 victims in the Palestinian Territories, and about 30 victims each in Sudan and Syria.

While Kaspersky was still examining Flame's modules, Bencsáth in Hungary contacted Raiu with news of a suspicious file found in Iran that someone had sent him. They had become well acquainted with Bencsáth when they had worked on Duqu, so it wasn't unusual for him to contact them. The file he had received from Iran turned out to be one of the same modules Raiu and his team had already been examining. Bencsáth also passed the file to Chien at Symantec, who began to examine the threat in parallel with Kaspersky. When the Symantec researchers added signatures to their antivirus engine to detect it, they uncovered more victims in Austria, Hungary, Lebanon, Russia, the United Arab Emirates, and Hong Kong.

More than 1,000 victims were eventually uncovered, many more than the 36 victims Duqu was known to have hit, although nowhere near the more than 100,000 machines that Stuxnet had struck. But that's because unlike Stuxnet, Flame couldn't spread automatically. All of its spreading mechanisms worked only when deployed and commanded by the attackers. So while the majority of Stuxnet's victims were collateral damage, everyone Flame hit was presumably an intended target. Raiu suspected the victims were infected in groups, based on whatever mission the attackers were conducting at the time.

There was no discernable pattern to the pool of victims—Flame targeted individuals, private companies, government agencies, and academic institutions. But it wasn't difficult to see what types of files the attackers were after, since the malware contained a list of file extensions it sought, including Microsoft Word documents, PowerPoint presentations, and Excel files. But also high on the list were AutoCAD drawings, which had been targeted by Duqu as well. Flame, notably, was also looking to steal digital certificates.

Although Flame had a long list of files it was seeking, it didn't steal every file it found. Instead, it extracted 1 KB of text from each and transmitted it back to one of the command servers. From there it was likely passed to another location, where Raiu suspected the attackers had a supercomputer set up to sift through all the text samples that came in and determine which files the attackers wanted to grab in full. Notably, a year later when the NSA documents leaked by Edward Snowden were published, they described a system codenamed TURBINE that was designed to do something very similar to this. (See page 218.)

With such an elaborate operation set up for Flame, it was no surprise that the attack had been around for a while. The earliest infection uncovered, on a machine in Europe, occurred in December 2007.[7] A machine in Dubai was struck in April 2008. Some of the domains the attackers used for their command servers were also registered around this time. A handful of others were registered in 2009 and 2010, but the majority were registered in 2011, after Stuxnet was exposed. All of this meant that Flame had been active in the wild infecting systems for at least five years before it was discovered and was active during the same time that Stuxnet and Duqu were being developed and unleashed.

A clear picture was beginning to emerge of a digital arsenal filled with spy tools and weapons created to attack not just Iran's nuclear program

---

7 The attackers were more careful with Flame to alter timestamps in files to prevent researchers from dating the work. Although some of the timestamps appeared to be accurate, others that indicated files had been compiled in 1994 and 1995 were clearly incorrect because the files contained code from libraries that hadn't been created until 2010.

but other targets as well. Two separate platforms had been used to create the malicious code discovered so far. One was the Flame platform, upon which the massive Flame spy tool had been built. The other was the Tilde-d platform, upon which Duqu had been built. The Flame platform was much more dense and complex than the Tilde-d platform, and had therefore probably been created in parallel by a different team. Both platforms, however, were used to develop Stuxnet at various stages.

Raiu surmised that the development of Flame likely began in 2005 or 2006, due to the fact that some of the custom code the attackers wrote for their command servers had been developed in December 2006.[8] Development of the spy tool likely reached maturity in early 2007. The earliest known dates for Duqu were August 2007, when one of Duqu's droppers was compiled, and November 2008, when Duqu's infostealer showed the first signs of being in the wild.

Raiu believed that when it came time to build Stuxnet, the attackers used Flame to jumpstart the digital weapon, then later switched to the Duqu platform for subsequent versions of the attack. He based this in part on the fact that Resource 207 found in the 2009 version of Stuxnet—which contained the Autorun code and the wallpaper exploit—looked a lot like an early version of Flame's main module. Flame would have already existed as a basic espionage tool by 2007, and when it came time to write the missile portion of Stuxnet in 2009, it appeared that the team behind Flame shared source code for Resource 207 with the Stuxnet crew, essentially kick-starting the creation of the missile code. The payload was already created by then, and the attackers just needed something to deliver it. "Probably there was some kind of urgency to get [Stuxnet] out the door, so that's why they took this already mature plug-in from Flame and used it in Stuxnet," Raiu says.

After this, however, Stuxnet and Flame diverged. The programmers

---

8 The server code actually had a liner note the programmers had inserted to identify the authors and date of creation. The note read: "@author OCTOPUS in 12/3/2006; @author DeMO (modifications)." The names were likely code names for the individuals or teams that set up the servers.

behind Flame continued to build their platform into a massive espionage tool, and in 2010 when the attackers behind Stuxnet prepared the next version of their code for a subsequent assault, they switched to the Tilde-d platform—which had already been used to create Duqu—to recraft the missile for launching their attack. The switch to the Duqu platform likely occurred because the missile portion of the variant Stuxnet 2010, with all of its zero-day exploits and additional spreading mechanisms, was much more complicated and required more code. And the Tilde-d platform was a much simpler and more compact tool to use.

The sequence of events determined by Raiu and his team seemed to match the scenario depicted by *New York Times* reporter David Sanger, who reported in his book *Confront and Conceal*, citing current and former government officials, that the earliest version of Stuxnet was developed by the United States, while later versions were developed by the United States and Israel. Raiu believed that Flame and the Flame platform were created by the United States, while Israel created Duqu and the Tilde-d platform. Both then used their respective platforms to build their portions of Stuxnet.

Whatever Flame's role in Stuxnet, the whole spy operation around it came crashing down on May 28, 2012, when Kaspersky and Symantec went public with news of its discovery in near-simultaneous announcements.[9] Once news of the spy tool was out, the response of Flame's operators was swift. Within an hour of the first news stories being published, command servers used for the spy tool went dark as the attackers shuttered their operation, thus ending a massively successful five-year espionage

---

9 While Kaspersky had been examining the Flame files it obtained, Symantec had been examining the one it received from Bencsáth as well as other modules they obtained from the machines of infected customers after adding detection to their antivirus tools. Neither of the teams communicated with each other about their work, though each secretly learned that the other was researching the code. When the Symantec researchers discovered that the Kaspersky researchers planned to publish their results on Memorial Day, they rushed to complete their analysis to publish the same day. The author was contacted by both companies separately—first by Kaspersky and then by Symantec—in advance of the announcements. See Kim Zetter, "Meet Flame, the Massive Spy Malware Infiltrating Iranian Computers," Wired.com, May 28, 2012, available at wired.com/threatlevel/2012/05/flame.

campaign in a matter of minutes. It was almost as if they had been waiting for the news to break.

Flame's reign was now over, but its effects would live on. Days after the servers went dark, Microsoft announced that it had found an even more disturbing discovery about the Flame attack that the Kaspersky and Symantec researchers had missed.

IT WAS THE Memorial Day holiday in the United States when news of Flame broke, and not many people at Microsoft headquarters in Redmond, Washington, were working. But when engineers in the company's Security Response Center learned that a new attack campaign, attributed to the same team behind Stuxnet and Duqu, had been uncovered, they immediately grabbed samples of the Flame files made available by researchers. They wanted to see if the new attack used any zero-day vulnerabilities in Windows, as Stuxnet and Duqu had done. But as they examined one of the files they received, they realized they were looking at something much worse than a zero day—Flame was performing a sophisticated attack against part of Microsoft's Windows Update system to spread itself between machines on a local network.

Windows Update is the automated system Microsoft uses to distribute software updates and security patches to millions of customers. To obtain the updates, a client-side tool sits on each customer machine and contacts the Microsoft servers to download patches whenever they're available.

For years, the security community had warned of the security nightmare that would occur if hackers ever hijacked the Windows Update system to deliver malicious code, threatening the security of millions of Windows customers. This attack didn't rise to that level exactly, but it was just as dangerous. Instead of subverting the actual Microsoft servers that delivered Windows software updates to millions of customers, it subverted the Windows Update tool that sat on customer machines. The distinction was subtle but important. If the attackers had subverted Microsoft's servers, they could have compromised machines on a global scale. But the way they performed the attack meant they could compromise machines only on specific networks that they targeted, leaving anyone else unaffected.

Like the Windows software, the update tool itself gets periodically updated by Microsoft. Each time the tool launches on a customer's machine, it sends out a kind of beacon to Microsoft servers to see if a new version of itself is available. Microsoft distributes the updates through a series of so-called .CAB files, signed with a Microsoft certificate to verify their legitimacy.

The attackers subverted this process by first infecting one machine on a victim's network with Flame. Then when the update client on any other machine on that victim's network sent out a beacon to Microsoft servers to check for updates to the Windows Update tool, the infected machine intercepted the beacon and sent a malicious Flame file, masquerading as a legitimate Microsoft .CAB file, to the new machine instead, thus infecting it with the spy tool. This wasn't the most sophisticated part of the attack, however. To pull off the hijack, the attackers had signed their malicious .CAB file with a legitimate Microsoft certificate—except in this case the certificate indicated that the company it belonged to was "MS," not Microsoft Corporation, as it should have said. When Microsoft's research team saw this, they immediately suspected something was wrong. The certificate appeared to have been issued and signed by Microsoft's Terminal Services Licensing Certificate Authority in February 2010, but it was clearly a rogue certificate, which the CA should not have generated and signed. Had Microsoft's server been compromised or its cert-signing key stolen? The engineers had to quickly figure out how the attackers obtained the cert before anyone else could repeat the feat. They put out a call for any colleagues available to work on the holiday and quickly assembled a team.

It turned out the attackers had pulled this off using something called an MD5 hash collision. An MD5 hash is a cryptographic representation of data—in this case the data on the certificate—generated by a cryptographic algorithm known as MD5. Hashes are supposed to function like a fingerprint, so that every data set run through the algorithm produced a unique hash. If the data changed, the algorithm would produce a different hash. The MD5 algorithm, however, had been found years earlier to have a weakness that would allow someone to create the same hash from different data sets.[10] This was called a hash collision. Many companies had stopped using the MD5 algorithm for this reason. But Microsoft hadn't changed the algorithm used for its Terminal Services (TS) Licensing service since 1999, when the system was architected.

TS Licensing is a system used by Microsoft corporate customers when setting up a server with Microsoft software running on it so that multiple employees or machines can use the software. The customer purchases licenses from Microsoft—say 100 licenses for 100 employees or machines—then submits a request for a certificate to Microsoft's Terminal Services Licensing Certificate Authority. Microsoft's CA generates a certificate with the customer's name on it, as well as a timestamp indicating when the certificate was issued and a serial number for the digital document.

When Microsoft issues the certificate, it runs all of the data on the certificate, including the timestamp and serial number, through the MD5 algorithm to create a hash, then signs the hash and sends the cert to the customer. The customer then uses the signed certificate to ensure that only authorized machines or people issued the certificate use the software licensed from Microsoft. But in this case, the attackers used the hash from Microsoft to sign their rogue certificate and then to sign their malicious .CAB files.

Before the attackers submitted their certificate request to Microsoft, they created a rogue certificate that contained information that they anticipated the real Microsoft certificate would contain, as well as some minor alterations—alterations that they had to be sure would produce a hash that was identical to the one Microsoft would issue. This was no easy task. Among other challenges, it required running thousands and thousands of different variations of the data on their rogue certificate through the MD5 algorithm to get one that produced an identical bit-for-bit hash as the legitimate Microsoft certificate that contained different data, a feat

---

10 Its weakness has been known since at least 2004.

that required a lot of computational power. It also required anticipating the serial number that Microsoft would give the certificate and the exact time when Microsoft's licensing server would sign the legitimate certificate, since the timestamp and serial number were part of the hash that Microsoft generates and signs.[11] If they estimated the wrong time by even a millisecond, the signed hash would not be transferable to their rogue certificate, since the two hashes would no longer match.[12] The attackers would have needed to research the Microsoft system extensively and test multiple certificates—possibly hundreds—before they got the timing and serial number right.[13]

The attackers then used the signed hash with their rogue certificate to sign their malicious .CAB files. It appeared to be a legitimate certificate, since it had the signed hash generated by Microsoft.

The Windows Update hijack was a brilliant feat that pushed the boundaries of mathematics and could only have been achieved by world-class cryptographers.[14] When the Kaspersky researchers learned of it, they

---

11 Generally a certificate is generated and signed within seconds after a request is submitted to Microsoft's servers. The attackers could have been able to gauge how long it took Microsoft to issue signed certificates by submitting a number of certificate requests to the company to detect a pattern. But one former Microsoft employee suggested to me that the attackers could also have been sitting on Microsoft's internal network watching the requests come in to see exactly how long it took for requests to arrive from outside and be processed. There's no evidence this is the case, however.

12 In addition to all of this work, they also had to modify the certificate to use it to install their malware on Windows Vista machines, since in its original form it would not have been accepted by any system using Vista or a later version of the Windows operating system. The modification involved getting rid of an extension on the certificate. They didn't remove the extension, which might have caused it to fail the computer's code-signing check; instead, they "commented out" a bit on the certificate—surrounded it with markers to make the machine simply ignore the extension. This allowed it to work on Vista machines. Only 5 percent of the machines that Kaspersky saw infected with Flame had Windows Vista installed, however. Most of the machines were using Windows 7 or Windows XP.

13 According to sources, Microsoft tried to investigate who had submitted the requests and how many requests for a certificate came in from this entity, but too much time had passed between when the certificate was issued—in February 2010—and when Flame was discovered in 2012. Microsoft's logs get rewritten over time, and the logs for that time period were no longer available.

14 Dutch cryptographer and academic Marc Stevens, who with colleague Benne de Weger developed one of the first practical MD5 hash collision attacks for research purposes in 2007, described the Flame attack as "world-class cryptanalysis" that broke new ground and went beyond the work they and others had done with collisions. Stevens and de Weger were part of a group of researchers, including Alexander Sotirov, who demonstrated a similar, though technically different, collision attack in 2008 at the Chaos Computer Club Congress—a hacker conference held annually

dubbed it the "God-mode exploit," since it was so technically astute and so much more potent than spreading malware via a zero-day exploit.[15] The only thing that would have made it more powerful and dangerous was if the attackers had actually subverted the Windows Update patch servers themselves.

Microsoft's engineers initially estimated it would take just twelve days for other well-resourced attackers to learn everything they needed to know about Microsoft's certificate and update system to pull off a copycat attack to spread their own malware. But when they did a test run, walking through all the steps someone would need to take to copy the Windows Update hijack, and timed themselves while doing it, they realized that someone could actually pull off a less-sophisticated version of the attack—one that didn't require an MD5 hash collision—in just three days.[16]

Working against the clock, Microsoft rushed out an emergency out-of-band patch to fix the vulnerabilities that allowed the attack to occur. The company had released only one out-of-band patch in all of 2011, the previous year, and reserved such releases for only the most significant vulnerabilities, so it was an indication of just how seriously Microsoft viewed the Flame exploit that it took this step.

The attackers behind Duqu and Stuxnet had already struck at the underpinnings of the validation system that made the internet possible—first by stealing individual security certificates from the companies in Taiwan to sign the Stuxnet drivers, then by sending Duqu to steal data from a

---

in Germany. They used a cluster of two hundred Playstation 3s to do their computational work to generate an identical hash for a certificate. Their certificate masqueraded as a different company, not as Microsoft. When they conducted their experiment, however, they kept guessing the wrong timestamp and had to generate a hash four times before they got it right. When the Flame attack was discovered in 2012, Sotirov estimated that it was ten to a hundred times more difficult to pull off than the attack he and his colleagues had done. Slides for the presentation by Sotirov and his colleagues can be found at events.ccc.de/congress/2008/Fahrplan/attachments/1251_md5 -collisions-1.0.pdf.

15 It should be noted that after going through all of this trouble to obtain their rogue certificate, the attackers should not have been able to use it to sign their malicious code. But they were able to do so because Microsoft had failed to implement certain restrictions so that the certificates it issued for TS Licensing would be designated for "software licensing" purposes only.

16 This low-rent certificate would allow the malware to at least slip past Windows XP machines, though not Windows Vista machines, which had stronger security.

certificate authority itself. But this exploit went even further than that by subverting the trust between the world's biggest software maker and its customers. Assuming that the perpetrators behind it were American, they likely justified the operation and even got legal approval for it by arguing that they weren't subverting the Microsoft Windows servers themselves—thereby putting all of Microsoft's customers at risk—but simply subverting the Windows client on individual customer machines. In this way, they could focus the attack on victims and machines that weren't in the States.[17]

But ultimately it mattered little that they hadn't subverted Microsoft's servers. Subverting the update client tool was enough to create customer mistrust in the integrity of the update service itself—which could lead users to disable the tool and prevent them from receiving the security updates that were critical for the safety of their systems.

Who *was* responsible for threatening this trust between Microsoft and its customers? About three weeks after the news of Flame broke, former US government officials claimed ownership, telling the *Washington Post* that Flame had been a joint operation between the NSA, the CIA, and Israel's military.[18]

The unnamed sources said Flame had been developed sometime around 2007—confirming the general timeframe Raiu and his team had established for it—to collect intelligence about Iranian officials and to map computer systems that were part of Iran's nuclear program. But the officials also suggested that Flame had been an early-generation tool that had since been surpassed by others.

"This is about preparing the battlefield for another type of covert ac-

---

17 Some would say, however, that this attack was even worse than subverting the Microsoft Windows Update servers to deliver malicious software, because in subverting those servers, although the attackers would be able to send malicious software to customers from Microsoft's servers, customer machines would reject the code if it wasn't also signed by Microsoft. But by undermining Microsoft's certificate process to sign their malicious code, the attackers didn't need Microsoft's Update servers. They could deliver their malware to machines from any server and pass it off as legitimate Microsoft code.

18 Ellen Nakashima, "U.S., Israel Developed Flame Computer Virus to Slow Iranian Nuclear Efforts, Officials Say," *Washington Post*, June 19, 2012.

tion," a former US intelligence official told the paper, adding that cyber collection against the Iranian program was "way further down the road than this." He may have been referring to things like the implants the NSA uses that can transmit stolen data via radio waves from infected machines. (See page 314.)

Notably, the *Post*'s sources also cleared up a mystery about the Wiper attack that had struck Iran earlier that year. They told the paper that the attack, which had erased hard drives on machines at Iran's oil ministry and had led to the discovery of Flame, was also a nation-state construct. But unlike Flame and Stuxnet, which had been joint operations of Israel and the United States, Wiper, one source said, had been launched against Iran by Israel alone. An official told the *Post*, in fact, that the United States had been caught off guard by the destructive attack.

THE REVELATIONS ABOUT nation-state attacks were coming at a rapid pace now, with one operation after another being exposed, after years of remaining stealth. And the revelations weren't done yet. The Kaspersky researchers would soon find evidence that still *more* malicious tools created by the same teams were lurking in the wild.

The key break came for them when they obtained access to some of the command servers used by Flame. They discovered that ten days before the news of Flame broke, the attackers had launched a massive cleanup campaign to cover their tracks and erase any trace of their activity from the servers, suggesting further that, indeed, the attackers had had advance notice that their operation was about to be exposed.[19] But they had made one big mistake that left a server in Malaysia with its data largely intact.

---

19 With Duqu, the attackers had launched their cleanup operation *after* news of the malware broke, but the fact that the team behind Flame launched their cleanup about ten days before news of Flame broke, suggested they had known in advance that their cover was about to be blown. The Kaspersky researchers had likely tipped them off inadvertently when they connected a test machine infected with Flame to the internet. As soon as the machine went online, the malware reached out to one of Flame's command servers. The attackers must have realized the machine wasn't on their list of targets and may even have identified it as a Kaspersky machine and concluded that Flame's days were numbered. In a panic, they wiped the command servers and sent out a kill module, called Browse32,

Several weeks before the cleanup operation, the attackers had carelessly changed the settings on the server and inadvertently locked themselves out. As a result, they weren't able to get back in to wipe it clean, leaving a wealth of forensic data for Kaspersky to find.[20]

Left intact was the control panel the attackers had used to deliver the Flame modules to infected machines and to process stolen data retrieved from them. The control panel was designed to resemble a publishing platform for a business called NewsforYou, so that if any outsiders got access to the server, they'd think it belonged to a newspaper or media company. Malicious modules the attackers planned to install on victim machines were stored in directories the attackers named "News" and "Ads," while a directory called "Entries" stored the data and files that were swiped from victim machines.

The Kaspersky researchers also found logs listing the IP address of

---

to infected machines to erase any trace of the malware so victims would never know they had been infected.

The cleanup campaign was successful for the most part. But Browse32 had a fatal flaw; it left behind one telltale file, ~DEB93D.tmp, that gave it away. This was a temporary file that got created whenever Flame performed a number of different operations on an infected machine. Once the operation was done, Flame was supposed to delete the temp file automatically. Because of this, the attackers hadn't put it on the list of files that Browse32 was supposed to delete, since they weren't expecting it to be on machines. In a twist of fate, however, if the Browse32 kill module arrived to a machine while Flame was still performing one of the operations that had created the temp file, the kill module erased Flame before it could delete the temporary file. Kaspersky found the orphan temp file abandoned on hundreds of systems that had been infected with Flame. It was this file, in fact, left behind on a machine in Iran, that led the Kaspersky researchers to stumble across Flame in the first place.

20 This wasn't the only mistake they made. They also botched the cleanup operation on the servers they could access. They had created a script called LogWiper.sh to erase activity logs on the servers to prevent anyone from seeing the actions they had taken on the systems. Once the script finished its job, it was also supposed to erase itself, like an Ouroboros serpent consuming its own tail. But the attackers bungled the delete command inside the script by identifying the script file by the wrong name. Instead of commanding the script to delete LogWiper.sh, they commanded it to delete logging.sh. As a result, the LogWiper script couldn't find itself and got left behind on servers for Kaspersky to find. Also left behind by the attackers were the names or nicknames of the programmers who had written the scripts and developed the encryption algorithms and other infrastructure used by Flame. The names appeared in the source code for some of the tools they developed. It was the kind of mistake inexperienced hackers would make, so the researchers were surprised to see it in a nation-state operation. One, named Hikaru, appeared to be the team leader who created a lot of the server code, including sophisticated encryption. Raiu referred to him as a master of encryption. And someone named Ryan had worked on some of the scripts.

every infected machine that had contacted the server. The server had only recently been set up, on March 25, but during a ten-day span of its operation, at least 5,377 infected machines in dozens of countries had contacted it. About 3,702 of these were in Iran, and another 1,280 in Sudan. Other countries had fewer than 100 infections.

Raiu and his team realized that if just one command server, out of more than eighty the attackers had registered, communicated with 5,000 infected machines in just ten days, and the malware had been in the wild since 2007 or 2008, the total number of victims had to be tens of thousands more than they originally calculated. They also found a file on the Malaysian server that was stuffed with 5.7 GB of data stolen from victim machines during the same ten-day period. If the attackers had purloined this much data in just ten days, Raiu suspected their total booty must have amounted to terabytes of data over the five-plus years that Flame had operated.[21]

But these revelations paled in comparison to another piece of evidence the Flame engineers left behind, which showed that the Malaysian server was configured to communicate with not just one piece of malware, but *four*. They were identified by the attackers as SP, SPE, FL, and IP, and had

---

21 The attackers seemed to have managed their project like a tightly run military operation, with multiple teams handling carefully compartmentalized tasks. There was a management team that oversaw the operation and chose the victims; there were coders who created the Flame modules and a command-and-control team who set up and managed the servers, delivered the Flame modules to infected machines, and retrieved stolen data from machines; and finally there was an intelligence team responsible for analyzing the stolen information and submitting requests for more files to be purloined from machines that proved to have valuable data. It was exactly the kind of setup that the Snowden documents suggested the NSA had.

The team operating the command servers had limited visibility into the overall operation and may not even have known the true nature of the missions their work facilitated. The process for uploading new modules to infected machines was tightly controlled so that neither they nor any outsiders who might gain access to the servers could alter the modules or create new ones to send to infected machines. The command modules, for example, were delivered to the servers prewritten, where they got automatically parsed by the system and placed in a directory for delivery to victims by the server team, who only had to press a button to send them on their way. Data stolen from victims was also encrypted with a sophisticated algorithm and public key. The private key to decrypt it was nowhere to be found on the server, suggesting that the data was likely passed to a separate team who were the only ones capable of decrypting and examining it.

been created in that order, with SP being the oldest. Each of them was designed to communicate with the command server using a different custom protocol the attackers had written.[22]

FL referred to Flame, but the other three attack codes were a mystery. The Kaspersky researchers knew for certain that SPE existed, because they had seen evidence of it in the wild. When they had created their sinkhole to intercept data headed for the Flame servers, about ninety machines in Lebanon, Iran, and France infected with the SPE code had contacted their sinkhole thousands of times attempting to communicate with it using that code's specific protocol. The other two malicious programs had yet to turn up, though. They hadn't been able to obtain a copy of SPE, so they still didn't know what it did.

But all of this confirmed that as shocking as the revelations about Stuxnet, Duqu, and Flame were, they likely were just the shallow tip of a stockpile of tools and weapons the United States and Israel had built.

Indeed, a couple of weeks after the news of Flame broke, Kaspersky stumbled upon yet another nation-state spy tool that had evaded detection for years.

Every time Raiu's team discovered new files or a little more information about Stuxnet, Flame, or Duqu, they would refine the signatures in their antivirus products and tweak the search terms they used to dig through their archive to see if they could find other variants of the same files. During one search of their archive, they found a suspicious file that had come in through their automated reporting system from a customer machine in the Middle East. The file had been flagged by the system as a Flame module and communicated with the same command-and-control servers as Flame. But it clearly wasn't Flame or any of the other three mysterious programs—SP, SPE, or IP.

They added signatures for the file to their antivirus engine and found about 2,500 victims infected with it in twenty-five countries. More than

---

22 The protocols were identified as Old Protocol, Old E Protocol, SignUp Protocol, and Red Protocol.

1,600 of the victims were in Lebanon. The next highest number, 482, were in Israel, and another 261 were in the Palestinian Territories. About 40 victims were in the United States, and only 1 was in Iran.

As they reverse-engineered the code and began to analyze it, they saw that it contained some of the same libraries, algorithms, and base code that Flame contained, which explained why their system had flagged it as such. The coders had even left path and project data in some of the files, which showed that the files had been stored on the attackers' machines in a directory they had called Flamer.[23]

The Kaspersky researchers dubbed this new attack "Gauss," after the name the attackers had given one of its main modules. The name appeared to pay tribute to noted mathematician Johann Carl Friedrich Gauss—since other modules were named Lagrange and Gödel, apparently after mathematician Joseph-Louis Lagrange and cryptographer Kurt Gödel. The reverence for math and cryptography became clear when the researchers discovered that the attack had a payload that used a highly complex and sophisticated encryption scheme worthy of a master cryptographer.

Like Flame, this new mystery malware was an espionage tool, but it was much smaller than Flame and was clearly part of a separate spy operation. The malware contained a handful of modules for stealing system passwords, recording configuration data, and swiping login credentials for social networking, e-mail, and instant-messaging accounts. There was also a module for infecting USB flash drives with the same .LNK exploit Stuxnet had used.

But there was something else the new attack had that the researchers had never seen in a nation-state tool before—a Trojan program for stealing login credentials to bank accounts. This wasn't a run-of-the-mill banking Trojan, though. Rather, it focused on customers of banks in Lebanon—the Bank of Beirut, EBLF, BlomBank, ByblosBank, FransaBank, and Credit Libanais. There was no sign the Trojan was being used to steal

---

23 Two names—Flame and Flamer—appeared in different parts of the code. Kaspersky decided to call the malware Flame, but Symantec opted to call it Flamer in their report about it.

money from the accounts, but some of Lebanon's banks were suspected of being used to launder funds for Iran's nuclear program and for the Iranian-backed Hezbollah, so the attackers may have been monitoring balances and transactions to map relationships between accounts and trace the movement of money.

There were two mysteries with the code that the researchers couldn't resolve—one involved a custom font file the attackers called Palida Narrow that Gauss installed on infected machines. Like Duqu's Dexter Regular, Palida Narrow was a fabricated font name. But unlike Duqu, the Palida Narrow file contained no exploit or malicious code. In fact, it appeared to have no functionality at all so the researchers were clueless as to why the attackers installed it.[24]

But a bigger mystery lay in an encrypted payload that Gauss deposited onto some machines, which was locked in an impenetrable shell.

Unlike Stuxnet, which delivered its payload to every machine it infected but executed the payload only on machines with a specific configuration, Gauss only delivered its payload to machines that had a specific configuration. It seemed the attackers had learned from mistakes made with Stuxnet. By limiting the number of machines to which they spread the Gauss payload, they greatly reduced the chance that it would be discovered.

Gauss delivered its warhead in a very restricted manner via USB flash drives. It would infect only one USB flash drive inserted into an infected machine and no more. When that flash drive then got inserted into another machine, it passed the payload to the machine only if the machine had the specific configuration Gauss was seeking. It also collected the configuration data from any machine it entered and stored it on the USB flash drive in a hidden file. If the flash drive was inserted into any other machine that was infected with Gauss and that was also connected to the internet,

---

24 It was possible that at one point Gauss might have contained the same Windows font exploit that Duqu had used to install itself on machines, though there was no sign of it. If it had been used, the attackers might have removed it after Microsoft patched the vulnerability it exploited in 2011.

Gauss transmitted the hidden file back to the attackers' command server. In this way, the attackers would know when Gauss had reached its target.

Gauss also took another precaution with its payload. Unlike Stuxnet, the keys for unlocking this mysterious payload were not stored in the malware. Instead, the warhead could only be decrypted with a key that was dynamically generated from the configuration data on the machine it was targeting.

But to generate the key, the malware went through a series of elaborate contortions to ensure that it wouldn't unload on the wrong machine and that no one would be able to unlock it using brute force. First it collected very specific configuration data from the targeted machine—information about directories, program files, and other resident data—then combined the names of each file, one by one, with the name of the top directory in the Windows Program Files folder on the machine. To this string of data it added a special value, then ran it through the MD5 hash algorithm 10,000 times, rehashing the resulting hash to produce a new hash each time.[25] If, at the end, it generated the correct hash it was seeking, the malware proceeded to the next step.

Even when Gauss arrived at the hash it was seeking, it didn't immediately unlock the payload. Instead, it recalculated the 10,000th hash using a different added value. The hash from *this* operation then became the key that unlocked the warhead. Once the payload was unlocked, Gauss used the same path and program data that produced the very first hash, added yet a new value to it, then decrypted a second section in the attack code, before repeating the same steps to decrypt yet a third section.

If you were trying to run an exceptionally careful and controlled operation, this was the way to do it. Stuxnet's payload had hardly been secured at all by comparison, allowing researchers to easily unlock it and

25 The attackers were checking to see whether a very specific program was installed on the machine, a program that was probably unique to the region in which it was located. The target program was unknown, but the Kaspersky researchers say it began with an odd character, and they believed, therefore, that the program might have had an Arabic or Hebrew name.

determine what it was doing. But the complex encryption scheme used for Gauss's payload ensured that the warhead remained locked in an impenetrable vault that no one could break.

Indeed, although the Kaspersky researchers tried millions of data pairings to uncover the configuration that unlocked Gauss's payload, they were unable to produce a key that could crack it. They had to wonder what was so special about Gauss's payload that the attackers had gone to so much trouble to secure it. They couldn't rule out the possibility that it was something destructive like Stuxnet or Wiper or that it was extra-sensitive because it had something to do with Gauss's banking Trojan and financial networks.

Gauss's locked payload prevented the researchers from fully deciphering the attack, but in the course of analyzing this threat, they stumbled upon another find that had eluded them until then: a sample of the mysterious SPE malware.

SPE was one of the four programs that communicated with Flame's command servers and that had contacted their Flame sinkhole months earlier. They discovered that it was actually a standalone module, instead of another attack entirely, that could be used either on its own or in conjunction with Flame or Gauss to expand the spying powers of either of these tools.[26] The module, which Kaspersky dubbed "mini-Flame," was the first direct link they found that connected Gauss and Flame. Previously they had believed the two attacks were entirely separate operations run by the same attackers, but mini-Flame proved otherwise. Kaspersky even found one machine in Lebanon that was infected with all three programs—Flame, Gauss, and mini-Flame.[27]

This junior Flame opened a back door onto infected computers and also operated as an infostealer, allowing the attackers to remotely examine the configuration of machines and map any other systems connected to

---

26 The discovery of SPE left two of the four pieces of malware used with the Flame servers undiscovered—SP and IP. Raiu guessed that SP was likely an early version of SPE that was not encrypted.

27 Gauss's files were named after elite mathematicians and cryptographers, but SPE adopted a more populist approach, using names such as Fiona, Sonia, Tiffany, Elvis, and Sam.

them. The attackers likely first infected a system with Flame or Gauss to collect basic intelligence about it and determine if it was a high-value target, then installed mini-Flame only on key machines belonging to high-profile victims when they needed to directly control the machine, swipe specific data from it, or further explore the victim's local network. Once mini-Flame was installed, the attackers likely sent out a module from their command servers to delete the larger Flame spy kit from the machine and thereby reduce their footprint.

Kaspersky found only about fifty victims infected with mini-Flame, located primarily in Iran and other parts of the Middle East, but also in Lithuania and the United States. Among the victims, they found six different variants of the module, all created between October 2010 and September 2011. But the development of the first mini-Flame module likely occurred in 2007, when Stuxnet, Duqu, and the larger Flame were created, since this is when the protocol that mini-Flame used to communicate with command servers was created. Oddly, though mini-Flame communicated with Kaspersky's sinkhole some 14,000 times over a four-month period in the summer of 2012, it completely halted communication with the sinkhole between July 4–7 of that year—a gap that Kaspersky could never explain.

WITH THE DISCOVERY of this last module, Kaspersky's work on code created by the Stuxnet gang began to wind down—in part because the detailed work that Raiu and his team had done to expose all of these covert nation-state tools was starting to bring the researchers unwanted attention.

As they released one finding after another, there were some in the security community who began to question their motives. Just as Symantec had been criticized for disloyalty to the United States in exposing Stuxnet and harming US national security interests, some wondered if the Moscow-based Kaspersky Lab was doing the bidding of Russian intelligence by exposing and sabotaging Western spy operations.

Raiu says, however, that they were never influenced or guided in their work by any government or intelligence agencies. He and his team considered their work above and beyond politics, and their only aim, like those of the Symantec researchers, was to exercise their reverse-engineering skills in the service of defending customers and contributing to the security of the computing community. In fact, their work exposing the Stuxnet and Flame gangs actually *conflicted* with their company's own business interests. Kaspersky Lab was in the midst of a major push to expand into the US market, and founder Eugene Kaspersky had been making a concerted effort to cultivate friends in Washington and Israel to this end. It was no help, then, that while he was courting these two governments, his researchers were busy exposing their covert operations.

But it wasn't just the company's business interests that were at risk of being affected by their work. The Symantec researchers had been worried during their analysis of Stuxnet that their work might be secretly monitored by Israel and the United States, or even by Iran, though they never saw any concrete signs that this actually occurred. Raiu, however, became certain that he was being followed while in Munich for a conference in the spring of 2012. It was shortly after they had discovered Flame, but before they'd gone public with the news. Raiu noticed someone lurking at the front desk of his Munich hotel when he checked in, as if trying to discover his room number. Later he noticed others tailing him when he went to the restroom or his hotel room. When he mentioned his concern to colleagues, they noticed it too. He suspected the people shadowing him were from a foreign intelligence agency, but he couldn't be sure. Then he was approached by three Israelis who wanted to speak with him about his work on Duqu, and by a woman who wanted to know if Kaspersky had the ability to recover wiped files from a hard drive. The latter question was a bit unsettling, since Kaspersky was in the midst of trying to recover files from systems in Iran that had been trashed with the Wiper malware.

It was yet another stark reality check that the world of virus hunting had changed dramatically with Stuxnet. Previously the only risk researchers faced from exposing digital threats was the wrath of cybercriminals who might take issue with them for interfering with their livelihood. But the dismantling of nation-state threats introduced a whole new world of concerns, and Raiu decided, for the sake of his young family, that he should lower his profile. After the incidents occurred at the Munich conference, he withdrew from speaking publicly about Kaspersky Lab's nation-state work and left it to colleagues to handle the media duties thereafter.

It was no coincidence then, when, not long after this, the Kaspersky researchers turned their attention away from the Stuxnet-Duqu-Flame family of threats to focus on other projects—in particular one believed to be the work of Russian actors. The operation, dubbed "Red October," targeted diplomats, governments, and research institutes, primarily in eastern Europe and central Asia, with the principal aim of collecting confidential documents and geopolitical intelligence. Raiu and his colleagues suspected it was the work not of nation-state actors but of Russian cybercriminals or freelance spies who were seeking the intelligence to sell it.

With the Red October operation, the Kaspersky team seemed to put the Stuxnet gang behind them for good. But this didn't mean that everyone had heard the last from Stuxnet. It turned out that the digital weapon still had one more surprise waiting to be revealed.

IT WAS NOVEMBER 2012, more than two years after Stuxnet had been discovered, when even Duqu and Flame were becoming distant memories, that the Symantec researchers stumbled upon a missing link that they had long given up hope they would ever find—an early version of Stuxnet that preceded all other known variants.

They found it while scouring their archive for any malicious files that had fingerprints matching Stuxnet's—something they periodically did with malware signatures to make sure they hadn't missed anything important. In doing this, a component popped up that they hadn't seen before. It had been sitting in their archive since November 15, 2007, when someone had submitted it to VirusTotal, which meant the first Stuxnet attack had been unleashed much earlier than previously believed.[28] As noted previously, they had always suspected other versions of Stuxnet existed, due to gaps in the version numbers of the 2009 and 2010 variants—1.001, 1.100, and 1.101. They had even suspected there might be an early version of Stuxnet that had preceded all other known ones. Now they had found it—Stuxnet version 0.5.

As they uncovered more files associated with the component, however, they discovered that this wasn't just any version of Stuxnet. It was one that contained the complete 417 attack code, fully intact and enabled.

Their previous attempt to unravel Stuxnet's attack against the Siemens S7-417 PLC had failed because the code was incomplete and disabled in later versions of Stuxnet. Symantec's Nicolas Falliere had thought perhaps the attackers had disabled it because they were waiting for a critical bit of configuration data to complete their attack. But now it was clear they had disabled it because they had decided to change their tactics. Although the later versions contained both the 315 and the disabled 417 attack codes, this early variant had no sign of the 315 attack code in it, just the code that attacked the Siemens 417 PLC. It was clear from this that the attackers had first focused their assault on 417 PLCs at Natanz and then for whatever reason—the attack hadn't achieved their aim or was taking too long to achieve it—had recalibrated and turned their sights on the 315 PLCs instead.

---

28 When malicious files are submitted to VirusTotal, the website will send a copy of the file to any of the antivirus companies whose scanner failed to detect the file, though it will also sometimes send files that do get detected as well. The VirusTotal record for the submission of this early Stuxnet file shows that the file was submitted at least twice to the site, on November 15 and 24. Both times, only one out of thirty-six virus scanners on the site flagged the file as suspicious, which would have been good news for the attackers. Oddly, there is information missing in the submission record that generally appears in the records of other files submitted to the site. The category indicating the total number of times the file was submitted to the site is blank, as is the category indicating the source country from where the file was submitted, which might have provided valuable intelligence about the location of the attackers, if they were the ones who submitted the file, or about the first victim, if the file was submitted by someone infected with the file. It's not clear whether that information was intentionally scrubbed from the record. VirusTotal was founded by a team of engineers in Spain, but Google acquired it in September 2012, just a couple of months before Symantec stumbled across this early Stuxnet version. Google did not respond to queries about why the data was missing from the record.

Now that the Symantec team—minus Falliere, who had left Symantec for a job at Google—had their hands on this early variant, they were finally able to determine what the 417 PLCs were controlling and what Stuxnet was doing to them. It turned out this version was targeting the valves that managed the flow of uranium hexafluoride gas into and out of the centrifuges and cascades at Natanz.[29] Stuxnet was opening and closing the valves to increase the pressure inside the centrifuges to five times its normal level. At that pressure, the gas would likely begin to solidify, ruining the enrichment process, and causing the centrifuges, spinning at high speed, to career dangerously off balance and crash into other centrifuges around them. Or at least this was likely the plan. It may not have worked as well or as quickly as the attackers had hoped, so in 2009 they changed tactics and focused on attacking the frequency converters instead—a more direct method of damaging the centrifuges.

Although Stuxnet 0.5 had no kill date and should have still been active when later versions of Stuxnet were released, researchers never found this version on any machines when Stuxnet was discovered in 2010.[30] This may have been because it got erased. One of the first things later versions of Stuxnet did when they landed on a machine was check for earlier versions of Stuxnet on the machine and replace them. So it was likely that Stuxnet 0.5 got automatically replaced on infected machines when the June 2009 version was launched.[31]

---

29 It was even easier to see from the configuration data in this version of Stuxnet than in later versions that Stuxnet was seeking the precise setup at Natanz. The code indicated it was seeking a facility where the systems it was targeting were labeled A21 through A28. Natanz had two cascade halls, Hall A and Hall B. Only Hall A had centrifuges in it when Stuxnet struck. The hall was divided into cascade rooms, or modules, that were each labeled Unit A21, A22, and so on, up to A28.

30 Stuxnet 0.5 had an infection kill date of July 4, 2009. Once this date arrived, it would no longer infect new machines, though it would have remained active on machines it already infected unless it got replaced by another version of Stuxnet. The next version of Stuxnet was released June 22, 2009, just two weeks before Stuxnet 0.5's kill date.

31 Like later versions of Stuxnet, this one had the ability to update itself on infected machines that weren't connected to the internet. It did this through peer-to-peer communication. All the attackers had to do was deliver an update from one of the command servers to a machine that was connected to the internet, or deliver it via a USB flash drive, and other machines on the local network would receive the update from that machine.

It's also possible that samples of Stuxnet 0.5 were never found because this version was much more tightly controlled than later ones and only infected a limited number of machines. Instead of using zero-day exploits to spread, it spread in just one way—by infecting Siemens Step 7 project files. These were the files that programmers shared among themselves that were used to program the Siemens S7 line of PLCs, making them ideal for getting Stuxnet onto the targeted PLCs. The fact that this version only spread via Step 7 files suggested the attackers had an inside track to get it onto core systems at Natanz. Stuxnet 0.5 was therefore likely never caught because patient zero—the first machine it infected—may have been one of the very programming machines the attackers were targeting. With later versions of the malware, they may have lost this access, which forced them to bulk up Stuxnet with extra spreading power to increase the odds of reaching their target.[32] Unfortunately, this spreading power in later versions, and the location of patient zero in an office outside of Natanz, were the factors that got Stuxnet caught.[33]

Stuxnet 0.5 was completely autonomous once unleashed, so the attackers had no need to control it. But if it found itself on a machine that was connected to the internet, it still contacted one of four command servers, from which the attackers could send new code to update the digital weapon if needed.[34] Stuxnet was programmed to stop communicating

---

32 One other note about this version is that it had a driver file that caused a forced reboot of infected Windows machines twenty days after they were infected. It's interesting to note that Stuxnet was discovered in 2010 after machines in Iran kept crashing and rebooting. Although the version of Stuxnet found on those machines was not 0.5, it raises the possibility that this version of Stuxnet or its driver might have been lurking on those machines and caused them to reboot repeatedly. Although VirusBlokAda never found Stuxnet 0.5 on the machines, they may simply have missed it.

33 After discovering Stuxnet 0.5 in their archive, the Symantec researchers did a search for it and found a number of errant and dormant infections in Iran but also in the United States, Europe, and Brazil.

34 The servers were set up in the United States, Canada, France, and Thailand. The command servers were designed to masquerade as an internet advertising firm called Media Suffix to conceal their true intention if someone were to gain access to them. The domains for the servers— smartclick.org, best-advertising.net, internetadvertising4u.com, and ad-marketing.net—each had the same home page for the fake advertising company, which had a tagline that read "Deliver What the Mind Can Dream." The home page read: "The internet is widely becoming the hottest advertising and marketing medium in the world. MediaSuffix focuses extremely in the internet segment of

with the servers on January 11, 2009, but by then the attackers were already preparing the next version of their assault—a driver they compiled January 1, 2009, for use with the next version of Stuxnet, which they unleashed five months later.

The submission of Stuxnet 0.5 to VirusTotal in 2007, along with other dates associated with the code, forced the researchers to revise their estimate of when work on Stuxnet began.[35] It appeared that preliminary work on the attack had begun as early as November 2005. This is when some of the domains for the command-and-control servers used with Stuxnet 0.5 were registered. Code for other command servers later used in the 2009 and 2010 Stuxnet attacks—the todaysfutbol.com and mypremierfutbol .com domains—was compiled in May 2006. Though Stuxnet itself wasn't unleashed in 2006—Bush's advisers proposed it to him only that year— the command infrastructure for controlling it was already being set up during this time. It's possible the command servers were initially set up to communicate with Flame, Duqu, or another spy tool the attackers used to collect intelligence for the operation, then were used again for Stuxnet. These early dates certainly coincided with when the Kaspersky researchers believed work on Flame began.

The dates also coincided with the period when the political situation over Iran's nuclear program was reaching a breaking point: In August 2005, two months after Ahmadinejad was elected president, international talks over Iran's nuclear program collapsed, and Iran announced it was withdrawing from the suspension agreement. Three months later, the attackers registered the command-and-control servers for Stuxnet 0.5.

Iran did have centrifuges installed at Natanz during this time, but only in the pilot plant. In February 2006, three months after the command servers were registered, Iran attempted to enrich its first batch of

---

advertising. MediaSuffix is ready to show your company how to capitalize on this unbelievable growing market. Don't be left behind. . . . We offer clients an unparalleled range of creative answers to the varied needs of our clients."

35 Stuxnet 0.5 may have been unleashed earlier than November 2007, but this is the first record of its appearance. According to the compilation date found in the Stuxnet component submitted to VirusTotal, it was compiled in 2001, though Chien and O'Murchu believe the date is inaccurate.

uranium in a small cascade at the pilot plant. But the operation didn't go well, since fifty of the centrifuges exploded. It's possible an early version of Stuxnet was responsible for this; Iranian authorities attributed the sabotage to UPSes from Turkey that they said had been manipulated to cause a sudden power surge.

Iran quickly recovered from that setback and in May announced that technicians had achieved 3.5 percent enrichment in a full-size cascade at the pilot plant. Plans to begin installing the first of 3,000 centrifuges in one of the underground cascade halls commenced. It took until early 2007, however, for the first centrifuges to be installed in the hall. By November that year, about 3,000 centrifuges were in place. That same month, Stuxnet showed up in the wild for the first time when someone submitted Stuxnet 0.5 to VirusTotal.

WITH THE DISCOVERY of this early version of Stuxnet, the researchers now had what was likely to be the most complete picture they were ever going to have about what occurred with this groundbreaking attack against Iran.

It had been a long and improbable ride that was made possible only by a series of unfortunate events and flubs that should never have occurred— from the zero-day exploits that launched Stuxnet on its wild odyssey through thousands of machines around the world to the crashing machines in Iran that first gave it away; from the green researchers in Belarus who lacked the skill and experience to tackle a threat like Stuxnet to the Symantec researchers who bumbled their way through the PLC code; from the Wiper tool in Iran that led the Kaspersky team to uncover Flame to the server in Malaysia that locked the attackers out and preserved a mountain of forensic evidence for the researchers to find. There were so many things that had to go wrong for Stuxnet and its arsenal of tools to be discovered and deciphered that it's a wonder any of it occurred.

When it was all done, the Kaspersky and Symantec researchers looked back over the two years of work they had put into reverse-engineering and analyzing the Stuxnet gang's malicious tools and were left to marvel at the level of skill and craftsmanship that went into building them. But they were also left scratching their heads at the shocking rapidity at which operations that had remained stealth for so many years had unraveled so quickly in their hands—like the errant string of a sweater that when yanked causes the entire garment to disintegrate.

The attackers had no doubt assumed, even counted on, the Iranians not having the skills to uncover or decipher the malicious attacks on their own. But they clearly hadn't anticipated that the crowdsourced wisdom of the hive—courtesy of the global cybersecurity community—would handle the detection and analysis for them.

With Stuxnet, a new world order was born in which security researchers and reverse-engineers became the unwitting draftees in a new kind of militia—one enlisted to dismantle and defend against the digital weapons that nations lobbed at one another. This new order created a host of new ethical and national security dilemmas for researchers caught between the needs of computer users and the interests of intelligence agencies and governments. If Stuxnet signaled the beginning of the militarization of cyberspace, it also signaled the beginning of the politicization of virus research.

"There's a new good guy/bad guy question here that puts us potentially in a very difficult position," Eric Chien said in 2012 after their analysis of Stuxnet was done. Their work on Stuxnet had been unmarred and unimpeded by political influences, and he hoped to never be in a position where they were forced to choose between customers and the interests of national security. But he wasn't so naïve to think that it would never come to that.

"It sounds a little cheesy, but we're just trying to help people and do what's right," he says. "If we get to a point where we have to ask that question, it's going to be a very hard question [to answer]. I think we'll be in a bad place if we get to that point."[36]

---

36 Author interview conducted with Chien, April 2011.

CHAPTER 16

OLYMPIC GAMES

In 2012, Chien may have been contemplating the dark and complicated future Stuxnet wrought, but four years earlier, the architects of the code were contemplating a different dark future if Iran succeeded in building a nuclear bomb.

In April 2008, President Ahmadinejad took a much-publicized tour of the enrichment facilities at Natanz, to mark the second anniversary of the plant's operation, and in the process gave arms-control specialists their first meaningful look inside the mysterious plant. Wearing the white lab coat and blue shoe booties of plant technicians, Ahmadinejad was snapped by photographers as he peered at a bank of computer monitors inside a control room, flashed an ironic "peace" sign at the cameras, and led an entourage of stern-looking scientists and bureaucrats down two rows of gleaming, six-foot-tall centrifuges standing erect at attention like military troops in full dress trotted out for inspection.

The president's office released nearly fifty images of the tour, thrilling nuclear analysts with their first peek at the advanced IR-2 centrifuges they had heard so much about. "This is intel to die for," one London analyst wrote of the images.[1]

---

1 The comment appeared in a post about Ahmadinejad's tour published on the Arms Control Wonk website. William J. Broad, "A Tantalizing Look at Iran's Nuclear Program," *New York Times*, April 29, 2008.

But among the retinue accompanying Ahmadinejad on his visit to Natanz was the Iranian defense minister—an odd addition to the party given Iran's insistence that its uranium enrichment program was peaceful in nature.

Iranian technicians had spent all of 2007 installing 3,000 centrifuges in one of the underground halls at Natanz, and during his visit Ahmadinejad announced plans to begin adding 6,000 more, putting Iran in the company of only a handful of nations capable of enriching uranium at an industrial level. It was a sweet triumph over the many obstacles Iran had faced in the past decade—including technical difficulties, procurement hurdles and sanctions, and all of the political machinations and covert sabotage that had been aimed at stopping its program. The success of the enrichment program now seemed assured.

But Natanz wasn't out of the woods just yet. Producing enriched uranium at an industrial scale required thousands of centrifuges spinning at supersonic speed for months on end with little or no interruption.[2] And while Ahmadinejad was taking his victory lap among the devices, something buried deep within the bits and bytes of the machines that controlled them was preparing to stir up more trouble.

IT WAS LATE in 2007 when President Bush reportedly requested and received from Congress $400 million to fund a major escalation in covert operations aimed at undermining Iran's nuclear ambitions. The money was earmarked for intelligence-gathering operations, political operations to destabilize the government and stimulate regime change, and black-ops efforts to sabotage equipment and facilities used in the nuclear program.[3] The latter included the experimental efforts to manipulate computer control systems at Natanz.

---

2 It took only a day or two for a batch of gas to run through a cascade and finish enriching, according to Albright, but centrifuges spin nonstop for years as new batches of gas are constantly fed into them.

3 Joby Warrick, "U.S. Is Said to Expand Covert Operations in Iran," *Washington Post*, June 30, 2008.

Although Bush's advisers had reportedly proposed the digital sabotage sometime in 2006, preparations for it had begun long before this, possibly even years before, if timestamps in the attack files are to be believed—the malicious code blocks that Stuxnet injected into the 315 and 417 PLCs had timestamps that indicated they had been compiled in 2000 and 2001, and the rogue Step 7 .DLL that Stuxnet used to hijack the legitimate Siemens Step 7 .DLL had a 2003 timestamp.[4]

It's likely, however, that the clock on the computer used to compile the files was out of date or that the coders manipulated the timestamps to throw forensic investigators off. But if the timestamps were accurate, it would mean the attackers had held the malicious code in reserve for three to six years while the United States waited to see how the diplomacy game with Iran played out, then pulled out the code only in 2006 when it was clear that negotiations and sanctions had failed.

Some of the attack code was generic to a lot of Siemens systems, and not specifically tailored to the ones at Natanz, so it *was* possible that parts of the attack code grew out of a general research project aimed at uncovering vulnerabilities in all Siemens PLCs, not just the ones at Natanz. Siemens control systems were used extensively throughout Iran in various industries—the oil and gas industries, as well as the petrochemical and mineral industries—not just in its nuclear program. They were also used extensively in other regions of the Middle East. With cyberwarfare already on the horizon in the late '90s, it would have made sense for the United States and Israel to invest in early research to uncover vulnerabilities in the Step 7 system and related Siemens PLCs—which came on the market in

---

4 The code that infected the OB1 and OB35 blocks in the PLCs—organizational blocks that controlled the reading of commands on the PLCs and the alarm system—had a compilation date of February 7, 2001. The code that sabotaged the frequency converters and manipulated the valves had similar timestamps. For example, there were thirty blocks of code in the 315 attack that sabotaged the Vacon and Fararo Paya frequency converters; two of these appeared to have been compiled in May 2000, while the timestamp for the remaining blocks was September 23, 2001. The code blocks used to manipulate the valves in the 417 attack had a timestamp from the same September day, though three hours later, as if the person compiling them had taken a dinner break, then returned to finish the job.

the mid '90s—in anticipation that the knowledge would come in handy later.

Not all of the code was so generically applicable to Siemens systems, however: the blocks targeting the frequency converters and valves were specific to the configuration at Natanz and would have required fore-knowledge of the exact components Iran planned to install at the plant, as well as intelligence about their precise configuration and operation. For the timestamps in these code blocks to be reliable, the programmers would have had to know in 2001 what equipment was going to be installed at a plant that wasn't even constructed yet.

That part is not as outlandish as it seems: Iran had already tested its uranium enrichment process in small cascades of centrifuges at the Kalaye Electric factory sometime around 1999. Furthermore, in 2000 and 2002, the CIA recruited key suppliers in the Khan network who provided the agency with intelligence about some of the components the network had supplied to Iran and other Khan customers. So by the time ground broke on Natanz in 2000, the intelligence agency may already have known what equipment Iran planned to install at the plant, including the Siemens con-trol systems.

David Albright of ISIS agrees that much of the information about Natanz could have been known in 2001.

"The cascade details, including the 164 centrifuges per cascade, num-ber of stages [in the cascade], most valves, pressure transducers, and pip-ing, could have been known [that early]," he says.[5] But information about the Vacon and Fararo Paya frequency converters may not have been avail-able then. "Frequency converters would be another matter, since Iran was acquiring them abroad back in that period from a variety of companies. So it would be hard to believe that Stuxnet's designers in 2001 could count on them being from Finland or domestically assembled [by Fararo Paya].

5 As noted previously, cascades are configured into a number of enrichment stages, with each stage containing a different number of centrifuges, depending on how many are needed for that stage in the enrichment process.

Moreover, the first module [of cascades installed at Natanz in 2007] was built with a range of imported frequency converters."[6]

In 2003, when the timestamp for the Step 7 doppelgänger indicates it was compiled, there was more information available about Natanz.

When IAEA inspectors paid their first visit to Natanz in February 2003, Iran already had a small cascade in place at the pilot plant and was preparing to install up to 1,000 centrifuges there by the end of the year. And as part of the IAEA's inquiry into Iran's nuclear program, Iran had to provide lists of equipment procured for Natanz and other nuclear facilities—lists that included machine tools, valves, and vacuum pumps.[7] Intelligence agencies also had been monitoring Iran's secret procurement activities and knew that a company named Neda Industrial Group—a leading industrial automation firm in Tehran—was involved in procurement for the nuclear program. The company worked with Kalaye Electric, the former watch factory that had been converted into a centrifuge factory, to install equipment at Natanz.[8] Neda was also Siemens's local partner in Iran, and in 2000 and 2001, according to the company's website, it had installed Siemens S7 PLCs in other facilities in the country—the same model of PLCs that Stuxnet attacked. It wasn't a stretch to think that if Neda installed these systems in other facilities, it had installed them at Natanz as well.

Siemens, in fact, did a brisk business selling automation equipment to various non-nuclear industries in Iran, but its machines found their way into nuclear ones as well. A 2003 letter from one Iranian firm to another, which Western sources later obtained, revealed that Siemens S7-

---

6 Author interview with Albright, November 2013. The first module of cascades, known as A24, is believed to have been struck by Stuxnet version 0.5, which targeted only valves on the centrifuges, not the frequency converters. Later versions that targeted the frequency converters are believed to have focused on a different module, A26, which Iran began installing in late 2007 or early 2008.
7 Iran has accused the IAEA of providing the United States and Israel with intelligence about its nuclear program. But even if the IAEA didn't provide information willingly, hacking IAEA computers to obtain information about Natanz was an option for Western and Israeli intelligence agencies. Recent news stories have revealed how US intelligence agencies spied on the UN Security Council, the IAEA's umbrella organization, and hacked into the videoconferencing system of the UN to glean information about UN activities.
8 See page 340 for more information about Neda.

300 and S7-400 controllers, along with the SIMATIC software needed to communicate with them, had been procured by a company named Kimia Maadan that was involved in uranium processing in Iran.[9] It was believed the controllers were purchased for Iran's Gachin mine, where Iran planned to mine natural uranium for processing in centrifuges.[10] All of this information would have been known to the United States and Israel.

Although the initial plot might have been hatched by US Strategic Command under Gen. James Cartwright, it was up to the cyberwarriors of the NSA and US Cyber Command, working in conjunction with coders from Israel's elite Unit 8200, to execute it.

To pull off the attack required a lot more intelligence than just knowledge of the equipment at Natanz. The attackers needed to know, for example, the exact frequency at which the converters operated and the exact configuration of the equipment. They couldn't rely only on old blueprints and plans that might be out of date. They also needed extensive knowledge about how the Step 7 system worked and how the computers at Natanz were networked in order to reassure White House legal advisers that the code wouldn't cause cascading effects on other systems. If they assumed there wasn't a connection with outside computers and there was, the code would break loose and spread to other machines, possibly damaging them

9 The contents of the document dated May 4, 2003, and titled, "Related to a PLC device Siemens TTE sold to Kimian Madaan [sic] for G'chin mine" was shared with me by someone who was given access to it. The letter was from Tehran Tamman Engineering to Kimia Maadan and indicated that Iran had obtained hardware and software for monitoring and controlling a SIMATIC S7-300 PLC in 2002. The next year, according to the document, Iran obtained another S7-300 and two S7-400s, as well as Siemens SIMATIC WinCC software to monitor the PLCs. The equipment was described in the letter as a "computerized system to monitor and control industrial process via information received from physical measurement transmitters, such as pressure, temperature, and controllers on valves, heating/cooling, using specialized software." The description closely matches what a control system for a cascade would do.

10 When Stuxnet was discovered in 2010 and it was revealed that the digital weapon was attacking Siemens controllers, many in the public wondered if Iran even had Siemens controllers installed at Natanz. But just the previous year, the British Navy had intercepted a secret shipment of 111 boxes of Siemens controllers at a port in Dubai that were apparently bound for Iran's uranium enrichment program. Siemens had shipped them to a buyer in China, where they were forwarded to Iran through Dubai. The discovery of the shipment caused a bit of an international incident—since the sale of technology for Iran's nuclear program is banned under UN sanctions—and eventually forced Siemens to announce in early 2010 that it would initiate no new business in Iran after the summer of 2010.

and exposing the operation. This is where tools like Flame and Duqu would have come in handy to gather data from the computers of systems administrators, who helped install and maintain the networks, and from contractors and others who programmed the PLCs. If Duqu was used, it could have been delivered via a phishing attack—like the one used to infect the Hungarian company. This worked for machines connected to the internet, such as a programmer's laptop. But buried in the PLCs that weren't connected to the internet was also configuration data about things like the number of Profibus cards connected to them and the model and number of frequency converters.

To get to that data, if it couldn't be obtained another way, the attackers needed a flash drive to jump the air gap and get their spy tool onto a machine connected to the PLCs. Since, as previously noted, PLC programmers generally work on laptops not connected to the control network, then connect their laptop physically to a machine on the PLC network or copy their programming files to a flash drive and carry it to a machine on that network, this would have been a simple way to achieve that. The attackers could have retrieved data about the PLCs and control network in reverse—using malware that recorded data from these systems onto the flash drive, which the programmer would have brought back to his internet-connected laptop, where it could be retrieved. It's also been reported that the intelligence agencies used special implants embedded in non-networked machines in Iran that transmitted data about infected systems via radio waves.[11]

It might have taken months to obtain the data the attackers needed. But some of the reconnaissance work could have been done as early as 2005, when the domains for the command-and-control servers used with Stuxnet 0.5 were registered. Although Stuxnet wasn't released until later, the domains could initially have been used to communicate with spy tools.

---

11 David E. Sanger and Thom Shanker, "N.S.A. Devises Radio Pathway into Computers," *New York Times*, January 14, 2014.

The reconnaissance also might have been done around May 2006, when researchers found that code for the command-and-control servers used with later versions of Stuxnet was created.

Once information about the systems was gathered, final work on the attack code could have occurred. Symantec estimated that two separate teams created the 315 and 417 attack codes based on the distinct ways they were written. Whether the United States and Israel worked on both of them together or the Israelis only worked on the missile portion while the Americans handled the payloads is unknown. A third team may have worked on the code that hijacked the Step 7 system to swap out the legitimate .DLL for Stuxnet's rogue one and inject the malicious commands into the PLCs. Symantec estimated that it took about six months to write this Step 7 portion of the code and a little less time to write the malicious PLC code blocks. The testing, however, would have also taken time.

Whoever was responsible for the actual code, this part of the operation had to be precise. There were so many ways for the attack to go wrong, but there was no room for error, and it would be difficult to gauge the effects of the code in the field or tweak it once it was unleashed. This meant the attackers had to do extensive testing—not only on a Siemens test-bed to make sure their code didn't brick the Step 7 system or the PLCs, but also, in the case of the variants unleashed in 2009 and 2010, on all versions of the Windows operating system to make sure the malware spread and installed seamlessly without detection.[12]

Most of all, the attackers needed precise knowledge of how each

---

12 In 2011, Ralph Langner suggested that tests the Idaho National Lab conducted in the summer of 2008 on the Siemens PCS7 system—which included the Step 7 and WinCC software and S7-400 PLCs—were used to uncover vulnerabilities for Stuxnet to attack. The tests were done as part of the lab's vendor-assessment program, whereby researchers examined various industrial control systems for security vulnerabilities. Langner first suggested the INL tests played a role in developing Stuxnet after he uncovered a PowerPoint presentation that INL had produced about the tests. But the INL tests were conducted between July and September 2008, and we now know that the earliest-discovered version of Stuxnet—Stuxnet 0.5—had been developed before these tests occurred and was already in the wild in November 2007, when someone had uploaded it to the VirusTotal website. And if the timestamp on Stuxnet's rogue Step 7 .DLL is to be believed, it was compiled in 2006. INL leaders insisted to reporters during a tour of the lab in 2011, in which the author participated,

change of the code would affect the centrifuges, particularly because what they were aiming for was not a brute-force attack but a finessed one. The tiniest mistake and they could destroy the centrifuges too quickly or destroy too many at once and expose the sabotage, blowing the operation.

To pull this off, they would have needed a team of material scientists and centrifuge experts who understood the density and strength of the aluminum rotors and centrifuge casings, and who understood how the bearings at the bottom of each centrifuge, which kept them spinning in balance, would respond to increased vibration. They also needed to calculate the normal wall pressure inside the centrifuges and determine how much it would increase as the gas pressure inside the centrifuges grew.[13]

To do all of this, they needed actual centrifuges against which to test the attacks. Luckily, as noted previously, the Department of Energy's Oak Ridge National Laboratory in Tennessee possessed a number of P-1 centrifuges, upon which the IR-1s at Natanz were based.

The story behind Oak Ridge's acquisition of the centrifuges began in August 2003, three years after the CIA infiltrated A. Q. Khan's illicit nuclear supply network and six months after the IAEA made its first visit to Natanz. The spy agency intercepted a shipment of black-market uranium enrichment components—including 25,000 centrifuge casings as well as pumps, tubes, and other components—headed from Malaysia to a secret enrichment plant in Libya. The seized crates were used by the West to confront Libyan dictator Muammar Gaddafi with evidence of his secret nuclear program and to pressure him into abandoning it. On December 19, Libya's foreign minister announced on national television that the country was renouncing its nuclear weapons and chemical weapons programs—programs it hadn't until then acknowledged possessing.

The IAEA learned there was more enrichment equipment already in

---

that it did not provide information about vulnerabilities in the Siemens system to anyone to develop Stuxnet.

13 It's been suggested by some that Germany and Great Britain, two countries in the Urenco consortium that produced the original centrifuges that served as the design for Iran's IR-1s, may have provided some assistance with understanding the centrifuges.

Libya that US authorities planned to dismantle and ship back to the Oak Ridge lab. So over the Christmas holiday, Olli Heinonen; his boss, Mohamed ElBaradei; and other IAEA colleagues raced to Tripoli to inventory the equipment before it disappeared. There they found more than one hundred tons of equipment worth about $80 million—including UPS regulators from Turkey (similar to the ones that would later be sabotaged in Iran in 2006), two hundred P-1 centrifuges from Pakistan that the Libyans had already assembled into a small cascade, as well as components for building about four thousand other centrifuges.[14] By March 2004, the seized equipment had been packed up and sent to the Y-12 National Security Complex at Oak Ridge, where it was protected by guards armed with assault rifles while put on display for journalists to see.

"By any objective measure," US Secretary of Energy Spencer Abraham told the assembled reporters at the time, "the United States and the nations of the civilized world are safer as a result of these efforts to secure and remove Libya's nuclear materials."[15] This may have been so, but what the captured booty really meant was that the United States now had the chance to assemble a secret plant to study the centrifuges and test an attack against them.[16]

THE OAK RIDGE National Laboratory, established in 1943 and located outside of Knoxville, is managed by UT-Battelle—a nonprofit company founded in 2000 by Battelle Memorial Institute and the University of Tennessee—and touts itself as a science facility focused on advanced materials research, nuclear science, clean energy, and supercomputing. But it's the lucrative classified national security work the lab does for the Defense

---

14 The numbers vary depending on the account. The United States told reporters that Libya had been caught with 4,000 centrifuges, but by ISIS's count, it was more like 200. The rest were simply components for centrifuges—the casings were there (the hollow aluminum cylinder) as well as other components, but they were missing the rotors to make them work.
15 Jody Warrick, "U.S. Displays Nuclear Parts Given by Libya," *Washington Post*, March 15, 2004.
16 William J. Broad, John Markoff, and David E. Sanger, "Israeli Test on Worm Called Crucial in Iran Nuclear Delay," *New York Times*, January 15, 2011.

Department, Department of Energy, and intelligence agencies—focused on nuclear nonproliferation, intelligence data mining, encryption cracking, and other areas—that really keeps it in business.

The secret centrifuge plant, part of a now decade-long classified program to research the destruction of centrifuges, was constructed sometime after 2005 on a backwoods lot on the 35,000-acre Oak Ridge Reservation, invisible and inaccessible to the majority of lab workers who held security clearances. Dubbed "the Hill" or sometimes "the chicken ranch" according to one person who knew about it, the covert facility was reached via an unmarked road that meandered for ten miles, blanketed on either side by a thick forest of trees, before delivering cars to first one security gate and then another.[17]

The Hill actually consisted of two facilities—one aboveground, the other beneath. The underground hall, a preexisting structure built long before for another purpose, was requisitioned for the first stage of the centrifuge program, which initially focused just on figuring out how the centrifuges obtained from Libya worked. The lab had obtained both P-1 and P-2 centrifuges from Libya to study, but the devices arrived for the most part as unassembled components without a manual. The researchers had drawers and drawers filled with the parts, but had no prior experience working with the designs and therefore spent a lot of their time initially just trying to figure out how to piece the components together and get them to work.

The researchers at Oak Ridge experienced some of the same problems the Iranians experienced in operating the temperamental and fragile devices. The scoops and ball bearings proved to be particularly problematic for them and delayed their progress for a while.

In the beginning, the program wasn't about building a virus to attack the centrifuges; it was simply about learning how the centrifuges and cascades worked in order to understand their capabilities and gauge how

---

17 Oak Ridge sits on former farmland, and "chicken ranch" may refer to a real chicken ranch that existed on the land in the 1940s before the farmers were displaced when the government bought up their land for the war effort.

far along the Iranians were in their enrichment program and to determine how close they might be to having enough enriched uranium to make a nuclear bomb. When the Oak Ridge scientists completed their initial research and testing, they estimated it would take Iran about twelve to eighteen months to produce enough fissile material for a bomb.

The study of centrifuges wasn't foreign to Oak Ridge. The lab has a long history of centrifuge research and development, having produced some of the first rotor centrifuges in the 1960s. But in 1985, its centrifuge program was terminated after lasers replaced centrifuges as the primary method of enriching uranium in the United States. The closure displaced thousands of skilled workers and researchers whose specialized knowledge was no longer needed.

Then in 2002, around the time the world was learning about Iran's secret enrichment facility at Natanz, centrifuge enrichment made a comeback, and Oak Ridge resurrected its program to design a new generation of centrifuges for the United States Enrichment Corporation, now a producer of enriched uranium for commercial nuclear power plants in the United States. To staff that operation, the lab pulled many of its former centrifuge experts out of retirement—some of them now in their seventies and eighties—to work alongside younger scientists.

After the cache of valuable centrifuges was seized from Libya, many of these scientists were reassigned to study the devices. According to someone familiar with the program, he believed the work was conducted under the auspices of the National Nuclear Security Administration (NNSA), a division of the Department of Energy that manages the security of the nation's nuclear weapons but also operates a nuclear nonproliferation research and development program known as NA-22.[18] The latter collects human intelligence about illicit nuclear operations and does remote sensing and en-

---

18 The NNSA is housed at Oak Ridge in the Multi-Program Research Facility, or MRF, a large SIGINT facility that contains a supercomputer in its basement that is used in part for doing data mining for the NSA. Other staff at the MRF, many of them former CIA and NSA employees, are technically astute and work on various other compartmentalized programs, including efforts to crack encryption and data fusion—what workers sometimes call "data diarrhea"—which involves fusing data from various branches of intelligence around the world.

vironmental testing to collect evidence of covert enrichment activity and nuclear detonations by rogue regimes and actors.[19]

The NNSA had been trying to get its hands on Iranian centrifuges for a while, so the shipment of P-1s and P-2s obtained from Libya in 2004, on which the Iranian centrifuges were based, was a huge boon.

Eventually, they also obtained parts directly from the Iranian program, via intelligence sources. These parts were highly valuable—North Korea was believed to be using centrifuges of the same general design— and workers were told to be very careful and expeditious in using the components because in some cases intelligence sources had given their lives to obtain them. In other words, there was no easy way to replace them and therefore every test on the equipment had to count.

Research on the devices was already under way in 2006, when Iran announced it would begin enriching uranium at Natanz, but the research was slow-moving, according to someone familiar with the program. But in 2007, the operation came together in earnest as Iran began installing its first centrifuges in the underground hall at Natanz.

In the meantime, the aboveground hall was constructed for the sole purpose of testing—and destroying—centrifuges. It's believed that some of this research may have initially focused on determining the possible destructive effects from a kinetic attack, such as an aerial bombardment on centrifuges buried deep underground, and that a cyberattack became part of the equation only later. Then when a digital operation *was* proposed, initially the goal wasn't to destroy the centrifuges at Natanz with a virus but simply to plant surveillance code in equipment at the plant to collect data that would help scientists determine where Iran was in its enrichment process. But at some point, the centrifuge destruction program and the reconnaissance operation merged to produce a plan for a digital kinetic at-

---

19 Various methods are used to do this, such as examining gas plumes from suspect factories for trace particles or measuring the temperature of water near suspect sites. Many nuclear facilities are built near rivers and other water sources and the temperature of the water can be indicative of nuclear activity. Another method involves measuring the flickering of lights in factory windows from long distances. Since centrifuges operate at specific frequencies, the pattern in flickering lights can sometimes provide clues as to the presence and kind of centrifuges being used in a building.

tack. Likely, most of the scientists testing the centrifuges never knew about the plan for such an attack but were simply focused on assessing the effects of various conditions on the centrifuges—such as increased and decreased speed or increased wall pressure inside the centrifuge—in a manner that was divorced from the causes of those conditions.

Inside the large testing hall, tall racks of control systems from Siemens and other vendors were arranged like stacks in a library at the front of the cavernous space, while more than a dozen man-sized centrifuges were spaced throughout the hall across from them. Jury-rigged cables attached to sensors snaked out from some of the centrifuges to record diagnostics and measure such things as the heat of the casing or the wobbling and vibration of the pin and ball bearing that kept the centrifuge balanced.

Some of the centrifuges spun for months, while data on them was collected. These were the research specimens, however. There were others whose fate was more dire. Just inside the entrance to the hall was a large reinforced cage made of acrylic and metal mesh—what a hospital baby-viewing room might look like if it were designed by the team from *MythBusters*—where condemned centrifuges went to die. Workers at the plant always knew when a centrifuge was being destroyed in the protective cage because it made a horrific explosive sound, accompanied by a rumbling in the ground.

The operation was in full swing by 2008, with centrifuges being destroyed sometimes on a daily basis. "You could tell the budget had jumped significantly," the source says. President Bush, perhaps not coincidentally, had just managed to obtain $400 million from Congress for covert operations against Iran's nuclear program.

While tests were being conducted at Oak Ridge, other tests were reportedly done on centrifuges at Israel's nuclear facility in Dimona. It's unclear how long all of these tests took or when officials decided they had enough conclusive data to conduct a successful attack.

During the 2006 testing, the development of the attack code was already under way. The exact timeline for that development is unclear, but the Symantec researchers found that a key function used in the attack code appeared to have been modified in May 2006. It was the code that Stuxnet used to initiate communication with the frequency converters in the attack on the 315 PLCs. And as noted, code used for the two command servers that were used with that version of Stuxnet—mypremierfutbol.com and todaysfutbol.com—was also compiled in May 2006. Other key functions in the attack code were modified in September 2007. Just two months after that, in November 2007, Stuxnet version 0.5 popped up on the VirusTotal website after it was submitted by either the testers or an infected victim.

At some point, some of the centrifuges at Oak Ridge or another lab were taken off for another kind of test—to directly measure the efficacy of the digital weapon against the centrifuges. When the proof-of-concept tests were done, officials reportedly presented Bush with the results of their labor—the detritus of a destroyed centrifuge that proved the outrageous plan might actually succeed.[20] Like the Aurora Generator Test, conducted by the Oak Ridge Lab's sister facility in Idaho in early 2007, the centrifuge test showed that heavy machinery was no match for a piece of well-crafted code.

HOW OR WHEN Stuxnet 0.5 was introduced to the computers at Natanz is still a mystery.[21] Because the industrial control systems at Natanz were not directly connected to the internet and this version of Stuxnet had few spreading mechanisms, the attackers had to jump the air gap by walking it into the facility or sending it via email. This version of Stuxnet had only one way to spread—via infected Step 7 project files. This meant it had to be introduced directly into a programmer's or operator's machine either with a USB flash drive—perhaps by an unwitting contractor who didn't realize he was a carrier for the worm or by a paid mole—or by emailing

---

20 David E. Sanger, *Confront and Conceal* (New York: Crown, 2012), 197.
21 Given that the first version of Stuxnet appeared in the field in November 2007, it suggests the sabotage might have begun that year. David Sanger writes that multiple versions of the worm were released while Bush was still in office; only one version from that period has been found by researchers. The others date from Obama's term in office.

an infected project file to someone at Natanz.[22] From a programmer's or operator's machine, it was just a step or two into the targeted PLC. Unlike subsequent versions that kept a log file of every system they infected, as well as a timestamp indicating when each infection occurred, researchers found no digital breadcrumbs to trace the path that Stuxnet 0.5 took.

This version didn't target the 315 PLC and frequency converters but instead attacked the 417 PLC and valves, opening and closing the latter to manipulate the flow of uranium gas.

Cascades at Natanz were configured into fifteen stages, with a different number of centrifuges installed at each stage; as the gas moved from one stage to the next, and the amount of gas being enriched diminished as it progressed through the stages, the number of centrifuges needed to enrich the gas also diminished.

Stage ten, for example, which was the "feed stage," where new batches of gas were pumped into the cascade, had twenty-four centrifuges. As the rotors inside the centrifuges spun at high speed and separated the isotopes, gas containing the U-235 concentrate was scooped out and sent to stage nine, which had twenty centrifuges, where it was further enriched, and then to stage eight, which had sixteen centrifuges. In the meantime, the depleted gas containing the concentration of U-238 isotopes got diverted to stage eleven, where it was further separated. The concentration of U-235 from this stage then got passed to stage eight when it was ready to join the other enriched gas. This continued until the enriched gas reached the final stage of the cascade and the final depleted gas was discarded. The last stage of the cascade, where the enriched uranium was sent, usually consisted of just one centrifuge and a spare in case it malfunctioned.

Each cascade had auxiliary valves that controlled the gas into and out of the cascade and into and out of each enrichment stage. Additionally,

---

22 In 2008, Iran hanged an Iranian electronics vendor named Ali Ashtari, who Iranian news reports say confessed to trying to introduce Mossad-produced viruses and GPS units into equipment used by members of the Revolutionary Guard. After Stuxnet was discovered, there were reports that said he helped get Stuxnet into Natanz. But news from Iran is often unreliable, since it generally comes from state-affiliated publications with an agenda. Over the years Iran has accused many people of being spies for the Mossad, often with little evidence to support the claim.

each IR-1 centrifuge had three narrow pipes at its top, with valves on each pipe that controlled the flow of gas into and out of the centrifuge. The feed valve opened to inject gas into the centrifuge, after which the enriched uranium got scooped out through the product valve, while depleted gas was extracted via the tail valve and pipe.

Stuxnet didn't attack all of the valves at Natanz. Rather, it was selective in its assault. The underground hall where the centrifuges were installed was divided into modules, or cascade rooms. Each module could hold 18 cascades containing 164 centrifuges each, for a total of about 3,000 cascades per room. At the time Stuxnet was unleashed, only one room in the underground hall was complete—filled with 18 cascades. But Stuxnet targeted only six cascades. Not all of the centrifuges in each cascade were affected, either. Stuxnet targeted the valves on only 110 of the 164 centrifuges in these cascades, leaving valves on the remaining 54 untouched.

Once this version of Stuxnet found itself on a system at Natanz, it lay dormant for about thirty days before launching its assault, conducting system checks to make sure that various valves, pressure transducers— for measuring the gas pressure—and other components were present and monitoring their activity.[23]

While it mapped the system, Stuxnet also recorded various data pertaining to the normal operation of the cascade to play it back to operators once the sabotage commenced, just as the 315 attack code did. For example, it briefly opened valves in the last stage of a cascade to take a pressure reading, then replayed this normal-pressure reading back to operators during the attack, to conceal the fact that the pressure had increased.

Once it collected all the data it needed, it waited until certain conditions on the cascade were met before proceeding. An individual cascade, for example, had to have been operating more than 35 days before the attack commenced, or all six of the targeted cascades—if they were all running—had to have been operating a total of 298 days or more.

---

23 Stuxnet 0.5 expected its target, for example, to have between two and twenty-five auxiliary valves and between three and thirty pressure transducers for measuring the gas pressure at each stage of the cascade.

Once it began, Stuxnet closed various valves, except the ones in the feed stage where the gas entered the cascade. In stage nine, for example, it closed the exit valves on only fourteen of the twenty centrifuges, and in stage eight, it closed the exit valves on thirteen of the sixteen centrifuges. The valves it closed in each stage were randomly chosen through a complex process.

With all of these valves closed, Stuxnet sat and waited for the pressure inside the centrifuges to increase as gas continued to pour into them but couldn't escape. It waited two hours, or until the pressure in the centrifuges increased fivefold, whichever was first. Once either of these effects was achieved, Stuxnet proceeded to the next step, opening all of the auxiliary valves except three valves believed to be near the feed stage. Then it waited about three minutes and fed more fake data to operators while preventing any changes from being made to the system for an additional seven minutes. Toward the end of the attack, it opened a set of about twenty-five valves. Albright and his colleagues at ISIS suspected these valves were in the "dump line." Each stage of the cascade had a pipe that connected to a dump line so that if something went wrong with the centrifuges or the enrichment process, the gas could be dumped from the cascade into a cooled tank. If Stuxnet opened valves for the dump line, then gas inside the cascade would exit into the tank, causing it to be wasted.

Once all of this was done, the attack ended and reset itself.

The fact that only some of the centrifuge valves were affected and that the attack lasted just two hours, during which operators were fed false readings, created great confusion among the technicians at Natanz, who would have seen problems occurring in the centrifuges over time, as well as a decrease in the amount of uranium that was enriched, without being able to spot a pattern or pinpoint the cause.

Researchers still don't know precisely which valves were opened and closed by Stuxnet, so it's impossible to say definitively what the effects were. But based on certain assumptions, Albright and his colleagues posited two scenarios. In one, the final product and tail valves at the end of the cascade were closed, so that gas would keep pumping into the cascade but couldn't get out. In this scenario, the pressure would increase rapidly, and once it reached five times the normal level, the uranium gas inside the centrifuges would begin to condense and solidify. As the resulting solid got caught in the centrifuge's spinning rotor, it would damage the rotor or cause it to become imbalanced and strike the wall of the centrifuge. This wobbling would also destabilize the bearings at the bottom of the centrifuge, causing the centrifuge to teeter off balance. A whirling centrifuge detaching itself from its mooring at high speed is a destructive thing and would take out other centrifuges around it.

In this scenario, the pressure would have built up in the later stages of the cascade faster than earlier ones, causing these centrifuges to fail first. Albright and his team estimated that such an attack might have destroyed about 30 centrifuges per cascade. It's believed that by focusing its effort on centrifuges in the later stages of the cascades, where the enriched uranium was most concentrated, the sabotage would have had more impact. If a centrifuge was destroyed near the feed stage, where the concentration of U-235 was the smallest, less time and work were lost than if the gas had passed through the entire cascade and been enriched nearly to the point of completion before the end centrifuges were destroyed and the gas was lost.

It's also possible, however, that Stuxnet didn't close the product and tail valves at the end of the cascade. If that's the case, Stuxnet's primary effect would have been more modest—it would have simply reduced the amount of gas being enriched. Gas would have been fed into the cascade, but with valves on 110 of the 164 centrifuges closed, it would only have been able to pass through the 54 centrifuges in each cascade that weren't affected by Stuxnet, which would have resulted in a smaller amount of gas being enriched and less enrichment achieved.

While Stuxnet conducted its sabotage and fed false data to operators, it also disabled a safety system on the cascade designed to isolate centrifuges before they could cause damage. The safety system was fairly elaborate and included an accelerometer on each centrifuge—to monitor the vibration of the centrifuge—as well as a couple dozen pressure transducers per cascade to monitor the pressure. If a centrifuge was at risk of crashing, the emergency response system acted rapidly—within milliseconds of detecting a problem—to close the valves on the centrifuge to isolate the gas inside it.[24] The kinetic energy from a troubled centrifuge would create a pulse of hot gas that, if not contained, would radiate out through the cascade and damage other centrifuges. The emergency response system was supposed to act quickly to halt the flow of gas from that centrifuge, but Stuxnet disabled that system so there was nothing to isolate the damage.

The assault capabilities of Stuxnet 0.5 then were multipronged—it increased the gas pressure to damage the centrifuges and spoil the gas, it dumped some of the gas from the cascade so that it couldn't be enriched, and finally it reduced the number of working centrifuges so that the amount of enriched uranium that came out of the end of the cascade was reduced. It is unclear just how successful this version of Stuxnet was. But judging by IAEA reports, it did appear to have some effect on the program.

THE INSTALLATION OF cascades at Natanz occurred in three stages, each of which the IAEA inspectors tracked during their visits.[25] First, the cascade infrastructure—pipes, pumps, and valves—was put in place. Next the centrifuges were installed, and their motors turned on to start them spinning. At this point, the vacuum pumps removed air that might cause excessive friction and heat. When the centrifuges reached optimal speed, the gas was piped in to begin enrichment.

Iran had begun installing centrifuges in Hall A, one of Natanz's two cavernous underground halls in early 2007. As previously noted, the hall was designed to have eight large rooms or units—A21 through A28—

---

24 Together, various systems constantly monitor the flow of electricity to the centrifuges, their speed and vibration, as well as the gas pressure and temperature, and the temperature of water used to heat or cool them.

25 The IAEA inspectors visited Natanz about twenty-four times a year. Every three months, the inspectors published a report listing the number of centrifuges during their most recent visit that were spinning and under vacuum—but did not yet have gas in them—and the number that were actually enriching gas. The reports also tracked how much gas the technicians fed into the cascades, and how much enriched uranium was produced from it.

with eighteen cascades in each. Each cascade was designed to hold 164 centrifuges, for a total of 2,952 centrifuges in each unit.[26]

Technicians began installing the first centrifuges in Unit A24 in February that year and planned to have all eighteen cascades in the unit by May. But that didn't happen.[27] By mid-August, only twelve were installed and enriching gas. It took until November to get the rest of them in place. But by then, there were signs of trouble. Technicians were feeding less gas into the centrifuges than they were designed to hold and were holding back some of the gas in a "process buffer," between the feed point and the cascades. From February to November, they fed about 1,670 kg of gas into the feed hull, but held 400 kg of it back in the buffer zone so that only 1,240 kg actually made it to the cascades. What's more, the gas that got into the cascades produced much less enriched uranium than expected. It should have produced 124 kg of low-enriched uranium—10 percent of the amount fed into the cascades. But instead the Iranians got only 75 kg out of it.[28] It's a trend that remained constant for most of 2007, with more feed going into the centrifuges than product was coming out. The level of enrichment was also low. Technicians claimed they were enriching at 4.8 percent, but IAEA tests indicated the gas was enriched to between 3.7 percent and 4.0 percent.

Was Stuxnet 0.5 at play, messing with the valves and the enrichment levels? It's hard to know for sure, but the problems didn't go unnoticed by outsiders. The 2007 National Intelligence Estimate released by the United States in December that year noted that Iran was having "significant tech-

---

26 See page 303, note 29 for previous discussion of the setup of Hall A, and Stuxnet's precise knowledge of it. Iran would later increase the number of centrifuges per cascade in November 2010, but until then, the number of centrifuges per cascade remained constant at 164.

27 IAEA Report to the Board of Governors, "Implementation of the NPT Standards Agreement and Relevant Provisions of Security Council Resolution 1737 (2006) in the Islamic Republic of Iran," February 22, 2007, available at iaea.org/Publications/Documents/Board/2007/gov2007-08.pdf.

28 IAEA Report to the Board of Governors, "Implementation of the NPT Safeguards Agreement and Relevant Provisions of Security Council Resolutions 1737 (2006) and 1747 (2007) in the Islamic Republic of Iran," November 15, 2007, available at iaea.org/Publications/Documents/Board/2007/gov2007-58.pdf.

nical problems operating" its centrifuges. Centrifuges were crashing at a rate 20 percent higher than expected. A senior IAEA official told David Albright that the breakage resulted in partially enriched gas being dumped into waste receptacles, which was likely the cause of the low production numbers.[29]

At the time, Albright and his colleagues attributed the high breakage rate to the poor centrifuge design and the fact that Iran was still "learning the difficulties of operating centrifuges in large numbers." But the problems were consistent with what would have occurred if the valves were being manipulated by Stuxnet 0.5.

Whatever the cause, Iran couldn't afford to waste uranium gas. It had a limited supply of uranium imported from abroad and its Gachin mine doesn't produce enough uranium to sustain its nuclear program.[30]

Between November 2007 and February 2008 technicians installed no new cascades in the hall and focused instead on trying to resolve whatever was creating the problems. Things appeared to turn around after February, however. By the time Ahmadinejad took his triumphant tour of the plant that spring, the cascades were operating in a more stable manner, with fewer breaking. Enrichment levels were hovering at a steady 4 percent, and where previously technicians had fed the centrifuges only half the amount of gas they could handle, they were now feeding them 85 percent of their capacity. Even the performance of individual centrifuges had increased.

By all accounts, Iran appeared to have mastered its problems with the cascades. Technicians began installing cascades at a breakneck pace—a pace that was much more rapid than reason or caution advised. As soon as one cascade was in place, they began feeding it gas, then moved on to the

---

29 An IAEA official told ISIS privately about the breaking centrifuges and the lost gas.
30 David Albright, Jacqueline Shire, and Paul Brannan, "Is Iran Running Out of Yellowcake?," Institute for Science and International Security, February 11, 2009, available at http://isis-online .org/publications/iran/Iran_Yellowcake.pdf; Barak Ravid, "Israel Slams Clinton Statement on Nuclear Iran," Ha'aretz, July 22, 2009; Mark Fitzpatrick, "Statement Before the Senate Committee on Foreign Relations," March 3, 2009, available at iranwatch.org/sites/default/files/us-sfrc-fitzpatrick -iranrealities-030309.pdf.

next cascade. In May 2008, Iran had 3,280 centrifuges enriching gas, but by August, the number had grown to 3,772, an increase of 500 centrifuges in three months.[31]

There was a lot of political pressure inside Iran to move quickly on the nuclear program. UN sanctions and the lack of progress in negotiations with the West irritated Iranian leaders, and they were tired of the delays. But the sudden ramp-up was ill-advised and likely was not supported by Iranian scientists and engineers. Even under normal conditions, installing centrifuges and getting them to run properly was a tricky business. Add to this the inherent fragility of the IR-1s and it didn't make sense to move this fast.

"From an engineering point of view, it's kind of a reckless procedure, because if you barely operated a 164-machine centrifuge cascade, why would you want to race and try to operate eighteen or thirty cascades all at once?" says Albright. "An engineer would say do this very slowly, and make sure that you've understood how to work all these things as a unit before you start scaling up like that."[32]

But few problems occurred during this period, and by the end of the summer, the technicians at Natanz must have begun to grow confident that they had put earlier troubles behind them. Then conditions began to go south again.

The IAEA reports told the story in a series of dry numbers.

During his April 2008 tour, Ahmadinejad had announced optimistically that technicians would soon add 6,000 centrifuges to the 3,000 centrifuges already installed in the underground hall. But after reaching just 3,772 centrifuges that August, the technicians stopped, and no new centrifuges were added in the next three months. Production levels were also

---

31 In addition to the eighteen cascades in A24 that were being fed gas, five cascades in A26 were being fed gas, another cascade was under vacuum, and construction on the remaining twelve cascades in that module was continuing. See IAEA Board of Governors Report, "Implementation of the NPT Safeguards Agreement and Relevant Provisions of Security Council Resolutions 1737 (2006), 1747 (2007) and 1803 (2008) in the Islamic Republic of Iran," September 15, 2008, available at iaea.org/Publications/Documents/Board/2008/gov2008-38.pdf.
32 Author interview with Albright, January 2012.

way down. Since the start of enrichment in early 2007, technicians had fed 7,600 kg of gas into the cascades, but by August 2008 the centrifuges had produced only 480 kg of enriched uranium, instead of the 760 they should have produced. The low production numbers continued the rest of 2008. Between August and November technicians fed 2,150 kg of gas into the cascades but produced only 150 kg of enriched uranium during that time. As in 2007, they appeared to be losing an unusual amount of gas.

Despite all of these problems, however, 2008 overall was a better year for Iran than 2007.[33] Whereas Natanz had produced only 75 kg of enriched uranium in all of 2007, by the end of 2008, this had jumped to 630 kg. Albright and his colleagues at ISIS estimated that with further enriching under optimal conditions, Iran could turn 700 to 800 kg of low-enriched uranium into 20 to 25 kg of weapons-grade uranium, enough for a crude nuclear weapon. Nonetheless, there was no getting around the fact that Iran's nuclear program wasn't at the level it should have been at that point.

The timing of the problems in late 2008 appeared to coincide with how Stuxnet 0.5 was designed to work. Once Stuxnet infected a 417 PLC, the sabotage took time to unfold. The reconnaissance stage took at least a month while Stuxnet recorded data to play back to operators, and the cascades had to be active for a period of time before the sabotage kicked in— at least 35 days in the case of a single cascade, or more than 297 days for all six cascades combined. Once the attack was finished, another 35 days passed before it began again. The problems in late 2008 seemed to be concentrated in unit A26, where technicians had begun to install centrifuges in the spring. If Stuxnet was introduced to controllers for that unit in late 2007 or early 2008, it could have taken months for the attack's negative effects—from the increase of pressure inside the centrifuges—to show.

Notably, around this time, a Canadian-Iranian man tried to purchase a batch of pressure transducers from two Western manufacturers to ship

---

33 David Albright, Jacqueline Shire, and Paul Brannan, "IAEA Report on Iran: Centrifuge Operation Significantly Improving; Gridlock on Alleged Weaponization Issues," September 15, 2008, available at isis-online.org/ publications/iran/ISIS_Report_Iran_15September2008.pdf.

to Iran. The devices were used for, among other things, measuring the pressure of gas inside a centrifuge. Between December 2008 and March 2009, Mahmoud Yadegari bought ten transducers at a cost of $11,000 and shipped two of them to Iran via Dubai. He placed an order for twenty more from a second firm, but the company rejected the order after he failed to certify the identity of the end recipient. He was arrested that April after authorities were tipped off about the suspicious order.[34] Was Iran attempting to purchase transducers to replace ones that appeared to be failing at Natanz or was there no connection between Yadegari's efforts and the problems that occurred at Natanz?

As Iran entered 2009, technicians began rapidly adding new centrifuges and cascades to unit A26. Nine cascades were under vacuum in this unit by February. But instead of being fed gas, the centrifuges sat in their cascades empty. In the past, technicians had begun to feed gas into new cascades as soon as they were installed, but for some reason now they weren't. At the same time, the number of separative work units—a measurement of how much work each centrifuge expends in the enrichment process—fell dramatically from .80 to .55 for the centrifuges that were enriching in A24 and A26. The level of enrichment also dropped from 4 percent, where it had hovered through most of 2008, to 3.49 percent. If the effects were caused by Stuxnet, it appeared the digital weapon was doing exactly what it was designed to accomplish.

But then the attackers decided to switch things up.

AS 2009 BEGAN, president-elect Barack Obama was invited to the White House to meet with President Bush for the standard debriefing that passed between incoming presidents and their predecessor as the two prepared to exchange the baton. During the conversation, Bush laid out the details of the digital attack and the subtle magic it had been working

---

34 Yadegari was convicted, and an explanation from the Ontario Court of Justice detailing the reasons for his conviction can be found on the website of the Institute for Science and International Security: isis-online.org/uploads/isis-reports/documents/Yadegari_Reasons.pdf.

over the last year to undermine the centrifuges at Natanz.[35] There had been progress in setting the Iranian program back a bit, but the operation needed more time to succeed. If it was to continue, however, it needed to be authorized by a sitting president, which meant Obama had to renew the Presidential Finding that approved it. Given that other options had failed up to then, and an airstrike was the only likely alternative, Obama ultimately needed little persuasion.[36]

In the summer of 2008, while still in the midst of his presidential campaign, Obama had made a whistle-stop tour in Israel, where he told the Israelis that he felt their pain. A nuclear-armed Iran, he said, would be "a grave threat" to peace not just in the Middle East, but around the world.[37] He promised that under his leadership all options would remain on the table to prevent Iran from obtaining nuclear weapons. Although in essence this meant a military option as well, Obama, like Bush, wanted to avoid a military engagement at all costs. Therefore, a covert operation that used bytes over bombs was a more welcome choice.

Coming into office, Obama already faced a lot of pressure on multiple fronts. Little progress had been made with Iran via diplomatic channels, and sanctions weren't having much of their desired effect either. And there was concern that the Israelis might take matters into their own hands if the United States didn't show results soon. For these and other reasons, Obama decided not only to reauthorize the digital sabotage program but to accelerate it. It was in this environment that he gave the green light for a new, more aggressive, version of Stuxnet to launch—the one that targeted the frequency converters at Natanz.

Why fire off a new attack when the first one seemed to be succeeding? The operation against the valves was effective but slow. Stuxnet's creators

---

35 Broad, Markoff, and Sanger, "Israeli Test on Worm Called Crucial in Iran Nuclear Delay."
36 Mike Shuster, "Inside the United States' Secret Sabotage of Iran," NPR.org, May 9, 2011, available at npr.org/2011/05/09/135854490/inside-the-united-states-secret-sabotage-of-iran. The meeting between President Bush and Barack Obama is described by Sanger, *Confront and Conceal*, 200–3.
37 Rebecca Harrison, "Obama Says Nuclear Iran Poses 'Grave Threat,'" Reuters, July 23, 2008, available at reuters.com/article/2008/07/23/us-Iran-usa-Obama-idUSL23104041320080723.

were running out of time and needed a faster attack that would target the centrifuges more directly and set Iran's program back more definitively. They also wanted to confuse technicians with a different set of problems.

The irony was that while Obama was authorizing this new attack against Iran's computer systems, he was also announcing new federal initiatives to secure cyberspace and critical infrastructure in the United States—to protect them, that is, from the very sort of destruction that Stuxnet produced.[38] The nation's digital infrastructure was a strategic national asset, he said during a speech weeks after his inauguration, and protecting it was a national security priority. "We will ensure that these networks are secure, trustworthy and resilient," he said. "We will deter, prevent, detect and defend against attacks and recover quickly from any disruptions or damage."[39]

While Obama was reauthorizing the covert operation, its details were already at risk of being exposed. It was no secret that the United States and its allies were engaged in efforts to sabotage Iran's nuclear program. In February 2009, the *Telegraph* in London reported that Israel had launched an extensive covert war against Iran's nuclear program that included hit men, front companies, double agents, and sabotage.[40] In the article, a former CIA officer seemed to hint at Stuxnet's existence by revealing that the sabotage was designed to slow the progress of the program in such a way that the Iranians would never know what caused it. The goal, he said, was to "delay, delay, delay until you can come up with some other solution or approach. . . . It's a good policy, short of taking them out militarily, which probably carries unacceptable risks."

Around the same time, the *New York Times* also revealed that a new covert campaign against Iran had been launched, but didn't go into detail.[41]

It's unclear if the Iranians saw these news stories or, if they did, con-

---

38 In May that year, he announced the creation of a cybersecurity czar position to help secure US critical infrastructure against cyberattacks.

39 Kim Zetter, "Obama Says New Cyberczar Won't Spy on the Net," *Wired*, May 29, 2009, available at wired.com/threatlevel/2009/05/netprivacy.

40 Philip Sherwell, "Israel Launches Covert War Against Iran," *Telegraph*, February 16, 2009.

41 David Sanger, "U.S. Rejected Aid for Israeli Raid on Iranian Nuclear Site," *New York Times*, January 10, 2009.

nected them to the problems they were having at Natanz. They were certainly well aware of the risks of sabotage, having already experienced it in 2006 with the power regulators from Turkey. But suspecting that something was being sabotaged was one thing. Homing in on the part or component that was causing it was another.

As the attackers were preparing to launch the next version of Stuxnet, Obama made good on another of the campaign pledges he'd made with regard to Iran. During the campaign, he had promised to engage in more robust diplomacy with the Islamic Republic. As part of this promise, he made the unprecedented move of directly addressing the Muslim world during his televised inauguration speech. "We seek a new way forward, based on mutual interest and mutual respect," he said. "To those leaders around the globe who seek to sow conflict, or blame their society's ills on the West—know that your people will judge you on what you can build, not what you destroy."[42]

He addressed Iranians directly again on March 20, when he appealed to the Islamic Republic's leaders and its people in a speech broadcast through *Voice of America* on Nowruz, the Persian New Year.

"In this season of new beginnings, I would like to speak clearly to Iranian leaders," he said. The United States was interested in pursuing constructive ties with Iran that were "honest and grounded in mutual respect," he said, and was seeking a future in which the Iranian people, their neighbors, and the wider international community could live "in greater security and greater peace." He closed his address with a quote from the Persian poet Saadi: "The children of Adam are limbs to each other, having been created of one essence." The United States, he said, was prepared to extend a hand in friendship and peace, "if you are willing to unclench your fist."[43]

But while Obama was extending one metaphorical hand in peace to the Iranian people, other hands were preparing a new round of digital attacks on Natanz.

---

42 See whitehouse.gov/blog/inaugural-address.
43 See whitehouse.gov/the_press_office/videotaped-remarks-by-the-president-in-celebration-of -nowruz.

CHAPTER 17

THE MYSTERY OF THE CENTRIFUGES

The two weeks leading up to the release of the next attack were tumultuous ones in Iran. On June 12, 2009, the presidential elections between incumbent Mahmoud Ahmadinejad and challenger Mir-Hossein Mousavi didn't turn out the way most expected. The race was supposed to be close, but when the results were announced—two hours after the polls closed—Ahmadinejad had won with 63 percent of the vote over Mousavi's 34 percent. The electorate cried foul, and the next day crowds of angry protesters poured into the streets of Tehran to register their outrage and disbelief. According to media reports, it was the largest civil protest the country had seen since the 1979 revolution ousted the shah, and it wasn't long before it became violent. Protesters vandalized stores and set fire to trash bins, while police and Basijis, government-loyal militias in plainclothes, tried to disperse them with batons, electric prods, and bullets.

That Sunday, Ahmadinejad gave a defiant victory speech, declaring a new era for Iran and dismissing the protesters as nothing more than soccer hooligans soured by the loss of their team. The protests continued throughout the week, though, and on June 19, in an attempt to calm the crowds, the Ayatollah Ali Khamenei sanctioned the election results, insisting that the margin of victory—11 million votes—was too large to have been achieved through fraud. The crowds, however, were not assuaged.

The next day, a twenty-six-year-old woman named Neda Agha-Soltan got caught in a traffic jam caused by protesters, and was shot in the chest by a sniper's bullet after she and her music teacher stepped out of their car to observe.

Two days later on June 22, a Monday, the Guardian Council, which oversees elections in Iran, officially declared Ahmadinejad the winner, and after nearly two weeks of protests, Tehran became eerily quiet. Police had used tear gas and live ammunition to disperse the demonstrators, and most of them were now gone from the streets. That afternoon, at around four thirty p.m. local time, as Iranians nursed their shock and grief over events of the previous days, a new version of Stuxnet was being compiled and unleashed.[1]

WHILE THE STREETS of Tehran had been in turmoil, technicians at Natanz had been experiencing a period of relative calm. Around the first of the year, they had begun installing new centrifuges again, and by the end of February they had about 5,400 of them in place, close to the 6,000 that Ahmadinejad had promised the previous year. Not all of the centrifuges were enriching uranium yet, but at least there was forward movement again, and by June the number had jumped to 7,052, with 4,092 of these enriching gas.[2] In addition to the eighteen cascades enriching gas in unit

---

1 A timestamp in the version of Stuxnet that was launched in June 2009 indicates that the attackers compiled the malware June 22 at 4:31 p.m. local time (the local time on the computer that compiled the code) and that it struck its first victim the following day at 4:40 a.m. (the victim's local time), an apparent difference of twelve hours, depending on the time zone the compilation computer was in. The infection time came from a log file that was buried in every sample of Stuxnet that was found. Each time Stuxnet infected a computer, it recorded the time (based on the computer's internal clock) in this log. It's not known if the attackers launched the attack right after they compiled it—and the malware then took twelve hours to reach its victim—or if they waited to launch it until the next day. 2 David Albright, *Peddling Peril: How the Secret Nuclear Trade Arms America's Enemies* (New York: Free Press, 2010), 202–3.

A24, there were now twelve cascades in A26 enriching gas. An additional seven cascades had even been installed in A28 and were under vacuum, being prepared to receive gas.

The performance of the centrifuges was improving too. Iran's daily production of low-enriched uranium was up 20 percent and remained consistent throughout the summer of 2009.[3] Despite the previous problems, Iran had crossed a technical milestone and had succeeded in producing 839 kg of low-enriched uranium—enough to achieve nuclear-weapons breakout capability.[4] If it continued at this rate, Iran would have enough enriched uranium to make two nuclear weapons within a year.[5] This estimate, however, was based on the capacity of the IR-1 centrifuges currently installed at Natanz. But Iran had already installed IR-2 centrifuges in a small cascade in the pilot plant, and once testing on these was complete and technicians began installing them in the underground hall, the estimate would have to be revised. It took 3,000 IR-1s to produce enough uranium for a nuclear weapon in one year, but it would take just 1,200 IR-2 centrifuges to do the same.

Cue Stuxnet 1.001, which showed up in late June.

To get their weapon into the plant, the attackers launched an offensive against computers owned by four companies. All of the companies were involved in industrial control and processing of some sort, either manufacturing products and assembling components or installing industrial control systems. They were all likely chosen because they had some connection to Natanz as contractors and provided a gateway through which to pass Stuxnet to Natanz through infected employees.

To ensure greater success at getting the code where it needed to go, this version of Stuxnet had two more ways to spread than the previous one.

---

3 David Albright and Jacqueline Shire, "IAEA Report on Iran: Centrifuge and LEU Increases; Access to Arak Reactor Denied; No Progress on Outstanding Issues," June 5, 2009, available at isis -online.org/publications/iran/Iran_IAEA_Report_Analysis_5June2009.pdf.
4 Albright, *Peddling Peril*, 202–3.
5 Albright and Shire, IAEA Report, June 5, 2009.

Stuxnet 0.5 could spread only by infecting Step 7 project files—the files used to program Siemens PLCs. This version, however, could spread via USB flash drives using the Windows Autorun feature or through a victim's local network using the print-spooler zero-day exploit that Kaspersky and Symantec later found in the code.

Based on the log files in Stuxnet, a company called Foolad Technique was the first victim. It was infected at 4:40 a.m. on June 23, a Tuesday.[6] But then it was almost a week before the next company was hit.

The following Monday, about five thousand marchers walked silently through the streets of Tehran to the Qoba Mosque to honor victims killed during the recent election protests. Late that evening, around 11:20 p.m., Stuxnet struck machines belonging to its second victim—a company called Behpajooh.

It was easy to see why Behpajooh was a target. It was an engineering firm based in Esfahan—the site of Iran's new uranium conversion plant, built to turn milled uranium ore into gas for enriching at Natanz, and was also the location of Iran's Nuclear Technology Center, which was believed to be the base for Iran's nuclear weapons development program. Behpajooh had also been named in US federal court documents in connection with Iran's illegal procurement activities.[7]

Behpajooh was in the business of installing and programming industrial control and automation systems, including Siemens systems. The company's website made no mention of Natanz, but it did mention that the company had installed Siemens S7-400 PLCs, as well as the Step 7 and WinCC software and Profibus communication modules at a steel plant in Esfahan. This was, of course, all of the same equipment Stuxnet targeted at Natanz.

---

6 Foolad Technique appears to operate under the domain name ISIE. It may be that ISIE was either acquired by Foolad or was a division of that company.

7 In 2006 an Iranian American was indicted for attempting to smuggle banned weapons technology into Iran. The defendant had purchased pressure sensors from a company in Minneapolis and sent them to a middleman in Dubai who was supposed to forward them to Behpajooh. See "Dubai Firm Implicated in Iran 'Bomb Component's Investigation in US," *Khaleej Times,* May 12, 2006.

At five a.m. on July 7, nine days after Behpajooh was hit, Stuxnet struck computers at Neda Industrial Group, as well as a company identified in the logs only as CGJ, believed to be Control Gostar Jahed. Both companies designed or installed industrial control systems.

Neda designed and installed control systems, precision instrumentation, and electrical systems for the oil and gas industry in Iran, as well as for power plants and mining and process facilities. In 2000 and 2001 the company had installed Siemens S7 PLCs in several gas pipeline operations in Iran and had also installed Siemens S7 systems at the Esfahan Steel Complex.[8] Like Behpajooh, Neda had been identified on a proliferation watch list for its alleged involvement in illicit procurement activity and was named in a US indictment for receiving smuggled microcontrollers and other components.[9]

About two weeks after it struck Neda, a control engineer who worked for the company popped up on a Siemens user forum on July 22 complaining about a problem that workers at his company were having with their machines. The engineer, who posted a note under the user name Behrooz, indicated that all PCs at his company were having an identical problem with a Siemens Step 7 .DLL file that kept producing an error message. He suspected the problem was a virus that spread via flash drives.[10]

When he used a DVD or CD to transfer files from an infected system to a clean one, everything was fine, he wrote. But when he used a flash

---

8 One of Neda's other customers was a gas pressurization station on Kharg Island in Iran, the site of one of the explosions that drew Eric Chien's attention in 2010 after Stuxnet was discovered. According to Neda's website, between 2008 and 2010 the company renovated control systems at the plant's Turbo Compressor units. There's no evidence that the explosion at the plant was caused by digital sabotage, but the fact that Stuxnet infected computers at Neda shows how simple it could be to conduct digital attacks against other types of facilities in Iran.

9 In 2004, a trading company in Dubai ordered 7,500 microcontrollers from an Arizona firm and diverted the shipment to Neda, evidently for use by Iran's military. The case is *US District Court, Mayrow General Trading et al., Indictment*, September 11, 2008, available at dodig.mil .iginformation/Mayrow%20Mayrow%20Superseding%20Indictment.pdf.

10 Although he posted his comments under the name Behrooz, he signed his messages at the bottom with "M. R. Tajalli." A search on Behrooz and the other name led to a LinkedIn profile and others identifying him as Mohammad Reza Tajalli, a control engineer who had been working for Neda since 2006. Tajalli specialized in control systems for the oil industry, according to his LinkedIn profile. He did not respond to queries from the author.

drive to transfer files, the new PC started having the same problems the other machine had. A USB flash drive, of course, was Stuxnet's primary method of spreading. Although Behrooz and his colleagues scanned for viruses, they found no malware on their machines. There was no sign in the discussion thread that they ever resolved the problem at the time.

It's not clear how long it took Stuxnet to reach its target after infecting machines at Neda and these other companies, but between June and August the number of centrifuges enriching uranium at Natanz began to drop. Whether this was the result solely of the new version of Stuxnet or the lingering effects of the previous version is unknown. But by August that year, only 4,592 centrifuges were enriching at the plant, a decrease of 328 centrifuges since June. The problem, again, was in unit A26, where previous issues had occurred. In June, there had been twelve cascades in this unit enriching gas. But by November, gas had been removed from half of them and only six of the A26 cascades were now enriching. The total number of centrifuges enriching at Natanz had dropped to 3,936, a decrease of 984 in five months. What's more, although new machines were still being installed, none of them were being fed gas. In A28 as well, seventeen cascades were now installed, but none of these nearly 3,000 centrifuges was enriching gas.

Clearly there were problems with the cascades, and technicians had no idea what they were. The changes mapped precisely, however, to what Stuxnet was designed to do.

This version of Stuxnet, as mentioned previously, increased the frequency of the centrifuge rotors to 1,410 Hz for fifteen minutes—a speed of almost 1,000 miles per hour—then after three weeks decreased it to 2 Hz for fifty minutes.[11] The changes, after a number of cycles, would have begun to damage the centrifuges and affect the level of enrichment in the gas.

But Albright and his colleagues determined that it would have taken the centrifuge motors longer than fifteen minutes to reach 1,410 Hz—the frequency that would have been most damaging to the centrifuges. They

---

11 See chapter 13, pages 235 and 246.

likely would only have reached 1,324 to 1,381 Hz in that time. Nonetheless, as the varying speed and constant acceleration and deceleration continued over time, it would have created incremental stress and damage to the centrifuge rotors. The increased speed would also have caused the aluminum centrifuges to expand and become imbalanced.

The IR-1s were already fragile by design, and the slightest imperfection could set them off—dust in the chamber, for example, could cause them to self-destruct. The head of Iran's Atomic Energy Organization, Gholam Reza Aghazadeh, revealed during an interview in 2006 that in the early days of the enrichment program, the IR-1s had disintegrated frequently due to *germs* on the machine. Initially, they couldn't figure out why the centrifuges were exploding, but he said they ultimately attributed the problem to technicians assembling the centrifuges without gloves. Microbes left behind on the machines literally pulverized them once the machines began to spin. "When we say a machine is destroyed," he told the interviewer, "we mean that it turns into powder."[12]

The centrifuges had bearings at their top and base that helped keep them steady, like a spinning top.[13] A spinning centrifuge had to be brought up to speed slowly. Once it was going, it was beautiful and elegant to watch. But in the blink of an eye everything could go wrong. If a centrifuge began to wobble, it would spiral quickly out of control. The centrifuge casing itself was hefty and wouldn't shatter, but it might split lengthwise, like a hot dog in a microwave, or bend and cause the caps at each end to blow out. And inside the casing, the rotor and other components would break apart.

The increased speed caused by Stuxnet could have induced vibrations that would have eventually worn down the bearings after a number of attack cycles, causing the centrifuges to become imbalanced and topple. But

12 William Broad, "A Tantalizing Look at Iran's Nuclear Program," *New York Times*, April 29, 2008.

13 The centrifuges have a cap at each end and balance precariously on a ball bearing attached to a pin or needle. The top part of the needle is attached to the cap that is located at the bottom of the centrifuge, while the bottom half of the needle, with the bearing, is inserted in a cup that is attached to a spring. This entire contraption allows the centrifuge to sway slightly as it spins while also keeping it stabilized. Too much movement, however, can destabilize the centrifuge and wear out these parts.

with false data being fed back to operators, they wouldn't have seen the destruction coming or have been able to figure out in the aftermath what had gone wrong.

The second attack sequence, which reduced the frequency of the centrifuges to 2 Hz for fifty minutes, made it appear the attackers were also trying to degrade the enriched uranium, not just damage the centrifuges. A centrifuge spinning at 1,064 Hz would take time to slow down to 2 Hz. In fifty minutes, it would likely only decrease to about 864 Hz, Albright and his team determined, before the sabotage ended and the speed returned to normal. But by reducing the speed of a centrifuge even just 50 to 100 Hz, Stuxnet could reduce the enrichment by half. In uranium enrichment, centrifuges need to spin consistently at high speed to separate the U-235 and U-238 isotopes in the gas. If the speed varies, particularly if it slows for fifty minutes, this disrupts the separation process. Technicians at Natanz would have been expecting to get one grade of uranium from the cascade but would have received something else instead. This effect was much more subtle than destroying centrifuges outright, and would not have been enough on its own to slow Iran's program. But combined with the other effects, it worked to sabotage the program from a different angle. In this attack sequence not only was the percentage of the enrichment affected, but the volume of the enriched uranium that was produced became erratic. In February 2009, the centrifuges had been producing about .62 separative work units, but in May this had dropped to .49. And in June and August, it varied between .51 and .55.

Back in the United States, Albright and his colleagues at ISIS read the IAEA reports, noting the changes at Natanz, and weren't surprised to see that Iran was having problems, given how rapidly technicians had installed the cascades in unit A26. He learned from sources that technicians at Natanz had reduced the speed of the centrifuges in an effort to address the problems, but Albright suspected that something more than routine breakage and technical difficulties was going on. He contacted sources in the government and at the IAEA to get a reading on what was happening but got no definitive answers.

As 2010 arrived, the numbers at Natanz continued to drop. The number of installed centrifuges was at 8,692, but the number of centrifuges actively enriching uranium now was down to 3,772, a drop of 1,148 since June. Until now, the problems had been confined to A26, but now they appeared to be spreading to A24 and A28 as well. The gas had been removed from one cascade in A24, for example.[14]

Most telling, however, was the fact that technicians had begun to disconnect and remove centrifuges from some of the cascades. In August, the IAEA had installed more cameras in the underground hall to keep pace with the facility's growth as technicians installed more cascades. Now they were capturing images of workers scurrying about as they removed centrifuges from the units. In January, the IAEA reported that technicians had removed an unspecified number of centrifuges from eleven of the cascades in A26 and had also removed all 164 centrifuges from a cascade in A28. None of the remaining sixteen cascades in A28 were enriching.[15] The *Washington Post* would later report that 984 centrifuges were replaced during this period, the equivalent of six entire cascades.

But Stuxnet's work still wasn't done.

AS 2009 CAME to a close, pressure on the United States to halt Iran's nuclear program was growing.

In late September, while the numbers at Natanz were dropping, President Obama announced at the UN Security Council Summit on Nuclear Nonproliferation and Nuclear Disarmament that a new secret uranium

---

14 In author interviews, several sources suggested that the centrifuges in A24 might have been configured differently than those in A26—that the frequency converters used to control them were a different model. If true, it's possible that Stuxnet 0.5, which targeted the valves on centrifuges and cascades, was used against A24, and that subsequent versions of Stuxnet, which targeted frequency converters, were used against the cascades in A26. This might explain why the cascades in A24 had problems in 2008, when Stuxnet 0.5 was released, but had fewer problems in 2009, when the later version of Stuxnet was performing its sabotage.
15 IAEA, "Implementation of the NPT Safeguards Agreement and Relevant Provisions of Security Council Resolution 1737 (2006), 1747 (2007), 1803 (2008) and 1835 (2008) in the Islamic Republic of Iran," February 18, 2010, available at iaea.org/Publications/Documents/Board/2010/gov2010-10.pdf.

enrichment facility had been discovered in Iran. This one was located on a military base, buried more than 150 feet beneath a mountain at Fordow, about 30 kilometers from the holy city of Qom.

The plant was much smaller than the one at Natanz and was designed to hold only 3,000 centrifuges, compared to Natanz's 47,000. But it was big enough to enrich uranium for one or two bombs a year, if Iran decided to use it for that purpose. "Iran has a right to peaceful nuclear power that meets the energy needs of its people. But the size and configuration of this facility is inconsistent with a peaceful program," Obama said during his announcement about Fordow.[16]

The Iranians told the IAEA's Mohamed ElBaradei that the plant was just a backup for Natanz, that the threat of a military strike against Natanz had prompted them to build it as a contingency. The new plant was still under construction and wasn't expected to be completed until 2011, but according to US intelligence, work on it had likely begun sometime between 2002 and 2004, which meant IAEA inspectors had passed the secret site numerous times on their way to Natanz over the years without knowing of its existence. Obama learned about the plant earlier that year during his pre-inauguration briefing at the White House, but intelligence agencies had known about it since at least 2007, when the head of Iran's Revolutionary Guard defected to the West and told the CIA that Iran was building a second secret enrichment plant somewhere within its borders. Since then, satellite reconnaissance had uncovered the site at Fordow.[17]

The Fordow plant, though smaller than Natanz, actually presented a

---

16 "Statements by President Obama, French President Sarkozy, and British Prime Minister Brown on Iranian Nuclear Facility," September 25, 2009, at the Pittsburgh Convention Center in Pittsburgh, Pennsylvania, available at whitehouse.gov/the-press-office/2009/09/25/statements -president-obama-french-president-sarkozy-and-british-prime-minister-Brown-on-Iranian-Nuclear -Facility.

17 Satellite images initially captured what looked like tunnels and underground construction occurring at Fordow, then in 2008 they captured workers stacking large cement pads outside the entrance to a tunnel. The pads resembled the cement platforms that are used in enrichment plants to hold cascades. The United States toyed with the idea of sneaking a special operations team into Iran to rig the pads so that they would destroy the centrifuges at a later date, but the risky endeavor never advanced beyond this. See David E. Sanger, *Confront and Conceal: Obama's Secret Wars and Surprising Use of American Power* (New York: Crown, 2012), 152, 155.

much graver danger than Natanz. With IAEA inspectors closely monitoring the latter site, it was unlikely Iran could secretly divert nuclear material from that plant to enrich it to weapons-grade material. Secret plants like Fordow, however, where weapons-grade enrichment could be done without the IAEA's knowledge, were far more worrying.

Fordow was also a particular concern because it was being built under more than a hundred feet of solid rock, putting it out of reach of the current crop of bunker-busting bombs and possibly even a new generation of bombs the United States was developing.[18]

The UK's prime minister, Gordon Brown, responded to the news of Fordow by calling Iran's nuclear program "the most urgent proliferation challenge that the world faces today." He said that the international community had no choice but to "draw a line in the sand" over Iran's "serial deception of many years."[19]

Iranian officials, however, seemed unperturbed by the revelations about Fordow, asserting defiantly that they planned to build ten more uranium enrichment plants in the coming decades to fuel a fleet of nuclear power plants they also planned to build.[20] The enrichment plants would all be buried deep under mountains to protect them from attack, the head of the AEOI said.[21]

In the wake of the Fordow news, Israel became more insistent that something had to be done about Iran's nuclear program. At a November meeting in Tel Aviv, an Israeli military leader told US officials that 2010

---

18 The Defense Science Board, which advised the Pentagon to build the weapon in 2004, wrote that a tunnel facility buried deep within rock could pose "a significant challenge" even to the new bombs. "Several thousand pounds of high explosives coupled to the tunnel are needed to blow down blast doors and propagate a lethal air blast," they wrote. William Broad, "Iran Shielding Its Nuclear Efforts in Maze of Tunnels," *New York Times*, January 5, 2010.

19 "Statements by President Obama, French President Sarkozy, and British Prime Minister Brown on Iranian Nuclear Facility," the White House.

20 A year later, in September 2010, while the Symantec researchers and Ralph Langner were still deciphering Stuxnet's payload, the Iranian dissident group that had exposed Natanz claimed it had information about yet another secret uranium enrichment plant being built near Abyek, about 120 kilometers west of Tehran. See David E. Sanger, "Dissidents Claim Iran Is Building a New Enrichment Site," *New York Times*, September 9, 2010.

21 Broad, "Iran Shielding Its Nuclear Efforts."

would be a "critical year" in the showdown with Iran. If they didn't act soon, Iran would harden its nuclear sites, and it would become more and more difficult to take them out.[22] The US had already secretly promised Israel a shipment of the new generation of bunker-busting bombs it was producing, but that ordnance was still six months away from delivery.

In January of 2010, the pressure mounted when a document leaked to the media disclosed a secret military branch of Iran's nuclear research program known as the FEDAT. The branch was said to be headed by Mohsen Fakhrizadeh, a professor at Imam Hossein University in Tehran.[23] The next month, the IAEA indicated it had received "broadly consistent and credible" information that Iran had been developing nuclear weapons. "This raises concerns about the possible existence in Iran of past or current undisclosed activities related to the development of a nuclear payload for a missile."[24]

On top of this, negotiations meant to ease concerns over Iran's growing stockpile of low-enriched uranium collapsed. For years, Iran had said it needed the uranium to produce fuel rods for its research reactor in Tehran to conduct cancer research and oncology treatments, but the United States and others had always been concerned that the uranium at some point would be further enriched for weapons. So in mid-2009, a White House adviser devised a clever compromise to resolve the West's concerns over the uranium. Under the White House plan, Iran would send most of this low-enriched uranium to Russia and France so that these two countries could turn it into fuel rods for the Iranian reactor. The proposal was an ingenious one because it would provide Iran with all the fuel it said it needed for its reactor, while robbing Iranian officials of the opportunity to further enrich their stockpile into weapons-grade material.

Iranian officials had said in 2009 that they needed time to consider

---

22 US State Department cable, "40th Joint Political-Military Group: Executive," November 18, 2009, published by WikiLeaks at wikileaks.org/cable/2009/11/09TELAVIV2500.html.

23 Dieter Bednarz, Erich Follath, and Holger Stark, "Intelligence from Tehran Elevates Concern in the West," Der Spiegel, January 25, 2010.

24 Erich Follath and Holger Stark, "The Birth of a Bomb: A History of Iran's Nuclear Ambitions," Der Spiegel, June 17, 2010.

the proposal. But on January 19, they announced that they were rejecting it. That wasn't all. They also announced that they had already taken some of the low-enriched uranium produced in the underground hall at Natanz and begun to further enrich it to nearly 20 percent in the pilot plant—a level they said they needed for medical research.[25]

Six days later, the team behind Stuxnet began preparations for a new round of attacks.

Throughout his first year in office, President Obama had kept close tabs on the digital weapon's progress. There was a lot riding on its success, and so far the news had been good. In fact, it was better than expected. Even though Stuxnet had targeted limited numbers of centrifuges, the Iranians were magnifying its effects by disabling entire cascades of centrifuges in their effort to uncover the source of the problems, thus contributing to further delays in their program. They still seemed to have no idea that the problems lay in the computers controlling their cascades, so there was no reason at this point to stop the sabotage. Particularly when the pressure to take military action against Iran was growing.

So on January 25, the attackers signed Stuxnet's two driver files with the digital certificate stolen from RealTek in Taiwan. On March 1, they compiled their code. Then they appeared to wait.

On March 20, Nowruz arrived, and Obama again delivered a pointed message about peaceful cooperation to the Iranian people as he'd done during the previous Persian New Year celebration. But this time, he spoke directly about Iran's nuclear program. "Together with the international community, the United States acknowledges your right to peaceful nuclear energy—we insist only that you adhere to the same responsibilities that apply to other nations," he said. "We are familiar with your grievances from the past—we have our own grievances as well, but we are prepared to move forward. We know what you're against; now tell us what you're for."

His tone grew darker as he made a veiled reference to Iran's recent

---

25 Olli J. Heinonen, "Iran Ramping Up Uranium Enrichment," Power and Policy blog, July 20, 2011, published by the Belfer Center at Harvard Kennedy School, July 20, 2011, available at powerandpolicy.com/2011/07/20/Iran-ramping-up-uranium-enrichment/#.UtM6Z7SYf8M.

rejection of the compromise proposal for nuclear fuel. "Faced with an extended hand," Obama said, "Iran's leaders have shown only a clenched fist."[26]

In the weeks prior to his speech, Iranian technicians had been working hard to recover from the problems created by Stuxnet, getting the number of cascades in unit A24 back up to capacity with all eighteen cascades enriching, and restoring centrifuges they had removed from several cascades in A26. They also increased the amount of gas they were feeding into the centrifuges that were still operating to make up for the lost time and to increase the output of enriched gas. But they had no idea they were about to get hit again.

Celebrations for the Persian New Year ran for thirteen days in Iran, though only the first four days were an official public holiday. It was on March 23, the fourth day of the holiday when most workers were still at home with their families and friends, that the next wave of Stuxnet struck. The payload was identical to the one unleashed the previous June, but this version included the larger collection of zero-day exploits and other spreading mechanisms, including the .LNK exploit that ultimately led to its discovery.

Despite all of these extra bells and whistles, however, the attackers appeared to target only a single company this time—Behpajooh. It's not clear when they unleashed their code, but it struck the first machines at Behpajooh around six a.m. on March 23. Behpajooh had been hit in the 2009 attack as well, and it would be hit in a subsequent attack that struck the following month, in April 2010. It was, in fact, the only company known to have been hit in all three rounds, suggesting it might have had a higher value as a conduit to reach the target computers at Natanz than the others. It was also, unfortunately, the victim that launched thousands of other infections in and outside Iran.

Over subsequent days, as vacationing workers returned to their offices,

---

26 "Remarks of President Obama Marking Nowruz," the White House, March 20, 2010, available at whitehouse.gov/the-press-office/remarks-president-obama-marking-nowruz.

the worm began to replicate wildly, spreading first through Behpajooh's offices in Iran, the UK, and Asia before breaking free and infecting other companies in those countries and beyond.[27] Later, when the Symantec researchers analyzed various samples of Stuxnet gathered from infected computers, they were able to trace thousands of infections back to these initial infections at Behpajooh.[28]

Why the attackers increased their firing power to reach their target at this point is unclear. Perhaps the two years they'd spent inside Natanz's computers had merely made them reckless, overconfident. But the most likely explanation is that the earlier versions of Stuxnet had been delivered via an insider or someone with close access to the target machines. If Stuxnet's creators had subsequently lost this access, they would've felt the need to ramp up the spreading power to improve their chances of reaching their target. One piece of circumstantial evidence supporting this explanation is the different delays between when the attacks were compiled and when they infected their first victims. In the June 2009 attack, only about twelve hours had passed between the time the worm was compiled and when it struck its first victim.[29] But the March 2010 version was compiled on the morning of March 1, then didn't infect its first machine until March 23. (The last known version to be released, in April, had a similarly long delay of twelve days between the compilation date and infection.) The short infection time in 2009 suggested that the attackers may have used

---

27 It spent nearly a month working its way through computers at Behpajooh and, on April 24, it struck gold when it hit a computer identified by the name "Manager 115." Stuxnet recorded that this computer contained a zip folder with Step 7 project files stored in it. Over the next couple of months, the malware broke out of Behpajooh's network and spread to other companies. The companies are identified in the log file only by their domain names, which may or may not also be the company's name. For example, they include MSCCO, Melal, and S-Adari.

28 There were ten "patient zeroes" at the five companies that were infected. That is, ten machines at these five companies were targeted by the attackers. And from these ten machines, the Symantec researchers were able to chart a constellation of about 12,000 other infections. Of these five companies, Behpajooh was responsible for 69 percent of those 12,000 infections.

29 Compilation and infection times aren't always accurate. The system clocks on either the compiling machine or the victim machine in this case could have been out of date or the code could have been compiled in a time zone different from the victim's time zone. In comparing the amount of time that elapsed between the time the three versions of Stuxnet were compiled and when they infected their first machines, the researchers assumed the compiling machine and the victim machines were in the same time zone.

an inside accomplice or unwitting victim who had been preselected for the operation. When it came time to unleash subsequent versions of Stuxnet, the attackers may have had to wait longer until an opportunity arose to unleash it.

As Stuxnet spread far and wide, it phoned home to its controllers via the command-and-control servers—and so it wasn't long before officials in Washington learned that their worm had gone rogue. At that point it became clear that an operation that had been one of the most tightly held secrets in Washington for more than three years was suddenly at risk of being exposed.

How had a digital weapon so carefully crafted and controlled for so long come undone now? Fingers pointed to Israel initially. In the spring of 2010 the White House, the NSA, and the Israelis had reportedly "decided to swing for the fences" with their sights on a specific group of 1,000 centrifuges they wanted to attack.[30] This likely was a group of six cascades in unit A26. The previous round of Stuxnet had reduced A26 from twelve cascades enriching uranium to just six. It may have been these final six that the attackers now wanted to take out. Six cascades of 164 centrifuges each added up to 984 centrifuges. The Israelis apparently added the final touches—the extra zero days and other spreading mechanisms—in order to supersize it. Sanger reports that sources told him that the worm was launched inside Natanz and escaped when an Iranian scientist connected his laptop to an infected control computer at the plant and then carried the infection out on his laptop to the internet. But this doesn't correspond to the forensic evidence researchers found in the code. As previously noted, each sample of Stuxnet contained a log file that tracked every machine it infected. These files showed that the first infections occurred at computers belonging to Behpajooh and the other companies, computers that appeared to be generic systems, not programming computers inside Natanz that contained Step 7 files or the Siemens software. It was possible that these were laptops belonging to contractors who were working inside Na-

---

30 Sanger, *Confront and Conceal*, 204.

tanz. But Sanger also writes that the worm should have recognized when its environment changed and it landed on machines outside of its target environment. There was nothing in any of the versions of Stuxnet that researchers examined, however, that served as a mechanism for recognizing this and preventing Stuxnet from spreading outside Natanz. The only limitations Stuxnet had were on where it ignited its payload, not where it spread.

It's important to note, however, that the operators who managed the command servers that communicated with Stuxnet *did* have the ability to halt the spread of the weapon once they saw it getting out of control. Stuxnet had a disinfect feature that allowed the attackers to remove it from an infected machine. As Stuxnet began to spread wildly out of control and the attackers started seeing infected machines reporting in to their server from Indonesia, Australia, and elsewhere, they could have sent out a disinfect command to delete the code from those machines. There were a limited number of possible reasons that they didn't do this. "Either they didn't care that it was spreading or it was spreading faster than they expected and they couldn't strike it down," says O'Murchu. O'Murchu doesn't think it was due to incompetence. "They had total control over infected machines, and I think it was a conscious decision to [do nothing]." Even after news of Stuxnet's spread made it back to Washington, a remarkable decision was made to let the operation continue with still no apparent attempt to halt its spread. Although, again, the details are murky, according to Sanger's sources, at least two more versions of Stuxnet were released after March, but were tweaked to remove the "bug" that caused the previous one to spread.

On April 14, the attackers did compile another version of Stuxnet, but the payload this time was exactly the same as the March one. Although the same spreading mechanisms were in this one, it didn't spread as far and wide as the March version.[31] No other versions of Stuxnet dating after this have been found in the wild.

---

31 Although the attack struck some companies multiple times, it was not always the same machine each time. The attackers might have been looking for better-placed machines each time or ones that gave them different routes of access to the target. It's not clear why the April version didn't spread as

It's possible that subsequent versions of Stuxnet were unleashed but were so much more tightly controlled that they've never been found. There was a hint of this when researchers found the random driver file in July 2010 that they thought was associated with Stuxnet. It was the driver discovered by ESET that had been signed with the certificate from J-Micron. As noted, the driver was found by itself, without any main Stuxnet file accompanying it, but it's believed this may have been part of another Stuxnet attack.

In the April attack, Foolad Technique was the first victim that was hit, as it had been in the June 2009 attack. The worm struck the company on April 26 and appeared to infect the same computer it had infected the previous year. Weeks later on May 11, the digital weapon was unleashed on three computers belonging to a company using the domain name Kala, believed to be Kala Electric or Kala Electronics, the front company that Iran used to manage Natanz and secretly procure components for its nuclear program—the same company that Alireza Jafarzadeh had mentioned in his 2002 press conference exposing Natanz.[32] Behpajooh was hit with this same version of Stuxnet on May 13.

Notably, although Neda Industrial Group doesn't show up in the logs for the 2010 infection samples that researchers examined, Behrooz, the control engineer who had posted to the Siemens user forum the previous year, popped up again complaining of continued problems. On June 2, he wrote that all Windows computers at his company were still experiencing the same problem they had the previous year.

Workers at other companies chimed in to say that they, too, were having the same problem. One user, who also wrote that all of the PCs at his company were infected, said the problem appeared to be confined to Iran. "[B]ecause you can see many people in Iran [on the forum] have the same problem from at least 1 [month] ago," he wrote. The discussion continued

---

widely as the March one did, since it had all of the same zero-day spreading mechanisms and also hit Behpajooh, the company hit in the March attack from which Stuxnet spread widely around the world. It's possible the machines hit in the April attack were not as broadly connected as the ones hit in March, reducing its spread.

32 The domain name of a computer can sometimes identify the name of the company that owns it, but not always.

throughout July, with Behrooz so frustrated at times that he ended some of his messages with an angry, red-faced emoticon. Then suddenly, on July 24, he posted a message saying finally the mystery had been solved. He included a link to a news article about Stuxnet, which had recently been publicly exposed, and ended his message with three grinning emoticons. Of course it would be several more months before he and the rest of the world learned what it was targeting.

UNLIKE THE 2009 assault, it's unclear what effect the attacks in 2010 had on Natanz. Sanger writes that after the attackers unleashed a third version of Stuxnet in 2010, it caused 984 centrifuges to come "to a screeching halt."[33] As noted previously, there were at this time exactly 984 centrifuges enriching in six cascades in unit A26, but there is no indication in IAEA reports that they stopped enriching. In September, there were still six cascades in unit A26 enriching gas and another six spinning under vacuum. It's possible that the centrifuges in question did halt and then recovered or were replaced at some point between the IAEA's May and September reports. It's also possible that Sanger's sources confused the dates and were referring to the 1,000 or so centrifuges that technicians removed in late 2009 and early 2010 that the IAEA had captured with their cameras.

It's difficult to know what exactly occurred with the centrifuges in 2010 because in June that year, officials in Iran began accusing the IAEA of leaking information to the press about its operations. In a June 3 letter, Iran warned the agency that if confidential information about the nuclear program "leaks, in any way, and/or [is] conveyed to the media," there would be consequences, the first being that Iran would withdraw its approval for some of the IAEA inspectors who were allowed to visit its

---

33 Sanger, *Confront and Conceal*, 206. Sanger writes that the NSA picked up intelligence intercepts indicating that the centrifuges had come to a halt.

nuclear facilities.[34] That same month, Iran made good on the threat and removed two names from its approved list of about 150 IAEA inspectors, citing "false and wrong statements" the IAEA had made in its May report. The report had claimed that some nuclear equipment had gone missing in Iran. Then in September, two more inspectors were banned, on grounds that they had leaked information to the media before the IAEA had released it publicly in its report.[35]

The rebuke appeared to have a detrimental effect on the amount of public information the IAEA published about Natanz thereafter. By November, the IAEA had stopped listing details about the centrifuges in its quarterly reports. Instead of listing the number of centrifuges installed and enriching in each unit, it aggregated the numbers from all three units—A24, A26, and A28—into a single count. This eliminated the primary means the public had for determining the effects Stuxnet had on the plant.[36]

---

34 Iran accused the IAEA of leaking information to Reuters for a May 14 story and to the Associated Press for a May 30 story.

35 Fereydoon Abbasi, who was appointed head of the Iranian Atomic Energy Organization after the attempt on his life in 2010, accused the West in a 2014 interview of using the IAEA reports about Iran's nuclear activities to "calibrate" its sabotage against the nuclear program and to "size up the level of destruction they have exerted" on Iran's nuclear machinery with each round of attack. "By accessing the leaked data from our reports they can tell how many centrifuges are operating in Iranian nuclear facilities and how many are about to be installed with what parts needed," he said. When Iran submits reports to the IAEA about the design of its nuclear facilities and the equipment it plans to procure for the program, intelligence agencies use the list to "booby-trap the devices" and "set up viruses in their control systems," he added. The Iranians got more careful over time about showing IAEA inspectors the exact equipment they installed in the cascade rooms—at one point they even placed stickers over brand names on equipment to prevent inspectors from identifying them. They also followed inspectors around with a camera to watch everything they did. Abassi also said that Stuxnet was not the first or the last such attack by the US and Israel against the nuclear program, and that they had repeatedly infiltrated the supply chain for Iran's nuclear program to sabotage vacuum valves, valve pumps, and other equipment. "Spy agencies adjust their attacks based on our needs; they obstruct conventional channels to our purchase and leave open only those that they can exert full control over to transfer their modified stuff to our facilities," he said, accusing Siemens of being complicit in the program. "This is how they penetrated our electronic infrastructures, bugged on us, and installed malwares like the Stuxnet. They set up the virus in the gauges we had purchased from Siemens and also [put] explosives in the devices." See "How West Infiltrated Iran's Nuclear Program, Ex-Top Nuclear Official Explains," *Iran's View*, March 28, 2014, www.iransview.com/west-infiltrated-irans-nuclear-program-ex-top-nuclear-official-explains/1451.

36 A former IAEA official told me the reason the reports changed in late 2010 had nothing to do with the accusations from Iran, but was due to uncertainty about the accuracy of the data collected. After the Iranians removed gas from some of the centrifuges in 2009 and 2010 and decommissioned

What we do know is that in July 2010, the centrifuges were still only producing at 45 to 66 percent capacity. ISIS noted for the first time in one of its reports, published in July, that "sabotage" might be the cause of some of the problems at Natanz.[37] Stuxnet had by then been discovered and publicly exposed, but its link to Iran's nuclear program and Natanz was still several months away.

It's also clear that the number of installed and enriching centrifuges fluctuated radically in 2010. In November 2009, at the plant's peak, Iran had 8,692 centrifuges installed. That number was down to 8,528 in May 2010 (with 3,936 enriching), but increased to 8,856 in September (with 3,772 enriching) before dropping to 8,426 in November (with 4,816 enriching). It's possible centrifuges continued to break during the year even after Stuxnet was discovered and that this was the reason for the fluctuation. Although the large jump of 1,000 centrifuges enriching from September to November suggests that the plant had recovered from the lingering effects of Stuxnet, Iran still had 3,600 centrifuges installed that were just sitting in cascades, not enriching.[38] This suggests at least some continuing problems. It wasn't long after this, on November 16, that officials at Natanz shut down the plant completely for six days following Symantec's revelation that Stuxnet was designed to sabotage frequency converters.[39] Some time that same month, they also added more centrifuges to six of the cascades, suggesting they may have

---

other centrifuges, they continued to operate some cascades with fewer than 164 working centrifuges in them. This made IAEA officials realize they had no way of knowing how many centrifuges in each cascade were actually functional and enriching gas at any one time, he said. They had simply assumed in the past that if a cascade was enriching uranium, all of the 164 centrifuges in the cascade were involved in enriching the uranium.

37 David Albright, Paul Brannan, and Andrea Stricker, "What Is Iran's Competence in Operating Centrifuges?" ISIS, July 26, 2010, available at isis-online.org/isis-reports/detail/what-is-irans -competence-in-operating-centrifuges/8.

38 Ivan Oelrich, with the Federation of American Scientists, notes that in fact there were more centrifuges enriching at this point, but they were only operating at 20 percent of their efficiency.

39 David Albright et al., "Natanz Enrichment Site: Boondoggle or Part of an Atomic Bomb Production Complex?" ISIS, September 21, 2011, available at isis-online.org/isis-reports/detail/ natanz-enrichment-site-boondoogle-or-part-of-an-atomic-bomb-production-comp.

been trying to alter the configuration of the cascades to thwart Stuxnet's payload.[40]

BACK IN WASHINGTON, conversations about Stuxnet had continued throughout 2010. Sometime during the early summer, CIA director Leon Panetta and Gen. James Cartwright had broken the news of the worm's out-of-control spreading to the president. The revelation prompted a lot of questions from Obama. Was there any sign that the Iranians had discovered it yet? If yes, could they determine what it was doing or trace it back to its source? He was also concerned about collateral damage to the machines infected outside Natanz. And taking all of this into account, should they now cancel the operation? His advisers reminded him that the worm was a highly targeted precision weapon that launched its payload only on machines that met a specific criteria; although it would affect other machines to a certain degree, simply by the nature of infecting them, it wouldn't harm them.

Satisfied that the operation was still in their control for the most part, Obama ordered them to proceed.[41]

Given Stuxnet's complexity and the long odds against it being uncovered or deciphered, the decision must have seemed completely reasonable

---

40 Sometime in November 2010, technicians increased the number of centrifuges in six cascades from 164 to 174. See IAEA Board of Governors, "Implementation of the NPT Safeguards Agreement and the Relevant Provisions of Security Council Resolutions in the Islamic Republic of Iran" (report, November 23, 2010), available at iaea.org/Publications/Documents/Board/2010/gov2010-62.pdf. Although some observers believe that Iran increased the number of centrifuges in order to increase the amount of gas they could enrich in the cascades—perhaps to make up for time lost to Stuxnet—an IAEA source told me that the centrifuges were added at the latter stage of the cascades, which wouldn't help increase the amount of gas that could be enriched in the cascade. He suggested that the additional centrifuges were simply meant to alter the configuration of the cascades in order to prevent any lingering copies of Stuxnet from working on them.

41 Sanger notes that the meeting between Panetta and Obama occurred midsummer, which would make it sometime in July, right around the time Stuxnet was exposed. But he also says within weeks after this meeting, the attackers unleashed two other versions of the worm. This suggests that new versions of Stuxnet were released after antivirus firms had already released signatures to detect it. As noted, no later version of Stuxnet has been found.

at the time. Indeed, even the initial reaction from Symantec and other security companies after Stuxnet was exposed seemed to confirm that their covert operation was safe—every sign indicated that the security community, stymied by the malware's complexity and unfamiliarity, had abandoned their work on the code after releasing signatures to detect it and had moved on.

But Washington hadn't counted on the dogged determination of the Symantec researchers to get to the bottom of the mysterious code or on Ralph Langner's blunt and vocal candor about what it was attacking. As the months went on and more information came out from Langner and Symantec, all anyone in Washington and Tel Aviv could do was sit and watch as each piece of the puzzle fell into place, until finally the picture was complete.

CHAPTER 18

QUALIFIED SUCCESS

A year after IAEA officials first began to notice technicians removing an unusual number of centrifuges from the underground hall at Natanz, the mystery behind the disappearing devices was at last solved. But with Stuxnet finally identified as the cause, and with details about the extensive resources behind it revealed, a couple of other questions begged to be answered: Just how successful had Stuxnet been at achieving its goals? And were the risks, costs, and consequences worth it?

"If Stuxnet's goal was the destruction of all the centrifuges [at Natanz]," then it had certainly failed, David Albright of ISIS noted in a 2010 report. But if the goal was to destroy a limited number of centrifuges in order to set Iran's uranium enrichment program back a bit, then "it may have succeeded," he wrote, "at least for a while."[1]

There was no doubt that Iran's nuclear program was not where it should have been in 2010 when Stuxnet was discovered. The two massive

---

1 David Albright, Paul Brannan, and Christina Walrond, "Did Stuxnet Take Out 1,000 Centrifuges at the Natanz Enrichment Plant? Preliminary Assessment," Institute for Science and International Security, December 22, 2010, available at isis-online.org/isis-reports/detail/did -stuxnet-take-out-1000-centrifuges-at-the-natanz-enrichment-plant.

underground halls at Natanz were capable of holding 47,000 centrifuges, yet more than a decade after their construction was complete, only one of the halls contained any centrifuges at all, and even that one was only one-third full. "Viewed from that perspective—what Iran had originally planned and where the program was now, the situation had worsened . . ." Albright wrote.

But how much of this was due to Stuxnet and how much to other causes—sanctions, diplomatic pressure, and the effects of other covert sabotage efforts—remains unclear. Ralph Langner believed the attack on Natanz was a huge success and had been "nearly as effective as a military strike" without all the risks and costs that a military strike entailed. The *New York Times* said Stuxnet appeared to be the "biggest single factor in putting time on the nuclear clock."[2]

But there were varying opinions about just how many centrifuges Stuxnet affected and how far Iran's nuclear program had been set back as a result.

Back in 2003, Israeli officials had warned that Iran would have enough enriched uranium for a bomb by 2007 if the nuclear program wasn't halted. But two voluntary suspensions and a host of other factors had pushed back the clock, causing the Israelis to revise the bomb time-line first to 2008 and then to 2010. Now post-Stuxnet, the timeline was pushed back again.

When Mossad's outgoing chief, Meir Dagan, left his job in early 2011, he told the Israeli Knesset that Iran now would not be able to produce a nuclear arsenal before 2015.[3] US officials were less generous in their estimate, however, saying the program had been set back only eighteen to twenty-four months, rather than four years. According to US Secretary of State Hillary Clinton, the nuclear program had been "slowed" by techno-

2 William J. Broad, John Markoff, and David E. Sanger, "Israeli Test on Worm Called Crucial in Iran Nuclear Delay," *New York Times*, January 15, 2011.
3 Yossi Melman, "Outgoing Mossad Chief: Iran Won't Have Nuclear Capability Before 2015," *Ha'aretz*, January 7, 2011.

logical problems and sanctions, but not to the point at which anyone could relax. "We have time," she said, "but not a lot of time."[4] Ivanka Barzashka, a research associate at the Centre for Science and Security Studies at King's College in London, believed the nuclear program had not been pushed back at all. She examined correlations between centrifuge numbers in the IAEA reports and the dates that Stuxnet was active in 2009, and found that evidence of the attack's impact was circumstantial and inconclusive. If Stuxnet did have an effect on the uranium enrichment program, it wore off quickly.

"If sabotage did occur, it was short-lived and most likely happened between May and November 2009," she concluded. "The malware did not set back Iran's enrichment programme, though perhaps it might have temporarily slowed down Iran's rate of expansion."[5]

The Iranians, in fact, showed a remarkable ability to recover from any damages and delays that Stuxnet and other factors had meted out.

In early 2010, for example, shortly after technicians at Natanz replaced the centrifuges that were causing them problems, they stepped up their enrichment activity, feeding more gas into the centrifuges to increase the output they produced. As a result, Iran's production of low-enriched uranium actually *increased* in 2010 and remained fairly steady thereafter. In the fall of 2008, for example, during the period that Stuxnet 0.5 was manipulating valves on the cascades, the centrifuges were producing only 90 kg of low-enriched uranium a month. At the end of 2009, when the next round of Stuxnet hit, the number dipped slightly to 85 kg a month. But in 2010, despite at least two more rounds of Stuxnet being released, the production level jumped to between 120 and 150 kg a month, and by

---

4 Mark Landler, "U.S. Says Sanctions Hurt Iran Nuclear Program," *New York Times*, January 10, 2011.

5 Ivanka Barzashka, "Are Cyber-Weapons Effective?" Royal United Services Institute for Defense and Security Studies, July 23, 2013, available at tandfonline.com/doi/pdf/10.1080/03071847.2013.7 87735. It should be noted that Barzashka only examined the IAEA reports for 2009 and did not take into consideration other rounds of attack by Stuxnet in 2008 and 2010.

2011, Iran was producing a steady 150 kg of low-enriched uranium per month.

It should be noted, however, that these production numbers were still well below what the centrifuges should have produced by design. In 2010, it took 4,820 centrifuges to produce this volume of enriched gas, but in 2011 Iran was using 5,860 centrifuges to produce the same amount, suggesting the centrifuges were working less efficiently than they had before, possibly due to lingering effects from Stuxnet.[6]

But in the end, Iran was still making progress and still producing enriched uranium. By mid-2011, the centrifuges had produced a total of 4,400 kg of low-enriched uranium.[7] What's more, Iran had transferred at least 1,950 kg of this to the pilot plant to be further enriched to 19.75 percent, and by the beginning of 2011, Iran had 33 kg of uranium enriched to this level and announced plans to triple this amount.

Officials began enriching the uranium to this higher percentage following the destruction of centrifuges by Stuxnet. Iranian officials claimed they needed the higher-enriched uranium for cancer treatment research. But the higher-enriched uranium created a bigger problem for those opposed to the enrichment program, because at 20 percent enrichment, Iran was closer to the 90-percent weapons-grade material it needed for a bomb. "Starting from this higher enrichment level means that Iran cuts its time by more than half to produce weapons-grade, highly enriched uranium at about 90 percent enrichment," noted Barzashka. In this regard, if "the purpose of [Stuxnet] was to decrease Iranian nuclear-weapons potential, it clearly failed."[8]

Meanwhile, technicians also began installing more advanced centrifuges at the pilot enrichment plant at Natanz—IR-2m and IR-4 cen-

---

6 David Albright and Christina Walrond, "Performance of the IR-1 Centrifuge at Natanz," Institute for Science and International Security, October 18, 2011, available at isis-online.org/isis -reports/detail/test1.
7 Olli J. Heinonen, "Iran Ramping Up Uranium Enrichment," Power and Policy blog, July 20, 2011, published by the Belfer Center at Harvard Kennedy School, July 20, 2011, available at powerandpolicy.com/2011/07/20/Iran-ramping-up-uranium-enrichment/#.UtM6Z7SYf8M.
8 Barzashka, "Are Cyber-Weapons Effective?"

trifuges. These centrifuges were much more efficient than the IR-1s. Whereas IR-1s could produce about 1.0 separative work units a day by design (though they seldom reached this level), the more advanced centrifuges could produce about three to five times this much. They were also more resilient than the IR-1s, which meant they were less prone to break under the kind of stress that Stuxnet produced.

Despite Iran's seemingly quick recovery from Stuxnet, the digital weapon did have at least two longer-lasting effects on the enrichment program. First, it cut into Iran's supply of uranium gas. Several tons of enriched uranium ended up in dump tanks during the period that Stuxnet was doing its sabotage. The waste likely wasn't all due to Stuxnet, since technicians experienced a number of varied problems with the centrifuges, but Stuxnet no doubt contributed to the loss. As previously noted, Iran had a limited supply of uranium on hand (some imported from abroad, some mined from its own land), and any gas that was wasted cut into these reserves.

But Iran also had a limited supply of centrifuges and materials to make new ones. With sanctions tighter than ever before, replacing damaged centrifuges now would become more challenging. In 2008, the IAEA estimated that Iran had enough components and materials on hand to build 10,000 centrifuges.[9] If Stuxnet destroyed 1,000 of these, this cut the stockpile of centrifuges by 10 percent. On top of this, Iran lost about 10 percent of centrifuges each year to normal wear and tear. At that rate of attrition, "after five years, these guys are cooked," says the IAEA's Olli Heinonen.[10]

But Heinonen in fact believed that more than 1,000 centrifuges were damaged by Stuxnet. He believed the number was closer to 2,000. He based his assessment on the fact that IAEA reports provided only a snap-

9 David Albright, Jacqueline Shire, and Paul Brannan, "Enriched Uranium Output Steady: Centrifuge Numbers Expected to Increase Dramatically; Arak Reactor Verification Blocked," Institute for Science and International Security, November 19, 2008, available at isis-online.org/publications/iran/ISIS_analysis_Nov-IAEA-Report.pdf.
10 Author interview with Heinonen, June 2011.

shot of conditions at Natanz during a three-month period and the fact that there had been problems with tamper-evident security seals at Natanz, which raised the possibility that Iran might have secretly replaced some of its damaged centrifuges without the IAEA knowing it.[11]

Although IAEA inspectors visited the plant twenty-four times a year on average, their reports were only publicly disclosed once a quarter, and the numbers in each report were based only on the number of centrifuges the inspectors observed at the plant during their most recent visit prior to each report. Thus, there were numerous opportunities in between visits for technicians to swap out centrifuges away from inspectors' prying eyes—as long as they did so out of the view of the IAEA cameras, which were, in theory, supposed to make such hidden swaps impossible.

Every time a new module of cascades was constructed at the plant, technicians placed portable walls around it, and made it accessible by only a single door—a door that an IAEA camera was positioned outside to monitor. Tamper-evident seals were also placed on the joints of the walls, to ensure that the door was indeed the single means of entry, and that technicians couldn't simply move the walls aside to remove centrifuges out of the view of the cameras. But there had been problems at Natanz with security seals mysteriously breaking.[12] Iranian officials said the breaks were accidental and that operators had been told "to exercise more vigilance." But Heinonen says "an unusual pattern" of broken seals emerged in Iran, raising the possibility that the walls might have been moved to furtively remove and replace damaged centrifuges.[13]

---

11 Heinonen left the IAEA in October 2010 before the centrifuges were removed, therefore he didn't have access to the inspector reports themselves to see the exact numbers, but he was certain the number of damaged centrifuges exceeded 1,000.

12 A July 2010 letter from the IAEA to Iran referenced "a number of incidents" involving broken seals at the plant. See IAEA Board of Governors, "Implementation of the NPT Safeguards Agreement and Relevant Provisions of Security Council Resolutions in the Islamic Republic of Iran" (report, September 6, 2010), 3; available at iaea.org/Publications/Documents/Board/2010/gov2010-46.pdf. The report does not specify whether the references are to seals placed on the walls or seals placed on gas canisters and other equipment, but an IAEA source told me they referred to wall seals.

13 An IAEA source told me that it was Iran who alerted inspectors to the broken seals, rather than the inspectors finding them on their own. The IAEA investigated the broken seals and found

But even if the number of damaged centrifuges exceeded 1,000, Stuxnet clearly wasn't the magic bullet it might have been had it been designed for more immediate and widespread destruction—to take out thousands of centrifuges in a single blow—rather than for slower, more incremental effects.

There were some, in fact, who wondered why Stuxnet *hadn't* been designed for more quick and severe damage. But the risk of repercussions for such an aggressive attack were greater. If Stuxnet had destroyed 3,000 to 4,000 machines at once, there would have been little question that the cause was sabotage, and Iran would likely have perceived it as a military assault to be responded to in kind. So Stuxnet's slow and stealthy attack was a compromise of sorts that made it harder to achieve more extensive results but also made it harder for Iran to make a case for striking back.

Questions remained, though, about what the digital weapon might have achieved had it not been discovered in 2010. Iran's enrichment program was just getting under way when Stuxnet struck, and the code was still in the early stages of mayhem when it was exposed. There was no telling what it might have accomplished over time as Iran installed more centrifuges and cascades. For this reason Barzashka believed the attackers made a mistake in unleashing Stuxnet too soon. Had it been held in abeyance until more centrifuges were installed and more uranium gas was in play, its effects on the program might have been more detrimental.

One thing was certain: it would now be harder for the attackers to repeat the feat. Stuxnet, as Langner had noted, was effectively a one-shot weapon: the attack, once discovered, had made the Iranians more cautious, thereby making future attacks by the same means more difficult to pull off. After this, anytime equipment at Natanz malfunctioned, the Iranians would immediately suspect sabotage and respond more swiftly.

---

no wrongdoing on Iran's part. But the investigation, he said, focused only on whether Iran might have broken the seals to remove nuclear material from the rooms out of the view of cameras, not on whether centrifuges might have been secretly removed from the rooms. When inspectors found that all of the uranium was accounted for, they concluded that the seals had not been intentionally broken for illicit purposes, but they left unexplored the possibility that they had been intentionally broken to remove broken centrifuges.

At the first sign of trouble, technicians would shut down the systems and examine them more closely for malware or manipulation.

But regardless of all the factors that limited Stuxnet's effects and cut its life short, the stealth attack made at least one group very happy.

"In the non-proliferation community, Stuxnet is just a welcome development," David Albright says. "It means we won't have to have a war with Iran."[14]

BUT EVEN IF the Stuxnet operation bought diplomatic negotiators a little more time, the weapon clearly didn't put an end to the political crisis or eliminate the possibility of war entirely. In 2011, a fifth round of UN sanctions was being levied against Iran, and the United States was planting Patriot missiles throughout the Middle East to protect its allies in the event of war. And Iran's adversaries continued to employ lethal measures against its scientists in an attempt to cripple the nuclear program. In July 2011, a thirty-five-year-old physicist named Darioush Rezaeinejad was shot in the throat while picking up his daughter from kindergarten in Tehran. The two gunmen reportedly escaped on motorcycles. The IAEA said Rezaeinejad had been involved in developing high-voltage switches for setting off explosions needed to trigger a nuclear warhead.[15]

Then in January 2012, just a day after Israel's military chief of staff said that 2013 would be a crucial year for Iran's nuclear program, motorcycle assassins struck again in Iran, this time killing Mostafa Ahmadi Roshan with an explosive attached to his car. Roshan was initially identified as a thirty-two-year-old chemist who worked at Natanz, but an Iranian official later revealed he actually managed the Natanz facility and also worked procuring specialized equipment for Iran's nuclear program.

14 Author interview with Albright, February 2011.
15 Ulrike Putz, "Mossad Behind Tehran Assassinations, Says Source," *Spiegel Online*, August 2, 2011, available at spiegel.de/international/world/sabotaging-iran-s-nuclear-program-mossad-behind -tehran-assassinations-says-source-a-777899.html. See also "Israel Responsible for Iran Killing: Report," *Global Security Newswire*, August 2, 2011, available at nti.org/gsn/article/israel-responsible -for-iran-killing-report.

Roshan's title was deputy for trade affairs at Kala Electronics Company, which provided parts for Natanz. Kala, of course, was one of the companies believed to have been struck by Stuxnet.[16]

A string of mysterious explosions also began to plague Iran. In November 2011, a massive explosion at a long-range-missile testing site killed more than thirty members of Iran's Revolutionary Guard, including the general said to be the architect of Iran's missile program.[17] Iran denied the explosion was the result of sabotage, insisting that it was an accident. But a Western intelligence source told the *New York Times* that the actual cause mattered little. "Anything that buys us time and delays the day when the Iranians might be able to mount a nuclear weapon on an accurate missile is a small victory," he said. "At this point, we'll take whatever we can get, however it happens."

That same month, a blast occurred at the uranium conversion plant in Esfahan, reportedly damaging a facility where raw materials for the uranium enrichment program were stored.[18] Then in August 2012, explo-

---

16 Roshan was given the title of "young nuclear martyr" after his death, and city streets and plazas were named after him. Saeed Kamali Dehghan and Julian Borger, "Iranian Nuclear Chemist Killed by Motorbike Assassins," *Guardian*, January 11, 2012. See also Zvi Bar'el, "Iran Domestic Tensions Boil as West Battles Its Nuclear Program," *Ha'aretz*, April 8, 2014. David Albright noted to me that when a scientist in the nuclear program is killed, the intent is to eliminate expertise and cripple the program. But killing someone involved in procurement for the program is meant to send a message and scare others from serving a similar role.

17 David E. Sanger and William J. Broad, "Blast That Leveled Base Seen as Big Setback to Iran Missiles," *New York Times*, December 4, 2011.

18 Sheera Frenkel, "Second Blast 'Aimed at Stopping Tehran's Nuclear Arms Plans'," *Times* (London), November 30, 2011. Iranian news agencies reported the blast initially, though the reports were later removed from websites, and officials retracted statements they had made confirming the blast. In February 2012, an Israeli ad was later pulled offline. The ad, for the Israeli cable TV company HOT, was later pulled offline. It featured members of an Israeli comedy series, *Asfur*, who sneak into Iran in drag dressed as Muslim women—likely a mock reference to the time former Palestinian leader Yasser Arafat was said to have escaped capture dressed as a Muslim woman. The three arrive in Esfahan, the site of the uranium conversion facility in Iran where the mysterious explosion occurred. As the comedians walk through town, a nuclear facility visible behind them, one of them spreads sunscreen on his face. When his companions look askance at him, he replies, "What? Don't you know how much radiation there is here?" The bungling travelers then encounter a bored Mossad agent sitting at an outdoor café who tells them he's been in town two months conducting surveillance and has been killing time watching on-demand episodes of *Asfur* on his Samsung Galaxy tablet, a gift his wife and he received for subscribing to HOT. "Nuclear reactor or no nuclear reactor, I'm not missing *Asfur*," he says. One of the travelers reaches toward the tablet and asks, "What's this application here?" As he presses something on the screen, a fireball explodes

sions took out power lines feeding electricity from the city of Qom to the underground enrichment plant at Fordow. News reports indicated that one of the explosions occurred when security forces found an electronic monitoring device disguised as a rock and tried to move it. The booby-trapped device was reportedly designed to intercept data from computer and phone lines at the enrichment plant.[19] In discussing the incident, an Iranian official revealed that power lines feeding electricity to the plant at Natanz were also taken out in a separate incident, though he didn't say when or offer further details.[20] Whatever Stuxnet's gains, they weren't enough to allow the West to relax.

None of this should have been a surprise to anyone, according to Henry Sokolski, executive director of the Nonproliferation Policy Education Center. Every president since Bill Clinton had tried covert operations to disrupt Iran's nuclear program, he noted to the *New Republic*, and none had succeeded. "Bush did it, Obama is doing it," he said. But covert action was never a substitute for sound foreign policy. It could only ever be "a holding action" not a solution, he said.[21]

Questions about the true nature of Iran's nuclear pursuits remained. Toward the end of 2011, an IAEA report, described as "the most damning report ever published" about Iran by the agency, declared that the Islamic Republic had been working on building a nuclear weapon since 2003, despite earlier assertions by US intelligence that Iran had abandoned its

---

behind them at the nuclear facility. His companions look at him in shock and he replies, "What? Just another mysterious explosion in Iran."

19 "Sources: Iran Exposed Spying Device at Fordo Nuke Plant," Ynet (online news site for the Israeli newspaper *Yediot Ahronot*), September 23, 2012, available at ynetnews.com/articles/0,7340,L-4284793,00.html.

20 Fredrik Dahl, "Terrorists Embedded in UN Nuclear Watchdog May Be Behind Power Line Explosion," Reuters, September 17, 2012, available at news.nationalpost.com/2012/09/17/terrorists-embedded-in-un-nuclear-watchdog-may-be-behind-power-line-explosion-iran. An Iranian official disclosed both incidents at the IAEA general conference in Vienna, accusing the IAEA of collusion. He noted that the day after the explosion that took out power lines feeding electricity to Fordow an IAEA inspector asked to conduct an unannounced inspection there. "Who other than the IAEA inspector can have access to the complex in such a short time to record and report failures?," the official asked.

21 Eli Lake, "Operation Sabotage," *New Republic*, July 14, 2010.

weapons program that same year.[22] The IAEA report wasn't based on new information but on earlier documents the agency had received, including ones from the Iranian mole known as "Dolphin." But although the information wasn't new, the IAEA's willingness to now assert that the documents were evidence of a nuclear weapons program was.[23] Israeli prime minister Benjamin Netanyahu once again renewed his call for a military strike against Iran. This time, however, the Iranians welcomed it. Iranian foreign minister Ali Akbar Salehi said defiantly that Iran was "ready for war" with Israel.[24]

IF THERE IS one thing to be said in Stuxnet's favor, it's that the digital attack, along with other covert operations, did succeed in staving off an ill-advised military attack against Iran. And despite continuing tension and gamesmanship, nobody has been willing to take that step in the wake of Stuxnet—a fact that ultimately left the door open for historic negotiations with Iran over its nuclear program that began in 2013. The initial discussions resulted in Iran agreeing to freeze core parts of its nuclear program—including halting the installation of new centrifuges and limiting the amount of enriched uranium Iran produces—in exchange for some loosening of sanctions against it.[25]

But any Stuxnet gains have to be weighed against the negative residual effects as well. At a time when the United States was battling an epidemic of cyber espionage attacks from China, attacking Iran made it harder to condemn other nations for cyber transgressions against the United States.

22 George Jahn, "UN Reports Iran Work 'Specific' to Nuke Arms," Associated Press, November 8, 2011, available at news.yahoo.com/un-reports-iran-specific-nuke-arms-184224261.html.
23 Ali Vaez, "It's Not Too Late to Peacefully Keep Iran from a Bomb," *The Atlantic*, November 11, 2011.
24 "Iran Says United and 'Ready for War' with Israel," *Ha'aretz*, November 3, 2011.
25 Anne Gearan and Joby Warrick, "Iran, World Powers Reach Historic Nuclear Deal," *Washington Post*, November 23, 2013, available at washingtonpost.com/world/national-security/kerry-in-geneva-raising-hopes-for-historic-nuclear-deal-with-iran/2013/11/23/53e7bfe6-5430-11e3-9fe0-fd2ca728e67c_story.html.

As the party that fired the first known digital weapon, the United States was no longer in a position to preach abstinence to others.

One final and more lasting consequence of Stuxnet also had to be weighed against its limited and uncertain benefits: the malware's release had launched a digital arms race among countries big and small that will alter the landscape of cyberattacks forever. Stuxnet's authors had mapped a new frontier that other hackers and nation-state attackers will inevitably follow; and when they do, the target for sabotage will eventually one day be in the United States.

CHAPTER 19

DIGITAL PANDORA

On May 30, 2009, just days before a new version of Stuxnet was unleashed on computers in Iran, President Barack Obama stood before the White House press corps in the East Room to address the grave state of cybersecurity in the United States. "We meet today at a transformational moment," he said, "a moment in history when our interconnected world presents us, at once, with great promise but also great peril."

Just as we had failed in the past to invest in the physical infrastructure of our roads, bridges, and railways, we had failed to invest in the security of our digital infrastructure, Obama said. Cyber intruders, he warned, had already probed our electrical grid, and in other countries had plunged entire cities into darkness. "This status quo is no longer acceptable," he said, "not when there's so much at stake."[1]

---

1 "Remarks by the President on Securing Our Nation's Cyber Infrastructure," May 29, 2009, available at whitehouse.gov/the-press-office/remarks-president-securing-our-nations-cyber -infrastructure. The claim that cyber intruders have plunged foreign cities into darkness has been repeated often by many officials, but has been disputed—though this hasn't prevented officials from continuing to repeat it. The claim was first made by CIA senior analyst Tom Donahue while speaking at a conference for cybersecurity professionals in 2008: "We have information that cyberattacks have been used to disrupt power equipment in several regions outside the US," he said. "In at least one case, the disruption caused a power outage affecting multiple cities." He also said the intrusions were "followed by extortion demands." (See Thomas Claburn, "CIA Admits Cyberattacks Blacked Out Cities," *InformationWeek,* January 18, 2008, available at informationweek .com/cia-admits-cyberattacks-blacked-out-cities/d/d-id/10635137.) Donahue never named the

How ironic his words turned out to be a year later when Stuxnet was discovered spreading in the wild, and the public learned that the United States had not only violated the sovereign space of another nation in an aggressive cyberattack, but in doing so had invited similar attacks upon vulnerable US systems in retaliation.

While Obama and other officials sounded the alarm about adversaries lurking in US systems and laying the groundwork for future attacks against the power grid, US military and intelligence agencies had been penetrating foreign systems in Iran and elsewhere, building stockpiles of digital weapons, and ushering in a new age of warfare, all without public discussion about the rules of engagement for conducting such attacks or the consequences of doing so. Perhaps it was knowledge of what the United States was doing in Iran and elsewhere that prompted the president's urgent warnings about the risks to US systems.

---

country where the attacks occurred, but in 2009 *60 Minutes* identified it as Brazil, asserting that a 2007 blackout in Espirito Santo that left 3 million people without power was caused by hackers. (See "Cyber War: Sabotaging the System," *60 Minutes*, November 6, 2009, available at cbsnews .com/news/cyber-war-sabotaging-the-system-06-11-2009.) Others have claimed Donahue was referring to a 2005 outage in Brazil instead. According to two sources I spoke with in 2009 who were interviewed by *60 Minutes* for their story, the newsmagazine sent a producer to Brazil to try to verify the hacker/extortion claim but was never able to do so, though viewers weren't told this. The Brazilian government disputed the claim after the *60 Minutes* show aired, pointing to a lengthy report about the 2007 outage that attributed it to soot and equipment failure. Furnas, the Brazilian energy company that experienced the blackouts, is a customer of Marcelo Branquinho, who operated the only ICS security firm in Brazil at the time. Branquinho told me there was no evidence the blackout was caused by anything but equipment failure. "We have full access to the documentation and [government reports investigating] what happened on these two blackouts," he told me in October 2011, referring to both the 2005 and 2007 incidents. "There is no single evidence that hacking activity happened here. Both events were due to hardware problems, not software problems." What's more, he says the substation that was affected in the 2007 blackout was not even an automated SCADA system that could be controlled by hackers. "It was only hardware, so it couldn't be hacked anyway," he says. "I'm not saying that we can't be hacked. We can be hacked; it's pretty easy. I believe that most of the electric installations—not only here, but worldwide— have very weak security if you compare them with a bank, for example, that has some good level of security infrastructure. But . . . in this case, the evidence tells us that we weren't hacked." It's possible the stories about the hacker blackout have been confused with a real cyberextortion incident that occurred in 2005 or 2006 but that had nothing to do with a blackout. Brazil's director of Homeland Security Information and Communication told Wired.com that in this case, attackers breached an administrative machine at a government agency using a default password and deleted files on the machine. They also left a ransom note for return of the data. But the incident involved no power outage. See Marcelo Soares, "WikiLeaked Cable Says 2009 Brazilian Blackout Wasn't Hackers, Either," Wired.com, December 6, 2010, available at wired.com/2010/12/brazil-blackout.

Michael V. Hayden, who was director of the CIA during the time Stuxnet was developed and unleashed, told a reporter after the digital weapon was exposed that "somebody had crossed the Rubicon" in unleashing it.[2] That somebody, it turned out, was the United States. And, as noted, where the United States led, others would follow.

Today there's a surge among nations around the world to expand existing cyber capabilities or build new ones. More than a dozen countries—including China, Russia, the UK, Israel, France, Germany, and North Korea—have digital warfare programs or have announced plans to build one. China began developing its offensive operations in the late '90s, at the same time the United States made its first forays into this new fighting domain. Even Iran is developing a cyberwarfare program. In 2012, Ayatollah Ali Khamenei announced the creation of a defensive and offensive cyber program and told a group of university students that they should prepare for the coming age of cyberwarfare with Iran's enemies.[3]

As for the United States, the Defense Department's Cyber Command currently has an annual budget of more than $3 billion and plans to increase its workforce fivefold, from 900 people to 4,900—covering both defensive and offensive operations.[4] The Defense Advanced Research Projects Agency, or DARPA, has also launched a $110 million research project called Plan X to develop cyberwarfare technologies to help the Pentagon dominate the digital battlefield. The technology wish list includes a continuously updated mapping system to track every system and node in cyberspace in order to chart the flow of data, identify targets to attack, and spot incoming assaults. The Pentagon also wants a system capable of launching speed-of-light strikes and counterstrikes using preprogrammed scenarios so that human intervention won't be necessary.[5]

---

2 David E. Sanger, "Obama Order Sped Up Wave of Cyberattacks Against Iran," *New York Times*, June 1, 2012.
3 "Iran's Supreme Leader Tells Students to Prepare for Cyber War," *Russia Today*, February 13, 2014, available at rt.com/news/iran-israel-cyber-war-899.
4 Ellen Nakashima, "Pentagon to Boost Cybersecurity Force," *Washington Post*, January 27, 2013.
5 Ellen Nakashima, "With Plan X, Pentagon Seeks to Spread U.S. Military Might to Cyberspace," *Washington Post*, May 30, 2012.

Of all the nations that have a cyberwarfare program, however, the United States and Israel are the only ones known to have unleashed a destructive cyberweapon against another sovereign nation—a nation with whom it was not at war. In doing so, it lost the moral high ground from which to criticize other nations for doing the same and set a dangerous precedent for legitimizing the use of digital attacks to further political or national security goals.

"This was a good idea," Hayden told *60 Minutes* about Stuxnet. "But I also admit this was a big idea too. The rest of the world is looking at this and saying, 'Clearly, someone has legitimated this kind of activity as acceptable.'"[6]

Digital assaults could now be considered a viable option by other states for resolving disputes.

Civil War general Robert E. Lee said famously that it was a good thing war was so terrible, "otherwise we should grow too fond of it."[7] The horrors and costs of war encourage countries to choose diplomacy over battle, but when cyberattacks eliminate many of these costs and consequences, and the perpetrators can remain anonymous, it becomes much more tempting to launch a digital attack than engage in rounds of diplomacy that might never produce results.

But the digital weapon didn't just launch a new age of warfare, it altered the landscape for all cyberattacks, opening the door to a new generation of assaults from state and nonstate actors that have the potential to cause physical damage and even loss of life in ways never before demonstrated. "My prediction is that we are all going to become nostalgic for the days of fame-seeking mass mailers and network worms," Symantec's Kevin Haley wrote of the post-Stuxnet future.[8] LoveLetter, the Conficker worm,

---

6 Interview with Michael V. Hayden, in "Stuxnet: Computer Worm Opens New Era of Warfare," *60 Minutes*, CBS, originally aired June 4, 2012, available at cbsnews.com/8301 -18560_162-57390124/stuxnet-computer-worm-opens-new-era-of-warfare/?tag=pop;stories.

7 Speaking in 1862 after the Battle of Fredericksburg.

8 Kevin Haley, "Internet Security Predictions for 2011: The Shape of Things to Come," Symantec blog, November 17, 2010, available at symantec.com/connect/blogs/internet-security-predictions -2011-shape-things-come.

and even the Zeus banking Trojan would become quaint reminders of the days when attacks were simpler and, by comparison, more innocent.

Stuxnet was a remarkable achievement, given its sophistication and single-minded focus. But it was also remarkably reckless. Because like the atomic bombs detonated over Hiroshima and Nagasaki, it introduced the use of a powerful technology that will have consequences for years to come. Kennette Benedict, executive director of the *Bulletin of the Atomic Scientists,* noted several parallels between Stuxnet and the first atomic bombs in an article she wrote for that publication about the lack of foresight that went into developing and unleashing both technologies. In both cases, government and scientific leaders raced to develop the weapons for the United States out of fear that adversaries would create and unleash them first. The long-term consequences of dropping the atomic bombs were also as poorly understood in the 1940s as the consequences of unleashing digital weapons are today—not only with regard to the damages they would cause, but to the global arms race they would create. "We have come to know how nuclear weapons can destroy societies and human civilization," Benedict wrote. "We have not yet begun to understand how cyberwarfare might destroy our way of life."

And in another parallel with atomic bombs, despite alarm bells sounded about their use, the United States continued to develop first atomic weapons and now digital ones without public discussion about how they should be used or their impact on global security and peace.[9] How ironic then, Benedict noted, "that the first acknowledged military use of cyberwarfare is ostensibly to prevent the spread of nuclear weapons. A new age of mass destruction will begin in an effort to close a chapter from the first age of mass destruction."

Despite the parallels, there is at least one crucial difference between the atomic bombs of the 1940s and Stuxnet. The bar was high for someone to build or obtain a nuclear weapon—or any conventional missile

---

9 Kennette Benedict, "Stuxnet and the Bomb," *Bulletin of the Atomic Scientists,* June 15, 2012, available at thebulletin.org/stuxnet-and-bomb.

and bomb, for that matter. But cyberweapons can be easily obtained on underground markets or, depending on the complexity of the system being targeted, custom-built from scratch by a skilled teenage coder, a task made simpler by the fact that every cyberweapon carries the blueprints for its design embedded within it. When you launch a cyberweapon, you don't just send the weapon to your enemies, you send the intellectual property that created it and the ability to launch the weapon back against you.[10] It would be comparable to a scenario where, if in 1945, it wasn't just radioactive fallout that rained down from the bombs onto Hiroshima and Nagasaki but all of the scientific equations and schematics for constructing them as well.

The nations, of course, that are most at risk of a destructive digital attack are the ones with the greatest connectivity. Marcus Ranum, one of the early innovators of the computer firewall, called Stuxnet "a stone thrown by people who live in a glass house."[11]

Stuxnet was proof that a digital attack, consisting of nothing more than binary commands, could achieve some of the same destructive results as a conventional bomb. But it also showed how even a powerful nation like the United States, with unmatched air and sea defenses, could be vulnerable to a similar assault from adversaries who never had to venture beyond their borders to launch an attack. As Mike McConnell, the former

---

10 There are ways to lessen this risk by carefully encrypting digital weapons to prevent random parties who get hold of the code from reverse-engineering it. A digital weapon has to decrypt itself in order to engage its payload once it finds the system it's targeting, but the keys for doing this don't have to be inside the weapon itself, as they were with Stuxnet. Instead, the better design is the one that Gauss used, which employed a complex encryption scheme that used the actual configuration of the system it was targeting to generate the decryption key. Gauss only delivered and decrypted its payload once it found this specific configuration. This won't work, of course, if the configuration on the targeted system changes, thereby defusing the digital weapon, but it will work in cases where the configuration of a system isn't likely to change. See the discussion of Gauss on pages 295–97. Also, to limit a digital weapon's exposure once it is decrypted on the system it's targeting, it could be designed to self-destruct upon completing its mission so that it won't linger on a system longer than necessary. This won't work for all weapons, however. Stuxnet needed to remain on a system for a long time to achieve its aim, for example. But it will work for other weapons that do their damage quickly.
11 Marcus Ranum, "Parsing Cyberwar—Part 4: The Best Defense Is a Good Defense," published on his Fabius Maximus blog, August 20, 2012, available at fabiusmaximus.com/2012/08/20/41929.

director of national intelligence, told a US Senate committee in 2011, "If the nation went to war today, in a cyberwar, we would lose. We're the most vulnerable. We're the most connected. We have the most to lose."[12]

The targets most in danger from a digital attack in the United States are not just military systems but civilian ones—transportation, communication, and financial networks; food manufacturing and chemical plants; gas pipelines, water, and electric utilities; even uranium enrichment plants.[13] "We now live in a world where industrial control systems can be attacked in the event of a crisis," Stewart Baker, former DHS assistant secretary has said. "We do not have a serious plan for defending our industrial control systems even though our entire civil society depends on it."[14]

Critical infrastructure has always been a potential target in times of war. But civilian infrastructure in the United States has long enjoyed special protection due to the country's geographical distance from adversaries and battlefields. That advantage is lost, however, when the battlefield is cyberspace. In a world of networked computers, every system is potentially a front line. There are "no 'protected zones' or 'rear areas'; all are equally vulnerable," Gen. Kevin Chilton, commander of the US Strategic Command, told Congress.[15]

The laws of war prohibit direct attacks on hospitals and other civilian infrastructure unless deemed a necessity of war, with military leaders subject to war crimes charges should they violate this. But the protections

12 Grant Gross, "Security Expert: US Would Lose Cyberwar," IDG News Service, February 23, 2010, available at computerworld.com/s/article/9161278/Security_expert_U.S._would_lose_cyberwar.

13 Though Siemens control systems aren't as widely used in the United States as they are in other parts of the world, the control systems that dominate facilities in the United States operate under the same design principles with some of the same flaws. An attacker would simply need to study the systems to find ways to attack them, which a number of security researchers have already done in the years since Stuxnet was released.

14 Gerry Smith, "Stuxnet: U.S. Can Launch Cyberattacks but Not Defend Against Them, Experts Say," Huffington Post, June 1, 2012, available at huffingtonpost/com/2012/06/01/stuxnet-us-cyberattack_n_1562983.html.

15 Prepared statement to the Strategic Forces Subcommittee of the House Committee on Armed Services, for a hearing on March 17, 2009, available at gpo.gov/fdsys/pkg/CHRG-111hhrg51759/html/CHRG-111hhrg51759.htm.

provided by law crumble when attribution is a blur. Since a hack from a cyber army in Tehran or Beijing can be easily designed to look like a hack from Ohio, it will be difficult to distinguish between a nation-state attack launched by Iran and one launched by a group of hackers simply bent on random mayhem or civil protest. Stuxnet was sophisticated and came with all the hallmarks of a nation-state attack, but not every attack would be so distinguishable.[16]

Some have argued that nation-state attacks would be easy to spot because they would occur in the midst of existing tension between nations, making the identity of the aggressor clear—such as the volley of denial-of-service attacks that disabled government websites in Georgia in 2008 in advance of a Russian invasion of South Ossetia. But even then it would be easy for a third party to exploit existing tension between two nations and launch an anonymous attack against one that appeared to come from the other in order to ignite a combustible situation.[17]

In November 2013, Israel held a simulated exercise at Tel Aviv University that illustrated the difficulties of identifying an attacker, particularly when third parties enter a conflict with the intention of escalating

---

16 In August 2012, a destructive virus called Shamoon struck machines at Saudi Aramco, Saudi Arabia's national oil and natural gas company, and wiped all the data from more than 30,000 machines—an attack that provided a stark reminder of how any machine on the internet can become ground zero for destruction in a political dispute and how difficult it can be to determine attribution afterward. The virus didn't just wipe data from the machines, it replaced every file on them with one containing an image of a burning US flag—though a bug in the code prevented the flag image from fully unfurling on infected machines. Instead, only a snippet of the image appeared when files were opened; the rest of the image was blank. US officials accused Iran of masterminding the attack, though offered no proof to back the claim. The attack may have been launched by Iran as retaliation for the Wiper attack that erased data from machines at the Iranian Oil Ministry and the Iranian National Oil Company four months earlier, or it may have been retaliation for Stuxnet, aimed at a US ally that was less capable of attacking back. Or it may simply have been the work of hacktivists opposed to US foreign policy in the Middle East (a group of hackers calling themselves the Cutting Sword of Justice took credit for the attack). It might even have been a "false flag" operation launched by another country to make it look like the perpetrator was Iran (NSA documents released by Edward Snowden disclose that the UK sometimes uses false flag operations to pin blame on third parties).
17 In August 2008, armies of computers with Russian IP addresses launched distributed denial-of-service attacks that knocked Georgian government and media websites offline, thwarting the government's ability to communicate with the public. The timing of the attacks, right before the Russian invasion of South Ossetia, was proof enough for many that the digital campaign was part of the military offensive.

hostilities between others. Using what were described as extreme but realistic scenarios, the war game pitted Iran and Iran-backed Hezbollah in Lebanon and Syria against Israel, and began with a series of simulated physical skirmishes against Israel that escalated into cyberattacks that threatened to pull the United States and Russia into the conflict to defend their allies.

The simulation began with an explosion at an offshore drilling platform, with rockets lobbed over the border from Lebanon into Northern Israel and blasts in Tel Aviv, and was followed by network disruptions that paralyzed a hospital in Israel. The cyberattacks were traced to an Iranian server, but Iran denied responsibility, insisting the Israelis were trying to put the blame on it in order to generate Western support for a strike against Tehran. Then the network attacks spread to the United States, forcing Wall Street trading to halt and shutting down air traffic control at JFK Airport. The White House declared a state of emergency after two planes crash-landed and killed 700 people. This time the attacks were traced first to a server in California, but then, puzzlingly, to Israel.

When the game ended, Israel was preparing to launch physical attacks against Hezbollah in Syria and Lebanon—over the cyberattacks attributed to them and Iran—and tensions between the United States and Israel had risen to a dangerous boil over questions about who was responsible for the cyberattacks against the United States.[18] "If we hadn't stopped when we did, the entire region could have been engulfed in flames," said Haim Assa, the game-theory expert who designed the exercise.

The simulation was instructive to participants on a number of levels. The United States "realized how difficult if not impossible it is to ascertain the source of attack," retired US Army Gen. Wesley Clark, who par-

---

18 The simulation designers revealed in the end that the bewildering web of attributions behind the cyberattacks had been a key part of their strategy. Under their plan, it was al-Qaeda that had actually launched the initial attacks against Israel in the hope of escalating tensions between Israel and the Iran-backed Hezbollah in Lebanon. But it was Iran that launched the attacks on the United States. The latter were done in a way to make it look as if Israel had launched with the intention of framing Iran for them. The US was supposed to think that Israel had played the ultimate dirty trick— launching an attack against the United States in order to point the finger at Iran and drum up US support for an Israeli airstrike against Tehran.

ticipated in the exercise, said. And an Israeli official noted "how quickly localized cyber events can turn dangerously kinetic when leaders are ill-prepared to deal in the cyber domain." To this end, they learned that the best defense in the digital realm is not a good offense but a good defense, because without a properly defended critical infrastructure, leaders were left with little room to maneuver in their decision making when an attack occurred. When civilian systems were struck and citizens were killed, leaders were under pressure to make quick decisions, often based on faulty and incomplete conclusions.[19]

IT'S EASY TO see why militaries and governments are embracing cyberweapons. Aside from offering anonymity and a perceived reduction in collateral damage, cyberweapons are faster than missiles, with the ability to arrive at their destination in seconds, and can be tweaked on the fly to combat counterdefenses. If a zero-day vulnerability gets patched, attackers can draw from a reserve of alternative exploits—as Stuxnet's developers did—or change and recompile code to alter its signatures and thwart detection.

"Cyber, in my modest opinion, will soon be revealed to be the biggest revolution in warfare, more than gunpowder and the utilization of air power in the last century," Israeli Maj. Gen. Aviv Kochavi has said.[20]

But cyberweapons have limited use. If tightly configured to avoid collateral damage in the way Stuxnet was, each one can be deployed only against a small set of targets without being reengineered. And unlike a bunker-busting bomb or stealth missile, a cyberweapon can instantly become obsolete if the configuration of a target system or network changes.

---

19 Barbara Opall-Rome, "Israeli Cyber Game Drags US, Russia to Brink of Mideast War," *Defense News*, November 14, 2013, available at defensenews.com/article/20131114/DEFREG04/311140020/ Israeli-Cyber-Game-Drags-US-Russia-Brink-Mideast-War.
20 "Israel Combats Cyberattacks, 'Biggest Revolution in Warfare,'" UPI, January 31, 2014, available at upi.com/Business_News?Security-industry/2014/01/31/Israel-combats-cyberattacks -biggest-revolution-in-warfare/UPI-24501391198261/.

"I am not aware of any other weapons systems in the history of warfare that can be disabled by their targets with a click of a mouse button," Marcus Ranum notes.[21] And any time a cyberweapon gets exposed, it isn't just that weapon that gets burned, but any other weapons that use the same novel techniques and methods it employed. "At this point, we can be sure that anyone who builds a gas centrifuge cascade is going to be a little bit more careful about their software than usual," said Thomas Rid, a war studies scholar at King's College, London.[22]

But another problem with digital weapons is that they can be difficult to control. A good cyberweapon should operate in a predictable manner so that it has a controlled impact and produces expected results each time it's deployed, causing little or no collateral damage. It needs precision design so that it executes only on command or automatically once it finds its target; and it should be recallable or have a self-destruct mechanism in case conditions change and a mission needs to be aborted. Andy Pennington, the former Air Force weapons system officer cited in an earlier chapter, likens an uncontrollable cyberweapon to a biological agent out of control. "If you don't have positive control over the weapon . . . you don't have a weapon, you've got a loose cannon. We created conventions and said we're not going to use biological and chemical warfare weapons, because we do not have accurate targeting, we do not have access control, they're not recallable and they're not self-destruct-capable."[23]

Stuxnet had some controls built into it, but lacked others. It was a targeted, precision weapon that unleashed its payload only on the specific systems it was designed to attack. And it had a time-release mechanism so that it initiated its sabotage only when certain conditions on the target machines were met. But once unleashed, Stuxnet couldn't be recalled, and it had no self-destruct mechanism—it only had an infection kill date that

---

21 Marcus Ranum, "Parsing Cyberwar—Part 3: Synergies and Interference," published on his Fabius Maximus blog, August 13, 2012, available at fabiusmaximus.com/2012/08/13/41567.
22 Thomas Rid, "Think Again: Cyberwar" *Foreign Policy*, March/April 2012.
23 Author interview with Andy Pennington, November 2011.

prevented it from spreading beyond a certain date three years in the future. And although the earliest versions of Stuxnet had limited spreading capabilities, the March 2010 version was clearly a "loose cannon," albeit a defused one, since although it spread uncontrollably to thousands of machines that weren't its target, it didn't sabotage them.

Would other digital weapons be as well designed or as lucky, though? Collateral damage in cyberspace has a longer reach than in the physical realm. A bomb dropped on a target might cause collateral damage, but it would be local. Computer networks, however, are complex mazes of interconnectivity, and a cyberweapon's path and impact once unleashed aren't always predictable. "We do not yet have the ability to scope collateral damage for all cyberattacks," Jim Lewis of the Center for Strategic and International Studies has noted. "For attacks that disable networks, there could be unpredictable damage not only to the target, but also to noncombatants, neutrals or even the attacker, depending upon the interconnections of the target network or machine. This makes the political risk of unintended consequences unpredictable (an attack on a Serbian network, for example, damages NATO allies' commercial activities) and carries with it the risk of escalating a conflict (an attack on North Korea damages services in China)."[24]

DESPITE THE APPARENT march toward digital warfare that Stuxnet initiated, it's fair to ask what the likelihood is that a catastrophic digital event will ever occur. Defense Secretary Leon Panetta has said the United States is in a "pre-9/11 moment," with adversaries plotting and preparing for the right opportunity to launch destructive cyberattacks on its systems. But Thomas Rid has called cyberwarfare "more hype than hazard"—the "shiny new thing" that has caught the attention of militaries like a gleaming new train set opened on Christmas morning. In reality, he thinks,

---

24 James A. Lewis, "Cyberwar Thresholds and Effects," *IEEE Security and Privacy* (September 2011): 23–29.

it will have much less impact than people imagine.[25] Any future use of digital weapons will likely be as an enhancement to conventional battle, not as a replacement for it. Critics of digital doomsayers also point to the fact that no catastrophic attack has occurred to date as evidence that the warnings are overblown.

But others argue that no passenger jets had been flown into skyscrapers, either, before 9/11. "I think to . . . say it's not possible, it's not likely, is really way too early. All sorts of things could happen over the next couple of years," says Jason Healey, head of the Cyber Statecraft Initiative at the Atlantic Council in Washington, DC, who was an original member of the military's first cyber taskforce. "As more systems get connected to the internet, and cyberattacks progress from simply disrupting ones and zeros to disrupting things made of concrete and steel, things will change, and the days when no one has died from a cyberattack or the effects of a cyberattack will be over."[26]

Some think the threat is overblown because most actors capable of pulling off an attack would be dissuaded by the risk of a counterstrike. In fact, some wondered after Stuxnet was discovered if it had been intentionally burned by Israel or the United States to send a message to Iran and other countries about the digital attack capabilities of these two countries. The fact that it had remained undetected for so long and was only discovered by an obscure antivirus firm in Belarus led some to believe that Stuxnet had not been discovered so much as disclosed. Gen. James Cartwright, former vice chairman of the Joint Chiefs of Staff—the man said to have played a large role in the Olympic Games operation in the United States—was in fact an advocate of making declarations about US cyber capabilities in the service of deterrence.

"For cyber deterrence to work," Cartwright said in 2012, "you have to believe a few things: One, that we have the intent; two, that we have the capability; and three, that we practice—and people know that we

---

25 Rid, "Think Again: Cyberwar."
26 This and other quotes from Healey come from author interview, October 2013.

practice."[27] Cartwright has since been investigated by the Justice Department for suspicion of leaking classified information about Stuxnet to the *New York Times*, though as of this writing he has not been charged with any wrongdoing and has denied the allegations.

But while deterrence of this sort might work for some nations—as long as they believe an attack could be attributed to them—irrational actors, such as rogue states and terrorist groups, aren't deterred by the same things that deter others. "The day a terrorist group gets cyberattack capabilities, they will use them," Jim Lewis told Congress in 2012.[28]

Lewis expects that in the future, limited digital conflicts that disrupt military command-and-control systems may arise between the United States and Russia or China, but these countries likely will not attack critical infrastructure, "because of the risk of escalation." But once countries like Iran and North Korea acquire cyberattack capabilities, a strike against civilian targets in the United States will be more likely. As US forces strike targets in their countries, they will feel "little or [no] constraint against attacking targets in ours," he wrote in a 2010 paper.[29] And threats of retaliation made by the United States to deter such attacks would have little effect on such groups since "their calculus for deciding upon an attack is based on a different perception of risks and rewards," he noted. Likewise, as smaller countries and non-state insurgents acquire the digital means to strike distant targets, "disruptions for political purposes and even cyber attacks intended to damage or destroy could become routine," he says. The Taliban in Afghanistan or Al-Shabaab in Somalia have little chance of launching a conventional retaliatory strike against the US homeland, but when they eventually acquire, or hire, the ability to launch effective cyberstrikes, this will change. "These strikes will be appealing to them as it

---

27 Julian Barnes, "Pentagon Digs In on Cyberwar Front," *Wall Street Journal*, July 6, 2012.

28 James A. Lewis in testimony before the Subcommittee on Cybersecurity, Infrastructure Protection and Security Technologies, March 16, 2012, available at homeland.house.gov/sites/homeland.house.gov/files/Testimony%20Lewis.pdf.

29 James A. Lewis, "Thresholds for Cyberwar," Center for Strategic and International Studies, September 2010, available at csis-org/publication/thresholds-cyberwar.

creates the possibility to bring the war to the U.S. homeland," Lewis notes. Although they may not acquire the ability to pull off massive attacks, "harassment attacks" aimed at specific targets like Washington, DC, Lewis says, will certainly be within their means, and depending on the severity of the attack or its cascading effects, essential systems and services could be lost for extended periods of time.

With cyberweapons in the hands of others, the United States may also find itself having to recalculate the risk of blowback when planning conventional attacks, Lewis notes. In 2003, US forces invading Iraq met with little resistance, but what if Iraq had possessed cyberweapons that it launched in retaliation? "These would not have changed the outcome of the invasion but would have provided a degree of vengeance [for Iraq]," he says.[30]

If there are disagreements about the likelihood of digital attacks against critical infrastructure occurring, there are also disagreements over the level of damage that such attacks can cause. Leon Panetta and others have warned about digital Pearl Harbors and cyber 9/11s that will strike fear throughout the land. But others note that the kind of digital destruction envisioned by the doomsayers isn't as easy to pull off as it seems. Conducting a disruptive attack that has long lasting effects "is a considerably more complex undertaking than flying an airplane into a building or setting off a truck full of explosives in a crowded street," notes W. Earl Boebert, a former cybersecurity expert at Sandia National Laboratories, whose job in part was to research such scenarios. Networks and systems can be brought down, but they can also be brought back up relatively quickly. "Considerable planning is required to raise the probability of success to a point where a rational decision to proceed can be made," he writes.[31] Though one can argue that the 9/11 attacks required at least as much

---

30 Ibid.
31 W. Earl Boebert, "A Survey of Challenges in Attribution," Proceedings of a Workshop on Deterring Cyber Attacks: Informing Strategies and Developing Options for US Policy. Published by the National Academy of Sciences at na.edu/catalog/12997.html.

planning and coordination as a destructive cyberattack would require, a well-planned digital assault—even a physically destructive one—would likely never match the visual impact or frightening emotional effect that jets flying into the Twin Towers had.

DESPITE THE RISKS and consequences of using digital weapons, there has been almost no public discussion about the issues raised by the government's offensive operations. Critics have pointed out that the Obama administration has been more open about discussing the assassination of Osama bin Laden than discussing the country's offensive cyberstrategy and operations. When questions about the rules of engagement for digital attacks were raised during the confirmation hearing for Gen. Keith Alexander to be made head of US Cyber Command in 2010, Alexander refused to address them in public and said he would only answer in a closed session.[32] And although there are numerous doctrinal manuals in the public domain that cover conventional warfare, the same is not true for digital warfare. Even some who have built their careers on secrecy have noticed the extreme secrecy around this issue. "This may come as a surprise, given my background at the NSA and CIA and so on, but I think that this information is horribly over-classified," former CIA and NSA director Gen. Michael Hayden has said. "The roots to American cyberpower are in the American intelligence community, and we frankly are quite accustomed

---

32 Rules of engagement are the military orders that take into consideration international law and US policy to draw up a single document that the military uses to conduct its operations. There are rules of engagement for different operations, since the rules will change whether it's a peacekeeping mission in Bosnia or an aggressive invasion of Iraq. Separately, there is an overarching set of rules of engagement that applies to the military's day-to-day operations. These latter standing rules, which are mostly classified, include cyber. According to Gary Brown, who was legal counsel for US Cyber Command from 2009 to 2012, these standing rules were being rewritten during his time with the command and he said in 2014 that he still didn't know if they were completed. The military was using the second version of the rules that were finished in 2005, known as the Bravo version when he was there. The third version, known as Charlie, should have been finished in 2010, but still wasn't completed when Brown left in 2012. The Bravo version addressed cyber, but only in broad terms. Version Charlie is supposed to address it in more specific terms.

to working in a world that's classified. I'm afraid that that culture has bled over into how we treat all cyber questions."[33]

Without more transparency, without the willingness to engage in debate about offensive operations, there is little opportunity for parties who don't have a direct interest in perpetuating operations to gauge their success, failure, and risks.

"Stuxnet let the genie out of the lamp in terms of how you could do this kind of attack. You can now target all kinds of other devices," says one former government worker. "Where does it end? It doesn't seem like there's any oversight of these programs. Sadly, the scientists are not pulling back the reins. They're excited that someone is giving them money to do this research. I don't think I ever saw anyone question what was being done. I don't think there was a lot of consciousness about it."

There have been no public discussions about the repercussions of the digital arms race launched by Stuxnet, or about the consequences of releasing weapons that can be unpredictable and can be turned back against the United States.

In a report to Congress in 2011, the intelligence community noted that the defenders of computer networks in the United States are perpetually outgunned by attackers and can't keep pace with the changing tactics they deploy. Exploits and exploitation methods evolve too quickly for detection methods and countermeasures to keep up, a problem that will only grow worse as nations develop and deploy increasingly sophisticated attack methods. Until now, the evolution of computer attacks has been driven by innovations in the criminal underground, but this will change as nation-state attacks like Stuxnet and Flame begin to drive future advancements. Instead of government hackers learning novel techniques from the underground, the underground will learn from governments. And as countermeasures for digital weapons are developed, the need to produce even more advanced weapons will grow, pushing further innovations in

---

33 Chris Carroll, "Cone of Silence Surrounds U.S. Cyberwarfare," *Stars and Stripes*, October 18, 2011, available at stripes.com/news/cone-of-silence-surrounds-u-s-cyberwarfare-1.158090.

weaponry. One US official has referred to Stuxnet as a first-generation weapon, on par with "Edison's initial light bulbs, or the Apple II," suggesting that more sophisticated designs have already replaced it.[34]

The criminal underground will benefit from the wealth of government-funded research and development put into digital weapons and spy tools, as they already have done from Stuxnet and the arsenal of tools used in conjunction with it. After Duqu was discovered in 2011, for example, exploits attacking the same font-rendering vulnerability that it attacked showed up in various readymade toolkits sold in the criminal underground. Within a year after Duqu used it, it was the most commonly targeted vulnerability that criminals used to surreptitiously install banking Trojans and other malware on machines.[35] But even when non-state hackers can't replicate a sophisticated government attack bit-for-bit, they can still learn and benefit from it, as shown by Microsoft's discovery that it would have taken just three days for criminal hackers to pull off a low-rent version of the Windows Update hijack that Flame performed.

Brad Arkin, senior director of product security and privacy for Adobe, has said that his company's primary security concern these days is not the criminal hacker but the high-level, state-sponsored hacker, who comes flush with wealth and a suitcase full of zero-day exploits to attack Adobe's software. "In the last eighteen months, the only [zero-day holes] found in our software have been found by . . . carrier-class adversaries," he said at a conference in 2011. "These are the groups that have enough money to build an aircraft carrier. Those are our adversaries."[36] The exploits used

---

34 David E. Sanger, "America's Deadly Dynamics with Iran," *New York Times*, November 5, 2011.
35 Duqu was publicly exposed in September 2011, and although Microsoft patched the font-rendering flaw it exploited, by late 2012 "attacks against this single vulnerability had skyrocketed," Finnish security firm F-Secure noted in its 2013 annual report. This vulnerability alone "accounted for an amazing 69 percent of all exploit-related detections report." See page 36 of "Threat Report H1 2013," F-Secure, available at f-secure.com/static/doc/labs_global/Research/Threat_Report_H1_2013.pdf.
36 Dennis Fisher, "Nation-State Attackers Are Adobe's Biggest Worry," ThreatPost, a security blog published by Kaspersky Lab, September 20, 2011, available at threatpost.com/nation-state-attackers-are-adobes-biggest-worry-092011/75673.

against Adobe products are "very, very expensive and difficult to build," Arkin said, and once they're designed and used by nation-state hackers, they trickle down to the crimeware tools.

The nation's chief cyberwarrior, NSA's General Alexander, acknowledged this trend to a Senate committee in 2013. "We believe it is only a matter of time before the sort of sophisticated tools developed by well-funded state actors find their way to groups or even individuals who in their zeal to make some political statement do not know or do not care about the collateral damage they inflict on bystanders and critical infrastructure," he said.[37] Alexander was referring to the well-funded tools that countries like China create to attack the United States, but no one on the committee asked him about the contributions his own agency was making to the pool of tools and techniques that criminal hackers and hacktivists would adopt. Nor did they ask about the ethics and consequences of stockpiling zero-day exploits and withholding information about security vulnerabilities from US system owners so the government can use them to attack the systems of adversaries.

Michael Hayden notes that there have always been strategic tradeoffs between building offensive capabilities and strengthening defenses. One of the core concepts the government has traditionally used in making tradeoffs in the kinetic realm—that also applies to the cyber realm—is something known as NOBUS, or Nobody But Us.

"Nobody but us knows it, nobody but us can exploit it," he told me. "How unique is our knowledge of this or our ability to exploit this compared to others? . . . Yeah it's a weakness, but if you have to own an acre and a half of Cray [supercomputers] to exploit it. . . ." If it was NOBUS, he said, officials might "let it ride" and take advantage of the vulnerability

---

37 Speaking to the Senate Committee on Appropriations, "Cybersecurity: Preparing for and Responding to the Enduring Threat," June 12, 2013, available at defense.gov/home/features/2013/0713_cyberdomain/docs/Alexander,_General_Keith_Testimony_6.12.13_Cybersecurity_Hearing.pdf.

for a while, at the same time knowing full well "that the longer this goes, the more other people might actually be able to exploit it."[38]

But given the state of computer security today, and the amount of hammering the United States is taking from cyberattacks, Hayden said he was prepared to acknowledge that it might be time to reevaluate this process.

"If the habits of an agency that were built up in a pre-digital, analog age . . . are the habits of an agency [that is] culturally tilted a little too much toward the offense in a world in which everybody now is vulnerable," he said, then the government might want to reassess.

In a report issued by a surveillance reform board convened by the White House in the wake of the Edward Snowden leaks, board members specifically addressed this issue and recommended that the National Security Council establish a process for reviewing the government's use of zero days. "US policy should generally move to ensure that Zero Days are quickly blocked, so that the underlying vulnerabilities are patched on US Government and other networks," the review board wrote, noting that only "in rare instances, US policy may briefly authorize using a Zero Day for high priority intelligence collection, following senior, interagency review involving all appropriate departments."[39] In almost all instances, they wrote, it is "in the national interest to eliminate software vulnerabilities rather than to use them for US intelligence collection." The group also recommended that cyber operations conducted by the US Cyber Command and NSA be reviewed by Congress in the same way the CIA's covert operations are reviewed to provide more accountability and oversight.

Richard Clarke, former cybersecurity czar under the Bush administration and a member of the panel, later explained the rationale for highlighting the use of zero days in their report. "If the US government finds a zero-day vulnerability, its first obligation is to tell the American people so

---

38 All quotes from Hayden here and next page come from author interview in February 2014.
39 The President's Review Group on Intelligence and Communications Technologies, "Liberty and Security in a Changing World" (report, December 12, 2013), 37. The report is available at whitehouse.gov/sites/default//files/docs/2013-12-12_rg_final_report.pdf.

that they can patch it, not to run off [and use it] to break into the Beijing telephone system," he said at a security conference. "The first obligation of government is to defend."[40]

In a speech addressing the review board's report, President Obama ignored both of the panel's recommendations for handling zero days and for conducting oversight. But during a confirmation hearing for Vice Adm. Michael Rogers in March 2014 to replace the retiring General Alexander as head of the NSA and US Cyber Command, Rogers told a Senate committee that the spy agency already had a mature equities process for handling zero-day vulnerabilities discovered in commercial products and systems and was in the process of working with the White House to develop a new interagency process for dealing with these vulnerabilities. He said it was NSA policy to fully document each vulnerability, to determine options for mitigating it, and to produce a proposal for how to disclose it.[41] In dealing with zero days, he said, it was important that the "balance must be tipped toward mitigating any serious risks posed to the US and allied networks." And in cases where the NSA opts to exploit a zero day rather than disclose it, he said the agency attempts to find other ways to mitigate the risks to US systems by working with DHS and other agencies.

A month later, news reports indicated that President Obama had quietly issued a new government policy on zero-day vulnerabilities in the wake of the Snowden revelations and the review board's report.[42] Under the new policy, any time the NSA discovers a major flaw in software, it must disclose the vulnerability to vendors and others so the flaw can be patched. But the policy falls far short of what the review board had recommended and contains loopholes.[43] It applies only to flaws discovered by the NSA, without mentioning ones found by government contractors, and

40 Clarke was speaking at the RSA Security Conference in San Francisco in February 2014.
41 "Advance Questions for Vice Admiral Michael S. Rogers, USN, Nominee for Commander, United States Cyber Command," available on the Senate Armed Services Committee website at armed-services.senate.gov/imo/media/doc/Rogers_03-11-14.pdf.
42 David E. Sanger, "Obama Lets N.S.A. Exploit Some Internet Flaws, Officials Say," *New York Times*, April 12, 2014.
43 Kim Zetter, "Obama: NSA Must Reveal Bugs Like Heartbleed, Unless They Help the NSA," Wired.com, April 15, 2014.

any flaw that has "a clear national security or law enforcement" use can still be kept secret by the government and exploited. The review board had said exploits should be used only on a temporary basis and only for "high priority intelligence collection" before being disclosed. Obama's policy, however, gives the government leeway to remain silent about any number of critical flaws as long as they can justify their use. There is also no mention in the policy about what the government plans to do with zero-day vulnerabilities and exploits already in its arsenal of digital weapons.

ONE ISSUE EVEN the review board didn't address, however, was the implication of subverting the trust of digital certificates and the Windows Update system to further offensive goals, as Stuxnet and Flame did.

The ACLU's Christopher Soghoian has likened the Windows Update hijack to the CIA subverting the trusted immunization system to kill Osama bin Laden. In that case, the spy agency reportedly recruited a doctor in Pakistan to distribute immunization shots to residents in a certain neighborhood so the doctor could surreptitiously collect DNA samples from people living in a walled compound where bin Laden was believed to reside.

In a similar way, the Windows Update hijack, and other attacks like it, undermine trusted systems and have the potential to create a crisis of confidence that could lead users to reject systems meant to protect them.

"Automatic security updates are a good thing. They keep us safe. They keep everyone safe," Soghoian told attendees at a conference after Flame's discovery.[44] "Whatever the short-term advantage of hijacking the Windows Update process, it simply isn't worth it."

But Hayden says that sometimes undermining a trusted system *is* worth it. He says he would have made the same decision CIA director Leon Panetta made to subvert the immunization system to locate bin

---

44 Soghoian was speaking at the Personal Democracy Forum in June 2012 in New York.

Laden. "What I'm telling you is, that [kind of decision-making] happened all the time," he says. Though he acknowledges that "[sometimes] we can get it wrong."[45]

If the United States was responsible for the Windows Update hijack in Flame, as reports indicate, there are questions about whether the hijack should have required some kind of notification and consent from Microsoft before it was done. US intelligence agencies can't do things that might put US businesses at risk unless they have high-level legal authorities sign off on the operation and the company consents. They can't, for example, make IBM an unwitting CIA accomplice by having an agent pose as an IBM employee without informing someone at the company who has fiduciary responsibilities. "The CIA *can* do it," says Catherine Lotrionte, a law professor at Georgetown University and a former attorney in the CIA's Office of General Counsel, "but [the agency has] to notify the CEO, because he or she has fiduciary duties owed to the [company's] board."[46]

If the use of Microsoft's digitally signed certificate was deemed an "operational use" of a US company—because it involved using a legitimate Microsoft credential to pass off a rogue file as a legitimate Microsoft file—then Microsoft might have needed to be put on notice. "It depends what is operational use in the technical world," Lotrionte says. "We know what it looks like when it's a human—[but] that technical business, that's a hard one."

When the malware was first exposed, some researchers wondered if Microsoft officials might have known about the Windows Update attack beforehand; but others note that if Microsoft had approved the operation, the attackers wouldn't have needed to go through the trouble of doing an

---

45 Author interview, 2014.
46 Lotrionte was with the CIA prior to 2002, followed by positions as counsel to the president's foreign intelligence advisory board at the White House and a position as legal counsel for the Senate Select Committee on Intelligence. She left government in 2006 around the time Stuxnet was being proposed and prepared.

MD5 hash collision to obtain the certificate—unless the MD5 hash gave Microsoft plausible deniability of cooperation.

"The question is, would Microsoft have allowed this?" Lotrionte asks. "That's what would concern me. The intelligence community will try everything, and I often wonder why companies put themselves at risk. I'm thinking if it was operational use and if they were put on notice, that's interesting."

Sources knowledgeable about the situation say that Microsoft was not notified and did not provide permission for the operation. "If that happened, it would be the end of the company," one said. "That's a gamble nobody [at the company] would take." He called government subversion of Microsoft's certification process "irresponsible" and "beyond shocking."

"It's very tricky waters we've sailed into," he said. "Guys who do this type of thing are going to create challenges for the private sector that I just don't think they've thought about."

But hijacking the trusted Microsoft system didn't just undermine the relationship Microsoft had with its customers, it also contradicted the government's stated commitment to strengthening computer security in the United States.

In 2011, the White House published its International Strategy for Cyberspace, a comprehensive document laying out the president's vision for the internet, which emphasized the government's responsibility to help make networks and systems more secure and resilient. It aimed to do this in part by establishing responsible norms of conduct and creating a system for sharing vulnerability information between public and private sectors to shore up systems. But Jason Healey says the government's actions call its sincerity into question.

"If you come out with a policy that subverts Microsoft certificates, subverts Windows Updates to spread malware, it's difficult to get yourself to a position where cyberspace is safer, more secure and resilient," he says. "In some ways I feel like the Fort Meade crowd are the Israeli settlers of cyberspace—it doesn't matter what the official policy is, they can go out and they can grab these hills, and they're changing the facts on the ground. . . . If we're ever going to get defense better than offense, some things should be more sacrosanct than others. . . . [But] if we have a norm that it's OK to go after these things, if we're creating this crisis of confidence . . . that's just going to bounce back at us."

Healey says a cavalier approach to offensive operations that erodes security and trust in critical systems creates the potential for the information highway to become dense with street skirmishes and guerrilla warfare. "We can think about attacks getting not just better, but way better. Where cyberspace isn't just Wild West, it's Somalia."

Not everyone would agree with Healey and Soghoian that some systems should be off-limits. There are parallels in the analog world, for example, where the CIA exploits vulnerabilities in door locks, safes, and building security systems to gain access and collect intelligence. No one has ever suggested that the CIA disclose these vulnerabilities to vendors so the flaws can be fixed.

But without lawmakers or an independent body asking the right questions to protect the long-term interests of security and trust on the internet, discussions about the nation's offensive operations occur only among insiders whose interests lie in advancing capabilities, not in curbing them, and in constantly pushing the limits of what is possible. "It's all people that have high-level security clearances [who are making these decisions], and there are probably few people [among them] that have ever worked a day in the real private sector where they had to really defend America's critical infrastructure," Healey says. "So it's very easy for them to make these decisions to keep going farther and farther . . . because the government accrues all the benefit. If we use a zero-day for Flame, the government gets the benefit of that. It's the private sector that's going to get the counterattacks and that's going to suffer from the norms the US is now creating that says it's OK to attack."

If the White House and Capitol Hill aren't concerned about how the government's actions undermine the security of computer systems, they might be concerned about another consequence of the government's offensive actions. As Stephen Cobb, a senior security researcher with security firm ESET, noted, "When our own government adds to the malware threat it adds to an erosion of trust that undermines the digital economy."[47]

BECAUSE THE GOVERNMENT'S cyber operations are so heavily classified, it's not clear what kind of oversight—by the military or by lawmakers—currently occurs to prevent mishaps, or what kinds of investigations, if any, are conducted after mishaps occur.

Hayden says the oversight is extensive. "When I was in government, cyberweapons were so over-watched, it was my view it would be a miracle if we ever used one. . . . It was actually an impediment getting in the way of the appropriate and proper use of a new class of weapons, it was so hard to get consensus."

But in 2009, long after Stuxnet had already been launched against systems in Iran, the National Academy of Sciences wrote that the "policy and legal framework for guiding and regulating US cyberattack capabilities was ill-formed, undeveloped, and highly uncertain."[48] Despite a decade of cyberoffensive planning and activity, little had been resolved regarding the rules of engagement for digital warfare since the first task force had been created in 1998.

The Pentagon and White House finally took steps to address this in 2011—more than three years after Stuxnet was first launched—when the Defense Department reportedly compiled a classified list of all the cyberweapons and tools at its disposal and began to establish a long-overdue framework for how and when they could be used.[49] The military regu-

47 Stephen Cobb, "The Negative Impact on GDP of State-Sponsored Malware Like Stuxnet and Flame," We Live Security blog, June 13, 2012, available at blog.eset.com/2012/06/13/impact-on-gdp-of-state-sponsored-malware-like-stuxnet-and-flame.

48 William A. Owens, Kenneth W. Dam, and Herbert S. Lin, (eds.), "Technology, Policy, Law, and Ethics Regarding US Acquisition and Use of Cyberattack Capabilities," National Academies Press, 2009, available at: steptoe.com/assets/attachments/3785.pdf.

49 Ellen Nakashima, "List of Cyber-Weapons Developed by Pentagon to Streamline Computer Warfare," Washington Post, May 31, 2011.

larly compiled a list of approved conventional weapons, but this was the first time cyberweapons were included on the list, a senior military official told the *Washington Post*, calling it the most significant development in military cyber doctrine in years.

Then in 2012, the president signed a secret directive establishing some policies for computer network attacks, the details of which we know about only because Edward Snowden leaked the classified document.[50] Under the directive, the use of a cyberweapon outside a declaration of war requires presidential approval, but in times of war, military leaders have advance approval to take quick action at their discretion. Digital attacks have to be proportional to the threat, as well as limit collateral damage and avoid civilian casualties—parameters that still leave the military a lot of discretion.[51] Any digital operation that could disrupt, destroy, or manipulate computers or is "reasonably likely to result in significant consequences" also requires presidential approval. Significant consequences include loss of life, damage to property, and serious economic impact, as well as possible retaliation against the United States or adverse effects on foreign policy.

Presidential authorization is also required to plant a logic bomb in a foreign system or a beacon marking it for later attack. But is not needed for espionage operations that are conducted for the sake of simply collecting data or mapping a network, unless the operation involves a worm or other malware that could spread. Notably, before taking action, the military has to weigh the possible effects an operation might have on the stability and security of the internet, and whether it would establish unwelcome norms of international behavior. Though some might argue that Stuxnet and Flame had already violated this guideline and established unwelcome norms of behavior, Herbert Lin, a cybersecurity expert with the National

---

50 Lolita Baldor, "Pentagon Gets Cyberwar Guidelines," Associated Press, June 22, 2011, available at usatoday30.usatoday.com/news/military/2011-06-22-pentagon-cyber-war_n.htm.
51 Glenn Greenwald and Ewen MacAskill, "Obama Orders US to Draw Up Overseas Target List for Cyber-Attacks," *Guardian*, June 7, 2013. Presidential Policy Directive 20 was issued in October 2012, according to the paper.

Research Council, points out that all the directive says is that military leaders have to ask questions about whether an operation might establish unwelcome norms, not that they can't proceed with it anyway. "Establishing an undesirable norm may in fact have been a price they were willing to pay to set back the Iranian nuclear program," he says of Stuxnet and Flame.[52]

The presidential directive addresses only the *military's* use of digital operations, however. A list of exceptions in the document excludes intelligence agencies like the NSA and CIA from it, as well as law enforcement agencies like the FBI and Secret Service. And although it establishes broad ground rules for conducting offensive military cyber operations, it does not address questions that are raised when the United States is faced with responding to a digital attack. In 2011, Pentagon officials took at least one step in this direction when they announced that any digital attack against the United States that took out portions of the electric grid or resulted in casualties would be considered an act of war and receive the appropriate response—even a kinetic military response, if the situation called for it, using "all necessary means."[53] In other words, as one military official put it, "If you shut down our power grid, maybe we will put a missile down one of your smokestacks."[54] At least they didn't assert, as the Joint Chiefs of Staff did in a statement of doctrine in 2004, that the United States reserved the right to respond to some cyberattacks with nuclear weapons. That wording has disappeared in subsequent statements of doctrine from the Joint Chiefs, Lin points out, but members of the Defense Science Board apparently hoped to revive it when they asserted in 2013 that the United States should not rule out a nuclear response. It's probably a good thing that the Science Board is just an advisory group and has no say in policy.

---

52 All quotes from Lin in this chapter come from an author interview in January 2014.
53 "International Strategy for Cyberspace: Prosperity, Security, and Openness in a Networked World," The White House, May 2011, available at whitehouse.gov/sites/default/files/rss_viewer/international_strategy_for_cyberspace.pdf.
54 Siobhan Gorman and Julian E. Barnes, "Cyber Combat: Act of War," *Wall Street Journal*, May 30, 2011.

Though the Snowden leak of the presidential directive hints at some of the questions the government has been asking internally about these issues, the public still has little understanding of what questions have been answered and which are still unresolved. Lin says that for the sake of transparency there are important conversations that could be made public without compromising classified operations. "We could in fact get into a discussion about what is possible without saying what the US is actually doing," he says. It would also be possible for US Cyber Command and the NSA to provide examples of circumstances under which they would use cyberweapons, or explain the circumstances under which they hoard information about zero-day vulnerabilities versus when they might allow disclosure of information about a security hole to get it fixed. And it would be important to know, at the very least, where the government draws the line in compromising trusted systems that are critical to the integrity of the internet—if it draws a line at all.

"Senators and congressmen need to be educated about this," Lin says, not to mention the public. "And there ought to be an accounting somewhere about all the cyberattacks that the US conducts for any purpose . . . that tells you what was attacked and under what circumstances. . . . It can be classified, but at least it would give the first step toward better understanding what the US is actually doing." Lawmakers like Rep. Mike Rogers (R-MI) insist that Congress *has* held private discussions on the government's cyber activities. But so far, Capitol Hill has shown little interest in holding even basic *public* discussions about the government's offensive operations.

"I do believe without question there needs to be a full conversation about doctrine and there needs to be a full conversation about rules of engagement," Air Force general Robert Kehler, the current head of US Strategic Command, said in 2011, before the presidential directive was signed. "I can't say all of that needs to be in the public domain."[55]

---

55 Carroll, "Cone of Silence."

———

AS THE UNITED STATES and other countries beat the drum of cyberwarfare, it's not just policy questions that are still unanswered, however. Many of the legal questions around digital operations are still unresolved.

Some, like Kaspersky Lab founder Eugene Kaspersky, have called for a cyber arms treaty to control the proliferation of digital weapons and set norms for their use. But as noted previously, there are obvious problems with trying to control the stockpiling of nonphysical weapons. Governments can sign treaties to halt the proliferation of nuclear weapons and use satellite imagery and UN inspectors to track the movement of nuclear materials. But satellites can't track the movement of illicit digital weapons, nor can custom inspections catch the smuggling of malicious code across borders. Nor can anyone monitor all of the rogue players who might emerge to exploit the vulnerabilities in critical infrastructure systems that Stuxnet exposed.

As for developing new laws to govern the use of cyberattacks by nations, the consensus among legal experts seems to be that existing laws of warfare will work just fine—it's just that new interpretations of these laws need to be developed to address cyber.

In 2013, a group of twenty international legal experts convened by a NATO-related institute attempted to do just this. The result was the three-hundred-page *Tallinn Manual*, designed to help military legal advisers in NATO member states develop cyber doctrine for their armies.[56] But despite the manual's length, it left many questions unanswered. The experts found that while some attacks in cyberspace have clear parallels to conventional attacks in physical space, others are murkier.

Under the UN Charter's Law of Armed Conflict, for example, they determined that hacking the control system of a dam to unleash water into a valley was the equivalent of breaching the dam with explosives.

———

56 Michael N. Schmitt, general editor, *Tallinn Manual on the International Law Applicable to Cyber Warfare*, NATO Cooperative Cyber Defence Centre of Excellence, available at ccdcoe/org/249.html.

And launching an attack from a proxy system located in a neutral country would be prohibited in the same way that an army couldn't march through a neutral country's territory to invade an enemy. They also determined that an attack had to cause physical or personal damage to qualify as an act of force—simply erasing hard drives, if it didn't result in physical damage or injury, didn't qualify. But what about an attack on Wall Street that damaged a nation's economy or aimed to do so? Here they found the legal waters less clear. Some of the experts believed such an attack qualified, while others were less convinced.

The experts also made a distinction between an act of force and an armed attack. Though the latter is considered more serious, it's not clearly defined. It's generally interpreted to refer only to the gravest uses of force, which are judged by the effects the attack has. Under Article 24 of the UN Charter, nations can respond to an act of force only with nonforceful countermeasures—such as applying economic sanctions or cutting off diplomatic ties with the offending nation.

Under Article 51, however, every state has the right to defend itself with lethal force—individually, or collectively on behalf of allies—if it or an ally suffers an armed attack, as long as the response is necessary and proportional to the initial attack and occurs while the threat of the original attack is ongoing or there is a threat of a future attack. As for what *level* of damage qualifies as an armed attack, and therefore justifies a lethal response—it's up to the victim to determine the threshold and defend its decision to the United Nations.[57] But what about an attack that

---

57 Many in the media and government have called the denial-of-service attacks against Estonian websites cyberwarfare, but they don't qualify as such. The attacks, launched by a botnet of 85,000 machines in 2007, persisted for three weeks and, at their peak, bombarded nearly sixty websites, knocking Estonia's largest bank offline as well as government sites. But when Estonia pointed the finger at Russia as the source of the attacks and sought help from NATO by attempting to invoke the collective self-defense agreement under Article 5 of the North Atlantic Treaty Organization, it was rebuffed. NATO determined that the attack did not constitute an armed attack under the treaty. The problem lay in the fact that the EU and NATO had not previously defined the obligations of its member states in the event of a cyberattack against one of them. NATO had also not defined a cyberattack as a clear military action, therefore Article 5 did not automatically come into play. Under Article 5 "an armed attack against one or more [members] in Europe or North America shall

is intended to cause great harm but fails to achieve it? A missile launched by one nation against another that gets diverted by a Patriot missile is still an attempted armed attack. Would the same hold true in the cyber realm? Catherine Lotrionte says no, since the effect of the attack is what matters, not the intent. But Gary Brown, senior legal adviser to the US Cyber Command from 2010 to 2012, says it likely *would* be considered an armed attack "if you can make an argument [with evidence] that it was going to have a kinetic effect."[58]

And what about espionage? Under international law and US policy, espionage is not an act of war. But since espionage could be the prelude to a destructive attack, as it was with Stuxnet and the spy tools the attackers used to collect intelligence for that operation, could the discovery of spy tools on a system indicate an intention to conduct an armed attack? Under current doctrine, an armed attack has to be current or imminent to merit a lethal use of force in response, but what determines imminence? After 9/11, the United States asserted that the invasion of Afghanistan was an act of self-defense, under Article 51, since the country was housing al-Qaeda leaders who were believed to be planning additional strikes against the United States.

One thing the *Tallinn* experts did agree on unanimously was that Stuxnet was an act of force that likely violated international law. They were split, however, on whether it constituted an armed attack. As an

---

be considered an attack against them all." In the event of such an attack, each member is expected to "assist the Party or Parties so attacked by taking forthwith, individually and in concert with the other Parties, such action as it deems necessary, including the use of armed force, to restore and maintain the security of the North Atlantic area."

Estonian prime minister Andrus Ansip challenged NATO's conclusion, however, asking, "What's the difference between a blockade of harbors or airports of sovereign states and the blockade of government institutions and newspaper websites?" (See Thomas Rid, "Think Again: Cyberwar," *Foreign Policy*, February 27, 2012, available at foreignpolicy.com/articles/2012/02/27/cyberwar.) The question is a valid one that has not been adequately resolved. If blocking commercial shipments can be an act of war, would thwarting e-commerce be the equivalent in cyberspace? And what kind of response would it merit? In 2010, NATO attempted to resolve the question by concluding that if an ally were hit with a cyberattack, NATO would help defend the victim's networks, but the assistance fell short of offering to help a victim conduct a counterattack.

58 Author interview with Brown, February 2014.

armed attack, Iran would have been within its rights to defend against the digital onslaught with a counterstrike—digital or kinetic—as long as it was proportional to the damage Stuxnet caused and occurred while the attack was ongoing. Once the attack subsided and there was no impending threat to the centrifuges or threat of another impending attack—that is, once the weapon was discovered and defused—the proper response was diplomacy or some other nonforceful measure.

It's important to note that official US policy, unlike the interpretation of the *Tallinn* experts, doesn't distinguish between an act of force and an armed attack—the two are considered the same. Under this interpretation, then, Stuxnet was an illegal armed attack, and Iran could have made a case for responding in self-defense. It also means, though, that if someone were to use a weapon like Stuxnet against the United States, the US government would consider it an armed attack, something Lotrionte says concerns her.[59]

There have been conflicting reactions to some of the *Tallinn Manual*'s conclusions. Martin Libicki, an expert on cyberwarfare with the RAND corporation, questions the wisdom of allowing cyber conflicts to be resolved with kinetic attacks. He wonders if it wouldn't be wiser to apply "Las Vegas rules" to cyberwarfare so that what happens in cyberspace stays in cyberspace. "Your escalation potential, if you go to the kinetic realm than if you stay in the cyber realm, is much greater," he says. "So a rule that says you can only match cyber with cyber puts a limit on your topside risk."[60]

Lotrionte, however, says the method of a counterattack doesn't matter, since escalation is controlled by the fact that a counterattack must be both necessary and proportional. "Necessary means you have to determine that

---

59 Harold Koh, former legal adviser to the State Department, speaking at the US CyberCom Inter-Agency Legal Conference at Fort Meade in September 2012, asserted that the government's position was that a use of force was the same as an armed attack. "In our view, there is no threshold for a use of deadly force to qualify as an 'armed attack' that may warrant a forcible response." See state.gov/s/l/releases/remarks/197924.htm.
60 Author interview with Libicki, October 2012.

there is no other way to resolve this threat," she says. "You can't talk, you can't sanction or call on the Security Council. If there is any other way to stop these attacks, you have to use that, and not use of force. That's how you stop escalation."[61]

Others point out the difficulty of applying the conventional laws of war to the cyber realm, where attribution is a problem. The Law of Armed Conflict requires that an attacker be identified to conduct a counterstrike. Though attribution in a digital attack can sometimes be determined— through intelligence means if not forensic ones—the anonymous nature of cyberattacks makes responding quickly to an attack, while the threat is current, complicated to say the least.

"Smoking guns are hard to find in the counterterrorism environment; smoking keyboards are that much more difficult," Frank Cilluffo, director of the Homeland Security Policy Institute at George Washington University told Congress. Cyberspace, he said, "is made for plausible deniability."[62]

If all of this wasn't enough to complicate the issue of cyberwarfare, there are further problems having to do with the lack of a clear understanding about what constitutes a cyberweapon. In the kinetic world, a weapon is something that damages, destroys, kills, or injures, which is something very different from an espionage tool. But Gary Brown notes that so many activities in cyber are carried out by "a guy sitting at a keyboard typing commands" and doing everything from installing malware and destroying data, to destroying and damaging a system or damaging equipment the system controls. "Does that mean that the software or technique we used to get access to the system turned into a weapon?" he asks. "That would mean everything [is a weapon]. It's a very complicated issue. I don't feel like we have a very good handle on it."

---

61 All quotes from Lotrionte come from author interview, February 2014.
62 Cilluffo was speaking at a hearing on the "Iranian Cyber Threat to the US Homeland" for a Joint Subcommittee Hearing of the Committee on Homeland Security, April 26, 2012, available at gpo.gov/fdsys/pkg/CHRG-112hhrg77381/pdf/CHRG-122hhrg77381.pdf.

Brown says the lack of clarity about what constitutes a digital weapon and what constitutes attack activity as opposed to espionage raises the risk of escalated responses, since the same techniques and tools used for espionage and damaging attacks in the digital realm can be indistinguishable to the victim.[63]

"Traditional espionage is less likely to be escalatory because it was better understood," he says. "Even if you cut through border-fence wire and tiptoed into an office and stole files . . . it doesn't look like we we're starting a war. . . . In cyber, if somebody got access to a critical system, maybe to the nuclear command-and-control . . . maybe they're just looking around. Or maybe they're planning to disable it and launch a nuclear attack. . . . It's that kind of escalation that worries me."

Clearly Stuxnet and the prospect of digital warfare has raised a host of issues that have yet to be adequately addressed. And if it seems the United States is late in getting around to looking at them, it's not the only one. "There are countries [in Europe] that are not even close to writing rules," says Lotrionte.

IN THE YEARS since Stuxnet was first exposed, a lot has changed—not just for the military but for malware hunters. For the researchers who spent so much time disassembling and analyzing Stuxnet—and its accompanying spy tools—deciphering the malware was an incomparable thrill that stretched the boundaries of virus research. But it also irrevocably changed the parameters of their profession by imbuing it with a degree of risk and politicization it had never known before.

In one of his team's final assessments of Stuxnet, Symantec's Eric Chien wrote that whether Stuxnet would usher in a new generation of

---

63 Brown has written a paper on the issue. See Gary D. Brown and Andrew O. Metcalf, "Easier Said Than Done: Legal Reviews of Cyber Weapons," *Journal of National Security Law and Policy*, published by Georgetown Law, February 12, 2014, available at jnslp.com/wp-content/uploads/2014/02/Easier-Said-than-Done.pdf.

real-world attacks that targeted critical infrastructure or was just a once-in-a-decade phenomenon, they couldn't say. But he was clear about his preference. It was the type of threat, he said, "we hope to never see again."

Thankfully, as of this book's publication there has been no sign yet of the counterstrikes against industrial control systems that Ralph Langner warned about, nor have there been signs of any other types of comparable digital attacks launched by the United States or anyone else. Stuxnet still holds the distinction of being the only known case of cyberwarfare on record. But that can change at any time, now that Pandora's digital box has been opened.

ACKNOWLEDGMENTS

When I first began writing about Stuxnet after its discovery in the summer of 2010, there was no way to know where it would lead. It wasn't until months later, after the Symantec researchers and Ralph Langner's team dug into it further, that it became clear that there was a larger story that needed to be told—not only about the attack on Iran's centrifuges and the discovery of the world's first digital weapon but about the security community and its changing nature at the dawn of the era of cyber warfare. It's a cliché to say that something is a game-changer, but Stuxnet really is. Everything in malware that occurred prior to its appearance might well be labeled BS—Before Stuxnet—since the code that came before it represented simpler, more innocent times when the motives and ambitions of attackers were more straightforward and easier to discern.

If Stuxnet was a challenge to decipher, the writing of this book was equally so. Combining a narrative structure with complex technical details and a political-historical context that was as convoluted as the code, while still offering a compelling read and doing justice to the intense labor that researchers invested in their analysis of the code, was not an easy task, especially when the subject of that narrative turned out to be a moving target.

As I began the book in earnest in early 2012, everything we thought we knew about Stuxnet had to be revised as one new discovery after another was made—first with Duqu, then with Flame, and then, in early 2013, with the unveiling of Stuxnet 0.5, the first known version of the digital weapon to be found. And the target is still moving today.

Stuxnet, and its ancillary espionage tools, were the state of the art at the time they were developed and unleashed, but that state has no doubt been surpassed by other digital tools developed in its wake that have yet to be detected and may not be for many years.

While the writing of this book was difficult, it was made easier by the enormous help and support I received from many people.

The book would not have been possible without the encouragement and support of my agent, David Fugate, who first reached out to me in 2007 following the publication of a three-part series I wrote for *Wired* about the digital underground of carding forums and the fascinating community of bank card thieves that inhabit them. Though I decided not to expand that series into a book, David remained in touch over the next few years, periodically reaching out to say he was still interested in collaborating and asking if I had any project in mind.

Throughout the proposal process and the writing of this book, he remained a steadfast supporter, providing valuable feedback and the seasoned perspective of a publishing veteran while lending the right amount of encouragement when needed the most. He's the kind of advocate every writer should have in his or her corner.

In addition to David, my editor at Crown/Random House, Julian Pavia, played a great role in helping to shape the book and keep it on path. This was a difficult project to wrangle, but Julian did it with grace and patience, even as the content unexpectedly changed and deadlines passed. Additionally, Julian did a masterful job of streamlining the technical details to balance the narrative flow and refine my sometimes jagged prose.

I'd also like to thank Kim Silverton, editorial assistant at Random House, for her timely and helpful feedback on the manuscript during the editing phase, as well as the publicity and marketing teams—Sarah Breivogel, executive publicist at Random House, Sarah Pekdemir, senior marketing manager, and Jay Sones, director of marketing at Crown—for their enthusiastic backing of the book.

The book would not exist, however, without all of the talented researchers who did the hard work of deciphering Stuxnet and its arsenal of tools and who provided me with untiring assistance to help me get the details right. These include Sergey Ulasen of VirusBlokAda and now Kaspersky Lab, and Oleg Kupreev of VirusBlokAda, who sounded the first alarm and got the rest of the world to take note of the strange code discovered in Iran.

They also include, of course, the brilliant and hard-working team at Symantec—Eric Chien, Liam O'Murchu, and Nicolas Falliere—whose curiosity, persistence, and skill provided the most important pieces of the Stuxnet puzzle and ensured that the code would not pass quietly into obscurity. The three of them were extremely generous with their time and endured many rounds of questions in the midst of busy schedules to share their views and expertise.

I cannot express enough gratitude to them and to the equally brilliant and tireless global research and analysis team at Kaspersky Lab—Costin Raiu, Aleks Gostev, Roel Schouwenberg, Kurt Baumgartner, Vitaly Kamluk, and the rest of the company's global group of researchers–who impressed me repeatedly with their skill and devotion to chasing down the tiniest details of very complex attacks, even though working with them often involved 6 a.m. phone calls on my end to accommodate the time difference with Eastern Europe. I'm particularly grateful to Costin for going beyond the call of duty, sometimes at the expense of time with his family, and for his remarkable wisdom, memory, and attention to detail, which helped me keep track of the many maddening facts that grew more extensive with each new discovery.

I'm also very grateful to Greg Funaro and Ryan Naraine at Kaspersky Lab who had an uncanny ability to anticipate what I needed before I knew I needed it and who had an unwavering commitment to leaving no question unanswered. Ryan's former job as a top security journalist, combined with his technical expertise, made him the perfect liaison with the research team.

In addition to the Symantec and Kaspersky research teams, the story of Stuxnet could not be told without the work of Ralph Langner and his colleagues Ralf Rosen and Andreas Timm. Ralph's passion for Stuxnet kept it alive in the press and brought it to the attention of mainstream media, while his extensive knowledge of industrial control systems helped the public understand Stuxnet's broader implications for the security of critical infrastructure. I'm grateful for the many hours he spent with me on the phone and in person to help me make sense of Stuxnet's broader context. His frank and straightforward manner cut to the heart of the issues and ensured that the public could not dismiss or overlook the importance of Stuxnet. I'm also grateful to Ralf Rosen for the time he gave to speak to me about their work on Stuxnet and for reviewing some of the completed text for accuracy.

Similarly, Boldizsár Bencsáth was immensely generous with his time and expertise, providing kind and invaluable assistance that helped me unravel a few mysteries and understand the ways in which all of the attacks were connected.

In addition to these researchers, I'm greatly indebted to David Albright at the Institute for Science and International Security, who helped not only me but also Symantec and Ralph Langner with understanding Stuxnet's effects on Natanz and the enrichment process. Both he and Olli Heinonen, formerly of the IAEA and now a senior fellow at Harvard's Belfer Center for Science and International Affairs, provided great insight into the Iranian nuclear program in general and to the enrichment process at Natanz in particular.

In addition, I'd like to thank Corey Hinderstein, now with the Nuclear Threat Initiative, for providing me with her firsthand memories of the press conference where Natanz was first exposed and her work uncovering the infamous satellite images.

I'd also like to thank Dale Peterson, Perry Pederson, Joe Weiss, and Mike Assante for helping me understand the wider effects of Stuxnet and weapons like it on critical infrastructure. Dale and Perry were especially helpful in reading the chapter on industrial control systems and providing feedback.

Similarly, I'd like to thank Jason Healey and Marcus Sachs for providing background information about the early days of the government's digital warfare program and to Jason for providing perspective on the implications of Stuxnet and Flame and where we go from here. I'd also like to thank Charlie Miller and Chaouki Bekrar for their frankness in discussing the zero-day market and helping me understand the motivations that drive this market.

In addition to all of these people, there are others who sat for interviews or read through chapters or parts of chapters to provide welcomed and helpful feedback. Some of them I have named here; many others have asked to remain anonymous.

One reader I'd like to thank in particular is Andrea Matwyshyn, a good and valued friend who has been supportive of my work and career for many years and who took some of these chapters with her to conferences and holidays to provide the feedback I needed in a timely manner. I'd also especially like to thank Cem Paya, another good friend and supporter of my work who took chapters on holiday to Turkey and even read various versions of chapters several times to ensure that the technical details were accurate and consistent.

This book on Stuxnet is the culmination of more than a decade of experience reporting on cybersecurity, hackers, and the security community, all of which helped sharpen my knowledge and understanding of these complex issues. I'd like to thank the many friends, family, and colleagues who have provided much support, inspiration, guidance, encouragement, good editing, and a voice of reason over the years, including Richard Thieme, Dan Goodin, Elinor Mills, and Rob Lemos, as well as my *Wired* colleagues past and present—Chuck Squatriglia, Jim Merithew, Kevin Poulsen, Ryan Singel, and David Kravets. I'd also like to thank David Zetter and Mark Zetter for their enduring support and many good memories.

INDEX

A

Abbasi, Fereydoon, 239–241, 355n35

Abdullah of Saudi Arabia, 191

Abraham, Spencer, 317

Abu Dhabi, 191

Acts of force, 401–403

Additional Protocol (IAEA), 71

Adobe, 388

Adobe Reader, 102

AEOI (Atomic Energy Organization of Iran), 35, 36, 43, 45–46, 50, 51, 69, 180, 240

AEP (American Electric Power), 160–161

AES, 267

Agha-Soltan, Neda, 337

Aghazadeh, Gholam Reza, 43, 69, 72–73, 74, 180, 342

Ahmadinejad, Mahmoud, 3, 67–68, 81, 126, 195–196, 240, 242, 305, 308–309, 330, 336–337

Air Force, U.S., 206, 207, 212, 213, 221–222

Albright, David, 41, 44, 84, 243–247, 311, 325, 326, 329, 330, 331, 341–342, 343, 359, 360, 366

Alexander, Keith, 151, 188, 202, 214–215, 386, 389, 391

Alfvén, Hannes, 45

Ali Khamenei, 336–337, 373

Alimohammadi, Massoud, 241n13

Al-Qaeda, 141, 217

American Civil Liberties Union, 113–114

American Electric Power (AEP), 160–161

Anonymous collective, 107, 113–114, 132

Antivirus firms. *See* Cybersecurity

Apple iOS, 102, 106

Arak, Iran, heavy-water production plant near, 35, 39, 77

Arkin, Brad, 388–389

Armed force, 401–404

Arquilla, John, 205–206, 215

Ashtari, Ali, 323n22

Assange, Julian, 180

Assante, Michael, 130, 160–164
Assassinations, of prominent Iranian nuclear personnel, 239–242, 366–367
Atomic bombs, 375–376
Atomic Energy Organization of Iran (AEOI), 35, 36, 43, 45–46, 50, 51, 69, 180, 240
Atoms for Peace, 45
Aurora Generator Test, 129–131, 142, 160–164
Australia, water treatment plant sabotage, 136–139
AutoCAD files, 267, 282
Automobile industry, 134
Autorun exploit, 9–10, 95, 96, 278–279, 283, 339

B
Backdoors, 145, 258, 298–299
Baker, Stewart, 377
Bank accounts, 295–296
Barzashka, Ivanka, 361, 362, 365
Behpajooh, 97, 98, 339–340, 349–350, 353
Behrooz (Neda Industrial Group engineer), 340–341, 353, 354
Bekrar, Chaouki, 108–113
Bell Atlantic, 135
Bencsáth, Boldizsár, 249–257, 260–261, 269–270, 281
Benedict, Kennette, 375
Benford, Gregory, 134n8
Beresford, Dillon, 144–146
Bin Laden, Osama, 392–393

Blackouts, 158–159
Boden, Vitek, 138–139
Boebert, W. Earl, 385
Boldewin, Frank, 17, 24
Booz Allen Hamilton, 106, 219–220
Bounty programs, 100, 102–103, 104
Brennan, John, 188
Brightmail, 22
Brown, Gary, 386n32, 402, 404–405
Browser exploits, 102, 103
Bryan, James D., 213
Budapest University of Technology and Economics, CrySyS Lab, 249–257, 260–261, 269–270, 281
Buffer-overflow vulnerability, 269–270, 278–279
Bulletin of the Atomic Scientists, 375
Bumgarner, John, 68n11
Bureau, Pierre-Marc, 16
Bush, George W., cyberstrategy of, 190, 191, 193–194, 201, 203, 321, 332–333
Bushehr, Iran, nuclear power reactor at, 34–35, 46–47, 50, 173–174, 176, 183–184
Buttyán, Levente, 255

C
C++ (programming language), 229, 266
C (programming language), 265–266
California Independent System Operator (Cal-ISO), 141–142, 158

Campbell, John H., 208, 209
Cartwright, James, 202, 214, 313,
    357, 383–384
Casey, William, 197
Center for Strategic and
    International Studies, 382
Central Intelligence Agency (CIA)
  on al-Qaeda's cyberterrorism
    interest, 141
  centrifuge shipment interception,
    316–317
  computer network attack policy
    exception, 398
  cyber operations, 216–217
  Cyber Storm III exercise, 186
  early digital sabotage efforts,
    197–201
  Flame responsibility, 290
  In-Q-Tel, 107
  Khan nuclear supply network
    infiltration, 77–80, 199–201
  Russian gas pipeline explosion
    plot, 125–126, 198–199
Centrifuges
  frequency converters, 232–235,
    245–246, 311–312
  IAEA inspectors' observations,
    72–73, 244
  Iran's acquisition of, 48–50, 77–
    78, 177
  Iran's concealment of, 83, 364
  Iran's first tests at Kalaye, 50–51,
    311
  Libyan shipments intercepted by
    CIA, 316–317
  Natanz facility installation, 83,
    84–85, 87, 309, 327–330, 337

Natanz facility production, 33,
    244–246, 328–329, 338, 341,
    344, 356–357, 361–362
Natanz facility replacement
    mystery, 1–3, 344
Natanz facility Stuxnet infection
    effects, 238, 246–247, 323–327,
    330–332, 341–343, 354–357,
    359–365
  number in Iran, 330, 337–338
Oak Ridge laboratory testing,
    317–322
operation of, 47–48
CERT-Bund, 169, 186
Certificate authorities, 261–262
Certs, 12, 15–16
CFIUS (Committee on Foreign
    Investment in the United
    States), 225
Chaos Computer Club Congress,
    288–289n14
Cheney, Dick, 191, 192n6
Chien, Eric, 22, 27, 28, 29, 30,
    31–32, 52–56, 58–59, 65, 67,
    68, 88–91, 117–118, 120, 126,
    127–128, 227–228, 229, 232–
    234, 237–238, 242–243, 245,
    246, 256–258, 269, 281, 307,
    405–406
Chilton, Kevin, 377
China
  Cal-ISO breach, 141–142
  cyberattacks against U.S., 369
  cyberwarfare program, 373
  Stuxnet responsibility speculation,
    16, 26, 31, 49, 51
  Telvent Canada attack, 149–150

China *(cont'd)*
  uranium supplied to Iran, 74
CIA. *See* Central Intelligence
    Agency (CIA)
Cilluffo, Frank, 404
Clandestine operations, 202
Clark, Wesley, 379–380
Clarke, Richard, 390–391
Clinton, Bill, 215, 368
Clinton, Hillary, 360–361
C-Media Electronics, 252, 262
CNA (computer network attack),
    107, 210–211, 220, 397–398
CND (computer network defense),
    220
CNE (computer network
    exploitation), 103, 217
CNN, 44, 135
Code Red worm, 59, 119
Cole, Juan, 67n9
Command-and-control servers
  Duqu's use, 251, 258–259
  military use, 384
  Stuxnet's use, 27–28, 61, 64, 305,
    314–315, 351
Committee on Foreign Investment
    in the United States (CFIUS),
    225
Computer network attack (CNA),
    107, 210–211, 220, 397–398
Computer network defense (CND),
    220
Computer network exploitation
    (CNE), 103, 217
Computer security. *See* Cybersecurity
Conficker worm, 20, 54, 92–93n5,
    107–108, 374

Congress, 309, 321, 390, 399
Control Gostar Jahed (CGJ), 97
Copycat attacks, 20, 182
Corporación Andina de Fomento,
    108
Counterattacks, 403–404
Crackme files, 119
Criminal underground, 388
Critical infrastructure facilities
  CAL-ISO attack, 141–142
  digital assault as act of war, 203–
    204
  electromagnetic pulse threat, 150
  Maroochy Shire incident as first
    cyberattack against, 136–139
  security of, 186, 223, 334
  vulnerability of U.S., 133–136,
    142–144, 146, 155–160, 182,
    377, 384–385
Crowley, Philip J., 241
CrySyS Lab, 249–257, 260–261,
    269–270, 281
C-SPAN, 34
CSX Corporation, 133
Cybersecurity. *See also specific firms*
  current situation, 387–390
  early years, 56–57
  government actions threatening,
    392–396
  Obama's agenda, 223, 334
  Stuxnet's impact on industry, 14,
    405–406
  zero-day exploit sales, 103, 106
Cyber Statecraft Initiative at the
    Atlantic Council, 383
Cyberwarfare
  atom bomb comparison, 375–376

attribution challenges, 377–380, 404

China program, 373

collateral damage, 382

cybersecurity effects, 392–396

cyberweapon definition, 404–405

digital weapons parts, 52

examples of operations, 215–218

expansion of, 219–221

historical development, 205–215

Iranian program, 373

legal issues, 400–405

limitations of, 380–382

oversight, 396–399

policy issues, 386–399

Stuxnet's impact, 374–375

U.S. government's lack of transparency, 386–387, 399

U.S. military response to cyberattack, 398

U.S. program, 221–226, 373–374

U.S. vulnerability to attack, 376–377, 382–386

D

Dagan, Meir, 241–242, 360

Dams, 151, 153, 400–401

DARPA (Defense Advanced Research Projects Agency), 373

Davis, Mike, 155–157

Davis-Besse nuclear power plant, 133

Debugging programs, 60

Def Con, 210, 220

Defense, U.S. Department of

cyber operations, 133, 208–210, 212–215, 396–398

early digital sabotage operations against Soviet Union, 197

Microsoft collaboration, 223–224

Oak Ridge National Laboratory's work for, 317–318

Stuxnet briefing, 188

vulnerabilities equities process, 224–226

Defense Advanced Research Projects Agency (DARPA), 373

Defense contractors, 106, 219–220, 391–392

Defense Science Board, 205, 398

Den Helder incident, 150

Denial-of-service attacks, 378, 401–402n57

Deterrence, 383–384

Dexter exploit, 270–271, 272

Digital arms dealers, 101

Digital arms race, 370

Digital bugs, 217–218, 220–221

Digital certificates, 11–13, 15–16, 95, 252, 282, 286–288, 393

Digital Globe, 39

Digital weapons. *See* Cyberwarfare

Diplomacy, 374

.DLL files, 24–25, 59, 61, 116–118, 121–122, 235, 310, 315, 340

DNS (domain name system) providers, 29

"Dolphin," 79–80, 369

Domain names, 28, 29

Donahue, Tom, 371–372n1

Drones, 216–217

Dubai, Flame attacks, 282

Duqu, 249–275
  cleanup operation, 291n19
  CrySyS Lab's discovery, 249–255
  Iranian "Stars" attack relationship,
    259–260
  Kaspersky Lab's analysis, 263–269,
    272–275
  life-span, 259
  naming of, 256
  Olympic Games operation, 314
  operation and spread of, 258–259,
    265–275
  Symantec's analysis and public
    announcement, 256–261
  targets and source, 261–262, 267,
    268n21, 272–275, 283
  versions, 259n7
Dynamic analysis, 122

E
"Easter eggs," 145n30, 270–271
eBay, 99
Egypt, 191
Eiland, Giora, 193
Eisenhower administration, 44–45
ElBaradei, Mohamed, 41, 69, 80n24,
    84, 317, 345
Electrical grid, 142, 155–164
Electromagnetic pulses, 150,
    201n25
Elghanian, Habib, 65–66
"Eligible Receiver" exercise, 207–208
Encryption, 23–25, 28, 60, 62–64,
    267, 274–275, 295, 376n10
Endgame Systems, 106–108

Energy, U.S. Department of, 129–
    131, 142, 318
Enrichment Technology Company,
    177
ESET, 15–16, 274, 353
Esfahan Steel Complex, 340
Esfahan uranium conversion plant,
    77, 78, 81, 367
Espionage
  Duqu as tool for, 259, 273
  Flame as tool for, 280, 283
  Gauss as tool for, 295
  legal issues, 402, 404–405
  presidential authorization, 397
  Stuxnet as tool for, 17, 26, 31–32,
    124, 125, 127
Esther (Jewish queen), 67
Estonia, denial-of-service attack of,
    401–402n57
EU3, 77, 78
Exploits, definition of, 6. See also
    specific exploits

F
Fakhrizadeh-Mahabadi, Mohsen,
    240, 347
Falliere, Nicolas, 27, 52, 53, 116–
    124, 127, 228–232, 234, 242,
    258, 302, 303
Fararo Paya, 233–234, 245
"Farewell Dossier," 197–198, 199
"Fearwall," 99–100
FEDAT, 347
Federal Bureau of Investigation
    (FBI), 197, 210, 216–217, 398

Federal Energy Regulatory
    Commission, 134, 160, 161
File paths, 66–67
Firmware, 145, 155–157
FirstEnergy, 159
Flame, 276–307
    cleanup operation, 291–292
    discovery of, 276–279
    end of, 284–285, 291–292
    Kaspersky Lab's analysis of
        Malaysian server, 291–299
    naming of, 279
    Olympic Games operation, 314
    operation and spread of, 280–290,
        292–295
    size of, 279–280
    targets and source, 280–283,
        290–291
    Windows Update system
        hijacking, 285–290, 392–394
    Wiper connection, 279n4
FL malware, 293–294. *See also*
    Flame
Florida Power and Light, 162
Font-parsing vulnerability, 269–
    270
Fonts, 269–270, 296
Foolad Technique, 97, 339, 353
Footprints, 65
Forbes, 105–106
Fordow plant, 344–346, 368
Fort Meade, 188–189, 214
France, Iranian nuclear reactor
    construction support, 46
Frank, Gideon, 83
Frequency converters, 232–235,
    245–246, 311–312

G
Gachin mine, 313, 329
Gallup poll, 191
Gamma Group, 106
GAO (Government Accountability
    Office), 216
Gas pipeline explosions, 125–126,
    127, 131, 150, 152–153, 198–199
Gates, Robert M., 86, 193
Gauss, 294–298, 376n10
GeCAD Software, 265
GENIE, 217
Georgia, denial-of-service attack,
    378
Germany
    CERT-Bund, 169, 186
    exploit sales regulation, 114
    Iranian nuclear reactor
        construction support, 46
    Iranian nuclear weapons program
        intelligence, 86
    Stuxnet responsibility speculation,
        247
    WWII, 225
Ghul, Hassan, 217
Google, 102, 112
Gostev, Alexander, 29n5, 263–264,
    265–266, 275, 279
Government Accountability Office
    (GAO), 216
Government agencies, zero-day
    exploit purchases, 101, 103–115
Government Communications
    Headquarters (GCHQ) (U.K.),
    218n33
Government contractors, 106, 219–
    220, 391–392

The Grugq, 105–106
GSMK, 179
Guardian Council, 337
Guava, 66–67, 68n11
Gulf War, 206

H
Hacking
  Def Con, 210, 220
  evolution of, 125
  Pwn2Own contest, 103, 109, 112
Hacking Team, 106
Haley, Kevin, 374
Haman, 67–68
Hamre, John, 209, 213
Harris, 106
Hassanpour, Ardeshire, 241n13
Hathaway, Melissa, 182
Hawaii, US Pacific Command
  "Eligible Receiver" exercise,
  207–208
Hayden, Michael, 214, 373, 374,
  386–387, 389–390, 396
HBGary Federal, 107
Healey, Jason, 383, 394–395
Heavy-water production plants, 35,
  39–40
Heinonen, Olli, 3, 41–43, 69, 72,
  73–74, 78–80, 317, 363–364
Hess, Markus, 206
Hibbs, Mark, 43n12
Hinderstein, Corey, 34, 35, 36,
  38–41, 73
Holocaust, Ahmadinejad's denial
  of, 81

Homeland Security, U.S.
  Department of, 142–143, 163,
  164, 185–186, 189, 223, 224,
  225–226
HOPE, 210
Hoz-e Sultan Lake, 72
HP TippingPoint, 100, 103
Hulsebos, Rob, 232–233
Hunter WaterTech, 137–138
Hussein, Saddam, 47, 71, 215
Hydroelectric plants, 151

I
IAEA. *See* International Atomic
  Energy Agency (IAEA)
ICS. *See* Industrial control systems
  (ICS)
ICS-CERT (Industrial Control
  Systems Cyber Emergency
  Response Team), 143, 145, 169,
  186, 187, 263n13
Idaho Falls, Idaho, Aurora Generator
  Test, 129–131, 142, 160–164
Idaho National Lab (INL), 142, 143,
  161
Immunity, 222–223
Implants, 217–218
India, Stuxnet infections, 30, 31
Indonesia, Stuxnet infections, 30
Industrial Control Systems Cyber
  Emergency Response Team
  (ICS-CERT), 143, 145, 169,
  186, 187, 263n13
Industrial control systems (ICS),
  129–165

nt'd)
et origin speculations, 64–
173–180
military support, 272
nctions against, 31, 83–84,
366
ith Iraq (1980–1988), 46–47
infections in, 276–277, 291
National Oil Company,
–277
Oil Ministry, 276–277
Passive Defense
anization, 183n18

r weapons development, 71
reactor strike, 192
ith Iran (1980–1988), 46–47
r, 85–86
stitute for Science and
rnational Security), 34, 35,
38–41, 44, 243–247

ke proposal to take out
anz facility, 190–194
nations of prominent
ian nuclear scientists
onsibility speculation, 240
uge testing, 321
ttack simulation exercise,
–380
responsibility, 262, 268n21,

responsibility, 290
infections, 295
ence leaks to IAEA, 37
rael relations, 369
d, 201n25, 241–242

Olympic Games operation
participation, 313
Stuxnet responsibility speculation,
31, 65–68, 247, 248, 284, 334,
351
Syrian Al Kibar cyberattack, 192,
215–216
tensions with U.S. over Iranian
nuclear program, 85, 346–347
"Wiper" infection responsibility,
291
Israel Atomic Energy Commission,
83
Ivry, David, 192n6

J
Jafari, Mahmoud, 183–184
Jafarzadeh, Alireza, 34, 35, 36–37,
38, 39–40, 50, 69
Jalali, Gholam-Reza, 259
Jalili, Saeed, 240
JMicron Technology, 15–16, 262,
273, 274, 353
Johnson's Shut-Ins State Park, 153
Joint Chiefs of Staff, 398
Joint Functional Component
Command–Network Warfare,
214
Joint Task Force–Computer
Network Defense (JTF-CND),
209–210, 212
Joint Task Force–Computer
Network Operations, 212–213
Joint Task Force–Global Network
Operations, 214

Aurora Generator Test, 129–131,
142, 160–164
malware targeting, 17
Maroochy Shire incident, 136–139
security, 171–172
vulnerability to attack, 132–136,
139–150, 155–160, 164–165
Weiss's warnings, 139–140, 143–
144
Industrial disasters, 150–154
"Information Operations Roadmap,"
213–214
Information warfare, 212–214. *See
also* Cyberwarfare
Inoculation values, 65
In-Q-Tel, 107
Institute for Science and
International Security (ISIS),
34, 35, 36, 38–41, 44, 243–247
International Atomic Energy Agency
(IAEA)
enrichment equipment intercepted
in Libya, 316–317
establishment of, 70
inspection reports, 244, 246–247,
343, 355, 364
Iran nuclear weapon development
awareness, 77–87, 347
Iran nuclear weapons status report
(2011), 368–369
Iran's accusation of press leaks by,
354–355
Iran's safeguards agreement with,
36, 75, 83–84
Natanz nuclear facility monitoring,
1–3, 41–44, 70–77, 83–84,
200–201, 312, 327n25, 344, 364

role an
satellite
Internatic
Internatic
Cybe
Internet,
conn
Internet l
IP addres
IPhone, 1
IR-1 centi
195,
338,
IR-2 centi
IR-2m cei
IR-4 centi
Iran. *See a*
assassina
persor
axis of e
CIA sab
route
cyberwa
Duqu in
273
Flame in
gas explo
Gauss in
Islamic F
Israel-Ira
nuclear p
190–19
309, 3:
president
336–3:
Stuxnet i
32, 97–

Iran (
Stu
6
Sud
UN
8
wai
Wi
Irani

Irani
Irani

Iraq
nu
O
wa
Iraq
ISIS

Isra
ai

a

c
c

Jumper, John, 212
Justice, U.S. Department of, 225, 384

K
Kala (Kalaye) Electric, 35–36, 50, 51, 74–75, 97, 311, 312, 353, 367
Kashan, Iran, 72
Kaspersky, Eugene, 300, 400
Kaspersky Lab, 91, 263–269, 272–275, 277–281, 288–289, 291–301
Kehler, Robert, 399
Kernel-level rootkits, 8–9
KGB, 206
Khan, Abdul Qadeer, 47, 48–50, 73, 77–78, 79, 199–200, 311, 316
Kharg Island fire, 126
Khatami, Sayyid Mohammad, 69
Khomeini, Ayatollah Ruhollah, 46, 47
Kill date, 259, 303, 381–382
Kimia Maadan, 313
Kingsley, Peter, 137n13, 139
Kochavi, Aviv, 380
Kosovo War, 215
Kraftwerk Union, 46
Krebs, Brian, 14
Kupreev, Oleg, 5, 8, 9
Kuwait, 81–82

L
Ladder logic, 168

Langner, Ralph, 166–179, 181–185, 189, 228–229, 230, 242, 245, 248, 315n12, 360, 365, 406
Larsen, Jason, 143
Lashkar Ab'ad nuclear site, 76
Law enforcement, 110
Lawrence Berkeley National Laboratory, 206
Lawson, Nate, 62–63
Lebanon, 295–296, 298
Lee, Robert E., 374
Levite, Ariel, 82
Lewis, Jim, 133, 382, 384–385
Libicki, Martin, 403
Libya
    CIA sabotage of nuclear parts in route to, 200
    cyberattack plans, 216
    enrichment equipment intercepted in, 316–317, 319, 320
Lin, Herbert, 397–398, 399
Live Free or Die Hard, 124–125
.LNK exploit, 9–10, 93–94, 95, 96, 222, 270, 279, 295
Lockheed Martin, 106
Log files, 97, 323, 351
Logic bombs, 54n1, 125–126, 172, 199, 397
Los Alamos National Laboratory, 200
Los Angeles Times, 141
Lotrionte, Catherine, 393, 394, 402, 403–404
Love Letter worm, 58
Low-enriched uranium, 72, 82, 87, 328, 331, 338, 347–348, 361–362
LulzSec, 132

M

MacOS, 102

"Magic marker," 123n2

Maiffret, Marc, 149

Malaysia, Kaspersky Lab's analysis of Flame-infected server in, 291–299

Malware

Code Red worm, 59, 119

Conficker, 20, 54, 92–93n5, 107–108, 374

Duqu. See Duqu

evolution of, 125

Flame. See Flame

Gauss, 294–298, 376n10

Melissa virus, 57–58

Morris worm, 57n2

RATs (remote-access Trojan), 258

self-replicating worms, 58n3

Shamoon virus, 378n16

Slammer worm, 133

Sobig virus, 133

Stuxnet. See Stuxnet

Zeus banking Trojan, 375

Zlob Trojan, 94–95, 222

Maroochy Shire incident, 136–139

Marsh Commission, 135–136

MC7, 229, 231

McAfee, 255, 261–262

McConnell, Michael, 86, 376–377

McGurk, Sean, 186–189

MD5 hash collision, 286–288, 394

Media coverage, 179, 354–355

MEK (Mujahedin-e Khalq), 37–38

Melissa virus, 57–58

Memory, malicious code placement, 25

Microsoft. See also Windows

bounty payments, 100, 102

Defense Department collaboration, 223–224

digital certificates, 11–12

Duqu threat notification, 255

Flame malware threat, 285–290, 393–394

RAV acquisition, 265

Stuxnet patch, 14, 18, 91, 279

Stuxnet threat notification, 13, 91, 263

Microsoft Outlook, 57–58

Microsoft Word, 57–58, 282

Military, U.S., 205–210, 396–398. See also Cyberwarfare; Defense, U.S. Department of

Military attacks, 190–194, 369, 374

Miller, Charlie, 103–105, 220

Milošević, Slobodan, 215

Mini-Flame, 298–299

Missouri, dam failure, 153

Mocana, 147

Mohammad bin Zayed, 191

Morris worm, 57n2

Mossad, 201n25, 241–242

Mousavi, Mir-Hossein, 336

Mozilla Firefox, 102

Mubarak, Hosni, 191

Myrtus, 66–68

N

NA-22 program, 319–320

Napolitano, Janet, 188

Natanz nuclear facility
Ahmadinejad's tour of (2008),
308–309
centrifuge installation, 83, 84–85,
87, 309, 327–330, 337
centrifuge replacement mystery,
1–3
construction of, 36, 72
IAEA monitoring, 1–3, 41–44,
70–77, 83–84, 200–201, 312,
327n25, 344, 364
international scrutiny, 31
ISIS's detection using satellite
imagery, 38, 44, 73, 244
Israel's air strike proposal to take
out, 190–194
NCRI press conference exposing,
34–38
production figures, 33, 244–246,
328–329, 338, 341, 344, 356–
357, 361–362
Stuxnet infection, 179–180,
228–229, 238, 242, 243–248,
302–306, 322–327, 330–332,
338–344, 351–352, 354–357,
359–365
underground buildings, 70
uranium enrichment at, 82–87
U.S. cyberattack plan, 202–204
National Academy of Sciences, 396
National Council of Resistance of
Iran (NCRI), 34–38, 76
National Cybersecurity and
Communications Integration
Center (NCCIC), 185–189
National Intelligence Estimate, 82,
85–86, 191, 328–329

National Nuclear Security
Administration (NNSA),
319–320
National Research Council, 397–398
National Security Agency (NSA)
computer network attack policy
exception, 398
computer network attack
techniques, 210–211
cyberattack tools, 219–220
cyber operations, 216–218
Cyber Storm III exercise, 186
electronic warfare team, 213
"Eligible Receiver" exercise,
207–208
exploit development, 106
Flame responsibility, 290
hackers contracted by, 219–221
Olympic Games operation
execution, 313
Snowden leaks, 216–217, 282
Stuxnet operations, 202, 351
VUPEN subscription, 109–110
zero-day exploits policy, 390–392
National Security Council, 197, 198
Nation-state attacks, 253–254, 378–
380, 388–389
NATO (North Atlantic Treaty
Organization), 110–111, 212,
215, 216, 262, 400
NCCIC (National Cybersecurity
and Communications
Integration Center), 185–189
NCRI (National Council of
Resistance of Iran), 34–38, 76
Neda Industrial Group, 97, 312,
340–341, 353–354

NERC (North American Electric Reliability Corporation), 129, 158n52

Netanyahu, Benjamin, 241

New Republic, 368

New York Times, 182, 247, 249, 334–335, 360, 367, 384

NNSA (National Nuclear Security Administration), 319–320

NOBUS (Nobody But Us), 389–390

Nonproliferation of Nuclear Weapons Treaty, 36, 45

Nonproliferation Policy Education Center, 368

North American Electric Reliability Corporation (NERC), 129, 158n52

North Korea, 206, 320

Northrop Grumman, 106, 219

NPR, 224

NSA. *See* National Security Agency (NSA)

Nuclear Regulatory Commission, 234

O

Oak Ridge National Laboratory, 247, 316–322

OB1 blocks, 310n4

OB35 blocks, 123, 310n4

Obama, Barack
  computer network attack policies, 397–398
  cyberattack target list, 219
  cyber operation reauthorization, 332–334
  on cybersecurity situation, 371–372
  cyberstrategy, 223, 348, 357, 386, 394
  diplomacy with Iran, 335
  Nowruz speech, 348–349
  UN Security Council Summit on Nuclear Nonproliferation and Nuclear Disarmament speech, 344–345
  zero-day exploit policy, 390–392

Oklahoma City bombing, 135

Olmert, Ehud, 85

Olympic Games cyber operation
  funding, 309, 321
  intelligence, 308–309, 311–317
  Oak Ridge National Laboratory contributions, 317–322
  Obama's reauthorization, 332–334
  planning, 194–196, 201–204, 310
  proposal to Bush, 194, 310

Olympic Pipe Line Company, 152

O'Murchu, Liam, 19–32, 52, 53, 54, 55, 59–64, 88–91, 116, 127, 227–228, 232–234, 242–243, 256–258, 260, 352

Operation Solar Sunrise, 208–209

P

P-1 centrifuges, 49, 77, 87, 245, 247, 316, 317, 318, 320

P-2 centrifuges, 318

Packers, 23–24

Pahlavi, Mohammad Reza, 44, 46, 66

Pakistan, nuclear weapons program, 38–39, 47, 48

Palestine, 281, 295

Panetta, Leon, 158, 357, 382, 385, 392–393

Pardis petrochemical plant explosion, 126

Passwords
  default vendor, 143, 149, 171
  Flame sniffer component, 277–278
  hard-coded, 91n3, 143, 145, 171
  Siemens vulnerability, 95, 145, 148
  Stuxnet hijacking, 91

Patches, 6, 14, 18, 147, 289

Peace Pipeline, 31

Pederson, Perry, 164

Peer-to-peer file sharing, 92

Pék, Gábor, 255

Pennington, Andy, 221–222, 223, 381

Persia, 66–67

Phishing, 259, 272, 314

Physics Research Center, 78

PLCs. See Programmable logic controllers (PLCs)

Poland, railway accident, 154

Power grid, 142, 155–164, 371–372, 398

Pr0f (hacker), 148–149

Presidential approval, 397–398

Print-spooler exploit, 90, 94–95, 222, 339

Proffit Mountain, 153

Profibus cards, 228, 232–233, 314, 339

Programmable logic controllers (PLCs). See also Siemens PLCs
  commercial operating system use, 134–135
  definition of, 17
  life-span of, 147
  origins of, 134
  programming of, 94, 149, 314
  Stuxnet infection, 117–118, 121–124, 166–167, 168, 172–173, 175
  uses for, 131–132
  vulnerability to attack, 144–146, 169, 171–172, 182

Programming language, 229, 265–266

Protective relays, 161–164

Proxy machines, 268

Pwn2Own, 103, 109, 112

Q

Qom, Iran, 72, 368

R

Railway accidents, 153–154

Raiu, Costin, 263–266, 274, 275, 277–278, 281, 282, 283, 284, 293, 294, 299–301

RAND, 205

Ranum, Marcus, 376, 381

RAT (remote-access Trojan), 258

RAV (Romanian Anti-Virus), 264–265

Raytheon, 106
RealTek Semiconductor, 11–13, 16, 95, 255, 262, 273, 348
"Red" networks, 55
Red October, 301
Reed, Thomas C., 198–199
Resource 207 (Stuxnet component), 278, 283
ReVuln, 106
Rezaeinejad, Darioush, 366
Rice, Condoleezza, 84
Rid, Thomas, 381, 382–383
Rieger, Frank, 179–180
Rogers, Michael, 391, 399
Rootkits, 6, 8–9, 60, 117
Rosen, Ralf, 169, 170, 171, 173, 174, 176, 177, 179, 185
Roshan, Mostafa Ahmadi, 366–367
Rouland, Christopher, 107
RTUs (remote terminal units), 68, 137, 138, 146n31
Rules of engagement, 386n32
Russia
 Bushehr plant equipment installation, 176
 CIA plot to install logic bomb in gas pipeline software, 125–126
 denial-of-service attacks against Georgian government, 378n17
 Iranian nuclear reactor construction support, 50
 malware-infected computers in, 107–108
 Sayano-Shushenskaya hydroelectric plant disaster, 151
 Siberian pipeline explosion, 127, 198–199
 Stuxnet responsibility speculation, 31

S
Saade, Tareq, 255
Sachs, Marcus, 210
Safety systems, 147–148
SAIC, 106
Salehi, Ali Akbar, 43, 240, 369
Samore, Gary, 247
San Bruno, Calif., gas pipeline explosion, 131, 152–153
Sanctions, 31, 83–84, 86, 191, 366
Sandia National Laboratories, 164, 385
Sanger, David, 284, 351–352, 354
Satellite imagery, 38–41, 44, 73, 244
Saudi Arabia, 191
Saudi Aramco, Shamoon virus attack, 378n16
Sayano-Shushenskaya hydroelectric plant disaster, 151
SCADA (Supervisory Control and Data Acquisition) systems, 131, 142, 148–150, 152–153, 161
Schaffer, Greg, 224
Schmidt, Howard, 222
SecurityFocus, 119–120
Self-replicating worms, 58n3
September 11, 2001, 213, 382–383, 385–386
Shahab-3 missiles, 80
Shahriari, Majid, 239–241
Shamoon virus, 378n16
Sharon, Ariel, 242

Siemens
automation equipment sales in
Iran, 312–313
Kraftwerk Union subsidary, 46
Langner's relationship with, 170
Stuxnet response, 168, 229–230
Siemens PLCs
Iranian Bushehr plant use, 176
Olympic Games operation attack
code, 310–311
Step 7-300 PLC, 313
Step 7-315 PLC, 59, 166, 175, 229,
234–235, 302, 315
Step 7-400 PLC, 313, 339
Step 7-417 PLC, 59, 166, 175, 229,
235–237, 245, 246, 302–303,
315, 323
Stuxnet infection, 17–18, 24, 28–
31, 53, 54, 59–62, 68, 91–94,
116–118, 121–124, 144–146,
166–169, 172–173, 175, 186–
187, 227–228, 229, 234–237,
304
Siemens SIMATIC, 17. See also Step
7 software; WinCC software
Signing keys (digital certificate), 12
Simulation exercise, Tel Aviv
University, 378–380
Sinkhole, 29, 281
60 Minutes, 164, 372n1, 374
Slammer worm, 133
Smart meters, 155–158
Smith, David, 57
Sniffers, 277–278
Snowden, Edward, 216–217, 218,
219, 282, 391, 397, 399
Sobig virus, 133

Soghoian, Christopher, 113–114,
392
Sokolski, Henry, 368
Sotirov, Alexander, 288n14
South Korea, 206
Soviet Union, 197–198, 206. See also
Russia
SPE malware, 293, 294, 298
SP malware, 293–294, 298n26
Spyware. See Malware
Stammberger, Kurt, 147
"Stars" attack, 259–260
Star Wars defense system, 206
State, U.S. Department of, 25, 38,
241
Static analysis, 122
Step 7 software, 17, 29n5, 59, 61, 62,
91–94, 116–117, 118, 121, 144–
145, 166–167, 186–187, 188n24,
227–228, 235, 304, 315, 322
Stevens, Marc, 288n14
STL (Statement List) programming
language, 229, 230–231, 233
Stringfellow, Robert, 137n13
Stuxnet
atomic bomb comparison, 375–
376
Conficker comparison, 54
control mechanisms, 381–382
copycat attacks, 182
cyberwarfare impact, 371–375,
387
discovery of, 5–14
Duqu relationship, 273–275
false claims, 256–257
file size, 20–21
illegality of, 402–403

Stuxnet *(cont'd)*
  Langner's analysis, 166–179,
    181–185, 189, 228–229, 230,
    242, 245, 248, 315n12, 360,
    365, 406
  launch of, 16–17
  motivations behind, 17–18
  naming of, 14
  NCCIC's analysis, 185–189
  operation and spread of, 23–30,
    59–64, 88–98, 121–124,
    229–238, 310–311, 313–316,
    321–327, 349–352
  security industry impact, 306–307
  size of, 279
  sophistication of, 388
  speculations about target and
    source, 16, 26, 31, 49, 51,
    63, 64–68, 97–98, 125–128,
    173–180, 187–189, 228–229,
    243–248, 283
  success of, 359–370
  Symantec's analysis of, 19–32,
    52–54, 59–68, 88–98, 116–128,
    228–238, 242–243, 350
  versions of, 183–184, 236–237,
    302, 353
  zero-day exploits, 88–98, 279
Stuxnet 0.5 (first version), 301–306,
  314, 322–327, 329–331, 350
Stuxnet 1.001 (June 2009), 3,
  16–17, 96n13, 97, 180n13, 237,
  278, 302, 303, 337n1, 338–344,
  350–351
Stuxnet 1.100 (March 2010), 17,
  95, 96, 97, 237, 279, 284, 302,
  349–350, 380, 382

Stuxnet 1.101 (April 2010), 17, 97,
  237, 275, 302, 349, 352
Substations, 159–160
Sudan, 272, 281, 293
Supreme National Security Council
  (Iran), 35, 36
Symantec
  Duqu analysis and public
    announcement, 256–261
  infection response time, 58
  Stuxnet analysis, 19–32, 52–54,
    59–68, 88–98, 116–128, 228–
    238, 242–243, 350
  Stuxnet version 0.5 discovery,
    301–306
  Threat Intelligence Lab in Culver
    City, 53–55
Syria, 192, 215–216, 281
Szor, Péter, 255, 261–262

T

Tabriz, Iran, gas pipeline explosion,
  126
Taghipour, Reza, 183
Tallinn Manual, 400–403
Tehran Nuclear Research Center,
  50
Tehran University, 45
Tel Aviv University, simulation
  exercise, 378–380
Telegraph, 334
Telvent Canada, 149–150
Temporary files, 62, 277–278
Tenenbaum, Ehud, 208
Tenet, George, 37n5

Terminal Services (TS) Licensing, 286–287

Terrorism, 140–141, 217, 383–384

Tilde-d platform, 274, 283, 284

Timm, Andreas, 169, 170, 173, 174, 176, 177, 179, 185

Transducers, 332

Treaties, 36, 45, 400

Trojan horses, 94–95, 222, 258, 375

Turkey
gas pipeline explosion, 126
uranium enrichment components obtained from, 82, 200–201, 233n4, 245, 306, 317, 335

U

U-235 isotope, 47–48, 75, 323

U-238 isotope, 48, 323

Ulasen, Sergey, 5–14, 18

United Kingdom
Government Communications Headquarters, 218n33
Stuxnet responsibility speculation, 247

United Nations. *See also* International Atomic Energy Agency (IAEA)
Charter's Law of Armed Conflict, 400–404
sanctions against Iran, 31, 83–84, 86, 366

United Nations Security Council Summit on Nuclear Nonproliferation and Nuclear Disarmament, 344–345

United States. *See also* Olympic Games cyber operation
on assassinations of prominent nuclear scientists, 240, 241
Chinese cyberattacks against, 369
cyberattack vulnerability, 376–377, 382–386
Duqu responsibility, 262
exploit sales regulation, 114
Flame responsibility, 284, 290–291
Gauss infections, 295
Iranian nuclear reactor construction support, 46
Stuxnet responsibility speculation, 31, 63, 187–188, 247–248, 284

United States Cyber Command, 214–215, 216, 313, 373, 386, 390

United States Enrichment Corporation, 319

United States Pacific Command, 207–208

United States Strategic Command, 202, 214, 313, 377, 399

University College Dublin, 21–22

University of Tennessee, 317

UPS (Uninterruptible Power Supply), 200–201, 306, 317

UPX (Ultimate Packer for eXecutables), 23

Uranium enrichment. *See also* Centrifuges; Natanz nuclear facility
complexity of, 82
Fordow plant, 344–346
Iranian production numbers, 330–331, 361–362

Uranium enrichment *(cont'd)*
  Iranian program, 35, 47–51, 77–
    87, 362–363
  nuclear reactor vs. weapon
    requirements, 75
  testing at Iranian facilities, 75–76
Uranium hexafluoride, 1, 47, 49, 51,
    73, 74, 77, 78, 81, 85, 203, 363
Uranium tetrafluoride, 80
URENCO, 47, 49, 50, 77, 177,
    247
USB flash drives, 9–10, 24, 60–61,
    93, 95, 96n14, 235, 295, 296–
    297, 322, 339, 340–341
US-CERT (United States Computer
    Emergency Readiness Team),
    186
UT-Battelle, 317
Utilities, attacks against, 136–139

V
Vacon frequency converters, 233–
    234, 245
Venezuela, malware-infected
    computers in, 108
VeriSign, 255
Vetrov, Vladimir Ippolitovich, 197,
    198
Viper (Wiper variation), 279n4
Virus-BlokAda, 5, 7, 10, 13, 15, 16,
    53, 94, 96n14
Viruses. *See* Malware
VirusTotal, 251n2, 275, 301–302,
    305
Voice of America, 335

Vulnerabilities equities process,
    224–226
VUPEN, 106, 108–113

W
Wallpaper exploit, 278–279, 283
Washington, D.C., Metro accident,
    154
Washington Post, 161, 202, 217, 290–
    291, 344, 397
Wassenaar Arrangement, 114
Water plants, 136–139, 141, 142,
    143, 148–150
Weger, Benne de, 288n14
Weiss, Gus, 197–198, 199, 201
Weiss, Joe, 137n13, 139–140, 143–
    144, 163, 181
White House National Security
    Telecommunications Advisory
    Committee, 136
WikiLeaks, 110, 180, 191
WinCC software, 17, 29n5, 30n8,
    59, 61, 117, 121
Windows
  Autorun exploit, 9–10, 95, 96,
    278–279, 283, 339
  .DLL exploit, 24–25, 59, 61,
    116–118, 121–122, 235, 310,
    315, 340
  industrial controls, 135, 147
  .LNK exploit, 9–10, 93–94, 95,
    96, 222, 270, 279, 295
  Stuxnet infection, 9–14, 60
  Update system hijacking, 285–
    290, 392–394

virus susceptibility, 57–58
zero-day exploit, 89–90, 102
"Wiper" infection, 276–277, 278,
    291
Worcester Airport, 135
World War II, 225
Worms. *See* Malware
Wurldtech Security, 146

Y

Yadegari, Mahmoud, 332
Yenisei River, 151
Yosef, Rav Ovadia, 68
Yugoslavia, NATO bombing of, 212

Z

Zero-day exploits
    commercial and government
        market for, 99–115, 219, 221–
        222
    definition of, 6
    in Duqu, 269–272
    government's stockpiling for
        offensive operations, 221–226
    life-span, 222–223
    price of, 101–104
    rarity of, 6–7
    regulation of, 114–115, 390–392
    in Stuxnet, 88–98, 279
Zeus banking Trojan, 375
Zlob Trojan, 94–95, 222